THE EUROPEAN UNION

THE
EUROPEAN
UNION

POLITICS AND POLICIES

FIFTH EDITION

JOHN MCCORMICK
JONATHAN OLSEN

**WESTVIEW
PRESS**

Westview Press was founded in 1975 in Boulder, Colorado, by notable publisher and intellectual Fred Praeger. Westview Press continues to publish scholarly titles and high-quality undergraduate- and graduate-level textbooks in core social science disciplines. With books developed, written, and edited with the needs of serious nonfiction readers, professors, and students in mind, Westview Press honors its long history of publishing books that matter.

Find us on the World Wide Web at www.westviewpress.com.

Every effort has been made to secure required permissions for all text, images, maps, and other art reprinted in this volume.

Westview Press books are available at special discounts for bulk purchases in the United States by corporations, institutions, and other organizations. For more information, please contact the Special Markets Department at the Perseus Books Group, 2300 Chestnut Street, Suite 200, Philadelphia, PA 19103, or call (800) 810-4145, ext. 5000, or e-mail special.markets@perseusbooks.com.

Typeset in 11.5 point Adobe Garamond Pro by the Perseus Books Group

Library of Congress Cataloging-in-Publication Data

McCormick, John, 1954–
  The European Union: politics and policies / John McCormick, Jonathan Olsen.—Fifth edition.
     pages cm
  Includes bibliographical references and index.
  ISBN 978-0-8133-4898-8 (pbk.)—ISBN 978-0-8133-4899-5 (e-book)
  1. European Union. I. Title.
  JN30.M37 2013
  341.242'2—dc23
                                                    2013003569

10 9 8 7 6 5 4 3 2 1

CONTENTS

Tables and Illustrations	*xi*
Preface and Acknowledgments	*xv*
About the Authors	*xix*
Acronyms and Abbreviations	*xxi*

Introduction   1

PART I

HISTORY

1 What Is the European Union?   **15**
Chapter Overview, 15
The Role of the State, 17
How Did the EU Evolve? 19
What Has the EU Become? 25
Questions to Consider, 32
Further Reading, 32
Notes, 33

2 Origins: The Road from Paris   **36**
Chapter Overview, 36
The Taming of Europe, 38

Economic Reconstruction and the Marshall Plan, 41
Security and the Cold War, 44
Opening Moves: Coal and Steel (1950–53), 47
Questions to Consider, 52
Further Reading, 52
Notes, 53

3 Emergence: To the Single Market and Beyond   **56**
Chapter Overview, 56
From Paris to Rome (1955–58), 58
Integration Takes Root (1958–68), 59
The Role of the United States, 61
Enlargement: Looking North and South (1960–86), 63
Toward Economic and Monetary Union (1969–93), 67
Completing the Single Market (1983–93), 69
Questions to Consider, 72
Further Reading, 73
Notes, 73

4 Consolidation and Crisis:
Maastricht, Lisbon, and the Eurozone   **76**
Chapter Overview, 76
From Community to Union (1970–93), 78
The Euro Arrives (1995–2002), 80
Changes to the Treaties: Amsterdam and Nice (1997–2001), 83
Shock Waves from Iraq (2003–05), 84
More Enlargement: Looking East (1994–2013), 87
From Lisbon to the Eurozone Crisis (2001–), 90
Questions to Consider, 92
Further Reading, 92
Notes, 93

PART II
INSTITUTIONS

5 The European Commission   **97**
Chapter Overview, 97
Evolution, 99
Structure, 100
How the Commission Works, 110
Questions to Consider, 115
Further Reading, 115
Notes, 116

6 The Council of the European Union   **118**
Chapter Overview, 118
Evolution, 120
Structure, 123
How the Council Works, 129
Questions to Consider, 133
Further Reading, 134
Notes, 134

7 The European Parliament   **136**
Chapter Overview, 136
Evolution, 138
Structure, 140
How Parliament Works, 148
Questions to Consider, 153
Further Reading, 153
Notes, 154

8 The European Court of Justice   **155**
Chapter Overview, 155
Evolution, 157
Structure, 160
Sources of European Union Law, 165
How the Court Works, 166

Questions to Consider, 171
Further Reading, 171
Notes, 172

9 The European Council and Other Institutions   **174**
Chapter Overview, 174
Evolution, 176
Structure, 177
How the Council Works, 179
Specialized Agencies, 182
Questions to Consider, 191
Further Reading, 191
Notes, 192

10 Representing Public Opinion   **194**
Chapter Overview, 194
An Emerging European Identity, 196
Referendums, 200
European Elections, 201
Political Groups, 205
Interest Groups, 210
Questions to Consider, 212
Further Reading, 212
Notes, 213

PART III

POLICIES

11 Public Policy in the EU   **217**
Chapter Overview, 217
The Policy Cycle, 219
Features of the Policy Process, 227
The Budget, 230
Questions to Consider, 235
Further Reading, 235
Notes, 236

12 Economic and Monetary Policy 238

Chapter Overview, 238
The Single Market and Europe 2020, 240
Justice and Home Affairs, 246
The Euro, 248
Questions to Consider, 254
Further Reading, 255
Notes, 255

13 Cohesion and Other Internal Policies 257

Chapter Overview, 257
Building a Level Playing Field, 259
Social Policy, 265
Education and Languages, 270
Questions to Consider, 274
Further Reading, 274
Notes, 275

14 Agricultural and Environmental Policy 277

Chapter Overview, 277
Agricultural Policy, 279
Environmental Policy, 287
Questions to Consider, 292
Further Reading, 293
Notes, 293

15 External Relations 296

Chapter Overview, 296
Toward a Common Foreign Policy, 298
Toward a Common Security Policy, 302
Trade Policy, 305
Developments in the Neighborhood:
    Eastern Europe and Russia, 307
Relations with a Rising Power: EU–China Relations, 312
Development Cooperation, 312
Questions to Consider, 314
Further Reading, 315
Notes, 315

16 The EU and the United States   **318**
   Chapter Overview, 318
   The Changing International System, 320
   The Transatlantic Relationship, 322
   A Litany of Disputes, 326
   Explaining the Differences, 328
   Questions to Consider, 334
   Further Reading, 334
   Notes, 335

Conclusions   **338**
   Notes, 342

Glossary   *343*
Appendix 1   *Chronology of European Integration*   *349*
Appendix 2   *Sources of Information*   *358*
Index   *361*

TABLES AND ILLUSTRATIONS

TABLES

0.1	The EU in Figures	8
4.1	Growth of the European Union Population	88
5.1	The European Commissioners, 2009–14	102
5.2	Presidents of the European Commission	104
5.3	Directorates-General and Services	108
5.4	Infringements of EU Law	114
6.1	Rotation of Presidencies of the Council of Ministers	127
6.2	Qualified Majority Voting in the Council of Ministers	131
7.1	Growth of the European Parliament	139
7.2	Recent Presidents of the European Parliament	143
7.3	Committees of the European Parliament	145
7.4	Distribution of Seats in the European Parliament, 2013	147
8.1	Judges of the European Court of Justice, 2012	162
8.2	Presidents of the European Court of Justice	164
9.1	Membership of the EESC and the CoR	189
10.1	Party Representation in the European Parliament, 2012	209
15.1	Membership of NATO	305

FIGURES

10.1 Identifying with the European Union   199
10.2 Turnout at European Parliament Elections, 2009   203
10.3 Party Balance in the European Parliament   207
11.1 The European Union Policy Process   224
11.2 The European Union Budget   233
13.1 Differences in Economic Wealth   261
13.2 Unemployment in the EU   269
15.1 The EU in the Global Economy   306
15.2 The EU Share of World Trade   308

BOXES

1.1   Stages in Regional Integration   22
1.2   NAFTA and the EU Compared   24
2.1   Two Crises that Changed Europe   46
2.2   Monnet and Schuman: The Fathers of Europe   49
3.1   The EFTA Sideshow   64
3.2   Intergovernmental Conferences   71
4.1   The Copenhagen Conditions   81
4.2   The Failed European Constitution   85
5.1   Barroso in Charge   106
5.2   European Union Law   112
6.1   The Case for an Upper Chamber   122
6.2   Meetings of the Council of the EU   132
7.1   Parliament's Multisite Dilemma   142
7.2   The Ordinary Legislative Procedure   150
8.1   The EU Charter of Fundamental Rights   159
8.2   Liquor, Beer, and the Single Market   167
9.1   European Summits   180
9.2   Specialized Agencies of the European Union   187
10.1 European Electoral Systems   204
11.1 Who Sets the European Agenda?   222
11.2 The Democratic Deficit   231
12.1 The Schengen Agreement   243
12.2 The Euro Crisis   252
13.1 Ireland: From Expansion to Contraction   263
13.2 The Erasmus Generation   272

14.1 The Common Fisheries Policy   282
14.2 The Climate Change Controversy   289
15.1 Europe's Soft Power Advantage   299
15.2 Who Speaks for Europe?   301
16.1 Transatlantic Economic Ties   325
16.2 Are Americans from Mars, and Europeans from Venus?   332

Maps

0.1   The European Union   4
2.1   Europe After World War II   42
3.1   Growth of the European Union, 1952–86   66
4.1   Growth of the European Union, 1990–2013   89
12.1 The Eurozone   250
15.1 The EU and Its Neighborhood   310

Preface and Acknowledgments

Although the crisis that broke in the eurozone in 2009 has given policy makers many sleepless nights, it also had the effect of drawing wider public attention to an entity about which many Americans knew little: the European Union (EU). Since the early 1950s, Europeans have been working to remove the political, economic, and social barriers that have long divided them, and the result has been the development of the world's newest superpower, the world's wealthiest marketplace and trading power, and the possible precursor to a United States of Europe.

Worries about the effects of the eurozone have combined with a growing public backlash against European integration to raise some deeply troubling questions about where the EU is headed, but it remains a powerful actor in the world—one that is important for Americans to understand: the EU is one of our biggest trading partners, it is our most influential and dependable ally in an uncertain world, and its emergence has been one of the defining events of the modern era, helping reorder the international system and bringing to Europe the longest spell of general peace that it has seen in centuries. Its achievements in this last regard were recognized in 2012 when it was awarded the Nobel Prize for Peace. The EU has helped promote democracy and economic development throughout Europe, it has helped more than half a billion Europeans overcome their political, economic, and social divisions, and it stands as a prime example of how peaceful means can bring lasting change.

But in spite of all this, it remains—for most people—a mystery and an enigma. Few Americans know much about it beyond the euro, and even Europeans are perplexed: most support the idea of "Europe" in principle, but also admit that they know little about how the EU works, or who makes the decisions, or how the EU has changed their lives. Enthusiasm for the EU is harder to find than ambivalence, indifference, or outright hostility. There are several reasons for the confusion:

- The EU is unique. There has never been anything quite like it before, and it fits few of our usual ideas about politics and government. Is it an international organization, a new European superstate, or something in between? How much authority does it have relative to its member states? How do its powers and structure differ from those of a conventional national government?
- It is not always well explained. Publishing on the EU has been a growth industry in the last decade, but much of it is bogged down in a morass of treaty articles and arcane jargon, and sidetracked by inconclusive debates over theory. The EU is one of today's most important and dramatic political and economic developments, full of fascinating characters and driven by conflicts, conspiracies, successes, crises, and failures, and yet much of the scholarly writing about the EU makes it sound dull, technocratic, and legalistic.
- The EU keeps changing. Just when we think we have begun to understand it, a new treaty comes along that gives it new powers, or its leaders agree to a new set of goals that give it a different character and appearance, or new member states join, changing its personality and its structure. Change is, of course, a core feature of politics and government everywhere, but the European target tends to move more quickly than most, with no certainty about where exactly it is headed.

Having taught courses on the EU for several years, and having worked with instructors teaching similar courses at other colleges and universities, we are familiar with the challenge of explaining the EU. As the power and influence of Europe grows, so does the importance of clear guidance through the complexities of the EU, and detailed analysis that offers observers the context they need to better appreciate the implications of European integration. It was concerns such as these that prompted the writing of this book, which sets out to help answer four fundamental questions:

- What is the EU?
- How did it evolve?
- What does it do?
- What difference does it make?

The first edition was written in 1993–95, when the European Union was still adapting to the near completion of the single market, struggling with preparations for the single currency, and mired in the fallout from the serial foreign policy embarrassments of the Gulf War and the Balkan conflicts. There was relatively little public or political interest in the EU at the time; there were few textbooks that provided an introduction to the EU and none written specifically for American students. Since then—reflecting the new levels of interest in the EU—many more textbooks have been written about the EU, but this fifth edition of *The European Union: Politics and Policies* retains its core goals of informing mainly American students, explaining how the EU functions from first principles, and explaining how and why the EU matters for those of us on this side of the Atlantic. It is also unusual because it is written more from the perspective of comparative politics and public policy than that of international relations; scholars from the latter subdiscipline have tended to dominate the research and writing on the EU for several decades.

The biggest change with the new edition is that Jonathan Olsen has joined John McCormick as co-author. As with previous editions, however, we have tried to keep the presentation simple enough for the introductory student (who most often is exposed to the EU in a one-semester course on European politics and the EU) yet detailed enough to provide a comprehensive overview of the EU's history, institutions, and policies. Every chapter begins with an overview and ends with a list of recommended readings that provides the most recent, readable, and enlightening Anglo-American sources. The book ends with a glossary of key terms, a chronology of events, and recommended sources of further information. The EU changes so much and so quickly that texts on it date quickly, so this new edition—while keeping the same basic structure as its predecessors—has been thoroughly overhauled and updated:

- Chapter 1 has been heavily revised in order to more fully explain the different theories of European integration and to give more attention to the importance of explanations coming out of comparative politics and public policy.

- The history in chapters 2–4 has been fine-tuned, with new material added on the transatlantic relationship and on the influence that the United States had on the evolution of the EU. Chapter 4 has been reorganized and rewritten to incorporate developments since 2008, including the new Lisbon Treaty and the crisis in the eurozone.
- The chapters on institutions (5–10) have been thoroughly revised to account for developments since 2008 and to inject new analytical material.
- The chapters on policy (11–15) have been overhauled to include all the latest developments in the different policy areas. The chapters on economic and foreign policy, and on EU relations with the United States, have been thoroughly revised, and those on agricultural, environmental, and cohesion policy substantially restructured. There is completely new material on topics such as justice and home affairs, the EU budget, climate change, sustainable development, the Bologna process and the Erasmus program, and the EU's relations with Russia, the Middle East, and China.
- A number of the boxes have been replaced, all the figures and tables have been updated, and the titles in the lists of Further Reading are mainly new.
- Throughout the book, more emphasis has been placed on the relationship between the United States and the EU: on what effects U.S. foreign policy has had on European integration; on changes in the relationship between the two actors; on the comparisons that can be made regarding their character, values, and places in the global system; and on what they mean for each other.

The biggest influence on this book has come from the students in the courses we have taught on European politics at our respective universities. It was their needs and concerns that drove the first edition, and their responses have since been the driving force in the revisions that came with each new edition. Both of us would like to thank the anonymous reviewers drafted by Westview to comment on this new edition, and Toby Wahl and the editorial team at Westview Press for their encouragement and their fine job on production. John gives his thanks and love to his wife, Leanne, and their two sons, Ian and Stuart, who are good at reminding him that there is life outside the academy. Jonathan thanks his wife, Molly, and their two children, Rose and Ian, for their love, patience, and understanding as he devoted many hours (including many weekend hours) to this project.

About the Authors

John McCormick is professor of political science at Indiana University Purdue University Indianapolis (IUPUI). His teaching and research interests lie in comparative politics and public policy, with particular interests in the politics of the EU, British politics, and transatlantic relations. He has held visiting positions at the universities of Exeter and of Sussex in Britain, and spent the first half of 2013 as the Fulbright Chair in EU-US Relations at the College of Europe in Belgium. His other publications include *The European Superpower* (Palgrave Macmillan, 2006), *Europeanism* (Oxford University Press, 2010), and *Why Europe Matters* (Palgrave Macmillan, 2013).

Jonathan Olsen is professor of political science at the University of Wisconsin–Parkside. He teaches courses in comparative politics and political theory, with a specialization in German politics and the politics of the European Union. He is a three-time Fulbright Scholar and has had visiting appointments at the University of Münster, Potsdam University, and the European University-Viadrina (Frankfurt-Oder). His books include *Nature and Nationalism* (Palgrave Macmillan, 1999) and (with Dan Hough and Michael Koß) *The Left Party in Contemporary German Politics* (Palgrave Macmillan, 2007) and *Left Parties in National Governments* (Palgrave Macmillan, 2010).

Acronyms and Abbreviations

ACP	African, Caribbean, and Pacific states
BEU	Benelux Economic Union
CAP	Common Agricultural Policy
CCP	Common Commercial Policy
CFSP	Common Foreign and Security Policy
CoR	Committee of the Regions
Coreper	Committee of Permanent Representatives
CSDP	Common Security and Defence Policy
DG	directorate-general
EADS	European Aeronautic Defense and Space Company
EAGGF	European Agriculture Guidance and Guarantee Fund
EAP	Environmental Action Program
EBRD	European Bank for Reconstruction and Development
EC	European Community
ECB	European Central Bank
ECJ	European Court of Justice
Ecofin	Economic and Financial Affairs
ECSC	European Coal and Steel Community
ECU	European currency unit
EDC	European Defense Community
EEA	European Economic Area or European Environment Agency
EEC	European Economic Community

EESC   European Economic and Social Committee
EFTA   European Free Trade Association
EIB   European Investment Bank
EMI   European Monetary Institute
EMS   European Monetary System
EMU   economic and monetary union
EP   European Parliament
EPC   European Political Community or European Political
        Cooperation
ERDF   European Regional Development Fund
ERM   Exchange Rate Mechanism
ESDP   European Security and Defense Policy
ESF   European Social Fund
ESM   European Stability Mechanism
EU   European Union
EU–15   the fifteen pre-2004 member states of the EU
EU–25   the twenty-five member states of the EU in 2004–2007
EU–27   the twenty-seven member states of the EU in 2007–2013
G8   Group of Eight industrialized countries
GAERC   General Affairs and External Relations Council
GATT   General Agreement on Tariffs and Trade
GDP   gross domestic product
GNP   gross national product
IGC   intergovernmental conference
IGO   intergovernmental organization
INGO   international nongovernmental organization
IMF   International Monetary Fund
IO   international organization
IR   international relations
JHA   justice and home affairs
MEP   Member of the European Parliament
NAFTA   North American Free Trade Agreement
NATO   North Atlantic Treaty Organization
OECD   Organization for Economic Cooperation and Development
OEEC   Organization for European Economic Cooperation
QMV   qualified majority vote
SEA   Single European Act
TEN   Trans-European Network
USSR   Union of Soviet Socialist Republics

VAT	value-added tax
WEU	Western European Union
WTO	World Trade Organization

EU Member States

AT	Austria
BE	Belgium
BG	Bulgaria
CY	Cyprus
CZ	Czech Republic
DE	Germany
DK	Denmark
EE	Estonia
EL	Greece
ES	Spain
FI	Finland
FR	France
HR	Croatia
HU	Hungary
IE	Ireland
IT	Italy
LT	Lithuania
LU	Luxembourg
LV	Latvia
MT	Malta
NL	Netherlands
PL	Poland
PT	Portugal
RO	Romania
SE	Sweden
SI	Slovenia
SK	Slovakia
UK	United Kingdom

A Note on Terminology

Anyone writing a book about the EU is faced with the challenge of deciding when and where to use the terms European Economic Community, European Community, and European Union. We have opted for the third except in cases of specific references to historical events where it would not make sense. We have also occasionally used Europe where European Union would be more accurate, mainly for stylistic reasons but also to make the point that the two terms increasingly have the same meaning. Finally, we have used the term Eastern Europe to refer to all those countries that were once behind the iron curtain, conscious that many in those countries like to make a distinction between Eastern and Central Europe.

INTRODUCTION

We cannot aim at anything less than the union of Europe as a whole, and we look forward with confidence to the day when that union will be achieved.
—WINSTON CHURCHILL, THE HAGUE CONGRESS, MAY 1948

That such an unnecessary and irrational project as building a European superstate was ever embarked on will seem in future years to be perhaps the greatest folly of the modern era.
—MARGARET THATCHER, *STATECRAFT: STRATEGIES FOR A CHANGING WORLD*, 2003

The European Union is the world's wealthiest capitalist marketplace, the world's biggest trading power, and—along with the United States—one of the two most influential political actors in the world. Its emergence has changed the character and definition of Europe, helped bring to the region the longest uninterrupted spell of general peace in its recorded history, and altered the balance of global power by helping Europeans reassert themselves on the world stage. By building a single market and developing common policies in a wide range of different areas, Europeans have come to relate to each other differently and have set aside many of their traditional differences in the interests of cooperation. The EU has brought fundamental changes to the way Europe functions, the way it is seen by others, and the way others—most notably the United States—work with Europe.

And yet the European project has raised many doubts and attracted many critics, even more so in the wake of a severe debt crisis that is testing the staying power of the euro, the EU's common currency. Some question the wisdom of European states transferring authority to a joint system of governance that is often criticized for its elitism and its lack of accountability and transparency. Others debate whether the EU works as efficiently as it might and whether it has outgrown itself. It is often faulted for its inability to reach common agreement on critical foreign and security policy issues and to match its economic and political power with military power.

Skeptics have routinely drawn attention to the EU's economic difficulties (such as sluggish economic growth and pockets of high unemployment), to its mixed record on dealing with ethnic and religious diversity, and to worries about demographic trends as birthrates decline and Europeans become older. For journalists and academics it has become almost de rigueur to talk and write of the crises in European governance, to point with alarm and foreboding at the latest example of a failure by European leaders to agree, and to question the long-term viability of the EU. Indeed, in the light of recent economic problems, some have even begun to doubt whether the European project will survive or whether the EU can truly be considered a world powerhouse.

In a recent editorial in the *New York Times*, Timothy Garton Ash argued that to include the EU with the United States and China in a "global Big Three" would be to invite laughter from elites in Beijing, Washington, or other world capitals. For Garton Ash, the crisis in the eurozone had demonstrated that the "five great drivers of European unification"—the legacy of "never again" left behind by World War II; the Soviet threat; the determination of Germany, as Europe's economic powerhouse, to sacrifice its own interests for those of "Europe"; the desire of Eastern European countries to belong to a common Europe; and the assumption that the EU would mean a continuous rise in living standards—have been exhausted. If the EU is really going to play the role it sees itself as playing, Garton Ash concludes, then it will have to pursue a course of more thoroughgoing integration, with a common identity and more comprehensive and muscular policies, from the social and economic spheres to—most especially—foreign affairs.[1]

Meanwhile, many Europeans are puzzled and uncertain about how the EU functions and what difference it makes to their lives. Americans are even more puzzled; many are—or at least have been, until recently—only vaguely aware of its existence and do not yet fully understand what difference it has made to Europe or to transatlantic relations. American political leaders are more attuned to its implications, as are corporate and financial leaders who have had to learn to deal as much with a twenty-eight-member regional grouping as with each of the individual states in the EU; even American tourists have noticed a difference as they use the euro in place of many different national currencies. But doubts remain about the bigger picture and about what difference the EU has made. To complicate matters, there is no agreement on just how we should define and understand the EU. It is not a European superstate, and suggestions that it might one day become a United States of Europe are greeted with a volatile mixture of enthusiasm and hostility.

The origins of the EU, and the motives behind European integration, are relatively clear. Frustrated and appalled by war and conflict, many Europeans argued over the centuries in favor of setting aside national differences in the collective interest. The first serious thoughts about a peaceful and voluntary union came after the horrors of World War I, but the concept matured following the devastation of World War II, when the most serious Europeanists spoke of replacing national governments with a European federation. They dreamed of integrating European economies and removing controls on the movement of people, money, goods, and services; they were driven by the desire to promote peace and to build a single European market that could compete with the United States.

The first tangible step came in April 1951 with the signing of the Treaty of Paris, which created the European Coal and Steel Community (ECSC), set up at least in part to prove a point about the feasibility and benefits of regional integration. Progress in the 1950s and 1960s was modest, but then the European Economic Community (EEC) was launched, membership began to expand, the goals of integration became more ambitious, and we now have today's European Union: an entity that has its own institutions and body of laws, twenty-eight member states and more than 500 million residents, a common currency used by more than half its members, and increasing agreement on a wide range of common policy areas. The Cold War–era political and economic divisions between Western and Eastern Europe have almost disappeared, and it is now less realistic to think of European states in isolation than as partners in an ever-changing European

Map 0.1 The European Union

Union. The fudge-word *integration* is used more often than *unification* to describe what has been happening, but those who champion the EU suggest that political union of some kind is almost inevitable. It may not be a United States of Europe, and it may turn out to be a loose association in which more power rests with the member states, but they find it hard to imagine a future in which European political union is not a reality.

Like it or not, the EU cannot be ignored, and the need to better understand how it works and what difference it makes becomes more evident by the day. Hence this book, written mainly for students in courses on European politics in the United States and Canada. In three parts it introduces the EU, goes through the steps in its development, explains how it works, and provides an overview of its policy activities.

Part 1 (chapters 1–4) provides context by first surveying the most important theories and concepts of regional integration and then showing how and why the EU has evolved. Giving the background on the earliest ideas about European unification sets the scene for the creation of the ECSC, whose founding members were France, West Germany, Italy, Belgium, the Netherlands, and Luxembourg. This was followed in 1957 by the signing of the two Treaties of Rome, which created the EEC and the European Atomic Energy Community (Euratom). With the same six members as the ECSC, the EEC set out to build an integrated multinational economy among its members, to achieve a customs union, to encourage free trade, and to harmonize standards, laws, and prices among its members. It witnessed greater productivity, channeled new investment into industry and agriculture, and became more competitive in the world market.

By the late 1960s, the EEC had all the trappings of a new level of European government, based mainly in Brussels, the capital of Belgium. Analysts refused to describe it as a full-blown political system, but it had its own executive and bureaucracy (the European Commission), its own protolegislature (the European Parliament), its own judiciary (the Court of Justice), and its own legal system. Over time, the word *Economic* was dropped from the name, giving way to the European Community (EC). Its successes drew new members, starting with Britain, Denmark, and Ireland in 1973, and moving on to Greece, Portugal, and Spain in the 1980s, East Germany joining via German unification, and Austria, Finland, and Sweden joining in the 1990s. The most recent round of enlargement came in 2004–07 with the addition of twelve mainly Eastern European member states, including Hungary, Poland, and the three former Soviet Baltic states, and Croatia became the EU's newest member in 2013. The character and reach of integration have been changed along the way with revisions to the founding treaties:

- In 1987 the Single European Act (SEA) led to the elimination of almost all remaining barriers to the movement of people, money, goods, and services among the twelve member states.
- In 1993 the Maastricht Treaty on European Union committed the EC to the creation of a single currency, a common citizenship, and a common foreign and security policy, and gave new powers over law and policy to the EC institutions. It also made the EC part of a broader new entity called the European Union.

- In 1998 and 2003 the treaties of Amsterdam and Nice built on these changes, fine-tuned the powers of the institutions, and helped prepare the EU for new members from Eastern Europe.
- An attempt was made in 2002–04 to provide focus and permanence by replacing the accumulated treaties with a European constitution. But the finished product was lengthy, detailed, and controversial, and it had to be ratified by every EU member state before it could come into force. When French and Dutch voters turned it down in 2005, there was another brief "crisis" before European leaders reached agreement in 2007 to draw up a new treaty based on much of the content of the failed constitution.
- The resulting Treaty of Lisbon fundamentally reformed several of the EU's institutions and attempted to give more coherence to the Union's policies, even while avoiding the language and trappings of a constitution that had been unpopular with many EU citizens.

The European Union today is the largest economic bloc in the world, accounting for one-fourth of global gross domestic product (GDP) and about 20 percent of global trade. It has replaced many of its national currencies with a new single currency, the euro, which has taken its place alongside the U.S. dollar and the Japanese yen as one of the world's primary currencies (its recent problems notwithstanding). There is now virtually unlimited free movement of people, money, goods, and services among most of its member states. The EU has its own flag (a circle of twelve gold stars on a blue background) and its own anthem (the "Ode to Joy" from Beethoven's Ninth Symphony); national passports have been replaced with a uniform EU passport, and in many ways Brussels has become the new capital of Europe.

Part 2 (chapters 5–10) looks at the European institutions, explaining how they work and how they relate to each other. Their powers and authority have grown steadily since the 1950s, although their work is often misunderstood by Europeans, and analysts continue to disagree over their character and significance. There are five main institutions:

- *The European Commission.* Based in Brussels, this is the executive and administrative branch of the EU, responsible for developing new EU laws and policies and for overseeing their implementation.
- *The Council of the EU.* Also based in Brussels, this is the major decision-making body of the EU, made up of government ministers

from each of the member states. Working with the European Parliament, the Council makes the votes that turn Commission proposals into European law.

- *The European Parliament.* Divided among Strasbourg, Luxembourg, and Brussels, the members of the European Parliament are directly elected to five-year terms by the voters of the member states. Although it cannot introduce proposals for new laws, Parliament can discuss Commission proposals, and it has equal powers with the Council of Ministers over adoption.
- *The European Court of Justice.* Based in Luxembourg, the Court interprets national and EU law and helps build a common body of law that is uniformly applied throughout the member states. It bases its decisions on the treaties, which in some respects function as a constitution of the EU.
- *The European Council.* This is less an institution than a forum, consisting of the political leaders of the member states. They meet at least four times per year to make broad decisions on policy, the details of which are worked out by the Commission and the Council of the EU.

Part 3 (chapters 11–16) focuses on the policies pursued by the European Union, looking at what integration has meant for the member states and for Europeans themselves. Covering economic, monetary, agricultural, cohesion, environmental, social, foreign, and security policies, this section examines the EU policy-making process, identifies the key influences on that process, and looks at its consequences and implications. The final chapter focuses on relations between the EU and the United States, which have blown hot and cold over the years.

Because European integration continues to be a work in progress, with a final destination that remains unclear, the relative balance of power among national governments and EU institutions is still evolving. That balance will continue to change as more countries join the EU and as integration reaches further into the lives of Europeans. All of this raises the key question: Why should Americans care about the EU? More specifically: What does it matter on this side of the Atlantic, and what effect will these changes have on our lives?

The most immediate implications are economic. Through most of the Cold War, the U.S. had it relatively good: it was the world's biggest national economy and national exporter, it had the world's strongest and

Table 0.1 The EU in Figures

	Area (Thousand Square Miles)	Population (Millions)	Gross Domestic Product ($ Billion)	Per Capita Gross National Income ($)
Germany	137	82.3	3,571	43,980
France	212	62.8	2,773	42,420
United Kingdom	94	62.0	2,432	37,780
Italy	116	60.5	2,195	35,330
Spain	195	46.0	1,491	30,990
Netherlands	16	16.6	836	49,730
Sweden	174	9.4	538	53,230
Poland	121	38.3	514	12,480
Belgium	12	10.7	512	46,160
Austria	32	8.4	418	48,300
Denmark	17	5.5	333	60,390
Greece	51	11.4	299	25,030
Finland	130	5.4	266	48,420
Portugal	36	10.7	238	21,250
Ireland	27	4.5	217	38,580
Czech Republic	30	10.5	215	18,520
Romania	92	21.5	180	7,910
Hungary	36	10.0	140	12,730
Slovakia	19	5.5	96	16,070
Croatia	21	4.4	64	13,850
Luxembourg	1	0.5	59	78,130
Bulgaria	43	7.5	54	6,550
Slovenia	8	2.0	50	23,610
Lithuania	25	3.3	43	12,280
Latvia	25	2.3	28	12,350
Cyprus	4	1.1	25	29,450
Estonia	17	1.3	22	15,200
Malta	0.1	0.4	9	18,620
TOTAL	1,691	504.8	17,616	33,982
United States	3,718	310.4	15,094	48,450
China	3,705	1,341.0	7,298	4,930
Japan	146	126.5	5,867	45,180
Brazil	3,286	195.0	2,477	10,720
Russia	6,593	143.0	1,858	10,400
India	1,269	1,225.0	1,848	1,410
Canada	3,852	34.0	1,736	45,560
World	57,309	6,894.6	69,971	9,488

Source: Population figures for 2010 from the UN Population Division, http://www.un.org/esa /population. Economic figures for 2011 from the World Bank, 2012, http://data.worldbank.org. Eurozone states indicated in boldface.

most respected currency, its corporations dominated the international marketplace and sold their products and services all over the world, and it led the world in the development of new technology. But much has changed in recent decades with the rise of competition first from Japan, then from Europe, and increasingly from China and India. The U.S. still has the world's biggest national economy, but the combined European market is nearly 20 percent bigger, and its population is nearly two-thirds bigger. European corporations are becoming bigger, more numerous, and more competitive; and the EU long ago displaced the U.S. as the world's biggest exporter and importer. And as one of the world's economic powers, naturally the EU's economic problems also have global economic significance.

All of this also applies to the bilateral relationship between the U.S. and EU. The U.S. does about one-fifth of its merchandise trade with the EU, which is the source of about two thirds of all the foreign direct investment in the United States and Canada, most of it coming from Britain, the Netherlands, and Germany. Subsidiaries of European companies employ several million Americans—more than the affiliates of all other countries combined—and account for about 15 percent of all manufacturing jobs in the United States and Canada. U.S. corporations, meanwhile, have made their biggest overseas investments in the EU. We often see and hear worried analysts in North America about the rise of China, but while the volume of Chinese imports to the U.S. is certainly catching up with that from the EU, Europe is still by far the most important economic partner of the United States.

The rise of the EU also has important political implications for North America. During the Cold War the most critical political relationship in the world was that between the United States and the Soviet Union—much else that happened in the world was determined by the attempts of the two adversaries to outwit and outmaneuver one another. With the collapse of the USSR and the end of the Cold War, it became usual to see the United States described as the world's last remaining superpower, and even perhaps as a hyperpower. But while the United States is unmatched in the size, reach, and firepower of its military, globalization has helped make political and economic relationships more important than investments in the ability to wage war. The U.S. spends almost as much on defense every year as the rest of the world combined, but this has not guaranteed its security, and in the view of many critics has actually made both the U.S. and the world less safe.

Meanwhile, the political influence of the EU has grown. Its economic might cannot be ignored, its policy positions are often less controversial than many of those taken by the United States (particularly toward the Middle East), and while the U.S. is associated (not always fairly) with hard power (coercion, threats, and the use of military force), the EU is associated with soft power (diplomacy, economic opportunity, and negotiation). The contrast is clear in the records of the U.S. and the EU on the promotion of democracy. Recent American leaders have made much of the importance of spreading democracy, but they have invested more time and money in using military means to achieve their objectives. Meanwhile, the promise of access to the European marketplace or even—for the select few—of membership in the European Union has arguably had a greater effect on promoting lasting democratic change and economic development, at least for Europe's closest neighbors. It was reasoning such as this that was behind the award to the European Union in 2012 of the Nobel Prize for Peace.

Just in the past few years, the relative roles of the United States and the European Union in the international system have been transformed. During the Cold War, Western Europe relied on the United States for security guarantees and economic investment. The two partners gave the impression that they saw eye to eye and made many public statements of solidarity. But behind the scenes there were tensions and crises as they disagreed over policy and over how to deal with the Soviet threat. Since the end of the Cold War, the disagreements have spilled into the open. The two are now economic competitors, Europeans are less willing to accede to U.S. policy leadership, and the two have become increasingly aware of what divides them. They differ not just over the use of military power but on how to deal with many international problems (including terrorism, climate change, nuclear proliferation, and the ArabIsraeli problem) and on a wide range of social values and norms. The result has been the emergence of two models of government, two sets of opinions about how the world works, and two sets of possible responses to pressing international concerns.

For all these reasons, we cannot ignore the European Union, nor can we understand the world today without understanding how the EU has altered the balance of global power. Not everyone is convinced that European integration is a good idea or that the EU has been able to fully capitalize on its assets and resources, but—like it or not—the changes it has wrought cannot be undone. The pace of global political and economic change is accelerating, and the results of the European experiment have fundamentally changed the way in which the world functions and the place of the United States in the international system.

Notes

1. Timothy Garton Ash, "Can Europe Survive the Rise of the Rest?," *New York Times*, September 2, 2012, B5.

PART I

HISTORY

1

What Is the European Union?

Chapter Overview

- Because the EU is a political arrangement that defies easy categorization, there has been much more vigorous theoretical debate about how to understand it than there has been for conventional states, such as the U.S.
- How we approach the EU still depends in large part on how we think about the role of the state. Consequently, there are at least five ways to conceptualize the EU—as an international organization, a regional integration association, a political system in its own right, a unique entity, or something that exhibits and combines all four of these.
- Theories analyzing the EU can be divided into two broad categories: those explaining how the EU evolved and those explaining what it has become. While the first category—which includes the theories of neofunctionalism and intergovernmentalism—was long dominated by scholars of international relations, the second category has increasingly become the province of scholars of comparative politics. The latter see the EU as a political system with its own

institutions, processes, procedures, and policies. In recent years the
term *multilevel governance* has emerged as one way to understand
the EU as a political system.

Numerous books have been published on national systems of politics
and government, but rarely do they begin with a chapter defining their
subject. No survey of the United States, for example, would begin by asking
"What is the United States?" We know that it is a country with an established and self-contained political system, with institutions bound together
by laws and political processes, and for which there is a multitude of ex-
planatory theories and an extensive political science vocabulary. But the
European Union is an animal of a different stripe: it is a unique political
arrangement that defies easy definition or categorization and does not fit
orthodox ideas about politics and government. It is clearly much more than
a conventional international organization, but it is less than a European
superstate. We do not even have a noun that comfortably describes the EU:
for some it is an "actor," but for others it is simply sui generis, or unique.

This uniqueness has spawned a vigorous debate over theory, which plays
a much greater role in the process of trying to understand the EU than it
does in trying to understand the United States. Initially, the debate was dominated by explanations generated by the subdiscipline of international relations
(IR). The EU was approached as an international organization, driven by
decisions made among the governments of the member states; European institutions were seen as less important than national institutions, although the
supranational element of the European Economic Community—those aspects
of its work and personality that rose above national interests—were not ignored. Since the 1990s there has been a reaction against the dominance of
IR, and new studies of the EU have been influenced by theories and analyses
arising out of the subfields of comparative politics and public policy. In other
words, rather than being portrayed as an international organization (albeit
one with unique features and powers), the EU is now increasingly seen as a
political system in its own right. More attention is being paid to the executive,
legislative, and judicial features of its institutions, to the channels through
which EU citizens engage with the EU (such as elections, referendums, and
the work of interest groups), and to its public policy processes.

The field of EU studies remains fluid, however, and there is no agreement
among either scholars or political leaders about how best to classify and
understand the EU, and no agreement on the balance of power between
EU institutions and member state governments. Although there is no short-

age of competing theories of European integration, there is no single, generally accepted theoretical framework. Undaunted, this chapter outlines the foundations of the debate by looking at a selection of the major concepts and theories of integration, divided into two broad categories: theories of how the EU evolved and theories of what it has become. It begins with a survey of the role of the state, then reviews attempts to understand how and why the EU emerged and developed. Finally, it looks at different analyses of the structure of the EU, focusing in particular on the federal and confederal qualities of the EU.

THE ROLE OF THE STATE

The EU scholar Ben Rosamond once suggested four possible approaches to the study of the EU.[1] First, we could try to understand it as an international organization, tying it to the substantial literature on such organizations. Second, we could study it as an example of regionalism in the global economic system, and compare it to other regional blocs such as the North American Free Trade Agreement (NAFTA) or the Latin American free-trade grouping named Mercosur. Third, we could approach it as an example of the dynamics of policy making in an attempt to better understand the process by which policy is made and how it is influenced by actors interested in the use of power. Finally, we could try to understand it purely on its own terms, as a unique organization that emerged out of a unique set of circumstances. But his list overlooked a critical fifth option: we could also try to understand the EU as a political system in its own right, and compare its structure and operating principles with those of conventional national political systems.[2] This approach to the EU figures prominently in the multilevel governance approach discussed below.

Of course, how we approach the EU depends in large part on how we think about the role of the state, which has for centuries dominated studies of politics and government. A state is usually defined as a legal and physical entity that (a) operates within a fixed and populated territory, (b) has authority over that territory, (c) is legally and politically independent, and (d) is recognized by its people and by other states. Most people—particularly when they cross international borders—identify themselves as citizens of a state and distinguish themselves from the citizens of other states by all the trappings of citizenship: legal residence, passports, allegiance to their national flag, protection by their home government, and a sense of belonging.

Just how long states have been important to an understanding of the ways in which societies are governed is debatable, but the 1648 Peace of Westphalia—which brought an end to two European wars and resulted in many territorial adjustments—is usually taken as a convenient starting point. Many states existed long before 1648, but Westphalia gave a new permanence to the idea of borders and sovereignty. As a result, the term *Westphalian* is often used as shorthand by political scientists to describe the international state system that has existed since then.[3]

In spite of its philosophical domination, the state has many critics. States are accused of dividing humans rather than uniting them and of encouraging people to place sectional interests above the broader interests of humanity. Identification with states is often associated with nationalism—the belief that every state should be founded on a nation and that national identity should be promoted through political action. But because few states coincide with nations, and most European states in particular consist of multiple national groups, nationalism can lead to internal instability, to a belief in national superiority, to ethnocentrism, racism, and genocide, and—in the worst cases—to war within and between states. Nationalism was at the heart of many of the disputes and wars that destabilized European politics for centuries, reaching their nadir with World War I and World War II.[4] In the 1990s, nationalist violence tore the former Yugoslavia into several pieces, and even today, several European states—Britain and Spain, for example—contain national minorities campaigning and agitating for greater self-government or even independence.

Americans have much less direct familiarity with the difficulties of nationalism than Europeans. The United States for most of its history has been relatively stable and united, avoiding the kinds of nationalist pressures and jealousies that have long brought stress to European societies. It had a civil war, it is true, but the conflict was primarily over policy differences—notably, attitudes toward slavery—and was fueled by economic pressures. Internal nationalist divisions have rarely been an issue for Americans, who—as a result—often find it difficult to understand nationalism in Europe. But it has long been at the core of European political, economic, and social developments.

Criticisms of the state contributed to the growth of international cooperation in the twentieth century, particularly after 1945. Seeking to reduce tensions and promote cooperation, states signed international treaties, reduced barriers to trade, worked together on shared problems, and formed a network of international organizations (IOs). Usually defined as bodies that promote voluntary cooperation and coordination between or among their members but have neither autonomous powers nor the authority to impose their rulings on their members, IOs are mainly a product of the second half of the twentieth century. By one estimate, there were fewer than 220 IOs in 1909, about 1,000 in 1951, and about 4,000 in 1972. Then came the era of growth: by 1989 there were nearly 25,000 IOs in the world, and today there are more than 50,000.[5] They include intergovernmental organizations (IGOs)—which consist of representatives of national governments and promote voluntary cooperation among those governments— and international nongovernmental organizations (INGOs)—consisting of individuals or the representatives of private associations rather than states.

The growth of IOs has led to the building of institutions in which states can attend to matters of mutual interest, the agreement of international treaties, the reduction and removal of trade barriers, and—in some cases— regional integration. This does not mean that states surrender their separate legal, political, economic, social, or national identities, but rather that they pool authority in selected areas and set up shared institutions with restricted powers. The ultimate expression of integration would be full political union, where states would create a new level of joint government and surrender or transfer most of their existing powers. This is what some hope will happen with the EU, while others regard it as the most dangerous risk of integration.

Integration involves the surrender, transfer, or pooling of sovereignty: the rights of jurisdiction that states have over their people and territory and that cannot legally be challenged by any other authority. Regional institutions are authorized to coordinate the making of new rules and regulations to which their member states are subject, although their work is restricted to the policy areas in which the member states have agreed that they should work together rather than separately, and the members collectively have the final say on the adoption of common rules and regulations. Regional institutions do not have powers of enforcement—they may be able to fine or embarrass members into action, but the execution of laws and policies is left to the governments of the member states.

How Did the EU Evolve?

The underlying motive behind European integration has always been peace. Exasperated by the frequency with which Europeans had gone to war over the centuries, and determined after 1945 to create a permanent peace, a number of thinkers outlined what they saw as the necessary conditions.

Federalists argued that postwar Europe needed to be rebuilt on the basis of a complete break with the past, replacing national states with a new European federation. Federalism was based on the idea that states had lost their political rights because they could not guarantee the safety of their citizens[6] and that political integration would be followed by economic, social, and cultural integration. The European Union of Federalists was created in 1946 with this view in mind, but their plan was too radical for the tastes of many, and by the time they met at their first Congress in 1948, national political systems were being rebuilt and the moment (assuming there ever had been one) had passed. All they were able to agree on was the creation of the Council of Europe, which had the more modest goal of intra-European cooperation.

A contrasting philosophical option was offered by David Mitrany, a Romanian-born British social scientist. He was interested in the achievement of world peace more generally, not with European integration—in fact, he was opposed to regional unification because he felt it would replace international tensions with interregional tensions—and yet his ideas formed the starting point for discussions about the road to integration. Mitrany saw nationalism as the root of conflict and argued that states should be bound together by a network of international agencies that built on common interests and had authority in functionally specific fields.[7] In other words, the economic and functional ties would precede the political ties. These agencies would be executive bodies with autonomous powers and would perform some of the same tasks as national governments, only at a different level; governments would slowly find themselves living in a web of international agencies and less capable of independent action.[8]

The idea behind functionalism was to "sneak up on peace" by promoting integration in relatively noncontroversial areas such as postal services or a particular sector of industry, or by harmonizing technical issues such as weights and measures.[9] Success in one area would encourage cooperation in others, and national sovereignty would gradually decline, to be replaced by a new international community. But the story did not unfold as Mitrany had hoped, because states did not give up significant powers to new international organizations.

American political scientists Ernst Haas and Leon Lindberg were among the first to try to understand European integration in particular, and their deliberations resulted in the adaptation of Mitrany's theories as neofunctionalism. Their thinking was in part a response to realism, then the dominant theory in IR, which argued that states were the most important actors in international relations, that domestic policy could be clearly separated from foreign policy, and that rational self-interest and conflicting national objectives led states to protect their interests relative to other states. Realists talked of an anarchic global system in which states used both conflict and cooperation to ensure security through a balance of power among states. By contrast, Haas tried to understand how and why states voluntarily mingled, merged, and mixed with their neighbors while acquiring new techniques for resolving conflict.[10] He saw territorially based governing organizations as important "agents of integration"[11] and argued that once governments had launched the process of integration, it would take on a life of its own (an "expansive logic") through the phenomenon of "spillover." Lindberg described this as a process by which "a given action, related to a specific goal, creates a situation in which the original goal can be assured only by taking further actions, which in turn create a further condition and a need for more action."[12]

Consider the following examples:

- *Functional spillover* implies that economies are so interconnected that if states integrate one sector of their economies, it will lead to the integration of other sectors.[13] Functional IGOs would have to be created to oversee this process, the power of national government institutions would decline, and there would eventually be economic and political union (see Box 1.1).

- *Technical spillover* implies that disparities in standards will cause states to rise (or sink) to the level of those with the tightest (or loosest) regulations. For example, Greece and Portugal—which had few environmental controls before they joined the EU—adopted such controls because of the requirements of EU law, which in turn had been driven by pressures from states with tight environmental controls, such as Germany and the Netherlands.

- *Political spillover* implies that once different functional sectors are integrated, interest groups (such as corporate lobbies and labor unions) will switch from trying to influence national governments to trying to influence regional institutions, which will encourage them in an attempt to win new powers for themselves. The groups will appreciate the benefits of integration, and politics will increasingly be played out at the regional rather than the national level.[14]

Box 1.1 Stages in Regional Integration

The concept of functional spillover has been applied to the process by which economic ties can move a group of states from limited economic integration to full political union. If there were a logical progression to this process, it might look something like this:

1. Two or more states create a *free trade area* by eliminating internal barriers to trade (such as tariffs and border restrictions) while keeping their own external tariffs against nonmember states. This happened in the European Economic Community (EEC) in the 1960s, and the United States, Canada, and Mexico have been engaged in a less ambitious attempt since 1994 with NAFTA.

2. The growth of internal free trade increases the pressure on the member states to agree to a *common external tariff;* otherwise all the goods coming in to the free trade area from outside would come through the country with the lowest tariffs. Agreement on a common external tariff creates a *customs union.* This happened in the EEC in 1968.

3. The reduction of internal trading barriers expands the size of the market available to agriculture, industry, and services, so these sectors want to expand their operations throughout the customs union. This increases investment in those countries and increases the demand for the removal of barriers to the movement of capital and labor, creating a *single market*. The European single market was more or less completed by the early 1990s.

4. With people moving more freely within the single market, pressure grows for coordinated policies on education, retraining schemes, unemployment benefits, pensions, health care, and other services. This in turn increases the demand for coordinated interest rates, stable exchange rates, common policies on inflation, and ultimately a *single currency*, thereby creating an *economic union*. This has happened with those EU states that have adopted the euro.

5. The demands of economic integration lead to growing political integration as the governments of the member states work more closely and more frequently together. The pressure grows for common policies in many other sectors, including foreign and defense policy, leading to *political union*. Although the EU has made progress in this direction, the idea of political union remains controversial.

Joseph Nye added a new dimension to the debate in 1971 by taking neofunctionalism out of the European context and looking at non-Western experiences. He concluded that regional integration involved an "integrative potential" that depended on several conditions:

- The economic equality or compatibility of the states involved.
- The extent to which the elite groups that control economic policy in the member states think alike and hold the same values.
- The extent of interest group activity, or pluralism. (The extent of interest group activity at the European level shows that many corporate and public interest groups see Brussels as an important focus for lobbying.)
- The capacity of the member states to adapt and respond to public demands, which depends in turn on levels of domestic stability and the capacity—or desire—of decision makers to respond.[15]

On almost all of these counts, the EU has long had a relatively high integrative potential, in contrast to the NAFTA parties. The United States and Canada may be strong motive forces for integration, but they are much wealthier than Mexico in both per capita and absolute terms. Elite groups in Mexico are more strongly in favor of state intervention in the marketplace than are those in the United States and Canada, labor unions in the United States have been critical of NAFTA, and public opinion in Mexico is more controlled and manipulated than it is in the United States and Canada. NAFTA has not had a significant impact on closing the gaps so far, and many obstacles remain to the development of the North American single market; not least of these is the fear north of the Rio Grande about immigration from Mexico, and the destabilizing effects of the Mexican drug war (see Box 1.2).

Neofunctionalism dominated studies of European integration during the 1950s and 1960s but briefly fell out of favor during the 1970s, which Haas explained by arguing that it lacked strong predictive capabilities.[16] However, there were two additional problems. First, the process of integrating Europe seemed to have ground to a halt in the mid-1970s, undermined in part by the failure of the European Commission (the Community's main executive body) to provide the kind of leadership that was vital to the idea of neofunctionalism. Second, the theory of spillover needed more elaboration. Critics of neofunctionalism argued that it was too linear, that it needed to

Box 1.2 NAFTA and the EU Compared

Although Europeans have traveled far along the road of regional integration, North Americans are at an earlier stage in the journey. The North American Free Trade Agreement (NAFTA) is a more modest exercise in free trade that has raised some of the same economic and political questions in the United States, Canada, and Mexico as have been raised in Europe by the EU.[16] It was an outgrowth of the Canada–U.S. Free Trade Agreement, which was signed in 1988 and came into effect on January 1, 1989, aimed at reducing barriers to trade between Canada and the United States. This evolved into NAFTA with the signing of a treaty in December 1992 that expanded free trade to Mexico, effective on January 1, 1994.

The original goals of NAFTA were to phase out all tariffs on textiles, apparel, cars, trucks, vehicle parts, and telecommunications equipment by 2004; to phase out all barriers to agricultural trade by 2009; to open up the North American advertising market; to allow truck drivers to cross borders freely; to allow banks, securities firms, and insurance companies total access to all three markets; and to loosen rules on the movement of corporate executives and some professionals. No institutions were created beyond two commissions that can arbitrate in disagreements over environmental standards and working conditions.

But progress has been modest. Trade between the U.S. and Canada is booming, but then they already had one of the world's biggest and most successful trade relationships before NAFTA was initiated. U.S.–Mexican trade has grown, leading to the creation of more jobs in the U.S., but how much of this is due to NAFTA and how much would have happened anyway is hard to say. There have been some job losses in the U.S., as labor unions predicted, but the trends were discernible before NAFTA was signed, the unemployment rate in the U.S. did not worsen as a result of NAFTA, and outsourcing has resulted in many more jobs moving to other parts of the world than to Mexico.

The opening of borders was slowed first by concerns about illegal immigration and international terrorism, and then by the drug war that broke out in Mexico in 2007. There is general political agreement in the U.S. that NAFTA has helped promote economic growth in Mexico, but there has been only limited economic convergence between Canada and the U.S. on the one hand and Mexico on the other; although significant progress has been made, Mexico still needs to do far more to free up its economy and to invest in education and infrastructure. There has also been no growth in common institutions: NAFTA has only small secretariats based in Washington, Ottawa, and Mexico City, and there has been little evidence of neofunctionalism at work in North America.

be expanded or modified to accommodate different pressures for integration, and that it needed to be seen in conjunction with other influences.[17]

One of the earliest responses to neofunctionalism was offered by Stanley Hoffmann, who in the mid-1960s argued that it concentrated too much on the internal dynamics of integration without paying enough attention to the global context. He instead argued that: the process was best understood as intergovernmental; while nonstate actors played an important role, the pace and nature of integration was ultimately driven by national governments pursuing national interests; that they alone had legal sovereignty, they alone had the political legitimacy that came from being elected, and they alone ultimately determined the pace of integration.[18]

A variation on this theme is liberal intergovernmentalism, associated with scholars such as Paul Taylor, Robert Keohane, and Andrew Moravcsik. Emerging in the 1980s and 1990s, it combines the neofunctionalist view of the importance of domestic politics with recognition of the role of the EU member state governments in making major political choices; in other words, the positions of the governments of the member states are decided at the domestic level, and then European integration moves forward as a result of intergovernmental bargains reached at the European level. As outlined by Moravcsik, integration advances as a result of a combination of factors such as the commercial interests of economic producers and the relative bargaining power of major governments.[19]

What Has the EU Become?

Most of the early theoretical debates about the EU focused on trying to explain how it had evolved. With time, the focus began to shift to attempts to explain what the EU had become and how it worked. But here too there have been many disagreements and few generally accepted conclusions. On the one hand, the EU has some of the qualities of an international organization: its members are nation-states, membership is voluntary, the balance of sovereignty lies with the member states, decision making is consultative, and the procedures used are based on consent rather than compulsion. On the other hand, the EU also has some of the qualities of a state: it has internationally recognized boundaries (even if these have changed quite dramatically over a short period of time as the EU has gone through cycles of enlargement), there is a European system of law to which all member states are subject, it has increasing authority to influence and control the lives of Europeans, in many policy areas the balance of responsibility and power has shifted to the European level, and in some areas—such as trade—it has become all but sovereign and is recognized by other states as an equal player.

However, it is neither one nor the other, and all we can say with any certainty—as noted earlier—is that it is more than a conventional international organization but less than a European superstate. The critical issues are (a) the relative powers of the member states and the EU institutions and (b) just where the EU sits on the continuum between intergovernmentalism (key decisions are made as a result of negotiations among representatives of the member states) and supranationalism (the EU is a network of autonomous governing bodies that have the power and authority to make decisions above the level of the member states and in the interests of the EU as a whole).

Some have questioned the assumption that intergovernmentalism and supranationalism are two extremes on a continuum. Mitrany argued that governments cooperated out of need and that this was "not a matter of surrendering sovereignty, but merely of pooling as much of it as may be needed for the joint performance of the particular task."[20] Keohane and Hoffmann agree, arguing that the EU is "an experiment in pooling sovereignty, not in transferring it from states to supranational institutions."[21] Leon Lindberg and Stuart Scheingold believe that the relationship between the EU and its member states is more symbiotic than competitive.[22] Haas argued that supranationalism did not mean that EU institutions exercised authority over national governments but rather that it was a process or a style of decision making in which "the participants refrain from unconditionally vetoing proposals and instead seek to attain agreement by means of compromises upgrading common interests."[23]

For its critics, the key problem with the intergovernmental/supranational debate is that it treats the EU as an international organization and diverts attention away from looking at the EU as a political system in its own right. Instead of being so much influenced by the thinking of IR, they argue, perhaps we should be looking more at the methods of comparative politics.[24] In 1994, Simon Hix argued that those methods could help us understand how governmental power was exercised in the EU, how Europeans related to EU institutions, and how European government was influenced by political parties, elections, and interest groups.[25] In other words, instead of studying the EU as a process, we should better understand how it actually works today.[26]

Hix was influenced by new institutionalism, an approach to the study of national and comparative politics that tried to revive the focus on the importance of institutions, overcome since the 1960s and 1970s by behavioralism, which had shifted attention away from institutions and toward political processes, such as the influence of interest groups. Behavioralists saw institutions as neutral arenas in which different groups competed for influence, but new institutionalists argued that structures and rules biased access to the political process in favor of some groups over others, and that institutions could be autonomous political actors in their own right.[27]

One of the handicaps faced by comparative politics approaches is the absence of a clearly identifiable European government. The term *government* typically applies to the institutions and officials (elected or appointed) that make up the formal governing structure of a state and have the powers to make laws and set the formal political agenda. But while the EU has a group of "governing" institutions and several thousand formally employed officials, there is no EU government as such. Instead, many prefer to use the term *governance* to describe the system of authority in the EU. This refers to an arrangement in which laws and policies are made and implemented without the existence of a formally acknowledged set of governing institutions, but instead as a result of interactions involving a complex variety of actors, including member state governments, EU institutions, interest groups, and other sources of influence. Taking this idea a step further, the term *multilevel governance* is used by some to explain how the EU is structured. This describes a system in which power is shared among the supranational, national, subnational, and local levels, with considerable interaction among them.[28]

In many ways, multilevel governance is just a more subtle and complex expression of the idea of federalism, which has been given relatively little attention by scholars of the EU; as Rosamond notes, there are no famous names in the academic debate about European federalism to compare with Mitrany and Haas,[29] in spite of the controversy that surrounds public debates in Europe about federalism. For its supporters, Europe has stopped disappointingly short of becoming a federal union, while for its critics federalism has become a code word for fears of the dangers inherent in the surrender of national sovereignty. This probably comes as a surprise to most Americans and Canadians, raised in federal systems that are at the core of an understanding of the American and Canadian political systems and are rarely seriously questioned (even if they are often misunderstood).

In addition to one of the most prominent federal states in the world—the United States—there are about two dozen federations today, including

Australia, Austria, Brazil, Canada, Germany, India, and Nigeria.[30] In each of these countries, national and local units of government coexist within a system of shared and independent powers, but none has supreme authority over the other. The national (or federal) government usually has sole power over foreign and security policy; there is a single currency and a common defense force; a national system of law coexists with local legal systems; there is a written constitution and a court that can issue judgments on disputes between the national and local units of government; and there are at least two levels of government, bureaucracy, and taxation: national and local.

In the U.S. system, federalism prohibits the states from having their own currencies, maintaining a military in peacetime, making agreements with other states or foreign nations, engaging in war, or—without the consent of Congress—levying taxes on imports or exports. The federal government cannot unilaterally redraw the borders of a state, impose different levels of tax by state, give states different levels of representation in the U.S. Senate, or amend the Constitution without the support of three-quarters of the states. Meanwhile, the states reserve all the powers not expressly delegated to the federal government or prohibited to them by the federal government. A key feature of federalism in the U.S. (and also in other strong democracies, such as Germany, Austria, and Australia) is the shared sense of identity of its citizens, the vast majority of whom place their primary loyalty to their country above their loyalty to the states, provinces, or region in which they live.

Federalism is comparatively poorly understood by most Europeans, partly because they have had little direct experience with the concept: only three EU member states (Austria, Belgium, and Germany) are federations. The EU itself is not a federation because its member states can still do almost everything that the states in the U.S. model (or provinces in the Canadian model) cannot do: they make treaties with other countries, make many independent decisions on interstate trade, operate their own currencies if they so choose, maintain their own armies, and go to war. The EU institutions, meanwhile, have few of the powers of the American or Canadian federal governments: they cannot levy taxes, they have no common security policy or military, they are not bound to people through a European citizenship, and they can negotiate with the rest of the world on behalf of the member states only in selected policy areas. And yet federalism is still an important analytical tool, because the EU has some of the features of a federal system of government:

- There is a system of European laws that coexists with national systems and is protected by the European Court of Justice.
- There is a directly elected European Parliament that coexists with national and subnational legislatures.
- There is a common budget, and a single currency in most of the member states.
- There is a common executive body (the European Commission) that has the authority to oversee external trade negotiations on behalf of all the member states and can sign international treaties on behalf of the member states.
- The member states of the EU are increasingly defined not by themselves but in relation to their EU partners.[31]

Federalism is not an absolute or a static concept, and it has taken different forms in different situations according to the relative strength and nature of local political, economic, social, historical, and cultural pressures. In the United States, for example, while the balance of power originally favored the states, there has been a gradual shift toward the center as a result of both historical trends toward greater national unity and the growth of federal government programs that have made states more dependent. In India, by contrast, political fragmentation in recent years has seen the states develop greater self-determination and a new prominence in national politics, particularly through the influence of regional political parties.

A second idea, which appears with even less frequency in debates about the EU, is confederalism. If a federation is a union of peoples living within a single state, then a confederation is a union of states.[32] *Confederalism* describes a system of administration in which two or more states pool limited amounts of authority in a common supranational government. In a federal system, power is divided between national and local units of government, both of which exercise authority over—and are answerable directly to—the citizens. In a confederal system, by contrast, power is held by independent states, the central government derives authority from the states, and there is no direct link between the central government and the citizens. The states transfer specified powers to a higher authority for reasons of convenience, collective security, or efficiency. Where federalism involves the local units giving up power over joint interests to a new and permanent national level of government, the units of a confederation are sovereign, and the higher authority is relatively weak; it exists at the discretion of the local units and can do only what they allow it to do.

Among the few examples of state confederalism in practice are Switzerland from the medieval era until 1789, and then again from 1815 to 1848; the Netherlands from 1579 to 1795; the United States from 1781 to 1789, and Germany from 1815 to 1866.[33] In the case of the United States, the assumption was that the original states might eventually cooperate enough to form a common system of government, but the 1781 Articles of Confederation created little more than a "league of friendship" that could declare war and conclude treaties, but could not levy taxes or regulate commerce, and the army depended on state militias for its support. There was no national executive or judiciary, and Congress (in which each state had one vote) met rarely.

For its part, Switzerland was more purely confederal until 1789, and although it now claims to be a federation, it has given up fewer powers to the national government than has been the case in the United States. The Swiss encourage direct democracy by holding national and local referendums, have a federal assembly elected by proportional representation, and are governed by a federal council elected by the assembly. One of the members of the council is appointed to a one-year term as head of state and head of government.

The European Union is confederal in several ways.

- Although authority has been transferred from the member states to the EU institutions, the member states still control the bulk of the power of negotiation and bargaining.
- The member states are still distinct units with separate identities, have their own national defense forces and policies, can sign bilateral treaties with other states, and can argue that the EU institutions exist at their discretion.
- It is a voluntary association. A member state could leave the EU if it wished, and its action would not legally be defined as secession. Attempts to leave federations, by contrast, have almost always been defined as secession and have usually led to civil war (as happened with the attempted secession of the Confederacy from the United States in 1861, of Chechnya from Russia since 1994, and of Kosovo from Yugoslavia in 1998).
- The only direct link between citizens and the EU institutions is the European Parliament. With the Commission, the Council of the EU, and the European Council, authority is derived mainly from the governments of the member states, and representation is indirect.

- There is no European government in the sense of elected leaders, such as a president, a foreign minister, and a cabinet, and there exists only a variable sense of European identity among the inhabitants of the EU.
- The EU may have its own flag and anthem, but most citizens still hold a higher sense of allegiance toward national flags, anthems, and other symbols, and progress toward building a sense of European citizenship has been mixed.

Surprisingly little has been published on confederation as a general concept, let alone on the EU as a confederation. Perhaps part of the problem is that confederalism falls short of what the most enthusiastic European federalists would like for Europe, while still going too far for most Euroskeptics. Another part of the problem may be that, in those few cases where confederalism has been tried, it has either failed or has evolved ultimately into a federal system. One study of Europe as a confederation was offered in 1981 by Murray Forsyth, who argued that studies of federalism seemed to have little connection with the realities of European integration and that the study of historical examples of confederations revealed that the EEC was clearly an economic confederation in both content and form.[34] Frederick Lister agrees, describing the EU as a "jumbo confederation" whose member states and governments continue to dominate the EU's institutions.[35]

Through all the debate over how the EU evolved, and what it has become, it is clear that there is little agreement among either scholars of the EU or European leaders about how best to understand the EU. Explanations coming out of IR still dominate, but it is clear that the EU has gone far beyond being an international organization and that there is more to its character than a series of intergovernmental bargains. Although many now believe that the EU should be seen as a political system in its own right, comparable in many ways to a conventional state, it is unclear just how far the comparisons can be taken. Paul Magnette, for example, is certain that the EU cannot become a state because its budget is too small, because its institutions tend to perpetuate divisions rather than override them, and because it is not a military power.[36] Just what final form the EU will take is anyone's guess, especially given the uncertainty that the crisis in the eurozone has engendered. It might remain a loose confederal association of states, or it might become a tighter United States of Europe with significant economic and political integration, or it might remain unique. The past offers little real certainty about the future.

Questions to Consider

1. In what ways does the EU today challenge traditional notions of the state and its importance to understanding the world of international politics? In what ways does the EU confirm the continuing importance of the state?
2. How might the proponents of neofunctionalism and the proponents of intergovernmentalism view the current European debt crisis and the EU's response to it?
3. How helpful is the US model of federalism—or the earlier Articles of Confederation—in understanding the political system of the EU?

Further Reading

Antje Wiener and Thomas Diez. *European Integration Theory*, 2nd ed. (Oxford: Oxford University Press, 2009).

> One of the most accessible and comprehensive of the different theoretical frameworks used to analyze European integration.

David Mitrany. *A Working Peace System* (Chicago: Quadrangle, 1966).

> Arguably the grandparent of them all; one of the first modern expositions of the idea of building peace through cooperation.

Ernst B. Haas. *The Uniting of Europe: Political, Social, and Economic Forces, 1950–1957* (Stanford, CA: Stanford University Press, 1958; repr., Notre Dame, Ind.: University of Notre Dame Press, 2004).

> Still widely seen as the starting point for modern ideas about the mechanisms and motives of European integration.

Simon Hix and Bjørn Høyland. *The Political System of the European Union*, 3rd ed. (London: Palgrave Macmillan, 2011).

> An outstanding analysis of the EU as a political system using the methods of comparative politics.

Anand Menon and Martin Schain, eds. *Comparative Federalism: The European Union and the United States in Comparative Perspective* (Oxford: Oxford University Press, 2006).

> A comparison of the European and U.S. models of federalism, with chapters on concepts, institutions, and policies.

Notes

1. Ben Rosamond, *Theories of European Integration* (New York: St. Martin's Press, 2000), 14–16.

2. Rosamond only refers to comparative politics later in his book, particularly on pages 105–8 and 157–64.

3. For a discussion of the effects of globalization on the Westphalian system, see Robert J. Holton, *Globalization and the Nation State*, 2nd ed. (New York: Palgrave Macmillan, 2011). For examples of some of the debates involved, see James Caporaso, ed., *Continuity and Change in the Westphalian Order* (Malden, MA: Blackwell, 2000).

4. For a useful reader on the history and meaning of nationalism, see Anthony D. Smith, *Nationalism: Theory, Ideology, History*, 2nd ed. (Cambridge: Polity Press, 2010).

5. Union of International Associations, www.uia.be.

6. Altiero Spinelli, "The Growth of the European Movement Since the Second World War," in Michael Hodges, ed., *Europe Integration: Selected Readings* (Harmondsworth, UK: Penguin, 1972).

7. David Mitrany, *A Working Peace System* (Chicago: Quadrangle, 1966), 27.

8. Mitrany, *A Working Peace System*, 27–31, 72.

9. Leon N. Lindberg and Stuart A. Scheingold, eds., *Regional Integration: Theory and Research* (Cambridge, MA: Harvard University Press, 1971), 6.

10. Ernst B. Haas, "The Study of Regional Integration: Reflections on the Joy and Anguish of Pretheorizing," *International Organization* 24 (1970): 607–46.

11. Ernst B. Haas, *The Uniting of Europe: Political, Social, and Economic Forces, 1950–1957* (Stanford, CA: Stanford University Press, 1958), 29.

12. Leon N. Lindberg, *The Political Dynamics of European Economic Integration* (Stanford, CA: Stanford University Press, 1963), 10.

13. For examples, see Ian Bache, Stephen George, and Simon Bulmer, *Politics in the European Union*, 3rd ed. (Oxford: Oxford University Press, 2011), 15.

14. Bache, George, and Bulmer, *Politics in the European Union*, 17.

15. Joseph S. Nye, "Comparing Common Markets: A Revised Neofunctionalist Model," in Lindberg and Scheingold, *Regional Integration*, 208–14.

16. Ernst B. Haas, *The Obsolescence of Regional Integration Theory* (Berkeley: Institute of International Studies, University of California, 1975).

17. See Gary Clyde Hufbauer and Jeffrey J. Schott, *NAFTA Revisited: Achievements and Challenges* (Washington, D.C.: Institute for International Economics, 2005); Stephen Clarkson, *Does North America Exist? Governing the Continent after 9/11 and NAFTA* (Toronto: University of Toronto Press, 2008); Sidney Weintraub, ed., *NAFTA's Impact on North America: The First Decade* (Washington, DC: Center for Strategic and International Studies, 2004).

18. Stanley Hoffmann, "The European Process at Atlantic CrossPurposes," *Journal of Common Market Studies* 3 (1964): 85–101, and "Obstinate or Obsolete? The Fate of the Nation State and the Case of Western Europe," *Daedelus* 95 (1966): 862–915.

19. Andrew Moravcsik, "Preferences and Power in the European Community: A Liberal Intergovernmentalist Approach," *Journal of Common Market Studies* 31 (1993): 473–524, and *The Choice for Europe: Social Purpose and State Power from Messina to Maastricht* (Ithaca, NY: Cornell University Press, 1998).

20. David Mitrany, "The Functional Approach to World Organisation," in Carol A. Cosgrove and Kenneth J. Twitchett, eds., *The New International Actors: The UN and the EEC* (London: Macmillan, 1970).

21. Robert O. Keohane and Stanley Hoffmann, "Conclusions: Community Politics and Institutional Change," in William Wallace, ed., *The Dynamics of European Integration* (London: Royal Institute for International Affairs, 1990), 277.

22. Leon N. Lindberg and Stuart A. Scheingold, *Europe's Would-Be Polity: Patterns of Change in the European Community* (Englewood Cliffs, NJ: Prentice-Hall, 1970), 94–95.

23. Ernst B. Haas, "Technocracy, Pluralism and the New Europe," in Stephen R. Graubard, ed., *A New Europe?* (Boston: Houghton Mifflin, 1964), 66.

24. See Alberta Sbragia, "Thinking about the European Future: The Uses of Comparison," in Alberta Sbragia, ed., *Euro-Politics: Institutions and Policymaking in the "New" European Community* (Washington, DC: Brookings Institution, 1992).

25. Simon Hix, "The Study of the European Community: The Challenge to Comparative Politics," *West European Politics* 17, no. 1 (1994): 1–30.

26. Simon Hix and Bjørn Høyland. *The Political System of the European Union*, 3rd ed. (London: Palgrave Macmillan, 2011).

27. For details, see Bache, George, and Bulmer, *Politics in the European Union*, 28–29.

28. Gary Marks, "Structural Policy and Multi-Level Governance in the EC," in Alan Cafruny and Glenda Rosenthal, eds., *The State of the European Community*, vol. 2 (Boulder: Lynne Rienner, 1993). For elaboration, see Lisbet Hooghe and Gary Marks, *Multi-Level Governance and European Integration* (Lanham, MD: Rowman and Littlefield, 2001).

29. Rosamond, *Theories of European Integration*, 23.

30. The study of comparative federalism has undergone significant growth in recent years. See, for example, Finn Laursen, ed. *The EU and Federalism: Polities and Policies Compared* (Aldershot: Ashgate, 2011); Michael Burgess, *Comparative Federalism: Theory and Practice* (London: Routledge, 2006); and Anand Menon and Martin Schain, eds., *Comparative Federalism: The European Union and the United States in Comparative Perspective* (Oxford: Oxford University Press, 2006).

31. Laursen, *The EU and Federalism*.

32. Frederick K. Lister, *The European Union, the United Nations, and the Revival of Confederal Governance* (Westport, CT: Greenwood, 1996), 106.

33. Murray Forsyth, *Unions of States: The Theory and Practice of Confederation* (Leicester, UK: Leicester University Press, 1981).

34. Forsyth, *Unions of States*, x, 183.

35. Lister, *The European Union, the United Nations, and the Revival of Confederal Governance*, chapter 2.

36. Paul Magnette, *What Is the European Union?* (New York: Palgrave Macmillan, 2005), 195–98.

2

Origins: The Road to Paris

Chapter Overview

- Although unity and cooperation had often been suggested as a solution to Europe's long history of conflict, a peaceful European community was really only possible after World War II. The main legacy of the war was a fundamental reordering of the international system into a new bipolar world dominated by the United States and the Soviet Union.
- The U.S. played a critical role in the new European drive toward unity. American economic leadership—embodied by the Marshall Plan and the new Bretton Woods economic system—ameliorated the continent's dire postwar economic needs and created the conditions for a prosperous Europe to emerge. Meanwhile, the security umbrella offered by the U.S. provided Europe with the crucial space it needed to start addressing its long-term political problems.
- Recognition of the relative decline of Europe's power also led its governments to seek a greater degree of cooperation that would, some argued, lead eventually to political and economic integration and a common European identity.

- A first step toward these goals was taken with the creation of the European Coal and Steel Community (ECSC), which pulled down some national tariff barriers and subsidies while creating a set of supranational governing institutions. The ECSC represents the first time European governments transferred significant powers to a supranational institution.

The roots of the European Union lie in soil created by hundreds of years of conflict among the peoples of Europe. Many had long dreamed of unity as an answer to Europe's divisions and conflicts, and proposals for the creation of institutions and processes that might help bring Europeans together date back to medieval times. But it was only after World War II that a broader and more receptive audience emerged. Although Europe enjoyed military and economic dominance before the war, World War II dealt these a severe blow. Subsequently, Europe found itself both divided and threatened by a cold war in which the main protagonists were external powers: the United States and the Soviet Union. The time was clearly ripe for Europeans to protect themselves from each other and to regroup in order to protect themselves from external threats potentially more destructive than any they had ever faced before.

The United States was to play a critical role in the emergence of the European Union, both intentionally and unintentionally. Intentionally, it offered at least three essential services that gave Europeans the luxury of more time and resources to address their internal problems. One was the economic opportunity offered by U.S. aid in the postwar reconstruction of Western Europe, embodied in 1948–51 by the Marshall Plan, which invested billions of dollars in helping address the devastation caused by war. The second was the economic leadership offered by the United States through the Bretton Woods system, which was underpinned by U.S. support for free trade and by the emergence of the U.S. dollar as the linchpin of the international monetary system. The third was the security umbrella offered by U.S. leadership in the defense of Western Europe against the Soviet threat, given substance in 1949 with the creation of the North Atlantic Treaty Organization (NATO).

Unintentionally, the United States helped Western Europe over the longer term by pursuing policies—particularly on the security front—that alarmed many Europeans. From the Korean War and continuing through the Suez crisis of 1956 and several major world events in the 1960s, transatlantic disagreements helped encourage Europeans to build stronger ties among themselves with a view to allowing Europe to build a stronger position as a global actor. Yet this meant that some way had to be found to encourage a greater sense of unity and common purpose than they had ever been able to achieve before. It was important not to be too ambitious and to develop a formula that could both encourage Europeans to see the logic behind cooperation and produce tangible results as quickly as possible. The first step toward this goal was taken with the creation in 1951 of the European Coal and Steel Community (ECSC), designed to prove a point about the feasibility of European integration.

THE TAMING OF EUROPE

Americans sometimes think of Europe as a continent restrained by the past, with centuries of history, timeless traditions, and relatively little social or political change. Nothing could be further from the truth. A long history it indeed has, but it is a history of constant change, of sometimes great political violence, and of almost unceasing social disturbance. Unity or cooperation often had been proposed as a solution to Europe's problems and conflicts, with suggestions for various kinds of international or regional bodies that might be the seeds of a European system of government. But national, social, or religious divisions always won out, and it was only brute force that ever took Europe close to the goal of regional unity.

The term *European* was not generally used until 800, when Charlemagne was crowned Holy Roman Emperor by the pope and was described in poems as the king and father of Europe. Later champions of European unity were often motivated by their belief that a united Christian Europe was essential for the revival of the Holy Roman Empire and by concerns about Europe's insecurity in the face of gains by the Turks in Asia Minor.[1] Among those thinkers and philosophers who explored the theme of peace through unity: Jean-Jacques Rousseau favored a European federation; Jeremy Bentham in 1789 proposed a European assembly and a common army; Immanuel Kant in 1795 argued that peace could be achieved through integration; and the Comte de Saint-Simon published a pamphlet in 1814 titled *The Reorganization of the European Community*, arguing the need for a federal Europe with common institutions, but within which national independence would be maintained and respected. Meanwhile, Napoleon tried to unify the continent by force, a project that ultimately failed as Europe by the end of the nineteenth century descended into nationalism and military rivalry between states.

The horrors of the Great War (1914–18) created an audience that was more receptive to the idea of European integration, the most enthusiastic proponents being smaller states that were tired of being caught up in big power rivalry. Yet prospects of a voluntary and peaceful European union were swept aside by economic recession and the rise of Nazi Germany, which was intent on correcting the "wrongs" of the Treaty of Versailles and creating a German *Lebensraum* (living space). Adolf Hitler spoke of a "European house," but only in the context of German rule over the continent.

The end of World War II in 1945 brought a fundamental reordering of the international system, which made the possibility of European unity much greater than ever before. Before the war, the world had been dominated by "great powers" such as Britain, France, and Germany, which were distinguished from other states mainly by the size and reach of their militaries[2] but also by their large economies, their strong positions in international trade, and their deep investments in the international system. Since the war had clearly resulted in the defeat of Germany, Britain and France continued to act like great powers, even though Europe's global role was diminishing, and a new bipolar order was emerging that was dominated by the United States and the Soviet Union. Their power and reach was so substantial that they represented a new breed of "superpower," the likes of which had never been seen before.[3]

The priority for Europe was to create the conditions necessary for peacetime reconstruction. For some this meant a rethinking of their systems of government; for others it meant a new focus on social welfare; and for all it meant taking a new view of international cooperation. But they had different sets of priorities, and different ideas about what needed to be done.

- France had been traumatized by the effects of wartime collaboration, and the only group that emerged with its credibility intact was the Resistance, whose spirit was embodied in Charles de Gaulle, leader of the Free French wartime government in exile. In 1946 the new constitution of the Fourth Republic went into force, but it was undermined by a lack of strong leadership and by foreign policy crises (see later in this chapter), and in 1958 de Gaulle came out of retirement to head the Fifth Republic, a new political system over which he was to preside until his resignation in 1969. Gaullism came to represent the ideas of French *grandeur* and independence, opposition to U.S. influence in Europe, and a new Europe dominated by a Franco-German partnership.

- Britain, it is often said, won the war but lost the peace. Britain's sense of national identity had been strengthened by its resistance to Nazi invasion; it was politically stable, its economy grew rapidly after the war, and it was wealthier and more powerful than France and Germany. However, its role in the world was being redefined. The new socialist Labour government of Clement Attlee embarked on a popular program of nationalization and welfare provision and signaled the beginning of the end of Britain's imperial status by granting independence to India and Pakistan in 1947. Many Britons still believed that their country was a major world power even while the security of Western Europe had to be based on the unchallenged leadership of the United States.[4] Cooperation with the rest of Europe was far from most British minds.

- Germany became introverted after 1945, not only because of the scale of its wartime devastation and the immediate challenges Germans faced simply to survive from day to day, but also because of shame over its role in starting the war and the actions it had taken during the war. The four postwar occupying powers disagreed on their plans for the new Germany, so by 1948 the country had effectively been split in two: a socialist eastern sector and three capitalist western sectors. The latter evolved into a new, democratic, "West" German state, and elections in 1949 were won by the conservative Christian Democrats. Chancellor Konrad Adenauer set about siding West Germany firmly with the Western Alliance and rebuilding West German respectability. Economic integration with its neighbors (especially France) accorded well with these goals.

- Italy, like Germany, emerged from the war both introverted and devastated, but was less successful than Germany in creating political stability. Although the Italian resistance came to be associated with the political left, Christian Democrats consistently won the biggest share of the vote following the creation of the Italian republic in 1946. Italy's integration with Europe was championed by the administration of Prime Minister Alcide de Gasperi, who saw European integration as a way of fostering peace and helping Italy deal with its internal economic problems.[5] Integration with Europe was eventually to contribute to Italy's "economic miracle" of the 1960s and 1970s by providing new markets for Italian industry.[6]

- The Benelux countries (Belgium, the Netherlands, and Luxembourg) had all been occupied by the Germans. Agreement was reached in 1944 among the three governments in exile to promote trilateral economic cooperation after the war. The Benelux customs union was duly created in 1948 with the abolition of internal customs duties and agreement on a joint external tariff. Cooperation was taken a step further in November 1960 with the creation of the Benelux Economic Union (BEU). All three countries retained many protectionist measures, but the BEU represented the first significant postwar experiment in European regional integration.

- For their part, the Scandinavian states had mixed wartime experiences but built on their postwar political stability with economic cooperation. Greece, Portugal, and Spain, meanwhile, remained relatively poor and politically unstable, and less interested in international cooperation than many of their neighbors. And all of Eastern Europe remained under the influence of the Soviet Union, experienced centralized political and economic control, and had little interest in cooperative arrangements with the West.

ECONOMIC RECONSTRUCTION AND THE MARSHALL PLAN

As Western European governments worried about domestic postwar reconstruction and adjustment, changes were taking place at the global level that demanded new thinking. During the war economists on both sides of the Atlantic had discussed the best means of achieving a stable and prosperous postwar world. Their views were crystallized in July 1944, when representatives from forty-four countries met at Bretton Woods, New Hampshire, to plan for the postwar global economy. They agreed on an Anglo-American proposal to promote free trade, nondiscrimination, and stable rates of exchange—goals that were to be underpinned by American economic and political leadership, and by the creation of three new international organizations: the General Agreement on Tariffs and Trade (GATT, forerunner to today's World Trade Organization), the International Monetary Fund (IMF), and the World Bank.[7] More immediately, though, Europe's economies had to be rebuilt and placed on a more stable footing.

World War II had spread through most of Europe, resulting in an estimated forty million deaths and leaving behind many pockets of devastation. Major cities lay in ruins, agricultural production was halved, food was rationed, and communications were disrupted because bridges, harbors, and railroads had been primary targets. Denmark, France, and the Benelux countries had suffered heavily under occupation. Many of Britain's major

Map 2.1 Europe After World War II

cities had been bombed, its exports had been cut by two-thirds, and its national wealth was cut by 75 percent. Before the war, Britain had been the world's second-largest creditor nation; by 1945 it was the world's biggest debtor nation. Germany and Italy were left under Allied occupation, their economies in ruins. In all of Europe, only Finland, Ireland, Portugal, Spain, Sweden, and Switzerland were relatively undamaged or unchanged.

When an economically exhausted Britain ended its financial aid to Greece and Turkey in 1947, President Harry S. Truman argued that the United States needed to step into the vacuum to curb communist influence in the region. The Truman Doctrine confirmed a new U.S. interest in European reconstruction as a means of containing the Soviets and discouraging the growth of communist parties in Western Europe.[8] At the same time, the U.S. State Department had begun to realize that it had underestimated the extent of the wartime economic destruction in Europe. Despite an economic boom during the late 1940s, sustained growth was not forthcoming, food rationing persisted (raising the prospect of famine and starvation), and there were fears of communist influence spreading across a destabilized Europe.

The U.S. had already provided more than $10 billion in loans and aid to Europe between 1945 and 1947, but something bigger and more structured was needed.[9] Into the breach stepped Secretary of State George Marshall, who proposed a new and more structured program of aid to Europe. His calculations were mainly political (a strong Europe would be a buffer to Soviet expansionism), but he made his argument more palatable to Congress by couching it in humanitarian terms. "Our policy is directed not against any country or doctrine," he announced in a speech at Harvard in June 1947, "but against hunger, poverty, desperation and chaos." Marshall argued that the initiative should come from Europe and that "the program should be a joint one, agreed to by a number, if not all European nations."[10] Many in the State Department and elsewhere felt long-term stability demanded coordinated regional economic management that would prevent the breakdown of Europe into rival economic and political blocs.[11]

The British and the French accepted the offer and approached the Soviets with the idea of developing a recovery plan. However, the Soviets suspected the United States of ulterior motives and bowed out. In July 1947, sixteen European countries met in Paris and established the Committee on European Economic Cooperation. They listed their needs and asked the United States for $29 billion in aid, much more than the United States had envisaged. With congressional approval, the European Recovery Program (otherwise known as the Marshall Plan) ultimately provided roughly $12.5 billion in aid to Europe between 1948 and 1951.[12] In April 1948 the same sixteen states created a new body—the Organization for European Economic Cooperation (OEEC), based in Paris—to coordinate the program.

Although the effects of the Marshall Plan are still debated even today, there is little question that it helped underpin the economic and political recovery already underway in Western Europe and helped bind the economic and political interests of the United States and Western Europe more closely together. It was a profitable investment for the United States, but it also had an important influence on the idea of European integration; as Western Europe's first permanent organization for economic cooperation, the OEEC encouraged Europeans to work together and played a key role in showing them how much mutual dependence existed among their economies.[13] It also helped liberalize inter-European trade and helped ensure that economic integration would be focused on Western Europe. But it ended up being based less on integration than on cooperation, and fell far short of promoting federalism or political unity.

SECURITY AND THE COLD WAR

In addition to economic concerns, there were also security concerns. U.S. policy on Europe after 1945 had initially been driven by President Truman's desire to pull the military out as quickly as possible. American public opinion favored leaving future peacekeeping efforts to the new United Nations, so within two years the U.S. military presence had been cut by 95 percent. However, it was increasingly obvious to European leaders that Joseph Stalin planned to spread Soviet influence in Europe, and that the Nazi threat had been replaced by a Soviet threat. Winston Churchill helped spark a change in U.S. public opinion with his famous March 1946 speech in Fulton, Missouri, in which he warned of the descent of an "iron curtain" across Europe.

The United States had hoped to share responsibility for security with the Western European powers, but it soon became clear that the Europeans lacked the resources to maintain their end of the bargain, and the dangers that Europe still faced were given new emphasis by events in Germany. Security concerns had encouraged Britain, France, and the Benelux states in March 1948 to sign the Brussels Treaty, creating a Western Union by which members would provide "all the military and other aid and assistance in their power" in the event of attack. In June, as a first step toward rebuilding German self-sufficiency, the Western Allies agreed to create a new West German state and a new currency for the three zones they were administering. In response, the Soviets set up a blockade around West Berlin. For the next year, a massive Western airlift was maintained to supply West Berlin. The Soviet threat was now clear, and the Berlin crisis led to the arrival in Britain in 1948 of the first U.S. bombers suspected of carrying nuclear weapons.

The U.S. Congress was wary of any direct commitments or entanglements in Europe but saw the need to counterbalance the Soviets and to ensure the peaceful cooperation of West Germany. In 1949 the North Atlantic Treaty was signed, under which the United States (entering its first ever peacetime alliance outside the Western Hemisphere) agreed to help its European allies "restore and maintain the security of the North Atlantic area." Canada also signed, as did the Benelux countries, Britain, France, Denmark, Iceland, Italy, Norway, and Portugal. The pact was later given more substance with the creation of the North Atlantic Treaty Organization (NATO), headquartered in Paris until it was moved to Brussels in 1966. The United States was now formally committed to the security of Western Europe.

Although NATO gave Europe more security and more space in which to focus on reconstruction, it soon became obvious that it was an unbalanced alliance: only 10 percent of NATO forces were American, but the United States exercised most of the political influence over NATO policy. NATO members agreed that an attack on one would be considered an attack on them all, but each agreed to respond only with "such actions as it deems necessary." The creation of NATO sent a strong message to the Soviets, but it was also designed to make sure that the United States would not immediately become involved in yet another European war.

Eager to encourage some kind of inter-European military cooperation, Britain invited its Brussels Treaty partners to join with West Germany and Italy to create the Western European Union (WEU).[14] The WEU obliged each member to give all possible military and other aid to any member that was attacked. The WEU also went beyond purely defensive concerns, and agreements signed by the seven founding members in Paris in October 1954 included the aim "to promote the unity and to encourage the progressive integration of Europe." Within days of the launch of the WEU in May 1955, and the coincidental admission of West Germany into NATO, the Soviet bloc created its own defensive alliance in the form of the Warsaw Pact. All of Central and Eastern Europe was firmly under Soviet control, the lines of the Cold War were now clearly defined, and its implications were clearly illustrated by events in Hungary.

In October 1956 the government of Imre Nagy announced the end of one-party rule, the evacuation of Russian troops from Hungary, and Hungary's withdrawal from the Warsaw Pact. As Britain and France were invading Egypt to retake the Suez Canal (see Box 2.1), the Soviets responded to the Hungarian decision by sending in tanks. The United States wanted to criticize the Soviet use of force and boast to the emerging Third World about the moral superiority of the West,[15] but it could not do so while British and French paratroopers occupied the Suez Canal. Britain and France were ostracized in the UN Security Council, British Prime Minister Anthony Eden resigned, and the Suez invasion was quickly abandoned.

BOX 2.1 TWO CRISES THAT CHANGED EUROPE

Two major events in the mid-1950s confirmed the new realities of the postwar international system, altered the way in which Western Europeans saw themselves, and gave a boost to supporters of European integration. The first came in French Indochina (now Vietnam, Laos, and Cambodia), which—except for its wartime Japanese occupation—had been under French colonial control since the late nineteenth century. Demanding independence, communist groups under the leadership of Ho Chi Minh launched an uprising in 1946, pulling the French into a bitter war. The end of the war came in May 1954 with the surrender of twelve thousand French troops besieged in the village of Dien Bien Phu. The loss of Indochina was a severe blow to French national pride and marked the beginning of the end of unilateral French influence outside Europe and Africa and the replacement of the French military presence in Southeast Asia by the United States.[16]

Two years later, events in Egypt marked the beginning of the end of Britain's role as a major world power. The Suez Canal had been built in 1856–69 by the British and the French, and had become a key conduit for British contacts and trade with India and the Pacific. Egypt became increasingly resentful about continued British control over the canal after World War II, especially after the 1952 coup that brought Gamal Abdel Nasser to power. Seeking a source of funds for his planned dam on the Nile at Aswan, Nasser nationalized the canal in July 1956. An outraged British government first responded with sanctions and then—with French and Israeli collusion—launched an attack on the canal zone in October 1956. The United States led international opposition to the attack, emphasizing the differences that had emerged between it and Britain regarding the new world order.

Indochina and Suez left the French more doubtful than ever about American trustworthiness and more convinced of the importance of European policy independence.[17] Meanwhile, Suez had the effect of drawing British attention away from its traditional links with Australia, Canada, and New Zealand, and encouraging Britain to begin (or to continue—opinion is divided) its slow turn toward Europe.[18] For Walter Hallstein, later president of the European Commission, Suez helped encourage greater European unity;[19] it was no coincidence that in 1957 the Treaty of Rome was signed (see chapter 3 for details).

The combination of France's problems in Indochina, the Suez crisis, and the Hungarian uprising had tumultuous consequences.[20] Britain and France began steady military reductions, finally recognizing that they were no longer world powers capable of significant independent action. Both countries embarked on a concerted program of decolonization; Britain began looking increasingly to Europe for its economic and security interests; and it became obvious to Europeans that the United States was the major partner in the Atlantic Alliance, a fact that particularly worried the French. West Germany, meanwhile, was alarmed about being caught in the middle of the Cold War, and many felt that a strong West German army would reduce the need for a nuclear defense strategy. West German public opinion changed somewhat after events in Hungary in 1956 and the 1957 launch of *Sputnik*, the first Soviet satellite, at which time there was also a massive buildup of U.S. nuclear warheads in Europe.

OPENING MOVES: COAL AND STEEL (1950–53)

Support for the idea of European cooperation after the war was reflected in the emergence (or reemergence) of several groups of pro-Europeanists. They included the United European Movement in Britain, the Europa-Bund in Germany, the Socialist Movement for the United States of Europe in France, and the European Union of Federalists. The spotlight fell particularly on Britain, which had led the resistance to Nazism and was still the dominant European power. In 1942–43, Churchill had suggested the creation of "a United States of Europe" operating under "a Council of Europe" with reduced trade barriers, free movement of people, a common military, and a high court to adjudicate disputes.[21] Yet it was clear that he felt this new entity should be based around France and Germany and would not necessarily include Britain. Britain, he once said, was "with Europe but not of it. We are interested and associated, but not absorbed."[22]

In an attempt to publicize the cause of European unity, pro-European groups organized the Congress of Europe in The Hague in May 1948. Within months the governments of Britain, France, Italy, and the Benelux countries had agreed to the creation of a new organization. The French and Italians hoped to call it the European Union, but the British insisted on the more ambiguous and noncommittal title Council of Europe.[23] It was founded in May 1949 with the signing of a statute in London by ten European states that agreed on the need for "a closer unity between all the like-minded countries of Europe." The Council of Europe made progress on human rights, cultural issues, and even limited economic cooperation, but it never became anything more than a loose intergovernmental organization and was not the kind of organization that European federalists wanted.

Among those who sought something bolder were two Frenchmen: an entrepreneur and public servant named Jean Monnet and French foreign minister Robert Schuman (see Box 2.2). Both were ardent Europeanists, both felt something practical needed to be done that went beyond the noble statements of organizations such as the Council of Europe, and both felt that the logical point of departure should be the perennial problem of Franco-German relations. One way of promoting reconstruction in Germany without allowing it to become a threat to its neighbors (particularly France) was to let it rebuild under the auspices of a supranational organization, thereby tying it into the wider process of European reconstruction. The congresses of the European Movement in early 1949 had suggested that the coal and steel industries offered strong potential for common European organization, for several reasons:[24]

- Coal and steel were the building blocks of industry, and the steel industry had a tendency to create cartels. Cooperation would eliminate waste and duplication, break down cartels, make coal and steel production more efficient and competitive, and boost industrial development.
- The heavy industries of the Ruhr Valley had been the traditional basis for Germany's power, and France and Germany had fought before over coal reserves in Alsace-Lorraine. Monnet argued that "coal and steel were at once the key to economic power and the raw materials for forging weapons of war."[25] Creating a supranational coal and steel industry would help contain German power.
- Integrating coal and steel would ensure that Germany became reliant on trade with the rest of Europe, bolstering its economic reconstruction and helping the French lose their fear of German industrial domination.[26]

Monnet felt that unless France acted immediately, the United States would become the focus of a new transatlantic alliance against the Soviet bloc, Britain would be pulled closer to the United States, Germany's economic and military growth would not be controlled, and France would be led to its "eclipse."[27] As head of the French national planning commission, Monnet knew from personal experience that intergovernmental

BOX 2.2 MONNET AND SCHUMAN: THE FATHERS OF EUROPE

The roll call of people throughout the centuries who have pondered the notion of European unity is impressive and includes William Penn, Jean-Jacques Rousseau, Jeremy Bentham, Immanuel Kant, Victor Hugo, and Winston Churchill. But it was two Frenchmen who outlined the ideas that led most immediately to the European Union as we know it today.

Jean Monnet (1888–1979) was an entrepreneur who spent many years in public service, notably during the two world wars. Born in Cognac in western France, Monnet worked for his family business before becoming an advisor to the French government during World War I, then working for the League of Nations. After the war he worked as a financier for an American investment bank, reentering public service during World War II. He was involved in post-war planning in France and was the architect of the Monnet Plan, a five-year strategy for investment and modernization. He became first president of the High Authority of the ECSC, from which he resigned in 1955.

Robert Schuman (1886–1963) had an altogether different career. Born to French parents in Luxembourg, he was raised in the province of Lorraine (which had been annexed by Germany in 1871 but was returned to France in 1918), attended university in Bonn, Munich, Berlin, and Strasbourg, and served in the German army during World War I. After the war he was elected to the French parliament and spent much of his time dealing with the legal problems of Alsace-Lorraine. He refused to serve in the French Vichy government during World War II, instead becoming an outspoken critic of German policy in Alsace-Lorraine. Schuman was imprisoned by the Gestapo, but he escaped and then worked for the French underground. Reelected to the new French legislature in 1945, he served as finance minister, briefly became prime minister, then served as French foreign minister from 1948 to 1952.[28]

Although the plan announced as the Schuman Declaration bears the name of the French foreign minister, it was actually Monnet's creation.[29] In fact, Monnet later claimed that Schuman "didn't really understand the treaty [the Treaty of Paris] which bore his name."[30] Nonetheless, the announcement of the plan was the spark that led to the European Union of today.

organizations tended to be hamstrung by the governments of their member states and to become bogged down in ministerial meetings. To avoid these problems, he proposed a new institution independent of national governments that would have a life of its own, and that would be supranational rather than intergovernmental. The proposal was discussed with West German chancellor Konrad Adenauer, and announced by Schuman at a press conference at the French Foreign Ministry in Paris on May 9, 1950. In what later became known as the Schuman Plan, he argued that Europe would not be built at once or according to a single plan but only through concrete achievements.

> The coming together of the nations of Europe requires the elimination of the age-old opposition of France and Germany. . . . With this aim in view, the French Government proposes that action be taken immediately in one limited but decisive point. It proposes that Franco-German production of coal and steel as a whole be placed under a common High Authority, within the framework of an organization open to the participation of the other countries of Europe.[31]

This, Schuman went on, would be "a first step in the federation of Europe" and would make war between France and Germany "not merely unthinkable, but materially impossible."[32] Few other governments were enthusiastic, however, and only four took up the invitation to join: Italy sought respectability and economic and political stability, and the three Benelux countries were in favor because they were small and vulnerable, had twice been invaded by Germany, and felt the only way they could have a voice in world affairs and guarantee their security was to be part of a bigger unit. They were also heavily reliant on exports and had already created their own customs union in 1948.

Undeterred by the less than enthusiastic response from other states such as Britain, the governments of the founding member states (the Six) opened negotiations and on April 18, 1951, signed the Treaty of Paris, creating the European Coal and Steel Community (ECSC). The new organization began work in August 1952, following ratification of the terms of the treaty in each of the member states. It was governed by four institutions:

- A High Authority with nine members (nominated for six-year terms) who were expected to work toward removing all barriers to the free movement of coal and steel and to represent the joint interests of the ECSC rather than national interests.

- A Special Council of Ministers representing the member states which would have equal power of decision making for the ECSC.
- A Common Assembly with advisory responsibilities, chosen on the basis of population from the national legislatures of the member states.
- A Court of Justice whose task it was to settle conflicts between states and to rule on the legality of High Authority decisions.

The creation of the ECSC was a small step in itself, but it represented the first time European governments had transferred significant powers to a supranational organization. It was allowed to pull down tariff barriers, abolish subsidies, fix prices, and raise income by imposing levies on steel and coal production. It faced some national resistance, but its job was made easier by the fact that much of the groundwork had already been laid by the Benelux customs union. The creation of the ECSC showed that integration was feasible, and its very existence obliged the Six to work together. It ultimately failed to achieve many of its goals (notably the creation of a single market for coal and steel),[33] but it had been established to prove a point about the feasibility of integration, which it did.

If the ECSC was at least a limited success, integrationists failed dismally with two much larger and more ambitious projects. The first of these was the European Defense Community (EDC), which was intended to promote Western European cooperation on defense while binding West Germany into a European security system. Echoing ideas outlined by Churchill in a speech to the Council of Europe in August 1950 a draft plan for the EDC was made public in October of that year.[34] It argued the need for a common defense and "a European Army tied to the political institutions of a united Europe and a European Minister for Defense."[35] On that understanding, the six members of the ECSC signed a draft EDC treaty in May 1952. Although West Germany, Italy, and the Benelux countries all ratified the treaty, there was clear resistance in Britain—wary of any kind of supranational security arrangement—and France. Plans for the EDC were finally abandoned in August 1954, when the French National Assembly voted it down on the grounds that giving up the right to a national army was too much of a restriction on sovereignty.

The second failed venture was the European Political Community (EPC), which was intended to be the first step toward the creation of a European federation. A draft plan was completed in 1953, based around a European Executive Council, a Council of Ministers, a Court of Justice, and a popularly elected bicameral parliament. With ultimate power resting with the Executive Council, which would represent national interests, the EPC was more confederal than federal in nature.[36] With the collapse of the EDC, however, all hopes for a European Political Community died, at least temporarily, and the plans were shelved. The failure of these two initiatives was a sobering blow to the integrationists, sending shock waves through the ECSC; Monnet left the presidency of the High Authority in 1955, disillusioned by the political resistance to its work and impatient to move on with the process of integration.[37]

Questions to Consider

1. What were the major obstacles to progress toward European unity and cooperation before World War II? What changed after World War II?

2. What was the impact of the Suez and Hungarian crises on U.S.–European relations and what role did this play in furthering European integration?

3. Why did Jean Monnet and Robert Schuman emphasize the Franco-German relationship in their ideas about a future European community? Why was the integration of coal and steel chosen as the foundation for this community?

Further Reading

Alan S. Milward. *The Reconstruction of Western Europe 1945–51* (Berkeley: University of California Press, 1984). Michael Hogan. *The Marshall Plan: America, Britain, and the Reconstruction of Western Europe, 1947–52* (Cambridge: Cambridge University Press, 1987).

> Two studies of the Marshall Plan and its contribution to European integration.

William I. Hitchcock. *The Struggle for Europe: The Turbulent History of a Divided Continent* (New York: Anchor Books, 2004). Tony Judt. *Postwar: A History of Europe since 1945* (New York: Penguin, 2005).

> Two valuable surveys of the history of postwar Europe.

Mark Gilbert. *European Integration: A Concise History* (Lanham, MD: Rowman and Littlefield, 2012). John Gillingham. *European Integration, 1950–2003: Superstate or New Market Economy?* (Cambridge: Cambridge University Press, 2003). Desmond Dinan. *Europe Recast: A History of European Union* (Boulder: Lynne Rienner, 2004).

Three of the best general histories of European integration; Gillingham is particularly critical, writing of missed opportunities and bad
decisions.

Wolfram Kaiser and Antonio Varsori, eds. *European Union History: Themes
and Debates* (New York/London: Palgrave Macmillan, 2010).

An excellent overview of how historians and social scientists have
conceptualized, written about, and debated the history of European
integration.

François Duchêne. *Jean Monnet: The First Statesman of Interdependence* (New
York: W. W. Norton, 1995).

A combined biography of Jean Monnet and history of European integration, written by Monnet's former speechwriter and press liaison
officer.

Notes

1. Derek Heater, *The Idea of European Unity* (New York: St. Martin's Press,
1992), 6.

2. Jack S. Levy, *War in the Modern Great Power System, 1495–1975* (Lexington, KY: University Press of Kentucky, 1983), 16–18.

3. For the first use of the term, see W. T. R. Fox, *The Super-Powers: The
United States, Britain and the Soviet Union—Their Responsibility for Peace* (New
York: Harcourt Brace, 1944), 20–21.

4. Stephen George, *An Awkward Partner: Britain in the European Community*, 2nd ed. (Oxford: Oxford University Press, 1997), 21.

5. Paul Ginsborg, *A History of Contemporary Italy: Society and Politics, 1943–
1988* (London: Penguin, 1990; repr., New York: Palgrave Macmillan, 2003),
16.

6. Paul Ginsborg, *A History of Contemporary Italy: Society and Politics, 1943–
1988* (London: Penguin, 1990; repr., New York: Palgrave Macmillan, 2003),
212–15.

7. Armand Van Dormael, *Bretton Woods: Birth of a Monetary System* (New
York: Holmes and Meier, 1978).

8. Michael J. Hogan, *The Marshall Plan: America, Britain, and the Reconstruction of Western Europe, 1947–52* (Cambridge: Cambridge University Press,
1987), 26–27.

9. Alan S. Milward, *The Reconstruction of Western Europe 1945–51* (Berkeley:
University of California Press, 1984), 46–48.

10. Office of the Historian, *Foreign Relations of the United States*, vol. 3 (Washington, DC: U.S. Department of State, 1947), 230–32.

11. Hogan, *The Marshall Plan*, 36.

12. Milward, *The Reconstruction of Western Europe 1945–51*, 94.

13. Derek W. Urwin, *The Community of Europe*, 2nd ed. (London: Longman, 1995), 20–22.

14. Urwin, *The Community of Europe*, 68–71.

15. Alan Sked and Chris Cook, *Post-War Britain: A Political History* (Harmondsworth, UK: Penguin, 1984), 135–36.

16. For details, see Martin Windrow, *The Last Valley: Dien Bien Phu and the French Defeat in Vietnam* (London: Weidenfeld and Nicolson, 2004).

17. Geir Lundestad, *The United States and Western Europe Since 1945* (Oxford: Oxford University Press, 2003), 115.

18. See Anthony Gorst and Lewis Johnman, *The Suez Crisis* (London: Routledge, 1997), 151, 160.

19. Roger Morgan, "The Transatlantic Relationship," in Kenneth J. Twitchett, ed., *Europe and the World: The External Relations of the Common Market* (London: Europa, 1976).

20. See Albert Hourani, "Conclusions," in William Roger Louis and Roger Owen, eds., *Suez 1956: The Crisis and Its Consequences* (Oxford: Clarendon Press, 1989).

21. Quoted in Michael Palmer et al., *European Unity: A Survey of European Organizations* (London: George Allen and Unwin, 1968), 111.

22. Quoted in Arnold J. Zurcher, *The Struggle to Unite Europe 1940–58* (New York: New York University Press, 1958), 6.

23. Mark Gilbert, *Surpassing Realism: The Politics of European Integration Since 1945* (Lanham, MD: Rowman and Littlefield, 2003), 34.

24. Milward, *The Reconstruction of Western Europe 1945–51*, 394.

25. Jean Monnet, *Memoirs*, trans. Richard Mayne (Garden City, NY: Doubleday, 1978), 293.

26. Monnet, *Memoirs*, 292.

27. Monnet, *Memoirs*, 294.

28. Drawn largely from Sherrill Brown Wells, "Robert Schuman (1886–1963)," in Desmond Dinan, ed., *Encyclopedia of the European Union* (Boulder: Lynne Rienner, 1998).

29. François Duchêne, "Jean Monnet," in Dinan, ed. *Encyclopedia of the European Union*, 347.

30. Roy Jenkins, *European Diary, 1977–1981* (London: Collins, 1989), 220.

31. Robert Schuman, "Declaration of 9 May 1950," in Peter M. R. Stirk and David Weigall, eds., *The Origins and Development of European Integration: A Reader and Commentary* (London: Pinter, 1999), 76.

32. Schuman, "Declaration of 9 May 1950," 76.

33. John Gillingham, *Coal, Steel, and the Rebirth of Europe, 1945–1955: The Germans and French from Rhur to Conflict to Economic Community* (Cambridge, UK: Cambridge University, 1991), 319.

34. Sir Anthony Eden, *Memoirs: Full Circle* (London: Cassell, 1960), 32.

35. Pleven Plan, reproduced in Stirk and Weigall, eds., *The Origins and Development of European Integration*, 108–9.

36. Urwin, *The Community of Europe*, 64–65.

37. Monnet, *Memoirs*, 398–404.

3

EMERGENCE: TO THE SINGLE MARKET AND BEYOND

CHAPTER OVERVIEW

- Although the ECSC was an important step toward creating an economic union, it was limited in scope. Accordingly, leaders of the ECSC signed the Treaty of Rome, which had as its intent a fuller economic integration of its member states and the creation of a single market. Rome also created institutions that continue to be used, in modified forms, in today's EU.
- The EU went through several rounds of enlargement, taking in the UK, Ireland, and Denmark in the 1960s, and Greece, Portugal, and Spain in the 1980s. Yet movement toward deeper integration slowed during the 1970s.
- The European project received new impetus with the creation of the European Monetary System, which aimed to coordinate macroeconomic policies and regulate exchange rates, and the Single European Act, which had as its goal the completion of the single

market. This treaty set the stage for even further economic and—more importantly—political integration that would come with the Maastricht treaty in 1992.

Europe after World War II found itself faced by two cardinal threats, one internal and one external. The internal threat was nationalism, which had been at the heart of repeated conflict over the centuries, and had most recently been glorified, abused, and discredited by fascism and Nazism. Because the German brand had been at the heart of three major wars in seventy years, many now argued that peace was impossible unless Germany could be contained and its power diverted to constructive rather than destructive ends. It had to be allowed to rebuild its economic base and its political system in ways that would not threaten European security; France was particularly eager to make sure this happened.[1] Perhaps if a new European identity could supersede multiple national identities, one of the recurring causes of conflict might be removed.

The creation of the European Coal and Steel Community had been a small first step toward this goal, but the organization was limited in its scope. Robert Schuman's original view was that any move toward political integration and a common European identity would depend upon further economic integration. Accordingly, in 1957 members of the ECSC—France, West Germany, Italy, and the three Benelux countries—took matters further by creating the European Economic Community (EEC), which had the more ambitious goal of creating a single European market. The institutions created by the Treaty of Rome can be seen as the forerunners of the institutions of the EU today: a commission that served as a quasi-executive, a Council of Ministers and a parliamentary assembly that performed legislative functions, and a Court of Justice that operated much like a supranational constitutional court. The kick-start given to economic integration by the Treaty of Rome brought new members to the European Community (EC): a first wave of enlargement added the UK, Denmark, and Ireland in the early 1970s, and a second wave in the 1980s added Greece, Spain, and Portugal.

However, moves toward fuller economic—not to mention political—integration were not as swift nor as straightforward as many European enthusiasts would have liked: the deepening of the European project appeared to stagnate during the 1970s, plagued by the member states' economic problems and reluctance to cede sovereignty on crucial economic issues. Yet economic risk created new opportunities and initiatives, and these came about in the form of the European Monetary System (EMS)—designed to help coordinate the macroeconomic policies of member states—and the Single European Act (SEA), which had as its goal the completion of a single market for the European Community by December 31, 1992. The SEA expanded the policy reach of European institutions, broke down some of the most difficult physical, fiscal, and technical obstacles to trade, and pushed the European Community toward a logic of political integration that would be given concrete shape by the Maastricht treaty.

FROM PARIS TO ROME (1955–58)

Although the six original members of the ECSC agreed that coal and steel had been a useful testing ground, it was difficult to develop those two sectors in isolation. For EU historian Desmond Dinan, the ECSC was "politically important and institutionally innovative, but economically insignificant," with little prospect of leading automatically to deeper integration.[2] When the foreign ministers of the Six met at Messina, Italy, in June 1955, they agreed to go further by working "for the establishment of a united Europe by the development of common institutions, the progressive fusion of national economies, the creation of a common market, and the progressive harmonization of their social policies."[3] A committee chaired by Belgian foreign minister Paul-Henri Spaak developed what he himself admitted was a plan motivated less by economic cooperation than by a desire to take another step toward political union.[4]

The Spaak committee report led to a new round of negotiations and the signing on March 25, 1957, of the two Treaties of Rome, creating the European Economic Community and the European Atomic Energy Community (Euratom). Following member state ratification, both came into force in January 1958. The EEC treaty committed the Six to several economic goals: the creation of a single market within twelve years through the removal of all restrictions on internal trade; agreement on a common external tariff; the reduction of barriers to the free movement of people, services, and capital; the development of common agricultural and transport policies; and the creation of the European Social Fund and a European Investment Bank. The Euratom treaty, meanwhile—mainly of interest only to the French—was aimed at creating a single market for atomic energy, but it was quickly relegated to focusing on research. When West Germany and Italy began developing their own nuclear power programs, Euratom funding was cut, and it rapidly became a junior actor in the process of integration.[5]

Although the EEC and Euratom inherited the same basic institutional framework as the ECSC, there were some changes:

- Instead of a High Authority, the EEC had an appointed nine-member quasi-executive Commission that had less power to impose decisions on member states and whose main jobs were to initiate policy and to oversee implementation.
- The EEC Council of Ministers was given greater power over decision making but still represented national interests. It had six members, but they shared seventeen votes (four each for France, Germany, and Italy; two each for Belgium and the Netherlands; and one for Luxembourg). Some decisions had to be unanimous, while others could be made by a simple majority or, more often, by a qualified majority of twelve votes from at least four states. This system made it impossible for the larger states to outvote the smaller ones.
- A single Parliamentary Assembly was created to cover the EEC, ECSC, and Euratom, with 142 members appointed by the member states. It could question or censure the Commission of the ECSC, but had little legislative authority. The Assembly renamed itself the European Parliament in 1962.
- A single Court of Justice was created with seven judges appointed for renewable six-year terms. It was responsible for interpreting the treaties and for ensuring that the three institutions and the member states fulfilled their treaty obligations.

Integration Takes Root (1958–68)

Given the long history of inter-European hostilities and war, the integration of six Western European states under the auspices of the ECSC, the EEC, and Euratom was a conspicuous achievement. There are still barriers to the single market even today, but internal tariffs fell quickly enough in the early years of the EEC to allow the Six to agree on a common external tariff in July 1968 and to declare an industrial customs union. The single market expanded as nontariff barriers to the movement of goods across borders were reduced, and standards and regulations on health, safety, and consumer protection were harmonized during the 1960s and 1970s. Quota restrictions fell, trade and productivity grew, and it was—in economist Barry Eichengreen's view—"a golden age of growth" for the EEC.[6]

There were other achievements as well:

- A fundamental goal of the Treaty of Rome had been agreement on a Common Agricultural Policy (CAP), which was achieved in 1968 with the acceptance of a watered-down version of a plan drawn up by the agriculture commissioner, Sicco Mansholt.[7] Its goals were to create a single market for agricultural products and to assure EEC farmers guaranteed prices for their produce. CAP initially encouraged both production and productivity, although it was also the largest single item in the budget and became enormously controversial (see chapter 14).
- Under the Common Commercial Policy agreed by the Treaty of Rome, the Six worked closely together on international trade negotiations and enjoyed influence they would not have had negotiating individually. The EEC acted as one, for example, in the Kennedy Round of GATT negotiations during the mid-1960s and in reaching preferential trade agreements with eighteen former African colonies under the 1963 Yaoundé Convention (see chapter 15).[8]
- Decision making was streamlined in April 1965 with the Treaty Establishing a Single Council and a Single Commission of the European Communities (the Merger treaty). The decision-making process was later given further authority and direction by the formalization in 1975 of regular summits of Community leaders coming together as the European Council (see chapter 9). The EEC was finally made more democratic with the introduction in 1979 of direct elections to the European Parliament.

But there were problems as well. Even Jean Monnet had warned that "Europe will be established through crises and . . . the outcome will be the sum of the outcomes of those crises."[9] The failure of the European Defense Community and the European Political Community had been early blows, but this was the result of a common core problem, which was that they were too ambitious. Then came the empty chair crisis of 1965, whose structural implications were more worrying because they showed how far some member states were prepared to go to protect national interests.

At the heart of this crisis were de Gaulle's attempts to discard the supranational elements of the Treaty of Rome and to build a Community dominated by France.[10] There were several sparks that set off the conflagration:

demands from the European Parliament for more power (especially concerning the budget), the fact that decision making by majority vote on certain issues in the Council of Ministers was scheduled to come into force
on January 1, 1966 (thereby taking away the national veto), and suggestions
by the European Commission that it replace its reliance on national contributions from EEC members with an independent source of income and
that more progress be made on the Common Agricultural Policy.

This all smacked of excessive supranationalism to the French, who insisted that EEC funding continue to come from national contributions, at
least until 1970. The other five states disagreed, so in June 1965 France
began boycotting meetings of the Council of Ministers, preventing any decisions from being made on new laws and policies and setting off the empty
chair crisis. De Gaulle even went so far as to cast doubts on the future of
the EEC unless the national veto was preserved. The crisis was ended only
with the January 1966 Luxembourg Compromise (actually an agreement
to disagree), by which the voting procedure in the Council of Ministers
was changed. Unanimity remained the ideal, but members would be allowed
to veto matters they felt adversely affected their national interests. This
curbed the growth of Commission powers and placed more power into the
hands of the member states (in the form of the Council of Ministers).

THE ROLE OF THE UNITED STATES

The United States was supportive of the idea of European integration. President John F. Kennedy announced in 1962 that the U.S. looked on "this
vast new enterprise with hope and admiration" and viewed Europe not as
a rival but as "a partner with whom we can deal on a basis of full equality."[11]
For the U.S., the Community not only promised valuable new trading opportunities, but might also help integrate West Germany into a peaceful
Western Europe, improve Western Europe's prospects of standing up to
the Soviets, and strengthen the transatlantic community.[12] But in spite of
the public show of transatlantic solidarity, there were transatlantic disagreements as well, and these contributed in their own way to European integration; Western Europeans pondered the motives and implications of U.S.
foreign policy, and some were moved to question the prospects for real
transatlantic agreement on key international problems.[13]

Early doubts had been raised by the Korean War. Europeans had initially
taken heart at the U.S.-led invasion to expel North Korean invaders from
the South, but were then alarmed by the invasion of the North, which set

off an intervention by China and threatened to generate Soviet hostility. Then came Suez, which saw the U.S. at odds with Britain and France over the shape of the postwar international system. Then a series of events in the 1960s and 1970s rattled Europeans again, emphasizing transatlantic policy differences and further convincing many Europeans of the need for the Community to develop policy independence from the United States:

- When the Berlin wall was built in 1961, cutting off the Soviet-controlled east from the Allied-controlled west, Europeans were disappointed that no stronger action was taken against the Soviets by the Kennedy administration.
- In October 1962 the world was taken to the brink of the nuclear abyss during the Cuban missile crisis, when decisions were made by the Americans with little reference to their European NATO partners.[14]
- The mid-1960s saw an escalation of the war in Vietnam, and it was the United States' turn to be disappointed in Europe: the Johnson administration hoped for political and military support from Europe but received none, and public demonstrations against the war were loud and vociferous in Western Europe; a 1967 poll found 80 percent of Europeans critical of U.S. policy.[15]
- Finally, when the Nixon administration suspended the convertibility of the U.S. dollar against gold in 1970 and then cut the link altogether in 1971—in both cases without reference to the Europeans—even pro-American European leaders began to argue that Europe needed to unite in order to protect its interests.[16]

Except for the anti-Vietnam demonstrations, European criticism of U.S. policy was muted. However, Europeans wondered how much they could rely on the Americans, and the Americans were disappointed at how often the Europeans seemed unwilling to understand or support the American view of the world and its major threats. The disputes were to continue to grow—over the Middle East, over détente with the Soviets, and over nuclear weapons. The doubts sown in the 1960s and 1970s eventually exploded into the open in 2003, when the U.S. invaded Iraq, and a newly assertive France and Germany made their opposition public (see chapter 16).

Perhaps the most telling indicator of the changing transatlantic balance was the growing assertiveness of the Community as a global trading power. Progress on the single market may have been mixed, there may have been difficulties with making agricultural policy work efficiently, and the road to economic and monetary union may have been bumpy (see chapter 4), but on the trade front the Community was making great strides, and no country felt the effects more than the United States. The Common Commercial Policy meant strength through unity; the Six—and later the Nine—wielded their combined powers and resources with considerable effect in the meeting chambers of GATT.[17] The Community and the U.S. were each other's biggest trading partners and biggest sources of foreign investment, and they were ultimately to become each other's biggest sources of commercial competition. Conflicts arose between the two sides over agricultural exports, the steel industry, government subsidies, and concerns from the U.S. about the rise of Fortress Europe, a unified trading bloc with external barriers working against U.S. trade interests.[18]

ENLARGEMENT: LOOKING NORTH AND SOUTH (1960–86)

There was a limit to how much the EEC could achieve with just six members, so the idea of enlargement was never far from the minds of its leaders. The country most obvious by its absence was Britain—still Western Europe's major power—but although Churchill had been a champion of European integration during both the war and his years in opposition (1945–51), neither the Labour government that ousted him in 1945 nor he upon his return to office in 1951 took this philosophy any further. Britain still saw its interests lying with its empire and with the United States, but the argument that joining the EEC might threaten its special relationship with the U.S. was undermined by the support that the U.S. gave to the idea of the Community.[19] Few in the British government felt that the EEC had much potential;[20] but then came Suez, which finally put to rest Britain's nostalgic idea that it was still a great power, shook the foundations of the Anglo-American relationship, and made clear that global political issues were being discussed and influenced bilaterally by the United States and the USSR.

After being diverted briefly by its creation of the European Free Trade Association (see Box 3.1), Britain began negotiating with the Six in early 1962, as part of a package deal that included Denmark, Ireland, and Norway. Denmark's motives for EEC membership were agricultural; it was producing three times as much food as it needed, and much of that was being exported to Britain. Furthermore, the EEC would be a big new market for Danish agricultural surpluses and would provide a boost for Danish

BOX 3.1 THE EFTA SIDESHOW

Dean Acheson, U.S. secretary of state during the Truman administration, described Britain's decision not to negotiate on membership in the ECSC as its "great mistake of the postwar period."[21] Certainly it began a British tradition of dragging its feet on Europe and typically arriving late to many of the most important decisions. But it has never been alone in this: several countries supported an early effort by Britain to organize an alternative to the EEC that would champion free trade without economic and political integration.

In January 1960, the European Free Trade Association (EFTA) was founded with the signing of the Stockholm Convention by Austria, Britain, Denmark, Norway, Portugal, Sweden, and Switzerland. Membership in EFTA was voluntary (unlike the contractual arrangements set up for the EEC by the Treaty of Rome), and EFTA had no political goals and no institutions beyond a Council of Ministers that met two or three times a year and a group of permanent representatives serviced by a small secretariat in Geneva. EFTA helped cut tariffs but achieved relatively little over the long term. Several of its members did more trade with the EEC than with their EFTA partners, and questions were soon raised about Britain's motives in pursuing the EFTA concept. It was a marriage of convenience, created to prove a point about the relative merits of a looser free trade arrangement with low tariffs.

It soon became clear that political influence in Europe lay with the EEC and that Britain risked political isolation if it stayed out. The continent had made impressive economic and political progress, and British industry wanted access to the rich European market.[22] So in August 1961, barely fifteen months after the creation of EFTA, Britain applied for EEC membership at the same time as Denmark and Ireland. They were joined by Norway in 1962. With three of its seven members now trying to defect, EFTA ceased to have much purpose, so the rest of its members—Austria, Portugal, Sweden, and Switzerland—all applied for associate membership in the EEC, followed by Malta and Spain. EFTA still exists today, but with just four members: Iceland, Liechtenstein, Norway, and Switzerland.

industrial development. Ireland saw the EEC as a potential boost for its industrial plans and as a means to reduce its reliance on agriculture and on Britain. Norway followed the British lead, owing to the importance of EEC markets.

All seemed set for success, but then the British application was tripped up by Charles de Gaulle. The French president, an Anglophobe who had plans for an EEC built around a Franco-German axis, saw Britain as a rival to French influence in the EEC, and resented Britain's lack of enthusiasm toward the early integrationist moves of the 1950s. He also felt that British membership would give the United States too much influence in Europe, a concern that seemed to be confirmed at the end of 1962 when Britain accepted the U.S. offer of Polaris missiles as delivery vehicles for Britain's nuclear warheads. For his part, Monnet was eager for British membership and even tried to convince West German chancellor Konrad Adenauer by suggesting that he refuse to sign a Franco-German Friendship Treaty unless de Gaulle accepted the British application. But Adenauer too was an Anglophobe and agreed that the development of the Franco-German axis was key.

In the space of just ten days in January 1963, de Gaulle vetoed the British application and signed the treaty with Germany. He upset Britain and some of his own EEC partners by reaching the veto decision unilaterally and making the announcement at a press conference in Paris. Since Britain's application was part of a package that included those of Denmark, Ireland, and Norway, they were turned down as well. Britain applied again in 1966 and was vetoed for a second time by de Gaulle, who was still worried about the influence within the EEC that British membership would afford to the United States, and also keen to ensure that French interests in the Common Agricultural Policy were not undermined. Following de Gaulle's resignation as president of France in 1969, Britain applied for a third time, and this time its application was accepted, along with those of Denmark, Ireland, and Norway. Following membership negotiations in 1970 and 1971, Britain, Denmark, and Ireland finally joined the EEC in January 1973; Norway would have joined also, but a Norwegian public referendum in September 1972 narrowly went against membership, thanks mainly to the concerns of farmers and fishing communities. The Six had now become the Nine.

A second round of enlargements, which came in the 1980s, pushed the borders of the EEC farther south. Greece had made its first overtures to the EEC during the late 1950s but was turned down on the grounds that its economy was too underdeveloped. It was given associate membership

Map 3.1   Growth of the European Union, 1952–86

in 1961 as a prelude to full accession, which might have come sooner had it not been for the Greek military coup of April 1967. With the return to civilian government in 1974, Greece applied almost immediately for full membership. The Commission felt that Greece's economy was still too weak, but the Greek government responded that EEC membership would help underpin its attempts to rebuild democracy. The Council of Ministers agreed, negotiations opened in 1976, and Greece joined in January 1981.

Portugal and Spain had requested negotiations for associate membership in 1962, but both were dictatorships. Although the EEC treaty said that "any European State may apply to become a member of the Community," democracy was—in practice—a basic precondition. Spain was given a preferential trade agreement in 1970 and Portugal in 1973, but only with the overthrow of the Marcelo Caetano regime in Portugal in 1974 and the death of Francisco Franco in Spain in 1975 was the possibility of EEC membership for the two states taken seriously. Despite their relative poverty, problems over fishing rights, and concerns about Portuguese and Spanish workers moving north in search of work, the EEC felt that membership would encourage democracy in the Iberian Peninsula and help link the two countries more closely to NATO and Western Europe. Negotiations opened in 1978 and 1979, and Portugal and Spain joined in January 1986, bringing EEC membership to twelve.[23]

The doubling of the membership of the EEC had several political and economic consequences: it increased the international influence of the EEC (which was now the largest economic bloc in the world), it complicated the Community's decision-making processes, it reduced the overall influence of France and Germany, and—by bringing in the poorer Mediterranean states—it altered the internal economic balance. Rather than enlarging any farther, it was deemed time to strengthen the relationships among the existing twelve members. Applications were made by Turkey (1987), Austria (1989), and Cyprus and Malta (1990), and although East Germany entered through the back door with the reunification of Germany in October 1990, there was to be no further enlargement until 1995.

TOWARD ECONOMIC AND MONETARY UNION (1969–93)

The Treaty of Rome had mentioned the need to "coordinate" economic policies but had given the Community no specific powers to ensure that this would happen, and coordination in practice meant little more than "polite ritualistic consultation."[24] Proposals to go further came up against concerns about loss of national sovereignty, and EEC leaders disagreed about whether to move first on economic union (the coordination of economic policies) or on monetary union (the creation of a single currency).[25] Following agreement on the principle of economic and monetary union (EMU) at a 1969 summit of EEC leaders at The Hague, it was decided to move on the economic and monetary fronts at the same time, with the achievement of fixed exchange rates in stages by 1980.[26] The Six accordingly agreed to work to hold exchange rates steady relative to one another and to hold the value of national currencies within ± 2.25 percent of the U.S. dollar in a structure known as the "snake in the tunnel" (a reference to the way values could go up an down within a defined band). They would meanwhile make more effort to coordinate national economic policies, with their finance ministers meeting at least three times annually.

The timing for this decision could not have been worse. The snake was launched in April 1972, just eight months after the Nixon administration took the United States off the gold standard, ending the Bretton Woods era of fixed exchange rates. Nixon blamed the problems of Bretton Woods largely on the protectionism of the Community and its unwillingness to take more responsibility for the costs of defense, when in fact the inflationary effects on the U.S. economy of the war in Vietnam were chiefly to blame.[27] The end of Bretton Woods brought international monetary turbulence, which was amplified in 1973 by an international energy crisis. In their anxiety to control inflation and encourage economic growth, several EC member states left the snake: Britain, Denmark, and Ireland left within weeks of joining; France refused to join, then joined, then left in 1974, then rejoined in 1975, then left again.[28]

A new approach was taken in March 1979, mainly on the initiative of the new West German chancellor, Helmut Schmidt, who was upset with the failure of the Carter administration in the United States to take action to strengthen the dollar.[29] The European Monetary System (EMS) replaced the snake with an Exchange Rate Mechanism (ERM) (operating on a similar basis) founded on a European currency unit (ECU). The goal of the EMS was to create a zone of monetary stability, with governments taking action to keep their currencies as stable as possible relative to the ECU, whose value was calculated on the basis of a basket of national currencies, weighted according to their relative strengths (the deutschmark made up nearly 33 percent, the French franc nearly 20 percent, the Dutch guilder 10 percent, and so on). The hope was that the ECUwould become the normal means of settling international debts between EC members, psychologically preparing them for the idea of a single currency.

EMU was taken a step further in 1989 with the elaboration by Commission President Jacques Delors of a three-stage plan:

1. The establishment of free capital movement and greater monetary and economic cooperation between the member states and their central banks.

2. Greater cooperation among central banks, close monitoring of the EMS, and coordination of the monetary policies of the member states.
3. The fixing of exchange rates and the creation of a single currency.[30]

The plan was approved by European leaders in June 1989, and it was later agreed that member states would have to meet several economic "convergence criteria" (including low inflation and interest rates) before they could adopt the single currency. If at least seven states met the criteria, a date would be set for stage three and a European Central Bank would be created and made responsible for setting monetary policy, paving the way for the single currency. This was easier said than done, however, and several member states found that the effort of controlling exchange rates caused their economies to overheat. Several exchange rate realignments were made to help member states build monetary stability, but turbulence in world money markets worsened in the early 1990s, and the deutschmark came under pressure following German reunification in October 1990.[31] In 1992 and 1993, the ERM came close to collapse: Britain and Italy joined, then pulled out, and Ireland, Portugal, and Spain devalued their currencies.

COMPLETING THE SINGLE MARKET (1983–93)

At the heart of the Treaty of Rome was the goal of building a single market that would pave the way for the "four freedoms": the free movement of people, money, goods, and services. Progress was made during the 1960s, but nontariff barriers persisted, including different technical standards and quality controls, different health and safety standards, and different levels of indirect taxation. Progress in the 1970s was handicapped by inflation and unemployment and by the temptation of member states to protect their home industries.[32] European corporations were also facing mounting competition from the United States and Japan, particularly in new technology. In response to these problems, a decision was made in 1983 to revisit the single market project. A 1985 intergovernmental conference took place to discuss the necessary steps (see Box 3.2), and a Commission white paper—the Cockfield Report—was published listing 282 pieces of legislation that would need to be agreed to and implemented in order to remove all remaining nontariff barriers and create a true single market.[33]

The result was the Single European Act (SEA), which was signed in Luxembourg in February 1986 and came into force in July 1987. The first formal expansion of Community powers since the Treaty of Rome,[34] its goal was to complete the single market by midnight on December 31, 1992, by creating "an area without internal frontiers in which the free movement of goods, persons, services and capital is assured." As well as relaunching "Europe" and creating the single biggest market and trading bloc in the world, the SEA brought many more specific changes:

- The Community was given responsibility over new policy areas, such as the environment, research and development, and regional policy.
- New powers were given to the European Court of Justice, whose workload was eased by the creation of the Court of First Instance.
- Legal status was given to meetings of heads of government under the European Council and to Community foreign policy coordination.
- Parliament was given more power relative to the Council of Ministers.
- Many internal passport and customs controls were eased or lifted.
- Banks and companies could do business and sell their products and services throughout the Community.
- Protectionism became illegal, and monopolies on everything from the supply of electricity to telecommunications were broken down.

Addressing the problem of physical, fiscal, and technical barriers to trade was one thing, but economic disparities within the Community acted as additional handicaps to the single market. During the mid-1960s per capita gross domestic product (GDP) in the Community's ten richest regions was nearly four times greater than that in its ten poorest regions. The gap closed during the early 1970s, but with the accession of Britain, Ireland, and Greece it grew to the point at which the richest regions were five times wealthier than the poorest.[35] The Commission-sponsored Thomson Report of 1973 concluded that these disparities were an obstacle to a "balanced expansion" in economic activity and to EMU.[36] France and West Germany saw regional policy as a means of helping Britain integrate with its new partners, while the government of Prime Minister Edward Heath saw it as a way of making EEC membership more palatable to Britons concerned about the potential costs of membership.[37] Agreement was reached in 1973 among the Six to launch the European Regional Development Fund

BOX 3.2 INTERGOVERNMENTAL CONFERENCES

One of the key intergovernmental qualities of the EU can be found in the convening of summit meetings at which representatives of the member states discuss and reach decisions on broad strategic matters. Known as intergovernmental conferences (IGCs), these take place outside the decision-making framework of the EU, typically over a period of weeks or even months. Depending on how they are defined, there have been as many as a dozen IGCs since 1950, but the most important have all been held since 1985.

The first IGC took place between June 1950 and March 1951 and focused on plans for the European Coal and Steel Community. Chaired by Jean Monnet, it led to the signing in April 1951 of the Treaty of Paris. The second IGC—which began in Messina, Sicily, in June 1955 and ended in Venice in May 1956—led to the signing in March 1957 of the two Treaties of Rome, creating the EEC and Euratom. Several more IGCs were held in the 1960s and 1970s, all dealing with more limited issues: a one-day IGC in April 1965 led to the Merger Treaty, another in 1970 discussed budgetary issues, and another in 1975 discussed the terms of the European Investment Bank.[38]

It was not until 1985 that the next substantial IGC was launched. Concerned about the lack of progress on integration and Europe's declining economic performance in relation to the United States and Japan, representatives of the Nine met between September 1985 and January 1986, discussing and agreeing on the framework of the Single European Act. Two more IGCs took place during 1991 to examine political and monetary union, paving the way for the signature in 1992 of the Treaty on European Union.

Institutional reform and preparations for eastward enlargement were the top priorities of IGCs in 1996, 1997, and 2000, which resulted in agreement on the Treaties of Amsterdam and Nice. Another IGC was convened in mid-2007 to discuss the content of the new Lisbon Treaty in the light of the failure in 2005 of the Constitutional Treaty, and a more recent IGC was convened in July 2012 to discuss Iceland's accession to the EU. In every case, the IGCs have been negotiated by national government ministers and permanent representatives, and so they continue to emphasize the extent to which decision making on the big initiatives of the EU still rests with the member states.

(ERDF), designed to match existing national spending on the development of poorer regions, and aimed at projects that would create new jobs in industry and services or improve infrastructure.[39]

With new attention focused in the 1980s on the reinvigoration of the single market, it became clear that social problems also had to be addressed, particularly those related to worker mobility, including industrial decline and long-term unemployment. The Single European Act now made "cohesion" a central part of economic integration, and new prominence was given to the Community's structural funds, including the ERDF, the European Social Fund, and the Cohesion Fund. Another boost for social policy came in 1989 with the Charter of Fundamental Social Rights for Workers (the Social Charter), promoting free movement of workers, fair pay, better living and working conditions, freedom of association, and protection of children and adolescents.

While structural funds accounted for only 18 percent of EC expenditures in 1984, they steadily moved up the budget and by 2007 made up about 46 percent of EU spending (about $62 billion). But despite the increased spending, regional disparities in the EU not only remain, they grew in 2004–07 as several relatively poor Eastern European states joined the EU. Meanwhile, neither the EU nor the member states have been able to deal effectively with unemployment, which in mid-2007, even before the current eurozone debt crisis, stood at 13 percent in Poland, 11 percent in Belgium, 8–9 percent in France, Germany, and Spain, and more than 7 percent in the eurozone as a whole, compared with 4 percent in the United States and Japan (see further discussion in chapter 13).

Questions to Consider

1. In what ways did the Treaty of Rome further European integration?
2. Two visions of European integration—widening, or EU enlargement, and deepening, or further economic and political integration of the existing members of the EU—are often seen as standing in tension with one another. How might this tension be illustrated in the development of the EU in the 1970s and 1980s?
3. Viewed from the perspective of today's EU, how important were the EMS and SEA? What did they do and what impact did they have on the European integration process?

Further Reading

Peter M. R. Stirk and David Weigall, eds. *The Origins and Development of European Integration: A Reader and Commentary* (London: Pinter, 1999).
Tells the history of European integration through documents, speeches, treaties, white papers, and excerpts from key texts.

Geir Lundestad. *The United States and Western Europe Since 1945* (Oxford: Oxford University Press, 2003).
An excellent survey of transatlantic relations, showing clearly how and why the Americans and the Europeans could not always agree.

Barry Eichengreen. *The European Economy Since 1945: Coordinated Capitalism and Beyond* (Princeton, NJ: Princeton University Press, 2007).
A detailed assessment of the impact of integration on European economic growth.

Charles Mulhearn and Howard Vane. *The Euro: Its Origins, Development and Prospects* (Northampton, MA: Edward Elgar, 2008).
Although now out of date with regard to the crisis in the eurozone, this concise volume provides a good overview of the euro against the backdrop of European integration and the steps leading to its introduction, including discussions of the ERM and EMU.

Notes

1. John Gillingham, "Jean Monnet and the European Coal and Steel Community: A Preliminary Appraisal," in Douglas Brinkley and Clifford Hackett, eds., *Jean Monnet: The Path to European Unity* (New York: St. Martin's Press, 1991), 131–37.

2. Desmond Dinan, *Europe Recast: A History of European Union* (Boulder: Lynne Rienner, 2004), 64.

3. Messina Resolution, cited in David Weigall and Peter Stirk, eds., *The Origins and Development of the European Community* (Leicester, UK: Leicester University Press, 1992), 94.

4. Derek W. Urwin, *The Community of Europe*, 2nd ed. (London: Longman, 1995), 76.

5. Urwin, *The Community of Europe*, 76–77.

6. Barry Eichengreen, *The European Economy Since 1945: Coordinated Capitalism and Beyond* (Princeton, NJ: Princeton University Press, 2007), 198.

7. See John Pinder, *European Community: The Building of a Union* (Oxford: Oxford University Press, 1991), 78–86; Urwin, *The Community of Europe*, 132–35.

8. Urwin, *The Community of Europe*, 131.

9. Jean Monnet, *Memoirs*, trans. Richard Mayne (Garden City, NY: Doubleday, 1978), 518.

10. Don Cook, *Charles de Gaulle: A Biography* (New York: Putnam, 1983), 370–71.

11. D. C. Watt, *Survey of International Affairs 1962* (London: Oxford University Press, 1970), 137.

12. U.S. State Department documents cited by Dinan, Europe Recast, 91.

13. For more details, see John McCormick, *The European Superpower* (New York: Palgrave Macmillan, 2006), chapter 2.

14. See Frank Costigliola, "Kennedy, the European Allies, and the Failure to Consult," *Political Science Quarterly* 110, no. 1 (spring 1995): 105–23.

15. Richard J. Barnet, *The Alliance: America, Europe, Japan; Makers of the Post-War World* (New York: Simon and Schuster, 1983), 264.

16. Roger Morgan, "The Transatlantic Relationship," in Kenneth J. Twitchett, ed., *Europe and the World: The External Relations of the Common Market* (London: Europa, 1976).

17. For details, see Sophie Meunier, *Trading Voices: The European Union in International Commercial Negotiations* (Princeton, NJ: Princeton University Press, 2005).

18. Klaus Heidensohn, *Europe and World Trade* (London: Pinter, 1995), 133–38.

19. Dinan, Europe Recast, 70–71. For a detailed analysis of British attitudes, see James Ellison, *Threatening Europe: Britain and the Creation of the European Community, 1955–58* (New York: St. Martin's Press, 2000).

20. Harold Macmillan, *Riding the Storm 1956–59* (New York: Harper and Row, 1971), 73.

21. Dean Acheson, *Present at the Creation: My Years in the State Department* (New York: W. W. Norton, 1969), 385.

22. Pinder, *European Community*, 46–47.

23. In February 1985 Greenland became the first territory to leave the EEC. As a colony of Denmark, it had become part of the Community in January 1973, in spite of voting against membership out of concern for losing control of its fishing rights. In May 1979 it was granted self-government by Denmark, clearing the way for a vote to leave the Community.

24. Tommaso Paddoa-Schioppa, *Financial and Monetary Integration in Europe: 1990, 1992 and Beyond* (New York: Group of Thirty, 1990), 18.

25. Derek W. Urwin, *The Community of Europe*, 2nd ed. (London: Longman, 1995), 155.

26. Commission of the European Communities, "Economic and Monetary Union in the Community" (the Werner Report), *Bulletin of the European Communities*, Supplement 11 (1970).

27. Tony Judt, *Postwar: A History of Europe Since 1945* (New York: Penguin, 2005), 454.

28. Barry Eichengreen, *The European Economy Since 1945: Coordinated Capitalism and Beyond* (Princeton, NJ: Princeton University Press, 2007), 248–49.

29. Mark Gilbert, *Surpassing Realism: The Politics of European Integration since 1945* (Lanham, MD: Rowman and Littlefield, 2003), 138–52.

30. European Commission, *Report of the Committee for the Study of Economic and Monetary Union* (Luxembourg: Office of Official Publications, 1989).

31. Gilbert, *Surpassing Realism*, 227–61.

32. For details on the development of the single market program, see Kenneth A. Armstrong and Simon J. Bulmer, *The Governance of the Single European Market* (Manchester, UK: Manchester University Press, 1998), chapter 1, and Gilbert, Surpassing Realism, chapter 6.

33. Commission of the European Communities, *Completing the Internal Market: The White Paper (the Cockfield Report)*, COM(85)310 (Brussels: Commission of the European Communities, 1985).

34. For an assessment of its initial results, see Michael Calingaert, "Creating a European Market," in Laura Cram, Desmond Dinan, and Neill Nugent, eds., *Developments in the European Union* (Basingstoke, UK: Macmillan, 1999).

35. Stephen George, *Politics and Policy in the European Community*, 3rd ed. (Oxford: Oxford University Press, 1996), 196.

36. Commission of the European Communities, *Report on the Regional Problems of the Enlarged Community (the Thomson Report)*, COM(73)550 (Brussels: Commission of the European Communities, 1973).

37. Dinan, *Europe Recast*, 149.

38. Alfred Pijpers, "Intergovernmental Conferences," in Desmond Dinan, ed., *Encyclopedia of the European Union* (Basingstoke, UK: Macmillan, 1998), 294.

39. For an assessment of the ERDF and regional policy, see James Mitchell and Paul McAleavey, "Promoting Solidarity and Cohesion," in Cram, Dinan, and Nugent, eds., *Developments in the European Union*.

4

CONSOLIDATION AND CRISIS: MAASTRICHT,
LISBON, AND THE EUROZONE

CHAPTER OVERVIEW

- The fall of the Berlin Wall and the end of the Cold War led to new rounds of expansion of the EU, taking the EU farther north and—most significantly—farther east.
- The post–Cold War era has also brought significant deepening—a new joint currency (the euro), far-reaching institutional changes, and a more independent and vigorous foreign policy.
- Nevertheless, the failed constitutional treaty of 2004 and the inability of the EU to take more decisive action in the wake of a severe global financial crisis and a crisis in the eurozone also exposed the limits of elite-led efforts to move the Union toward further integration.

By 1989 membership of the European Economic Community had grown to twelve, and the EEC had become known as the European Community (EC, or simply the Community). Its member states had a combined population of 322 million and accounted for just over 20 percent of world trade. The Community had its own administrative structure and an independent body of law, and its citizens had direct representation through the European Parliament (EP), which also gave them a greater psychological and political stake in the work of the Community. While progress on integration remained patchy, the Single European Act (SEA) had begun to address barriers to the free movement of people and capital that were preventing European businesses from reaching fully across borders and undermining their attempts to compete with their Japanese and American counterparts. The SEA also expanded the Community's responsibilities over new policy areas, strengthened the powers of the European Court of Justice and the EP, and gave formal recognition to foreign policy coordination and the summit meetings of heads of state. The effect was to push the European Community toward a logic of greater political integration.

With the fall of the Berlin Wall and the end of the Cold War, the European project acquired a renewed importance and the EC began to evolve in new and fundamental ways. It began to prepare for expansion to include the states of Eastern Europe (including the territory of the former East Germany) once under the Soviet imperium, a move that would be a potent symbol of the end of the Cold War. But it also deepened with the signing of the 1992 Treaty on European Union—popularly known as the Maastricht treaty—seeking to further integrate the states of what was now to be known as the European Union (EU) both politically and economically. Economic integration was later given its most substantial, as well as symbolic, expression in the creation of a new joint currency, the euro. Yet successful enlargement also created its own challenges, as the institutional machinery designed for twelve states was not quite up to the task for two dozen or more. Further tinkering with institutional arrangements in the Treaties of Rome and Nice were seen as insufficient, and thus a new European constitutional treaty was envisaged that could provide an institutional framework—and an overarching vision—commensurate with the importance and power of the EU. The rejection of the treaty by French and Dutch voters in 2005 indicated that EU elites may have reached too high; accordingly, a more modest, if not substantially different, framework was provided by the Treaty of Lisbon in 2009.

The EU today is a very different actor on the international stage than it was in its early years. It is a global powerhouse: the world's largest economy, its second largest exporter and importer, and—with a population of more than 500 million—significantly larger than the United States. It has acquired newfound independence in foreign policy, having had a serious falling out with the U.S. over the war on terror and the invasion of Iraq, while also remaining a key strategic American ally. The most recent rounds of enlargement have transformed the EU from a Western European economic club to one that includes most of Europe, such that when one speaks of "Europe" today what is meant is the EU.

At the same time, the global financial crisis which began in 2007, and soon after spilled over into a deeply troubling sovereign debt crisis in the eurozone, demonstrated that in some ways the EU is still not significantly more than the sum of its parts. The EU's attempts starting in 2010 to stave off an economic meltdown in Greece—and, to a lesser extent, in Ireland, Spain, Italy, and Cyprus as well—exposed weaknesses in the EU's ability to act quickly, decisively, and with one voice. Although forecasts of the death of the euro (not to mention the EU as a whole) were not just premature but misplaced, it remains unclear whether the EU's reflexive, ad hoc approach to the crisis will be adequate to the gravity of the challenge it faces or whether the debt crisis will ultimately spur the EU to an even greater level of political and economic integration.

FROM COMMUNITY TO UNION (1970–93)

The controversial idea of political integration received less attention from Community governments because of a prevailing feeling that there was little hope of building political union without first achieving economic union. A 1970 report authored by Belgian diplomat Etienne Davignon argued that foreign policy coordination would be a useful first step, especially given the growing divergence between U.S. and Western European policies, made painfully obvious by Vietnam. He recommended quarterly meetings of the six foreign ministers, liaison among EC ambassadors in foreign capitals, and common EC instructions on certain matters for those ambassadors.[1] This so-called European Political Cooperation (EPC) achieved some early successes, such as the 1970 joint EC policy declaration on the Middle East, the signing of the Yaoundé Conventions on aid to poorer countries, and collective European responses during the 1980s to the war in the Falklands, developments in Poland and Iran, and apartheid in South Africa.[2] But it was more reactive than proactive, its weaknesses becoming particularly clear during the 1990–91 Persian Gulf crisis, when EC member states were divided over their response to the U.S.-led response to Iraq's invasion of Kuwait (see chapter 15). Differences also became clear in December 1991, when Germany unilaterally recognized Croatia and Slovenia without conferring with its EC partners.

Political union had been given a new focus in 1984 by President François Mitterrand of France, who was determined to reassert the leadership of his country in the EC. This acquired special importance in the wake of the fall of the Berlin Wall and its resulting "German question," that is, what the consequences of the reunification of Germany would be for the future of the EU. Mitterand's goals for the EC now included a more thoroughgoing political union alongside its economic one so that reunified Germany would remain firmly tied to the fortunes of its western allies. The result was the 1990–91 IGC on political union (meeting alongside an IGC on economic and monetary union), which led to the Treaty on European Union, agreed to at the Maastricht European Council summit in December 1991 and signed in February 1992. Changes brought by the treaty included the following:

- The creation of a new European Union, based on three pillars: a reformed and strengthened European Community, a Common Foreign and Security Policy (CFSP) that would replace EPC, and new policies on justice and home affairs.
- A timetable and conditions for the creation of a single European currency.
- The extension of EU responsibility to new policy areas such as consumer protection, public health, transportation, education, and social policy.
- More cooperation on immigration and asylum, the creation of a European police intelligence agency (Europol) to combat organized crime and drug trafficking, and more regional funds for poorer member states.
- New rights for European citizens and the creation of an ambiguous European Union "citizenship," including the rights of citizens to live wherever they liked in the EU (subject to some limitations) and to vote in local and European elections.

Mark Gilbert argues that Maastricht represented an "unprecedented voluntary cession of national sovereignty," and that it was "less an international treaty than a tentative constitutional act."[3] The stakes were emphasized by the debate over the wording of the draft treaty, which had originally mentioned the goal of federal union but was changed on British insistence to "an ever closer union among the peoples of Europe, in which decisions are taken as closely as possible to the citizen." Problems also came during ratification, when Danish voters caused political shock waves by rejecting the treaty in a June 1992 national referendum. Following agreement that Denmark could opt out of the single currency, common defense arrangements, European citizenship, and cooperation on justice and home affairs, a second referendum was held in May 1993, and Danes accepted the treaty. Following ratification in the other eleven states, the Maastricht treaty came into force in November 1993, nearly a year late.

THE EURO ARRIVES (1995–2002)

Meanwhile, political agreement on the single currency was building in spite of doubts raised by the lessons of the ERM, and a decision was made in 1995 to call it the "euro." While supporters argued that a single currency would further economic integration by eliminating the cost of exchanging currency for both producers and consumers while removing exchange rate risks, critics charged that the new eurozone—the group of countries within the EU using the euro as a currency—did not qualify as an optimum currency area: national economies were too different from each other and labor flexibility and wage flexibility within the eurozone were too low.[4] Moreover, the fact that monetary policy (including the setting of interest rates and money supply) was to be directed by the EU through the European Central Bank, while fiscal policy (i.e., taxing and spending) was left in the hands of the member states, suggested some possible future conflicts.

Leaders of the member states met in May 1998 to decide which applicants met the criteria outlined under Maastricht to join. It was decided that all but Greece were either ready or were making good progress,[5] but Britain, Denmark, and Sweden decided not to adopt the euro, at least initially. In June 1998 the new European Central Bank became responsible for monetary policy in the eurozone, and in January 1999 the euro was launched when participating states permanently fixed their currency exchange rates relative to one another and to the euro.

The monumental task of preparing consumers and businesses in the eurozone for the physical switch to the euro proceeded, as did the printing of 14 billion new euro banknotes and 56 billion euro coins. There was much discussion about the designs of the banknotes, which could not be tied to any one country but instead had to capture general European themes.

Box 4.1 The Copenhagen Conditions

With the institutional and policy change coming out of Maastricht, the time was ripe for new consideration of enlargement. The territory of the EU had expanded in 1990 as a result of German reunification, but this was a domestic matter rather than a broader issue of enlargement. Nonetheless, it added a new dimension to discussions about the eventual possibility of EU membership for Eastern European states, which was given new meaning by the end of the Cold War and the drawing aside of the iron curtain. It was always informally understood that countries applying for membership in the European Community should be European, although there was doubt about exactly what this meant. There was little question of rejecting an application from Morocco in 1987, while the eight remaining non-EU Western European countries all had strong prospects for joining. But further east the lines became fuzzy. Assuming that Europe's eastern border is marked by the Ural Mountains (deep inside Russia), eighteen more countries theoretically qualified for membership in 1992: seven in Eastern Europe, six former Soviet republics, and five former Yugoslavian states.

More focus was provided in June 1993 when the European Council—meeting in Copenhagen—agreed on a set of terms for membership. The so-called Copenhagen conditions required that applicant states must:

- be democratic, with respect for human rights and the rule of law;
- have a functioning free market economy and the capacity to cope with the competitive pressures of capitalism;
- be able to take on the obligations of the *acquis communautaire* (the body of laws and regulations already adopted by the EU).

In 1990, negotiations began on the creation of the European Economic Area (EEA), under which the terms of the SEA would be extended to the seven members of the European Free Trade Association, in return for which they would accept the rules of the single market. The proposal made economic sense, given that 55 percent of EFTA exports went to the EC and 26 percent of EC exports went to EFTA.[6] The EFTA states were also stable and wealthy and would have to make relatively few adjustments to integrate themselves into the single market. Negotiations on the EEA were completed in February 1992, but because the Swiss turned down membership in a December 1992 referendum, only six EFTA states joined when the EEA finally came into force in January 1994: Austria, Finland, Iceland, Liechtenstein, Norway, and Sweden. Almost before it was born, however, the EEA had begun to lose its relevance because all but Iceland and Liechtenstein[7] had already applied for Community membership. Negotiations were completed in early 1994, referendums were held in each country, and all but Norway (where once again the vote went against membership) joined the EU in January 1995. This increased EU membership to fifteen, expanded its land area by one-third, and for the first time gave it a common border with Russia.

The final solution was to use designs based on styles of architecture that were found throughout Europe. As for the coins, one side had a common design while the other had designs peculiar to the participating states: so, for example, the Belgians, the Dutch, and the Spanish chose images of their monarchs, Ireland chose the Celtic harp, France used an image of Marianne (a mythical icon of liberty), and Germany used the German eagle.

On January 1, 2002, the final switch to the euro began, as consumers and businesses turned in their old coins and banknotes and were issued euros. The original plan was to make the transition in a period of six months, but within a month the euro was accounting for 95 percent of cash payments in participating countries, and the switch was largely complete by the end of February. After years of often heated discussion, the single currency was finally a reality. Gone were deutschmarks, drachmas, escudos, francs, guilders, lire, markkas, pesetas, punts, and schillings, and for the first time since the Roman era, much of Europe had a single currency. It was a remarkable achievement, and it stood as one of the most substantial steps yet taken in the process of European integration.

Denmark and Sweden turned down membership in the euro in national referendums, so the focus of interest now switched to Britain, where debate about whether or not to join was heated. The government of Tony Blair set five criteria that would have to be met (including assurance that there would be no negative impact on jobs, financial services, or foreign investment) and insisted that a national referendum would have to be held on the issue. Blair himself was in favor, but opinion polls regularly found a large majority opposed to adopting the euro, and the referendum was repeatedly postponed. In January 2007, Slovenia became the thirteenth country to adopt the euro, with Cyprus and Malta following in 2008, Slovakia in 2009, and Estonia in 2011.

With the single market almost complete (there are still some remaining barriers to the free movement of people—see chapter 12) and the euro circulating in the majority of EU member states, the core goals of economic and monetary union should have been close to being met. There were unresolved concerns about low productivity and high unemployment, to which the EU responded with the launch in March 2000 of the Lisbon Strategy. This was aimed at making the EU "the most competitive and dynamic knowledge-based economy in the world" within ten years, with the specific goals of liberalizing telecommunications and energy markets, improving European transport, and opening up labor markets.[8] But these high hopes did not anticipate the global financial crisis that broke out in

2007, followed by the sovereign debt crisis in the eurozone in 2008. Policy makers would be sent reeling, and nothing would ever be the same again.

CHANGES TO THE TREATIES: AMSTERDAM AND NICE (1997–2001)

The ink had barely dried on the Maastricht treaty before EU leaders agreed that a new IGC should be convened to take stock of the progress of European integration and to discuss the institutional and policy changes that many felt were needed in light of the projected growth of the EU to a membership of twenty countries or more. The result was the Treaty of Amsterdam, which was signed in October 1997 and came into force in May 1999.[9] Much was expected of the treaty, but it fell short of moving Europe closer to political union, and the leaders of the member states were unable to agree on substantial changes in the structure of EU institutions. Plans were confirmed for enlargement of the EU to the east, the goal of launching the single currency in January 1999 was confirmed, and more focus was given to policies on asylum, immigration, unemployment, social policy, health protection, consumer protection, the environment, and foreign affairs.

Another set of changes to the treaties was agreed to by EU leaders at a summit meeting in Nice, France, in December 2000. Less radical and headline making than either the SEA or Maastricht, the key goal of the Treaty of Nice was to make the institutional changes needed to prepare for eastward expansion of the EU, and to make the EU more democratic and transparent. It proved to be a disappointment, though, doing little more than tinkering with the structure of the institutions to anticipate future enlargement; hence the size of the Commission was to be increased, with no country having more than one commissioner, the distribution of votes in the Council of Ministers was to be changed, agreement was reached on a redistribution and capping of the number of seats in the European Parliament, and changes were made to the Court of Justice and the Court of First Instance. Agreement was also reached on a Charter of Fundamental Rights of the European Union (see chapter 8, Box 8.1), including an early warning mechanism designed to prevent breaches of the rights of member states.

The Treaty of Nice was signed in February 2001, and like the earlier treaties was to come into force when it was ratified by all the member states. But a surprise came in June 2001, when voters in Ireland—where the constitution requires a referendum on all new EU treaties—rejected the terms of Nice. Opponents argued that it involved the surrender of too much national control; they were particularly concerned about the implications for Irish neutrality. Part of the problem, however, was simply low voter turnout: just 33 percent of voters cast a ballot, and just 54 percent of those said no. A second vote was taken in Ireland in October 2002, following assurances that Ireland's neutrality on security issues would be respected, and this time turnout was a more respectable 48 percent, and the treaty was accepted by a 63 percent majority.

Nice came into force in February 2003, but it went largely unnoticed because there had already been broader discussions in the European Council in 2001 about the need to make the EU more democratic and to bring it closer to its citizens. At the Laeken European Council in December a decision was made to establish a convention to debate the future of Europe, and to draw up a draft constitutional treaty designed to simplify and replace all the treaties, to determine how to divide powers between the EU and the member states, to make the EU more democratic and efficient, to determine the role of national·parliaments within the EU, and to pave the way for more enlargement (see Box 4.2).

SHOCK WAVES FROM IRAQ (2003–05)

Enlargement and revisions to the treaties had taken place against a background of changes in the international order that were to have important implications for European integration. The goals of the Common Foreign and Security Policy outlined by Maastricht had been only loosely defined, with vague talk about the need to safeguard "common values" and "fundamental interests," to "preserve peace and strengthen international security," and to "promote international cooperation." The continuing weaknesses in European foreign policy were emphasized by the absence of a coordinated European military and by the often halfhearted response to security problems, such as the wars in the Balkans, U.S.-led attempts to put pressure on the Saddam Hussein regime in Iraq in 1998, and the violent suppression by the Yugoslav government of the secession movement among ethnic Albanians in Kosovo the same year.

The end of the Cold War had both heightened the expectation that the EU would take the lead in building bridges to the east and weakened the EU's alliance with the U.S. by removing the one project that had kept it together for so long: offsetting Soviet influence around the globe. If events in the Balkans emphasized the weaknesses of Europe, its strengths were revealed in a growing litany of trade disputes with the United States (see

BOX 4.2 THE FAILED EUROPEAN CONSTITUTION

The accumulation of treaties over the years created a messy semi-constitutional basis for the EU, which many felt needed to be cleaned up with a codified constitution. With this in mind, a convention took place in 2002–03 under the presidency of former French president Valéry Giscard d'Estaing. It had 105 members, including government representatives from the fifteen EU member states and thirteen applicant countries. The result of its deliberations was a draft constitutional treaty,[10] published in July 2003, that included the following proposals:

- A new president of the European Council, elected by its members for a two-and-a-half-year term—replacing the system under which a country holds the presidency for a six-month term.
- A new foreign minister for the EU, appointed by the European Council.
- A limit of seventeen on the membership of the European Commission, selected on a rotating basis.
- A common EU foreign and security policy.
- More decision-making power for the European Parliament.
- A legal personality for the EU, by which its laws would cancel out national laws in areas where the EU had been given competence.
- Freedom for member states to leave the EU.

By the time the treaty was sent to the member states for consideration in 2004, the membership of the EU was up to twenty-five, and it was agreed that all twenty-five had to approve before it could come into force. Generally speaking, bigger countries were happier with the draft than were smaller countries, which were concerned that their voices would not be heard. Some countries declared that government ratification would be enough, while others opted for national referendums. Eight countries endorsed the treaty in late 2004 and early 2005, including Germany, Italy, and Spain, but then shock waves were generated by negative public votes in France and the Netherlands in May and June 2005. By February 2007 eighteen member states had endorsed the treaty,[11] but in its existing form it was dead, and debates had already begun about where to go next. The end result was the Treaty of Lisbon.

chapter 16); the EU may have been uncertain on the military front, but on the trade front it was flexing its muscles with growing confidence. Then came the September 2001 attacks on New York and Washington, DC, which showed that international terrorism was a critical new threat and also led to an almost unparalleled degree of transatlantic solidarity. Every EU leader expressed unqualified support and sympathy for the United States, the French newspaper *Le Monde* famously declaring that "Nous sommes tous Americains" (We are all Americans), and EU foreign ministers declaring the assaults to be attacks "against humanity itself." The EU and the U.S. were also generally in agreement about the need to act quickly against the Taliban in Afghanistan, a country which had become a haven for terrorists. But when the Bush administration prepared to launch a pre-emptive invasion of Iraq, accusing Saddam Hussein of possessing weapons of mass destruction and being a threat to neighboring states and U.S. interests, everything changed.

European governments split into two camps: supporters of U.S. policy included Britain, Denmark, Italy, the Netherlands, Spain, and many in Eastern Europe; opponents included Austria, Belgium, France, Germany, and Greece. U.S. Defense Secretary Donald Rumsfeld caused much baffled head scratching when in January 2003 he dismissed France and Germany as "old Europe" and as "problems" in regard to the Iraq question, contrasting them with the Eastern European governments that supported U.S. policy. But whatever their governments said and thought, Europeans themselves were deeply critical of the March 2003 invasion. Opinion polls found that 70 to 90 percent were opposed in Britain, Denmark, France, and Germany and even in "new" European countries such as the Czech Republic and Hungary. Several pro-war governments—notably those in Britain and Spain—found themselves in trouble with their electorates, and massive antiwar demonstrations were held in most major European capitals, including Berlin, London, and Rome. Most remarkably, an October 2003 survey found that 53 percent of Europeans viewed the United States as a threat to world peace, on par with North Korea and Iran.[12]

This was more than a dispute over Iraq. The EU had been struggling for decades to reach agreement on common foreign and security policies but had found itself both divided internally and obliged to follow the U.S. lead, not always with much enthusiasm. Even after the end of the Cold War, it found itself unable to agree or to provide leadership, it had been embarrassed by its weak response to the first Gulf War and the Balkans, and it had been reminded in both words and actions that the United States could now lay claim to being the world's last remaining superpower. But the growth of European economic strength gave it a new sense of identity and purpose, and Iraq was the catalyst that finally encouraged Europeans to publicly express their opposition to U.S. policy and to reveal to themselves and to others what might be possible were the EU to find the means to present a united front to the rest of the world. Many doubted that the EU had the ability to do this, holding on to the argument that the U.S. was unparalleled as a world power and pointing to the absence of a European military and a European security policy as the EU's greatest handicaps. But others argued that U.S. power was declining and that EU power—with its emphasis on civilian rather than military means to address international problems—was in the ascendancy.[13]

MORE ENLARGEMENT: LOOKING EAST (1994–2013)

Perhaps nowhere was the new power and influence of the EU more obviously on show than in the attraction it held for its Eastern European neighbors, many of which were now anxious to join the club. Just as Community membership had helped bring stability to Greece, Portugal, and Spain, so there were hopes that extending membership to former Eastern bloc countries would promote their transition to capitalism and democracy, open up new investment opportunities, and pull Eastern Europe into a strategic relationship with the West that could be useful if problems in (or with) Russia worsened. But the challenge was substantial, and the hurdles to be jumped were high; the *Economist* argued that it was as though the United States had agreed to welcome into the union several Mexican states, with a commitment to bring them up to American standards of infrastructure and social provision.[14] The EU nonetheless signed agreements between 1994 and 1998 with several Eastern European countries that allowed for gradual movement toward free trade and were designed to prepare its co-signatories for eventual EU membership. In 1997 the EU launched Agenda 2000, a program that contained a list of all the measures that the European Commission felt needed to be agreed to in order to bring ten Eastern European states into the EU.

Negotiations on membership began in 1998–2000 with Bulgaria, Cyprus, the Czech Republic, Estonia, Hungary, Latvia, Lithuania, Malta, Poland, Romania, Slovakia, and Slovenia. Following the completion of negotiations in December 2002, all but Bulgaria and Romania were invited to join the EU. All accepted, and all but Cyprus held referendums that came down in favor of membership. In May 2004 ten new members joined the EU, pushing membership up to twenty-five and for the first time bringing in former Soviet republics (Estonia, Latvia, and Lithuania). The population of the EU grew by nearly 20 percent, but—given the relative poverty of the new members—its economic wealth grew by just 5 percent. In a second phase of eastern enlargement, Bulgaria and Romania joined the EU in January 2007, while Croatia completed negotiations for accession in 2011 and joined the EU in July 2013 (See Table 4.1 and Map 4.1.)

Eastward expansion provided final and emphatic confirmation of the end of the Cold War division of Europe, was a decisive step in the transformation of former Soviet bloc states from communism to liberal democracy, and gave new meaning to the word *European*. Until 2004 the European Union had ultimately been a Western European league, and the absence from its membership of its eastern neighbors reflected the political, economic, and social divisions of the continent. By 2007, almost all of Europe had finally been brought together under the aegis of the European Union.

Iceland, Macedonia, Montenegro, Serbia, and Turkey have been accepted as candidate countries, meaning that membership has been agreed to in

Table 4.1 Growth of the European Union Population

Year	Member States	Cumulative Population
1952	Belgium, France, Italy, Luxembourg, Netherlands, West Germany	160 million
1973	Britain, Denmark, Ireland	233 million
1981	Greece	249 million
1986	Portugal, Spain	322 million
1990	East Germany (via German reunification)	339 million
1995	Austria, Finland, Sweden	379 million
2004	Cyprus, Czech Republic, Estonia, Hungary, Latvia, Lithuania, Malta, Poland, Slovakia, Slovenia	470 million
2007	Bulgaria, Romania	500 million
2013	Croatia	504 million

Map 4.1 Growth of the European Union, 1990 2013

principle, while Albania and Bosnia-Herzegovina have applied for membership and have signed "stabilization and association" agreements with the EU. But the prospects for further enlargement any time soon are slim, given that many of these states face significant political and economic problems, there is political and public resistance in the EU to more integration in the short-term, and the EU faces many economic problems that need first to be resolved.

From Lisbon to the Eurozone Crisis (2001–)

With the failure of the constitutional treaty in 2005, EU governments pondered how best to move forward, eventually deciding to revive much of the content of the treaty in the form of what was ultimately named the Treaty of Lisbon. It was discussed at an IGC in Lisbon in 2007 and signed there the following December. Its key provisions were:

- The creation of the positions of president of the European Council and a High Representative of the Union for Foreign Affairs and Security Policy—an EU foreign minister in all but name.
- Formal establishment of the European Council as an institution in its own right.
- Abolition of the pillar structure of Maastricht and of the European Community.
- A new formula for qualified majority voting within the Council of Ministers.
- New powers for the European Parliament, including giving it and the Council of Ministers equal power over proposals for almost all EU legislation.
- Recognition of the rights laid out in the Charter of Fundamental Rights (see chapter 13 for more details).
- A single legal personality for the EU.

While every other state in the EU took the position that Lisbon was simply an amendment to past treaties (and therefore ratified it through parliamentary means), Ireland once again put the issue to the voters in a referendum, where it was rejected in June 2008. Its defeat owed much to false information put out by the treaty's opponents, who claimed that Lisbon would endanger Irish neutrality, would mean far-reaching changes in tax policy, and would legalize abortion in Ireland. To placate the Irish, new protocols to the treaty were added which not only attempted to assuage any fears that these things might happen but also walked back some institutional changes, such as the proposal to reduce the number of commissioners. A new vote on the treaty was held in Ireland in October 2009, and this time the result was an overwhelming 67 percent in favor. The following month, Czech president Vaclav Klaus (a well-known Euroskeptic who had held up ratification pending the Irish referendum and his own satisfaction as to the treaty's provisions) signed on to ratification and the treaty came into force.

Then, whatever residual concerns had existed about the way the Treaty of Lisbon had been designed and approved were swept aside when a crisis broke out in the eurozone—the most serious crisis that the EU has faced in its history, one whose implications will continue to play themselves out for years to come. The problems can be traced back to (a) flaws in the design of the euro (where the European Central Bank was given control over monetary policy but not over fiscal policy), (b) the breaking of the rules of membership in the euro by several states (including Germany), and (c) a global financial crisis that began in the United States and quickly moved across the Atlantic.

The crisis and resulting sharp recession in the United States affected all of the EU states to one degree or another. Ireland was the first to feel its effects, with the bursting of its housing bubble. Then Spain, Italy, and Cyprus all experienced ripple effects that would only fully surface with the virtual implosion of the Greek economy under the weight of economic recession, a staggering debt load (brought on largely by mismanagement of the economy by various Greek governments), and subsequent withdrawal of confidence in Greece by international investors.[15] Greece's extreme economic straits not only threatened its continued solvency but acted as an accelerator for the crisis in other EU states, with the future of the euro and eurozone even coming into question. The EU needed to respond decisively, and fast. Germany's initially uncompromising position toward Greece (the former insisting that a radical austerity program by the Greeks would be all that was needed) divided the EU, with some states (such as the Netherlands, Finland, and Latvia) supporting this position and others (mostly those states with more dire economic outlooks) arguing for an EU bailout and a more lenient approach.[16] Under Chancellor Angela Merkel, Germany had set the tone for the EU's response to the crisis, but the defeat of Nicolas Sarkozy in the French presidential election in the late spring of 2012 removed a powerful ally.[17] Under pressure from France's new president, François Hollande, as well as from Spain's prime minister Mariano Rajoy and Italy's prime minister Mario Monti, Merkel made important concessions in an IGC in late June 2012. Although still refusing to countenance the idea of Eurobonds—common bonds issued by the EU that would have securitized much of its member states' debt (which was anathema to German taxpayers)—she agreed to a modest anti-austerity economic growth pact, a future banking union and bank oversight, and—most importantly—a plan to recapitalize at-risk banks in the eurozone (most especially in Spain) directly through the EU's new European Stability Mechanism (ESM), all of this of course still contingent on Greece getting its own financial house in order.[18]

Observers were divided on the potential impact of the IGC: while some saw it as a decisive and historic step toward greater economic and political integration (this group including, it appears, the markets, as the euro received an immediate boost), others were skeptical, seeing the moneys spent as too modest, the plans for oversight too vague, and the steps toward further integration too timid.[19] Given the different national interests, however, less rather than more could have been expected, and in that sense the IGC was at least a modest success. Whether it represents a first step in a series of significant steps or merely another example of the EU simply muddling through, only time will tell.

Questions to Consider

1. What effects has eastern enlargement had on the development of the EU in terms of its institutional arrangements, economic development, and identity?
2. Why did the constitutional treaty fail? Did its failure ultimately matter?
3. In light of the EU's problems in dealing with recent economic crises, can the euro be considered a success or were early critics of the euro right after all?

Further Reading

Maria Green Cowles and Desmond Dinan, eds. *Developments in the European Union 2*, 2nd ed. (New York: Palgrave Macmillan, 2004).
    An edited collection on developments in EU institutions and policies, including issues such as enlargement.
Nicolas Jabko and Craig Parsons, eds. *The State of the European Union*, vol. 7: *With US or Against US? European Trends in American Perspective* (New York: Oxford University Press, 2005). Sophie Meunier and Kathleen R. McNamara, eds. *The State of the European Union*, vol. 8: *Making History: European Integration and Institutional Change at 50* (Oxford: Oxford University Press, 2007).

The most recent additions to a series of assessments of the EU, one focusing on U.S. perceptions of Europe and the other reflecting on the first fifty years of integration.

Alexander Stubb. *Negotiating Flexibility in the European Union: Amsterdam, Nice and Beyond* (Basingstoke, UK: Palgrave Macmillan, 2003).

An assessment of the negotiations that led up to the treaties of Amsterdam and Nice by a Commission staff member who took part.

Peter Poole. *Europe Unites: The EU's Eastern Enlargement* (Westport, CT: Praeger, 2003). Neill Nugent, ed. *European Union Enlargement* (Basingstoke, UK: Palgrave Macmillan, 2004). John O'Brennan. *The Eastern Enlargement of the European Union* (London: Routledge, 2006).

Three of the large number of assessments of enlargement that have been published in recent years.

Notes

1. Derek W. Urwin, *The Community of Europe*, 2nd ed. (London: Longman, 1995), 148.

2. Brian White, *Understanding European Foreign Policy* (Basingstoke, UK: Palgrave Macmillan, 2001), chapter 4.

3. Mark Gilbert, *Surpassing Realism: The Politics of European Integration since 1945* (Lanham, MD: Rowman and Littlefield, 2003), 212.

4. For a concise discussion, see Madeleine O. Hosli, *The Euro: A Concise Introduction to European Monetary Integration* (Boulder: Lynne Rienner, 2005), 15–16.

5. For details, see Amy Verdun, "The Euro and the European Central Bank," in Maria Green Cowles and Desmond Dinan, eds., *Developments in the European Union 2*, 2nd ed. (New York: Palgrave Macmillan, 2004).

6. Rene Schwok, "EC–EFTA Relations," in Leon Hurwitz and Christian Lequesne, eds., *The State of the European Community, vol. 1: Policies, Institutions, and Debates in the Transition Years* (Boulder: Lynne Rienner, 1991).

7. Liechtenstein is a principality between Austria and Switzerland with a population of thirty-five thousand. It is in a monetary and customs union with Switzerland, which also manages its diplomatic relations. It is one of several microstates within Europe that are independent but generally regarded as part of the larger states they border. (The others are Andorra, Monaco, San Marino, and Vatican City.)

8. See Anthony Wallace, "Completing the Single Market: The Lisbon Strategy," in Cowles and Dinan, eds. *Developments in the European Union 2*.

9. For an analysis of the origins, negotiation, and conclusion of the Treaty of Amsterdam, see Desmond Dinan, "Treaty Change in the European Union: The Amsterdam Experience," in Laura Cram, Desmond Dinan, and Neill Nugent, eds., *Developments in the European Union* (Basingstoke, UK: Macmillan, 1999).

10. For details, see Desmond Dinan, "Reconstituting Europe," in Cowles and Dinan, eds. *Developments in the European Union 2.*

11. Those countries which had postponed or cancelled making a decision were the Czech Republic, Denmark, Ireland, Poland, Portugal, Sweden, and the UK.

12. Flash Eurobarometer 151, "Iraq and Peace in the World" (poll), November 2003, http://ec.europa.eu/public_opinion/flash/fl151_iraq_full_report.pdf.

13. For more details, see John McCormick, *The European Superpower* (New York: Palgrave Macmillan, 2006), chapter 1.

14. "Europe's Mexico Option," *The Economist*, 5 October 2002, 36.

15. "Going to Extra Time," *The Economist*, 16 June 2012, 26–28.

16. Regarding Germany's position on the euro crisis see for example Hans-Werner Sinn, "Why Berlin Is Balking on a Bailout," *New York Times*, 13 June 2012, A23; see also Nicholas Kulish, "Germany Is Open to Pooling Debt, with Conditions," *New York Times*, 5 June 2012, A1.

17. For a discussion of the French-German relationship after the election of François Hollande, see "The Feeling's Mutual," *The Economist*, 26 May 2012, 54.

18. Nicholas Kulish, "At Outset of Brussels Summit Meeting, the One Thing Missing Is Confidence," *New York Times*, 28 June 2012, A12; Paul Wiseman and David McHugh, "Europe Reaches a Deal," *Associated Press*, 30 June 2012.

19. "Inching towards Integration," *The Economist*, 7 July 2012, 16.

PART II
INSTITUTIONS

5

THE EUROPEAN COMMISSION

CHAPTER OVERVIEW

- The most supranational of the EU's institutions, the Commission performs executive and bureaucratic functions within the EU.
- The College of Commissioners operates much like a cabinet in a parliamentary system, with commissioners having significant authority over their portfolios, or areas of policy responsibility, and a president acting as the first among equals for the entire college.
- Although Euroskeptics have always had the Commission in their sights, seeing it as a powerful and unchecked institution, the reality is that the Commission's powers have never been as formidable as some critics have said they are. This has become all the more apparent in recent years as other EU institutions have gained power at its expense, and Commission presidents have been criticized for showing too little leadership.

The European Commission is the executive-bureaucratic arm of the EU, responsible for generating new laws and policies, overseeing their implementation, managing the EU budget, representing the EU in international negotiations, and promoting the interests of the EU as a whole. Headquartered in Brussels, the Commission consists of a college of appointed commissioners who function collectively much like a national government cabinet in a parliamentary system, and several thousand full-time European bureaucrats assigned to one of the Commission's directorates-general (DGs), the functional equivalent of national government departments. There is a DG for each of the major policy areas in which the EU is active, and each is supported by services that provide policy advice, research support, and legal expertise. Confusingly, both the commissioners and the European bureaucrats are separately and collectively described as "the Commission."

As the most visible and supranational of the EU institutions, the Commission has long been at the heart of European integration. As a result, its powers are routinely overestimated: Euroskeptics like to grumble about waste and meddling by the Commission, complain that commissioners are not elected, and charge that the Commission has too little public accountability. For some, "Brussels" is synonymous with the Commission and has become a code word for some vague and threatening notion of government by bureaucracy, or creeping centralization, much like "Washington" figures in some American political discourse.

But this is unfair. The Commission has much less power than its detractors suggest, because the final decisions on new laws and policies rest with the Council of the EU and the European Parliament. With new initiatives and powers given to these institutions over the last several years, the argument could be made that there has been a decline in the Commission's power. Furthermore, there is no reason why the Commission should be elected; bureaucracies all over the world consist of career employees, with the heads of government departments appointed by government leaders in much the same way as commissioners are appointed. Finally, the Commission is quite small given the size of its task; it had just over thirty-eight thousand employees in 2011 (a ratio of about 1:13,000 EU residents), compared with more than four million federal bureaucrats in the United States (1:77 U.S. residents). [1]

At the same time, the Commission deserves credit for the rich and creative role it has played in the process of European integration. It has not only encouraged member states to harmonize their laws, regulations, and standards in the interest of bringing down barriers to trade, but it has also been at the heart of some of the defining European policy initiatives, including the single market, efforts to create a single currency, efforts to build common foreign policy positions, and enlargement. Like all large institutions the Commission suffers occasionally from waste, mismanagement, and bureaucratic excess, but it is honest about its own shortcomings, and given the size of its task it has been remarkably productive. Europeans misjudge the Commission when they think of it as remote, intrusive, and powerful.

EVOLUTION

The origins of the European Commission can be traced back to the High Authority of the ECSC. Based in Luxembourg, the nine members of the Authority were nominated for six-year terms by the national governments of the member states. Their job was to oversee the removal of barriers to the free movement of coal and steel, and their powers were checked by a Special Council of Ministers and a Common Assembly (the forerunners, respectively, of today's Council of Ministers and European Parliament).

The Treaties of Rome created separate nine-member Commissions for the EEC and Euratom, which were nominated by national governments for four-year terms. Under the terms of the 1965 Merger Treaty, the three separate Commissions were merged in 1967 into a new Commission of the European Communities, more commonly known as the European Commission. As the Community expanded, the number of commissioners grew; it was originally nine but by the time of the 1995 accession of Austria, Sweden, and Finland it had risen to twenty.

The Commission has always been at the heart of the debate over the balance of power between the EU and its member states. With its supra-nationalist tendencies it has engaged in an ongoing tug-of-war with the intergovernmental Council of the EU. European federalism was championed by the Commission's first president—Walter Hallstein of Germany—in the face of Charles de Gaulle's preference for limiting the powers of the EEC. The 1965 empty chair crisis began when de Gaulle challenged the right of the Commission to initiate the policy process and it tried to collect receipts from the Community's common external tariff.[2] This would have given the Commission an independent source of funds and would have loosened the grip of the member states. Although the Luxembourg Compromise obliged the Commission to consult more closely with the Council of Ministers, and de Gaulle was able to veto the reappointment of Hallstein in 1967, the crisis ironically confirmed the right of the Commission to initiate policies.

Despite this history, the Commission became less ambitious and aggressive and lost powers with the creation in 1965 of the Committee of Permanent Representatives (see chapter 6), the creation in 1974 of the European Council (see chapter 9), and the introduction in 1979 of direct elections to the European Parliament. After enjoying a newly assertive phase under President Jacques Delors during the late 1980s and early 1990s, and winning responsibilities for developing laws in a growing range of new policy areas, the Commission saw its powers continuing to decline relative to those of the Council of Ministers and the European Parliament.

Preparations for the 2004 enlargement of the EU forced a rethinking of the size and role of the Commission. The failed European constitution included a proposal that the Commission would be reduced in 2014 to seventeen voting members, with no more than one commissioner from each state. Reflecting the extent to which member states wanted to retain their own commissioners, and the extent to which national interests are still protected even in the Commission, the proposal was widely criticized, particularly by smaller member states. Consequently, Lisbon retained the current formula of one commissioner per member state and proposed capping the number of commissioners from 2014 on at no more than two-thirds of the number of member states (thus, if there are thirty member states, there will be twenty commissioners). Small states continued to balk at this idea, so one of the concessions made to Ireland as it looked for guarantees prior to its second referendum on Lisbon in October 2009 was confirmation of the rule of one commissioner per state.

STRUCTURE

The European Commission is based in Brussels with a headquarters in the Berlaymont building, a distinctive piece of 1960s Belgian government architecture with a star-shaped floor plan that provided a strong visual image for the Commission. Most of the staff work in buildings sprinkled in and around the European Quarter in Brussels. When it was discovered in 1992 that the Berlaymont had high levels of asbestos, instead of the less expensive option of tearing it down, it was renovated at a cost of nearly $800 million. Commission staff were relocated to various new and existing buildings around the city until the new Berlaymont was ready in in 2004.

The Commission has five main elements: the College of Commissioners, the president of the Commission, the directorates-general and services, the Secretariat General, and a network of committees.

The College of Commissioners. The European Commission is led by a group of commissioners (twenty-eight in 2013), who function something like a cabinet for the EU system, taking collective responsibility for their decisions. Each has a policy portfolio for which he or she is responsible (see Table 5.1), and each serves renewable five-year terms, which begin six months after elections to the European Parliament (EP). Commissioners are nominated by their national governments, which—in practice—usually means by the prime minister or the president. The nominations are made in consultation with the president of the Commission, and nominees must be acceptable to the president of the Commission (who has the power of veto), the other commissioners, other governments, the major political parties at home, and the EP.[3]

All nominees are required to attend hearings before the relevant committees of the EP, but Parliament does not have the right to accept or reject them individually; instead, it must approve or reject the College as a whole. Under the circumstances, it is unlikely to reject the College unless it has serious reservations about one or more of the nominees. This happened in 2004 when the nominee from Italy—Rocco Buttiglione, who was to have been the new justice commissioner—commented before an EP hearing that homosexuality was a "sin" and that "the family exists in order to allow women to have children and to have the protection of a male who takes care of them." The resulting outcry led to Buttiglione being replaced as the Italian nominee by Franco Frattini. Bulgarian nominee Rumiana Jeleva withdrew in 2010 after facing hard questions about her financial declaration and failing to impress Members of the European Parliament (MEPs) with her qualifications for the job; she was replaced by Kristalina Georgieva.

Parliament also has the power to remove the College in midterm through a motion of censure, although it has never done this. The closest it came was in January 1999, when—after several years during which stories had circulated about fraud, nepotism, and cronyism in the Commission—Parliament tried to dismiss the College. It was unable to find the necessary two-thirds majority, but a committee was appointed to investigate the allegations, resulting in the surprise resignation of the College just hours after the committee report was published on March 16.

Despite the way they are appointed, commissioners are not expected to be national representatives; they must be impartial in their decision making and must swear an oath of office before the European Court of Justice agreeing "neither to seek nor to take instructions from any Government or body." In reality, it is difficult for commissioners to detach themselves

Table 5.1 The European Commissioners, 2009–14

Name	Member State	Portfolio
José Manuel Barroso	Portugal	President
Siim Kallas	Estonia	VP, Transport
Antonio Tajani	Italy	VP, Industry and Entrepreneurship
Viviane Reding	Luxembourg	VP, Justice, Fundamental Rights and Citizenship
Neelie Kroes	Netherlands	VP, Digital Agenda
Maros Šefčovič	Slovakia	VP, Inter-Institutional Relations and Administration
Joaquin Almunia	Spain	VP, Competition
Catherine Ashton	UK	VP, High Representative of the Union for Foreign Affairs and Security Policy
Johannes Hahn	Austria	Regional Policy
Karel De Gucht	Belgium	Trade
Kristalina Georgieva	Bulgaria	International Cooperation, Humanitarian Aid and Crisis Response
Androulla Vassiliou	Cyprus	Education, Culture, Multilingualism and Youth
Štefan Füle	Czech Republic	Enlargement
Connie Hedegaard	Denmark	Climate Action
Olli Rehn	Finland	Economic and Monetary Affairs
Michel Barnier	France	Internal Market and Services
Günther Oettinger	Germany	Energy
Maria Damanaki	Greece	Maritime Affairs and Fisheries
László Andor	Hungary	Employment, Social Affairs, and Inclusion
Máire Geoghegan-Quinn	Ireland	Research and Innovation
Andris Piebalgs	Latvia	Development
Algirdas Šemeta	Lithuania	Taxation and Customs Union
John Dalli	Malta	Health and Consumer Policy
Janusz Lewandowski	Poland	Budget
Dacian Cioloş	Romania	Agriculture and Rural Development
Janez Potočnik	Slovenia	Environment
Cecilia Malmström	Sweden	Home Affairs

As this book went to press, the commissioner from Croatia had not yet been appointed.

completely from national interests, but it helps that (for now, at least) all member states are "represented" and that all commissioners have just one vote each. Their independence is also promoted by the fact that they cannot be removed in midterm by their home governments. However, they can be recalled at the end of their terms if there is a change of political leadership at home or a disagreement with their national leaders.

There are no formal rules on the qualifications of commissioners, but most tend already to have national political reputations at home.[4] At one time, many were political lightweights whose usefulness at home had ended, so they were "kicked upstairs" to the Commission. As the powers of the Commission increased and the EU became a more significant force in European politics, postings to the Commission became more desirable and important, and the quality of the pool of potential candidates improved.[5] Commissioners now tend to come to the job with senior national government experience, and they usually count among their number a host of former foreign ministers, finance ministers, labor and trade ministers, and several former MEPs.

At the beginning of each term, all commissioners are given policy portfolios, which are distributed at the prerogative of the president. Just as in national cabinets, there is an internal hierarchy of positions: the key posts in the Commission are those dealing with the budget, agriculture, trade, and external relations. As the membership of the College has expanded, it has become more difficult to find significant portfolios; when the Bulgarian and Romanian commissioners arrived in January 2007, the best that could be found for them was—respectively—consumer protection and multilingualism.

In making appointments, the president will be influenced by three main factors:

- The abilities, political skills, and professional backgrounds of individual commissioners.
- Lobbying by commissioners and their home governments.[6] The latter are obviously keen to see "their" commissioner win a good portfolio or one of particular interest to their country, so political influence is often brought to bear.
- Recognition and promotion in the case of returning commissioners. A commissioner with a strong reputation in a particular area will normally keep the same portfolio or at least be brought back for another term.

Every commissioner has a *cabinet* (French)—a small personal staff of assistants and advisers—which is headed by a *chef* (chief) *de cabinet* and provides advice and the basic information and services that help commissioners do their jobs. The quality of the *cabinet* staff can have a major bearing on the performance of a commissioner, and the *cabinets* collectively have become a key influence on the operations of the Commission.[7] The *chefs de cabinet* meet every Monday to prepare the weekly meeting of the College, which takes place every Wednesday. Most *cabinet* members once came from the same country as the commissioner and were usually recruited from the same national political party as the commissioner or from the national bureaucracy. But recent changes to the rules have required that every *cabinet* should include at least three different nationalities.

The President. The dominating figure in the Commission is the president, the person who—at least until the Treaty of Lisbon created a president of the European Council—comes closest to being able to claim to be leader of the EU. The president is technically no more than a first among equals and can be outvoted by other commissioners, but he or she is one of the most visible of the "leaders" of the EU institutions, and—as with prime ministers in parliamentary systems—holds a trump card in the form of the power of appointment: the ability to distribute portfolios is a potent tool for patronage and political influence.

Table 5.2 Presidents of the European Commission

Dates	Name	Member State	Ideology
1958–1967	Walter Hallstein	West Germany	Christian Democrat
1967–1970	Jean Rey	Belgium	Centrist
1970–1972	Franco Maria Malfatti	Italy	Christian Democrat
1972–1973	Sicco Mansholt (interim)	Netherlands	Social Democrat
1973–1977	François-Xavier Ortoli	France	Conservative
1977–1981	Roy Jenkins	United Kingdom	Social Democrat
1981–1985	Gaston Thorn	Luxembourg	Socialist
1985–1994	Jacques Delors	France	Socialist
1995–1999	Jacques Santer	Luxembourg	Christian Democrat
1999–2004	Romano Prodi	Italy	Centrist
2004–	José Manuel Barroso	Portugal	Centrist

Appointed for renewable five-year terms, the president of the Commission oversees meetings of the College, decides on the distribution of portfolios, represents the Commission in dealings with other EU institutions, represents the EU at meetings with national governments and their leaders, and is generally responsible for ensuring that the Commission gives impetus to the process of European integration. In these areas, the president has the same executive function as the president of the United States. But Commission presidents have only a fraction of the powers of a U.S. president, and in some ways have the same status as nineteenth-century U.S. presidents, who had less of a role in government than either Congress or the states and were more clearly executives rather than leaders. However, the presidency of the Commission took on a new and more forceful character from the mid-1980s onward thanks mainly to one man: Jacques Delors.

The most productive, controversial, and well-known of all Commission presidents, Delors came to the job in 1985 with experience as a banker, a labor leader, an MEP, and the economics and finance minister of France.[8] He was single-minded, hardworking, demanding, and sometimes short-tempered; a fellow commissioner once described his management style as a form of "intellectual terrorism," and a British government minister described the Delors Commission as "practitioners of Rottweiler politics."[9] The Delors Commission will be remembered for at least four major achievements: the completion of the single market, the plan for economic and monetary union, promotion of the Social Charter, and the negotiations leading up to Maastricht. Delors left the Commission at the end of 1994 at age sixty-eight, and surprised many by turning down the opportunity to run for president of France.

There are few formal rules regarding how the president is appointed. Before the Treaty of Lisbon the selection process was labyrinthine, inasmuch as the successful nominee could be vetoed by any national leader within the EU. Current president José Manuel Barroso was the product of just such a situation in 2004. Several names had been touted, including Belgian prime minister Guy Verhofstadt, Austrian chancellor Wolfgang Schuessel, and former NATO chief Javier Solana. Verhofstadt was the favored candidate of France and Germany but was opposed by Britain because he was considered too much a European federalist. In the end, Barroso—dismissed by some as a "lowest common denominator" compromise—was approved unanimously. For France and Germany he had sufficient pro-European credentials, and as a supporter of the war in Iraq he was acceptable to Britain and Italy.

Box 5.1 Barroso in Charge

José Manuel Barroso took over the presidency of the Commission at a time of great change and uncertainty, moving to Brussels in November 2004: the latest and perhaps riskiest round of enlargement of the EU had recently been completed, the conversion to the euro was still in its early stages, EU–U.S. relations were in deep trouble, the debate over Turkish membership in the EU was heating up, and votes in France and the Netherlands had finally brought a halt to progress on the draft European constitution just a few months before. He was faced with the challenge of reviving public confidence in the Commission, and he spoke of his desire to "open a new chapter of European integration" and to fight public apathy toward the EU. Despite—or perhaps because of—the perception that he had not been a particularly strong or inspirational leader, he was confirmed for a second term in 2009, just as the crisis in the eurozone was gathering pace.

Born in Lisbon in 1956, Barroso studied law at the University of Lisbon and politics at the University of Geneva, at one time embracing far-left Maoist political ideas. He also started—but did not finish—a Ph.D. at Georgetown University. He joined the Social Democratic Party in 1980 and was elected to the Portuguese Parliament in 1985, serving six terms and being appointed Portuguese home affairs minister at the age of twenty-nine, then moving on to become foreign minister. He became prime minister in 2002, supporting the war in Iraq and hosting a meeting between George W. Bush and Tony Blair in the Azores on the eve of the war. He suffered low approval ratings for an austerity package he forced on Portugal in order to help it meet the terms of membership in the euro. He was confirmed as the eleventh president of the Commission in June 2004, stepping down as prime minister of Portugal in order to take up his new job.

Barroso was reported to have initially turned down the idea of becoming president, but ultimately he proved a worthy compromise candidate. He came from a small country with a global reach (more people speak Portuguese as a first language than speak French), and it helped that he is fluent in both English and French. The most serious issue he has faced thus far is the European debt crisis, where he has tended to take a supporting role to the work of the leaders of Germany and France, and has—as a result—been criticized for a failure to fully participate in the efforts to resolve the crisis.

The Treaty of Lisbon led to a significant change in this selection process: starting in 2014 commission presidents must be proposed by the European Council using the qualified majority vote (QMV; see chapter 6) and must be confirmed by the European Parliament, a process not dissimilar (minus QMV, of course) to that used in the U.S. Senate for presidential nominees to the cabinet, courts, and other offices. If the first candidate is rejected, then the Council proposes a second within a month's time. Using QMV prevents any one national leader from blocking the nomination of a candidate acceptable to other member states and should change the dynamics involved in the selection of the commission president considerably.

As the reach of the EU has expanded, so competition for appointments to the presidency has strengthened, and the quality of the pool of nominees has deepened. Experience as a government minister was once enough, but the last three presidents have all been former prime ministers: Jacques Santer (Luxembourg), Romano Prodi (Italy), and Barroso (Portugal). As with most positions of leadership in government, the nature of the job depends to a large extent on the character of the officeholders and the management style and agenda they bring to their task.[10] Like U.S. presidents, incumbents have proved quite different in their styles and abilities; Walter Hallstein, Roy Jenkins, and Jacques Delors are remembered as the most active, and the remainder as relatively passive.

Directorates-General and Services. Below the College, the European Commission is divided into twenty-six directorates-general (DGs) and several services (see Table 5.3). The DGs—each of which is headed by a director-general—are the equivalent of national government departments in that each is responsible for a specific policy area. (Although DGs are tied to commissioners, the list of policy areas does not exactly match.) Employees consist of a mixture of full-time bureaucrats known as *fonctionnaires*, national experts attached from the member states on short-term contracts, and supporting staff. The Commission is required to ensure balanced representation by nationality at every level, but nearly one in four Eurocrats is Belgian, mainly because of locally recruited secretarial and support staff. Although the people who eventually become directors-general theoretically work their way up through the ranks of the Commission, appointments at the higher levels are based less on merit than on nationality and political affiliation.

About two-thirds of Commission staff members work on drawing up new laws and policies or on overseeing implementation, while the rest are involved in research, translation, and interpretation; although the

Table 5.3 Directorates-General and Services

Directorates-General

Agriculture and Rural Development
Budget
Communication
Competition
Development
Economic and Financial Affairs
Education and Culture
Employment, Social Affairs and Equal Opportunities
Energy and Transport
Enterprise and Industry
Environment
External Relations
Health and Consumers
Informatics
Information Society and Media
Internal Market and Services
Interpretation
Justice, Freedom and Security
Maritime Affairs and Fisheries
Personnel and Administration
Regional Policy
Research
Taxation and Customs Union
Trade
Translation

Services

Administration and Payment of Individual Entitlements
Bureau of European Policy Advisors
Data Protection Officer
EuropeAid–Co-operation Office
European Anti-Fraud Office
Eurostat
Internal Audit Service
Joint Research Center
Legal Service
Publications Office

Commission mainly uses English and French in daily operations, all key documents must be translated into all twenty-three official EU languages. The Commission's services deal with a variety of external matters and internal administrative matters. They include the European Anti-Fraud Office (which fights fraud and corruption within EU institutions), Eurostat (the statistical office of the EU that generates much useful comparative data on the EU), and the Legal Service (which acts as an in-house source of legal advice for the Commission, most notably checking through legislative proposals before they are sent to the College of Commissioners for a decision). About three-fourths of Commission staff members work in offices in and around Brussels, the balance working in Luxembourg and other parts of the EU.

Recruitment is both complex and competitive. Several hundred new positions typically become vacant each year, for which there are literally thousands of applicants. (A competition launched in May 2003 to recruit staff from the ten new, mainly Eastern European member states attracted nearly thirty-eight thousand applications.[11]) A university degree and fluency in at least two EU languages are minimum requirements, and specialist professional training (in law, business, finance, or science, for example) is increasingly required. Entrance exams (the *concours*) are held in all the member states, but the overall process is so convoluted and detailed that applicants may have to wait as long as three years to find out whether or not they have been accepted. Once appointed, Commission staff are well paid, and redundancies are rare. An affirmative action policy has made sure that women are well represented at the lower levels of the Commission and increasingly at the higher levels as well, although the College has been dominated by men. The first two women commissioners were Vasso Papandreou of Greece and Christiane Scrivener of France, appointed in 1989. The 1995–99 and 1999–2004 Colleges both had five women members, and the 2009–14 College has nine.

The Secretariat General. The administration of the Commission is overseen by a Secretariat General with a staff of about seven hundred. The job of the Secretariat General is to provide technical services and advice to the Commission, prepare the annual work program of the Commission, and organize and coordinate the work of the DGs and services. The secretary general chairs the weekly meetings of the *chefs de cabinet*, sits in on the weekly meetings of the commissioners, directs Commission relations with other EU institutions, and generally makes sure that the work of the Commission runs smoothly.[12] The position was held for nearly thirty years by

Emile Noël of France, and since 2005 has been held by Catherine Day of Ireland, former director-general for the environment.

Committees. Most of the work of discussing and sorting out the details of proposed laws and policies is left to a series of advisory, management, and regulatory committees, participating in a phenomenon known as "comitology." There are several hundred such committees and subcommittees, chaired by the Commission and made up of small groups of officials from government departments in the member states. The committees have no formal powers to prevent the Commission from taking action, but the Commission is expected to take seriously the opinions of advisory committees in particular.

In addition, the Commission will work with expert committees consisting of national officials and specialists appointed by national governments, and consultative committees consisting of members with sectional interests, set up and funded directly by the Commission.[13] For example, if the Commission is thinking about a proposal for a new law on air pollution, it might have a meeting at which representatives from interest groups, the transport lobby, vehicle manufacturers, energy producers, consumer organizations, and other interested parties are invited to share their thoughts. Members are typically nominated by EU-wide organizations, but any interest group or lobbyist seeking to influence EU policy is well advised to give testimony before one of these committees.

How the Commission Works

The core responsibility of the Commission is to be the "guardian of the treaties," meaning that it must ensure that EU policies are advanced in light of the treaties. It does this in four ways.

Powers of Initiation. The Commission is legally obliged to make sure that the principles of the treaties are turned into practical laws and policies. In this respect it is sometimes described as a think tank and policy formulator, and it is expected to provide leadership for the EU.[14] It has the sole "right of initiative" on new European legislation and can also draw up proposals for entire new policy areas (as it did with the Single European Act and the Delors package for economic and monetary union) and pass them on to Parliament and the Council of Ministers for consideration.

The Commission can take any initiative that it considers appropriate for advancing the principles of the treaties, but in reality most of its proposals are responses to either legal obligations or technical issues that need to be addressed. The Commission can also be prompted into action by other institutions; although neither Parliament nor the Council can formally initiate the lawmaking process, informal pressure and influence are brought to bear on the Commission. A proposal may also come from a commissioner or a staff member of one of the DGs, or may come as a result of a ruling by the Court of Justice. Member-state governments, interest groups, and even corporations can exert direct or indirect pressure on the Commission. Increasing numbers of policy suggestions have also come from the European Council (see the section on agenda setting in chapter 11).

Typically, a proposal for a new European law will start life as a draft written by middle-ranking Eurocrats in one of the directorates-general. It will then be passed up through the ranks of the DG, referred to other interested DGs, vetted by the Commission's Legal Service, and discussed by *cabinets* and advisory committees, being amended or revised along the way. The draft will eventually reach the College of Commissioners, which meets at least once each week to go through the different proposals. Meetings usually take place on a Wednesday in Brussels, or in Strasbourg if Parliament is in plenary session. Meetings are not open to the public, but agendas and minutes are posted on the Commission website.

By a majority vote, the College can accept a law, reject it, send it back for redrafting, or defer making a decision. Once passed by the College, it will be sent to the European Parliament and the Council of Ministers for a decision. It may take months or even years for the process to be completed, and Commission staff members will be involved at every stage, consulting widely with national bureaucrats and interest groups, working with and making presentations to the Council of Ministers and the European Parliament, and carrying out their own research into the implications of the new law (see Box 5.2).

Powers of Implementation. Once a law or policy has been accepted, the Commission is responsible for ensuring that it is implemented by the member states. It has no power to do this directly but instead must work through national bureaucracies. The Commission has the power to (a) collect information from member states so that it can monitor progress on implementation; (b) take to the Court of Justice any member state, corporation, or individual that does not conform to the spirit of the treaties or follow subsequent EU law; and (if necessary) (c) impose sanctions or fines if a law is not being implemented. Every member state is legally obliged to report to the Commission on the progress it is making in meeting deadlines and incorporating EU law into national law, but detection can be

BOX 5.2 EUROPEAN UNION LAW

The foundation of the EU legal order is provided by the nine major treaties: Paris (now expired), the two Treaties of Rome, the Merger treaty, the Single European Act, Maastricht, Amsterdam, Nice, and Lisbon. Each results in changes to the one that came before, and cumulatively they set out the basic goals and principles of European integration and describe—as well as place limits on—the powers of EU institutions and of member states in their relationship with the EU. They have also spawned thousands of individual laws, which come in five main forms.

Regulations. These are the most powerful EU legislative tools. Usually fairly narrow in intent, they are often designed to amend or adjust an existing law. A regulation is binding in its entirety on all member states and directly applicable in the sense that it does not need to be turned into national law.

Directives. These are binding on member states in terms of goals and objectives, but it is left up to the states to decide how best to achieve those goals. Most focus on outlining general policy goals, while some are aimed at harmonization. The governments of the member states must tell the Commission what they plan to do to achieve the goals of a directive.

Decisions. These are also binding and can be aimed at one or more member states, at institutions, and even at individuals. They are usually fairly specific in intent and have administrative rather than legislative goals. Some are aimed at making changes in the powers of the EU, and others are issued when the Commission must adjudicate disputes between member states or corporations.

Recommendations and Opinions. These have no binding force, so it is debatable whether or not they have the effect of law. They are used mainly to persuade or to provide interpretation on the application of regulations, directives, or decisions.

The Commission has also relied on two additional tools for the development of policies. *Green papers* are discussion papers on specific policy areas, addressed to interested parties and designed to elicit their input. Recent topics have included energy efficiency, promoting healthy diets and exercise, European policy on illegal drugs, public access to EU documents, and a tobacco-free Europe. *White papers* contain official proposals for Community policies and actions, and they usually follow a green paper. A recent example was the 2012 white paper on pension systems across the member states, designed to provide a comprehensive strategy at the EU and national levels to meet the challenges of aging populations.[15]

difficult; governments and industries have been known to collude to hide the fact that they are breaking the law or not implementing a law. For this reason, the Commission also relies on whistle-blowing: individuals, corporations, and interest groups will occasionally report to the Commission that laws are being broken or that there are failures in implementation.

The Commission adds to the pressure on member states by publicizing progress on implementation, hoping to embarrass the slower states into action. It was particularly busy in the two to three years leading up to the 2004 enlargement, checking to make sure that the Eastern European states were keeping up with the schedule to implement the large body of EU law. A report issued by the Commission just months before enlargement warned that all ten countries faced problems and were running the risk of fines, export bans, and losses of EU subsidies unless their records improved. Poland had the worst record, being criticized for its performance in areas as diverse as farm subsidies, inadequate standards at meat and dairy plants, corruption, and its fishing industry. At the other end of the scale, the Commission announced that Lithuania and Slovenia had made the most progress.[16]

If a member state falls behind schedule, the Commission can issue a warning (a Letter of Formal Notice) giving it time to comply—usually about two months. If the member still fails to comply, the Commission can issue a Reasoned Opinion explaining why it feels there may be a violation. If there is still noncompliance, the state can be taken to the European Court of Justice for failure to fulfill its obligations. Greece and Italy have been the worst offenders over time, with more proceedings started against them as an annual average than any other member state (see Table 5.4). Most cases of noncompliance come less from a deliberate avoidance by a member state than from differences in interpretation or differences in the levels of efficiency of national bureaucracies; the latter accounts, for example, for many of Italy's infringements because its national bureaucracy is notorious for delay, inefficiency, and corruption.

Managing EU Finances. The Commission ensures that all EU revenues are collected, plays a key role in drafting and guiding the budget through the Council of Ministers and Parliament, and administers EU spending, especially under the Common Agricultural Policy and the structural funds. Collection involves working with national agencies to make sure that they understand where income is to be generated and ensuring that the member states make their required contributions. The administration of EU spending is undertaken in cooperation with the Court of Auditors (see chapter 9);

Table 5.4 Infringements of EU Law

Actions for failure of a member state to fulfill obligations, annual average

Greece	12.6	Sweden	3.2
Italy	10.5	Czech Republic	3.2
Spain	9.0	Netherlands	2.3
Austria	8.1	Malta	2.0
France	6.7	Estonia	1.0
Portugal	6.7	Hungary	1.0
Belgium	6.0	Denmark	0.9
EU–27	5.3	Slovakia	0.8
Ireland	5.2	Cyprus	0.6
Germany	4.4	Lithuania	0.4
Luxembourg	4.3	Slovenia	0.4
Poland	4.0	Bulgaria	0
UK	3.4	Latvia	0
Finland	3.4	Romania	0

Source: Figures calculated by authors from data in the Annual Report of European Court of Justice, http://curia.europa.eu. Figures show the annual average for each member state since it joined the EEC/EU.

the Commission is involved in authorizing spending, ensuring that it has gone for the purposes intended, and evaluating the effectiveness of spending.[17]

External Relations. The Commission acts as the EU's main external representative in dealings with international organizations such as the United Nations, the World Trade Organization, and the Organization for Economic Cooperation and Development.[18] Discussions on global trade are overseen by the Commission acting on behalf of EU member states; thus the Commission has increasingly become the most common point of contact for U.S. and Japanese trade negotiators. The Commission has also been a key point of contact between the EU and the rest of the world. As the power and significance of the EU have grown, more than 140 governments have opened diplomatic missions in Brussels accredited to the EU, and until the creation of the new European External Action Service (see chapter 15) the Commission operated more than 130 offices in other parts of the world. The growing significance of the EU and the Commission can be seen in the numbers of foreign leaders who regularly visit Brussels (which is also the headquarters of NATO).

The Commission oversees the process by which applications for full or associate membership in the EU are considered. Although the applications initially go to the Council of Ministers, the Commission examines all the implications and reports back to the Council. If the Council decides to open negotiations with an applicant country, the Commission oversees the process.

Questions to Consider

1. What are the significant changes Lisbon made to the Commission? What effect, if any, have these changes had on the Commission's power?
2. Should the College of Commissioners be selected in the same way that executives are in parliamentary systems, that is, by the "winner" of elections in the European Parliament? What would be the advantages and disadvantages?
3. In what ways is the Commission similar to and different from the executive branch in the United States, especially its bureaucracy?

Further Reading

David Spence, ed. *The European Commission*, 3rd ed. (London: John Harper, 2006).

    A dense but thorough collection looking at the Commission, its relations with other institutions, and its work in key policy areas.

Neill Nugent. *The European Commission* (Basingstoke, UK: Palgrave Macmillan, 2000).

    Although it is beginning to show its age, this is still the most thorough single-authored study of the structure and workings of the Commission.

George Ross. *Jacques Delors and European Integration* (New York: Oxford University Press, 1995). Helen Drake. *Jacques Delors: Perspectives on a European Leader* (London: Routledge, 2000).

    Two studies of the Commission under Delors, the first written by a scholar who was given unparalleled access to its meetings and documents.

Hussein Kassim, John Peterson, Michael W. Bauer, Sara Connolly, Renaud Dehousse, Liesbet Hooghe, and Andrew Thompson. *The European Commission of the Twenty-first Century* (Oxford: Oxford University Press, 2013). A detailed study of the bureaucracy of the Commission, relationships between its different structures (such as the cabinet and services), and the similarities and differences between the Barroso Commission and previous Commissions.

Notes

1. By some estimates, the size of the U.S. federal bureaucracy—when contract employees are taken into account—is actually much bigger. See Paul C. Light, *The True Size of Government* (Washington, DC: Brookings Institution Press, 1999).

2. See Derek W. Urwin, *The Community of Europe*, 2nd ed. (London: Longman, 1995), 107–13.

3. For details of the nomination and appointment process, see David Spence, "The President, the College and the Cabinets," in David Spence, ed., *The European Commission*, 3rd ed. (London: John Harper, 2006), 34–38.

4. For more details, see Andrew MacMullen, "European Commissioners: National Routes to a European Elite," in Neill Nugent, ed., *At the Heart of the Union: Studies of the European Commission*, 2nd ed. (New York: St. Martin's Press, 2000).

5. Neill Nugent, *The European Commission* (Basingstoke, UK: Palgrave Macmillan, 2001), 88–91.

6. Nugent, *The European Commission*, 105–6.

7. Spence, "The President, the College and the Cabinets," 60–72.

8. For a short assessment of the Delors presidency, see Helen Drake, "The European Commission and the Politics of Legitimacy in the European Union," in Nugent, ed., *At the Heart of the Union*, 238–44. See also Helen Drake, *Jacques Delors: Perspectives on a European Leader* (London: Routledge, 2000).

9. George Ross, *Jacques Delors and European Integration* (New York: Oxford University Press, 1995), 51.

10. Michelle Cini, *The European Commission: Leadership, Organization and Culture in the EU Administration* (Manchester, UK: Manchester University Press, 1996), 109.

11. European Commission press release, 1 July 2003. europa.eu/newsroom/index_en.htm.

12. For more details see Hussein Kassim, "The Secretariat General of the European Commission," in Spence, ed., *The European Commission*.

13. Nugent, *The European Commission*, 244–45.

14. Cini, *The European Commission*, 18–22.

15. European Commission, *White Paper: An Agenda for Adequate, Safe, and Sustainable Pensions*, COM(2012) 55, 16 February 2012, www.ec.europa.eu /social/BlobServlet?docId=7341&langId=en.

16. "Stark Warning to New EU Members," *BBC News*, 5 November 2003, http://news.bbc.co.uk/2/hi/europe/3242941.stm.

17. Nugent, *The European Commission*, 287–88.

18. See Michael Smith, "The Commission and External Relations," in Spence, ed., *The European Commission*, chapter 12.

6

The Council of the European Union

Chapter Overview

- The Council of the EU, one of the most powerful (and inter-governmental) of the EU's institutions, is the forum in which government ministers from the member states meet to make decisions on EU policies. Confusingly, it consists of multiple councils, each responsible for a specific policy area.
- The Council performs legislative, as well as some executive, functions and can be considered to be something of an upper house of parliament for the EU.
- Although Lisbon cannot be said to have affected the power of the Council, it did alter its organizational structure: it reduced the number of councils, redefined the role of the General Secretariat, changed the future method of voting within the councils, and—while keeping a presidency for most of the councils—now has a foreign policy council chaired by the EU's High Representative of the Union for Foreign Affairs and Security Policy.

The Council of the European Union (long known more usually as the Council of Ministers, and usually referred to simply as "the Council") is the forum in which national government ministers meet to make decisions on EU law and policy. It is the primary champion of national interests and one of the most powerful of the EU institutions. Once the Commission has proposed a new law, the Council of the EU—in conjunction with the European Parliament (EP)—is responsible for accepting or rejecting the proposal. The Council also approves the EU budget, a responsibility it shares with the EP; coordinates the economic policies of the member states; champions the Common Foreign and Security Policy; coordinates police and judicial cooperation on criminal matters; and concludes international treaties on behalf of the EU. In short, it has a mix of legislative and executive functions. In some ways, its legislative power makes the Council of the EU something like the U.S. Senate, with the European Parliament playing the role of the U.S. House of Representatives.

The name *Council of the EU* is misleading, because while all its decisions are credited to "the Council" (singular) it actually consists of several different groups of ministers, membership depending on the topic under discussion. Thus foreign ministers will meet to deal with foreign affairs, environment ministers to discuss proposals for environmental law and policy, and so on. Despite its powers, the Council is less well known and more poorly understood than either the Commission or Parliament. Its meetings are closed (although most are broadcast on the internet), there has been surprisingly little scholarly study of its structure and processes, and when most Europeans think of the EU, they think of the Commission, forgetting that the Commission can achieve little without the support of the Council.

Before Lisbon, the Council of the EU and the European Council (see chapter 9) were both chaired by government representatives occupying the presidency on a six-month rotation. But Lisbon created a new position of president of the European Council, so now only meetings of the Council of the EU are chaired through the rotating presidency. This rotation has the advantage of providing member states with the opportunity to bring their pet issues to the agenda, to make a mark on the work and direction of the EU, and to lead the EU in its dealings with other countries. Meanwhile, the day-to-day work of the Council is overseen—and most of its key decisions mapped out—by the Committee of Permanent Representatives (known by its French acronym, Coreper). Made up of the permanent representatives of the member states, Coreper is one of the most influential institutions in the EU system of governance, and yet most Europeans are barely aware of its existence.

Opinion is divided on whether the Council is intergovernmental or supranational, with debate complicated by its changing role, powers, and methods. Changes in its voting procedures have altered the Council's priorities over time, obliging member states to work together on achieving agreement and tending to push the Council more toward supranationalism. At the same time, however, there has been a tendency in recent years for the Council to develop greater influence at the expense of the Commission, thereby strengthening the intergovernmental flavor of the EU.

EVOLUTION

The Council of the EU grew out of the Special Council of Ministers of the ECSC, which was created at the insistence of the Benelux countries to defend their national interests in the face of the dominance of France, Germany, and Italy.[1] Because its members consisted of national government ministers, the ECSC Council provided an intergovernmental balance to the supranational qualities of the High Authority (precursor to today's European Commission).

A separate Council of Ministers was created for the EEC in 1958, where the idea of defending national interests was taken a step further with a weighted system of voting designed to prevent the bigger member states from overwhelming the smaller ones. The EEC Council had only six member states, but among them they had seventeen votes: four each for the three largest countries, two each for Belgium and the Netherlands, and one for Luxembourg. In the case of simple majority voting, the big three could easily outvote the small three, but some votes required a qualified majority, meaning that a measure needed twelve votes from at least four states to pass. This not only protected small states and large states from each other, but also encouraged them to work together. As a result of the Merger treaty, a single Council of Ministers was created in 1967. Its name was formally changed to Council of the EU in 1993 following the passage of the Maastricht treaty, but it is still interchangeably known as the "Council of Ministers."

Speaking at the first session of the ECSC Council of Ministers in September 1952, West German Chancellor Konrad Adenauer argued that the Council stood "at the crossroads of two kinds of sovereignty, national and supranational. . . . While it must safeguard the national interests of the member states, it must not regard this as its paramount task . . . which is to promote the interests of the Community."[2] The Council has been torn ever since between these two goals, which some see as compatible and others as contradictory. It is dominated by national government ministers with their own parochial concerns, so its work is ultimately the sum of those concerns. But the search for compromise can also encourage ministers to reach decisions that promote the broader interests of the EU.

It was assumed that as Europe integrated and the member states learned to trust one another, the Council would become less important, and the Commission would be able to initiate, decide, *and* implement policy. But in fact the power and influence of the Council grew because member states were disinclined to give up powers to the Commission. The result was a perpetuation of the idea of the EEC as an intergovernmental organization, which displeased those who supported a federal Europe. Several other developments added to the power and influence of the Council:

- It increasingly adopted its own nonbinding agreements and recommendations, which the Commission has found difficult to ignore.
- As the interests and reach of the EU have spread, both the Commission and the Council became involved in new policy areas not covered by the original treaties.
- The presidency of the Council of the EU became an increasingly important part of the EU decision-making system and the source of many key initiatives on issues such as economic and monetary union, and foreign policy.[3]

At the same time, however, both the European Council and the European Parliament have made inroads into the power of the Council of the EU . The former—which is similarly torn between European and national pressures—has more power in deciding the broad goals of the EU, and the latter has demanded and won an equal say with the Council of the EU in decision making. Even though the Luxembourg Compromise introduced the power of veto into the Council, it was rarely used, and decision making became increasingly consensual and less nationalistic. More of its decisions have also been subject to qualified majority voting, which has obliged member states to put EU interests above national interests. Thanks to changes introduced since the Single European Act—and most especially, Lisbon— the Council of the EU has had to share its decision-making authority with Parliament, and the two have effectively become the co-legislatures of the EU (see Box 6.1).

Box 6.1 The Case for an Upper Chamber

Most national legislatures are either unicameral (consisting of one chamber) or bicameral (consisting of two chambers). In small or homogeneous countries, there is rarely a need for two chambers—fair representation is usually achieved by a single chamber, which can also move more quickly through the legislative agenda. But bigger or more heterogeneous countries usually need a second, upper chamber that offers a different level of representation and helps resolve differences where there are significant regional, social, or cultural divisions. Few political communities are bigger or more diverse than the European Union, so is there a case for converting the Council of the EU into a second legislative chamber?

All federations have bicameral legislatures, the obvious example being the United States. During the Constitutional Convention of 1787, one of the most controversial points of debate related to the allotment of power among the states, which varied substantially in size. The solution reached, known as the Great Compromise, included the creation of two chambers: the House of Representatives would be based on population size, with the number of representatives given to each state determined by its population, while the Senate would give each state equal representation, regardless of size. This protected small states from bigger states, while also preventing small states from slowing down the process of government. Other federations have opted for variations on the U.S. model; thus Germany has a Bundestag based on population and a Bundesrat that represents the *Lander* (states), while Canada has a House of Commons and a Senate, and Russia has a State Duma and a Federation Council.

The Council of the EU is an upper legislative chamber in all but name. Much like the U.S. Senate, it shares powers over lawmaking (with the European Parliament) while also making sure that the interests of the member states are given reasonable representation regardless of size. Given its role in decision making, is it time to consider converting it into a full-fledged elected upper chamber, with an equal number of representatives from each member state?

STRUCTURE

The Council of the EU is based in the Justus Lipsius building in the European Quarter of Brussels, across the road from the Berlaymont, the seat of the European Commission. Named for a sixteenth-century Flemish humanist, the Justus Lipsius is a large, marble-clad building that was opened in 1995. The Council has four main elements: the councils of ministers themselves, the Committee of Permanent Representatives, the presidency, and the General Secretariat.

The Councils. While there were once nearly two dozen different so-called technical councils (or "configurations") that came under the general heading of the Council of the EU, the number has now been reduced to ten:

- Agriculture and Fisheries
- Competitiveness
- Economic and Financial Affairs (Ecofin)
- Education, Youth and Culture
- Employment, Social Policy, Health and Consumer Affairs
- Environment
- Foreign Affairs
- General Affairs
- Justice and Home Affairs
- Transport, Telecommunications and Energy

Although supposedly equal in terms of their status and powers, some are more influential than others and have more well-defined identities.[4] The most important is the General Affairs Council, which prepares and ensures follow-up meetings of the European Council. Other influential councils include the Foreign Affairs Council (dealing with external relations, trade and development issues), the Economic and Financial Affairs Council (Ecofin), the Justice and Home Affairs Council, and the Agriculture and Fisheries Council. These five councils meet most often (usually monthly for General Affairs and Foreign Affairs), while the other councils meet two to four times per year. The number of meetings is determined by the country holding the presidency, and altogether the councils now meet about fifty to sixty times each year. Most meetings are held in Brussels, but during April, June, and October they are held in Luxembourg. Sessions usually last no more than one or two days, depending on the agenda, the volume of work, and the level of formality.

In a perfect world, each of the councils would consist of the relevant and equivalent ministers from each member state, but this does not always happen, for two main reasons. First, member states sometimes send deputy ministers or senior diplomats instead of their ministers; the relevant minister may have more urgent problems to deal with at home, may want to avoid political embarrassment on some issue, or may not think the meeting is important enough to attend. However, by the terms of the Lisbon treaty, every delegate to a Council meeting should be authorized to act on behalf of his/her member state. Second, not every member state has an identical set of ministers, and each divides policy portfolios differently. For example, some member states have ministers of women's affairs, while others do not. The result is that Council meetings are often attended by a mixed set of ministers with different responsibilities. The Commission and the European Central Bank are invited to send representatives to relevant meetings, but the Council may decide to meet without either institution being present.

Permanent Representatives. The ministers may be the most visible element of the Council hierarchy, but its heart and soul is the powerful and secretive Committee of Permanent Representatives (Coreper). Undoubtedly the most underrated and most often overlooked part of the entire EU decision-making process, Coreper is the meeting place for the permanent representatives—the heads of the Permanent Representations (or embassies) of the member states in Brussels. It undertakes the detailed work of the Council, attempting between meetings of the ministers to reach agreement on as many proposals as possible.

Thanks to Coreper, as much as 90 percent of the work of the Council is resolved before the ministers even meet.[5] Only the most politically sensitive and controversial proposals are normally sent to the ministers without a decision having been reached by Coreper. One former British government minister, Alan Clark, put it colorfully (if not entirely accurately) when he noted in his diaries that "it makes not the slightest difference to the conclusions of a meeting what Ministers say at it. Everything is decided, and horse-traded off by officials at Coreper. . . . The ministers arrive on the scene at the last minute, hot, tired, ill, or drunk (sometimes all of these together), read out their piece and depart."[6]

No mention of Coreper was made in the Treaty of Paris, but a Coordinating Committee helped prepare ministerial meetings in the ECSC, and member states began to appoint permanent representatives to the EEC in 1958.[7] Coreper was finally recognized in the 1965 Merger treaty, by which time the growing workload of the Council had led to a decision to create two committees: permanent representatives constitute Coreper II and deal with broad issues coming before General Affairs, Ecofin, and Justice and Home Affairs, and with the preparatory work of the European Council, while their deputies constitute Coreper I and concentrate on the work of the other councils.[8]

The permanent representatives act as a valuable link between Brussels and the member states, ensuring that the views of the member states (or at least their governments) are expressed and defended and that the capitals are kept informed of what is happening in Brussels. Because they work with each other so much and come to know each other well, the representatives are occasionally torn between defending national positions and trying to ensure that their meetings lead to successful conclusions.[9] At the same time, they know each other better than do the ministers and so are better placed to reach compromises and to negotiate deals, often informally over lunch. They also play a key role in organizing Council meetings by preparing agendas, deciding which proposals go to which council, and deciding which of the proposals are most likely to be approved by the Council with or without discussion. Meetings of Coreper II are prepared by senior members of the national delegations, known as the Antici Group (for Paolo Antici, the Italian diplomat who chaired its first meeting in 1975).

Much like a national legislature, the Council of the EU also has a complex network of committees and working parties that does most of the preparatory work and tries to reach agreement on proposed legislation before it goes to the Council. There are several standing committees (including those on energy, education, and agriculture), each made up mainly of national government officials but occasionally including representatives from interest groups (for example, the Committee on Employment includes representatives from industry). The working parties are organized along policy lines (so, for example, the environment working party will look at environmental proposals) and bring together policy specialists, national experts, members of the Permanent Representations, and staff from the Commission. They usually meet several times each week to review Commission proposals and try to identify points of agreement and disagreement. (Working parties are not to be confused with political parties; see chapter 10.)

The Presidency. As mentioned earlier, while Lisbon placed the European Council under the direction of an appointed president, it did not fundamentally alter the structure of the presidency of the Council of the EU:

each such presidency continues to be held not by a person but by a country, with every EU member state taking a turn for a term of six months, beginning in January and July each year. The only exception to this, again courtesy of Lisbon, is that the Foreign Affairs Council is chaired by the High Representative of the Union for Foreign Affairs and Security Policy (who is also a member of the College of Commissioners). The presidency has several responsibilities:[10]

- It prepares and coordinates the work of the Council of the EU, and sets the agendas for about two thousand meetings, the most important of which are those of the ministerial councils.
- It arranges and chairs meetings of the Council of the EU and Coreper and represents the Council in relations with other EU institutions. An active presidency will lean heavily on Coreper to push its favorite proposals and to ensure that agreement is reached.[11]
- It mediates and bargains and is responsible for promoting cooperation among member states and for ensuring that policy development has consistency and continuity. Presidencies are measured according to the extent to which they are able to encourage compromise and build a consensus among the EU members, and by how many agreements they fail to broker.

At one time, the rotation among member states was alphabetical, but as membership of the EU grew, a more complex arrangement was developed to make sure that the work load was more fairly spread and that there was a mix of big and small countries. Lisbon formalized the practice whereby the Council uses a troika system in which ministers from the incumbent presidency work closely with their predecessors and their successors. This has in effect created an eighteen-month, three-state "team presidency," albeit with one of the member states chairing all meetings for a six-month period and formally holding the position of president. Each troika should reflect the diversity and geographical balance of member states within the Union (see Table 6.1). Just how much one member state (or the troika) can actually achieve is debatable, because despite the importance attached to the job by the holder, and the grand plans that each member state typically has for its turn at the top, much of what happens is outside the control of the presidency. The day-to-day work of running the EU continues regardless, the key decisions being made by bureaucrats in Brussels. As the *Economist* once put it, "Holding the presidency for six months lets a country

Table 6.1 Rotation of Presidencies of the Council of Ministers

	First Half	*Second Half*
2010	Spain	Belgium
2011	Hungary	Poland
2012	Denmark	Cyprus
2013	Ireland	Lithuania
2014	Greece	Italy
2015	Latvia	Luxembourg
2016	Netherlands	Slovakia
2017	Malta	UK
2018	Estonia	Bulgaria
2019	Austria	Romania

and its leader host a few summits, chair a lot of meetings and enjoy an unusual share of the international spotlight. But it is rare that six-month presidencies decisively affect the Union's direction."[12]

The main advantage of holding the presidency is that it allows a member state to convene meetings and launch strategic initiatives on issues of particular national interest, to try to bring those issues and initiatives to the top of the EU agenda, and to earn prestige and credibility (assuming the president does a good job). The presidency also allows the leaders of smaller states to negotiate directly with other world leaders—which they might otherwise rarely be able to do—and contributes to European integration by making the EU more real to the citizens of that country; it helps them to feel more involved and to see that they have a stake in the development of the EU.

The main disadvantage of the job is the sheer volume of work involved, a burden that is especially onerous on member states with limited resources and small bureaucracies. A member state can pass up its turn as president, as Portugal did immediately after it joined the Community in 1986 on the grounds that it was not yet in a position to do a good job. A member state can also ask another state to help bear some of the workload. Ireland, for example, has won respect for its presidencies but has had difficulty meeting its foreign policy obligations. Officially neutral, Ireland has full-time embassies in barely thirty countries, which means it lacks an intelligence-gathering system and a pool of foreign policy experts; the Irish Parliament does not even have a foreign affairs committee. Ireland's low-key approach led to the old joke that its most useful role in international relations lay in occupying the seat between Iraq and Israel at international gatherings.

Different states have different approaches to the presidency, depending upon a combination of their national administrative and political cultures, their attitudes toward the EU, and their policy priorities. This was described in colorful terms by the *European* when it likened an Italian presidency to "a bus trip with the Marx brothers in the driver's seat," while the subsequent Luxembourg presidency was more like "being driven by a sedate couple who only take to the road on Sundays and then infuriate other motorists by respecting the speed limit."[13] The records of some recent presidencies illustrate the often contrasting styles and priorities different member states bring to the job, as well as the difficulties they have in really achieving their goals.

For example, when Germany's Angela Merkel took the reigns of the presidency in January 2007, trends in unemployment and economic growth at home were positive, and the primary issue on her agenda was what to do about the failed European constitution. She began her presidency by emphasizing the importance of the EU having a constitutional treaty, but she also asserted that the EU needed to strengthen its foreign policy, reduce European red tape, and deal with issues such as energy security and climate change. Matters came to a head at the Brussels European Council meeting in June that year, when hours of debate that ended at 5 a.m. on the final day produced agreement not on the constitutional treaty that Merkel had hoped for, but instead on a compromise reform treaty (which evolved into the Lisbon treaty). Merkel nonetheless declared herself "very, very satisfied with what we have been able to conclude."[14]

In contrast, when Denmark took over the presidency in January 2012, the crisis in the eurozone—of which Denmark is not a member—was accelerating. Prime Minister Helle Thorning-Schmidt listed four priorities for the Danish presidency: the economy, growth, the environment, and security. Deals were made on energy efficiency and patents, the latter a key part of twelve measures the Commission identified as essential in making the single market work better. By the end of the Danish presidency, however, the eurozone crisis overshadowed almost all of the other policy accomplishments of the EU in the first half of 2012. To be sure, the initial inability of the EU to act more quickly and decisively was hardly a result of any weakness of the Danish presidency. However, it did demonstrate the declining role of the Council presidency and the ability of any country in the presidency to successfully meet its declared priorities.

The General Secretariat. This is the bureaucracy of the Council, consisting of about three thousand staff members based in Brussels, most of whom are translators and service staff. The office is headed by a secretary general appointed for a five-year term. The General Secretariat prepares Council meetings, advises the presidency, provides legal advice for the Council and Coreper, briefs every Council meeting on the status of each of the agenda items, keeps records, manages the Council budget, and generally gives the work of the Council some continuity. In 1999, the secretary general was given new powers when the position was combined with the new office of the High Representative for the Common Foreign and Security Policy and in so doing, became a hub for the development of the EU's foreign and security policies.[15] But Lisbon changed this, and with the High Representative now chairing the Foreign Affairs Council (and serving as a vice-president in Commission as well) the role of secretary general is similar to its pre-1999 incarnation.

HOW THE COUNCIL WORKS

The Council of the EU has a cluster of specific responsibilities, including overseeing attempts to coordinate the economic policies of the member states (which is done mainly through Ecofin), signing international treaties on behalf of the EU, approving (in conjunction with the EP) the EU budget, promoting the Common Foreign and Security Policy of the EU (through the High Representative and the Foreign Affairs Council), and coordinating cooperation between national courts and police forces on criminal matters. Its primary responsibility, though, is to decide—in conjunction with Parliament—which proposals for new European laws will be adopted and which will not. The European Commission may have a monopoly on proposing new laws and policies, but the Council and Parliament can encourage it to investigate an issue and to submit proposals for new policies or laws. The Council has exploited loopholes in the treaties to expand this power over the years, and the struggle between the Council and the Commission for power and influence has become one of the most important internal dynamics of EU decision-making.[16]

What happens to a Commission proposal when it reaches the Council depends on its complexity and urgency, and on the extent to which problems have already been ironed out in discussions between Council and Commission staff. The more complex proposals usually go first to one or more of the Coreper working parties, which look over the proposal in detail and identify points of agreement and disagreement.[17] The proposal then goes to Coreper itself, which considers the political implications and tries to clear up as many of the remaining problems as it can, ensuring that meetings of ministers are as quick and as painless as possible. The proposal moves on to the relevant Council; if agreement has been reached by working parties or by Coreper, the proposal is listed as an "A point," and the Council will usually approve it without debate. If agreement has not been reached, or if the item was left over from a previous meeting, it is listed as a "B point." The Council must discuss B points and try to reach a decision.

The method of voting in the Council of the EU has changed dramatically over the years: although unanimity was once the rule it is now all but unknown, and while a simple majority continues to be used for many procedural or narrow policy issues, most issues are decided by qualified majority voting, or QMV. The idea behind QMV in its various forms is to prevent big states from having too much power and to encourage states to form coalitions. It also reduces the tendency toward nationalism inherent in the way the Council of the EU is structured.

Under the rules of QMV devised by the Treaty of Nice, each EU member state (or more properly, minister in the council) is given several votes roughly in proportion to its population (see Table 6.2) for a total of 352 votes. To be successful, a proposal must win a triple majority: a majority of states must be in favor, and they must have a total of at least 260 votes (slightly under 74 percent of the total) from states whose cumulative population represents 328 million people (representing just under 65 percent of the EU population). Lisbon has revised these rules: from November 2014 the qualified majority will be 55 percent of the vote from a minimum of 15 member states home to at least 65 percent of the population. A blocking minority will also be incorporated: four states representing 35 percent of the population of the EU will be able to block legislation.

The issue of the allocation of votes under QMV has been a regular bone of contention. It was, for example, one of the main causes of the failure of the European Council to agree to the draft constitution for Europe in December 2003. Agreement had been reached under the Treaty of Nice to give Poland twenty-seven votes, just two votes short of Germany, which had twice the population and an economy more than ten times as large. There was talk of cutting the number of Polish votes, but Poland was unwilling to give up the clear advantage it had won under the formula agreed to at Nice, and it successfully held out for twenty-seven. During the debate

Table 6.2 Qualified Majority Voting in the Council of Ministers

Germany	29	Belgium	12	Croatia	7
UK	29	Hungary	12	Lithuania	7
France	29	Portugal	12	Latvia	4
Italy	29	Austria	10	Slovenia	4
Spain	27	Bulgaria	10	Estonia	4
Poland	27	Sweden	10	Cyprus	4
Romania	14	Slovakia	7	Luxembourg	4
Netherlands	13	Denmark	7	Malta	3
Greece	12	Finland	7		
Czech Republic	12	Ireland	7	**Total**	**352**

Member states by size of population. To pass, a proposal must normally have a 55 percent majority of countries in favor, from states which must be home to more than 65 percent of the EU population.

at the June 2007 European Council over what would become the Lisbon treaty, Polish president Lech Kaczynski balked at proposals to change the voting system from a triple majority to a double majority, claiming that it would hurt Poland to the benefit of large states such as Germany. He shocked his peers by arguing that Poland would have a much bigger population were it not for the ravages of World War II, claiming that "Poles like Germans, while Germans do not like Poles."[18] In the end, he was placated by an agreement to delay switching to the new voting system until 2014, and then to phase it in over a period of three years.

Since the Luxembourg Compromise, each member state has possessed an implied national veto. Although rarely used, its very existence can be employed as a threat, and governments can use it to convince their citizens that national sovereignty has not been compromised by EU membership. There have been a number of attempts since the 1980s to invoke it, usually in connection with votes on agricultural prices, but they have generally failed for lack of political support. Typically, a vote will not be called if the threat of veto exists.[19]

Once the Council is faced with having to make a decision, it has three main options available (see chapter 7 for details):

Box 6.2 Meetings of the Council of the EU

Meetings of the Council can often seem chaotic and unwieldy, with national delegations of perhaps half a dozen members each, delegations from the Commission and the General Secretariat, and a phalanx of interpreters. The number of participants was high even before the 2004–07 enlargement, and it has only continued to climb since then.

The delegations are seated at a table in order of the rotation of the presidency, with the Commission delegation at one end and the delegations from the presidency and the General Secretariat at the other. The member state holding the presidency not only chairs the meeting but also has separate national representation. National delegations are normally headed by the relevant minister, backed up by national officials and experts. The performance of individual ministers is influenced by several factors, including national interests, the ideological leanings of the minister, public opinion at home (especially if an election is in the offing), and the individual personalities and relationships in the room.

In addition to general discussions, there are regular postponements and adjournments, huddles of delegates during breaks, regular communication with national capitals, and a constant flow of ministers and officials coming and going. When negotiations are becoming bogged down, the president might use a device known as a *tour de table*, during which the heads of delegations are asked in turn to give a brief summary of their positions on an issue. This procedure can be time consuming, but it also gives every delegation the chance to take part in discussions, it can focus the discussion, and it helps raise possible new points of agreement and compromise.

Council meetings are not the only forum in which discussions take place and decisions are made. In addition to the preparatory committee and working party meetings, Council meetings also break for lunches attended only by ministers and translators, and agreements are often reached over a meal. Meetings of the Council are not open to the public except when Commission proposals are sufficiently important that the Council decides to allow the public to watch and listen.

- Under the *consultation procedure*—once the most common method of decision making—the Council asks Parliament for its opinion, and Parliament can either accept or reject the proposal, or ask for amendments. If amendments are needed, they are made by the Commission, and the new proposal is sent to the Council, which then decides whether to accept or reject the proposal, to which it can make additional changes if it wishes.
- Under the *ordinary legislative procedure*—once known as the co-decision procedure—the Council shares legislative powers with Parliament. Both institutions read and discuss the proposal twice and must agree on a common final draft. If they fail, a Council–Parliament conciliation committee is formed, an agreeable wording is developed, and the proposal goes back to both institutions for a third reading and a vote. The proposal is either rejected or becomes law.
- Under the *consent procedure*, Parliament must agree before a proposal is passed. Unlike the consultation procedure, where it can suggest amendments, with the consent procedure it must either accept or reject the proposal.

Because the Council of the EU is a meeting place for national interests, the keys to understanding how it works are found in terms such as *compromise*, *bargaining*, and *diplomacy*. The ministers are often leading political figures at home, so they are clearly motivated by national political interests.[20] And because they are also ideologically driven, Council decisions will be influenced by the relative weight of left-wingers, right-wingers, and centrists. The authority of different ministers will also depend to some extent on the stability of the governing party or coalition in their home states. All of these factors combine to pull ministers in many different directions and to deny the Council the kind of consistency and regularity enjoyed by the Commission.

Questions to Consider

1. What are some ways in which intergovernmentalism is reflected in the way the Council functions? Does the Council also reflect supranational tendencies as well?

2. How has the relationship between the European Parliament and the Council of the EU changed over the years, and what difference has this made to how the EU operates?

3. How does QMV—and the different ways in which it is calculated—affect the balance of power within the Council? Could something like this work for the U.S. Senate, and if so, would it be a good idea?

Further Reading

Fiona Hayes-Renshaw and Helen Wallace. *The Council of Ministers*, 2nd ed. (Basingstoke, UK: Palgrave Macmillan, 2006). Martin Westlake and David Galloway. *The Council of the European Union*, 3rd ed. (London: John Harper, 2004). Tim Veen. *The Political Economy of Collective Decision-Making: Conflicts and Coalitions in the Council of the European Union* (Berlin: Springer, 2011).

     The first two texts present very good overviews but are out of date and do not completely convey the political drama of Council operations; the third uses a (rather dense) theoretical model to explain policy outcomes for different member states within the Council.

Philippa Sherrington. *The Council of Ministers: Political Authority in the European Union* (London: Continuum, 2000).

     An analysis of the work of the Council, based on interviews with key officials and with national government ministers.

Ole Elgström, ed. *European Union Council Presidencies: A Comparative Perspective* (London: Routledge, 2003).

     A comparative study of several Council presidencies, explaining why different member states have different styles, strategies, and priorities.

Notes

1. Desmond Dinan, *Europe Recast: A History of European Union* (Boulder: Lynne Rienner, 2004), 51.

2. Quoted in Jean Monnet, *Memoirs*, trans. Richard Mayne (Garden City, NY: Doubleday, 1978).

3. Thomas Christiansen, "The Council of Ministers: Facilitating Interaction and Developing Actorness in the EU," in Jeremy Richardson, ed., *European Union: Power and Policy-Making*, 3rd ed. (New York: Routledge, 2006), 155–59.

4. See Fiona Hayes-Renshaw and Helen Wallace, *The Council of Ministers*, 2nd ed. (Basingstoke, UK: Palgrave Macmillan, 2006), 34ff.

5. Fiona Hayes-Renshaw and Helen Wallace, "Executive Power in The European Union: The Functions and Limits of the Council of Ministers," *Journal of European Public Policy* 2, no. 4 (1995): 559–82.

6. Alan Clark, *Diaries* (London: Weidenfeld and Nicholson, 1993).

7. Fiona Hayes-Renshaw, Christian Lequesne, and Pedro Mayor Lopez, "The Permanent Representations of the Member States of the European Communities," *Journal of Common Market Studies* 28, no. 2 (December 1989): 119–37.

8. For more details on the work of Coreper, see Hayes-Renshaw and Wallace, *The Council of Ministers*, 72–82.

9. Hayes-Renshaw, Lequesne, and Mayor Lopez, "The Permanent Representations of the Member States of the European Communities."

10. See Ole Elgström, "Introduction," in Ole Elgström, ed., *European Union Council Presidencies: A Comparative Perspective* (London: Routledge, 2003), 4–7.

11. Guy de Bassompierre, *Changing the Guard in Brussels: An Insider's View of the EC Presidency* (New York: Praeger, 1988), 48.

12. "Turbulence for Silvio Berlusconi, at Home and Abroad," Economist, 5 July 2003, 42.

13. *The European*, 28–30 December 1990.

14. "EU Leaders Agree on Reform Treaty," BBC News Online, 23 June 2007, http://news.bbc.co.uk/2/hi/europe/6232540.stm.

15. Christiansen, "The Council of Ministers," 164–67.

16. See Hayes-Renshaw and Wallace, *The Council of Ministers*, chapter 8.

17. For a more detailed explanation of the process, see Hayes-Renshaw, Lequesne, and Mayor Lopez, "The Permanent Representations of the Member States of the European Communities."

18. "Poles in War of Words Over Voting," BBC News Online, 21 June 2007, http://news.bbc.co.uk/2/hi/europe/6227834.stm.

19. Philippa Sherrington, *The Council of Ministers: Political Authority in the European Union* (London: Pinter, 2000), 63–65.

20. B. Guy Peters, "Bureaucratic Politics and the Institutions of the European Community," in Alberta Sbragia, ed., *Euro-Politics: Institutions and Policy-making in the "New" European Community* (Washington, DC: Brookings Institution, 1992), 79.

7

The European Parliament

Chapter Overview

- The European Parliament is one of the two legislative bodies of the EU, similar to a lower house in parliamentary systems, or the U.S House of Representatives.
- The EP consists of 754 Members of the European Parliament (MEPs) elected to renewable five-year terms, with seats divided among the member states based on population. It is headed by a president elected by its members, and has a number of standing and special committees.
- The EP has won new powers over the years, and while it still lacks some of the defining features of a legislature, changes in the treaties have made it an equal legislative partner to the Council of Ministers. Nevertheless, although it is the only directly elected EU institution, it remains relatively unknown or misunderstood by EU citizens.

The European Parliament (EP) is one of the legislative bodies of the EU, sharing responsibility with the Council of the EU for debating, amending, and voting upon proposals for new EU laws. Splitting its time between Strasbourg in France and Brussels, it has 754 members elected from the twenty-seven EU member states on a fixed five-year electoral rotation. (Twelve appointed MEPs from Croatia were added to the ranks in July 2013.) Although it has the moral authority that comes from being the only directly elected EU institution, it lacks three of the typical defining powers of a legislature: it cannot directly introduce proposals for new laws, it cannot decide alone on the content of laws, and it cannot raise revenues. However, the EP can ask the Commission to propose a new law or policy, it shares powers with the Council of the EU on the approval of legislative proposals and the EU budget, it must approve and can remove the Commission, and it can veto membership applications from aspirant EU members.

Most of the EP's handicaps stem from the unwillingness of the governments of the member states to surrender their powers of lawmaking or to give up their grip on decision making in the Council of Ministers. The idea that national legislatures—to which most voters have stronger psychological attachments—should be losing their lawmaking powers is a cause for concern among those who worry about growing EU powers. Parliament also has a credibility problem: few Europeans know (or much care) what it does. Also, European party groups still compete in European elections on national platforms and have not yet developed a strong European identity, with the result that most voters in EP elections are making their choices on the basis of domestic rather than European issues. The EP's powers and credibility are further undermined by low voter turnout: few voters are interested in what it does because of its limited powers, but its powers are limited in part because so few voters are interested in what it does.

In fairness, Parliament is a much more substantial body than most Europeans realize. With increasing confidence, it has used arguments about democratic accountability to win more powers and to be taken more seriously. Instead of simply reacting to Commission proposals and Council votes, the EP has launched its own initiatives and forced the other institutions to pay more attention to its opinions. As well as winning more powers to amend legislation and to check the activities of the other institutions, it has been a valuable source of ideas and new policy proposals, and it has acted as the democratic conscience of the EU. The use of direct elections since 1979 has given Parliament an advantage over the other institutions, because it is the only one that is directly elected. This has given it a critical role in building bridges across the chasm that still separates EU citizens from EU institutions.

EVOLUTION

The European Parliament began life in September 1952 as the Common Assembly of the ECSC. The Assembly met in Strasbourg in northeastern France, and although the Treaty of Paris held out the possibility that the Assembly's members could eventually be directly elected, it initially consisted of seventy-eight members appointed by the national legislatures of the six ECSC member states. The Assembly had no power to make law for the ECSC, nor could it even influence the lawmaking process, which rested with the Council of Ministers. Its only significant power was the ability to force the High Authority of the ECSC to resign through a vote of censure, but it never used this power and ended up being little more than an advisory forum for the discussion of High Authority proposals.[1] But its very creation and existence paved the way for what would later become the European Parliament.[2]

The Treaties of Rome did not create separate assemblies for the EEC and Euratom, but instead transformed the ECSC Common Assembly into the joint European Parliamentary Assembly. Its powers were expanded to give it joint responsibility with the Council of Ministers over the budget, but its suggestions for amendments to EEC law and policy were nonbinding. In 1962 the Assembly was renamed the European Parliament, but despite the symbolism of the change, it still consisted of members appointed by national legislatures from among their own numbers, an arrangement that had two important effects. First, only pro-European legislators volunteered for appointment to the Parliament. Second, since members of the European Parliament (MEPs) were also members of national legislatures, they placed national interests above European interests, mainly because their jobs at home depended on the support of voters. As a result, the European Parliament was seen as a junior European institution, and it has since had to work hard to change its image and to win more power and credibility.

Parliament was a keen supporter of the idea of direct elections, provision for which had been made by the Treaty of Rome, but the Council of Ministers remained opposed throughout the 1960s and early 1970s. At stake were concerns about the tendency toward supranationalism and the determination of the Council (and of national leaders such as Charles de Gaulle) to keep a firm grip on decision-making powers. It was only in 1976 that the European Council finally changed its mind, and elections were held for the first time in June 1979. This was a watershed: now that MEPs were directly elected and met in open session, they could argue that as the elected representatives of the citizens of the EU, they should be allowed to represent the interests of the voters.

As new countries joined the EEC/EU, membership of the EP grew, from 410 members in 1976 to 785 in 2007 (see Table 7.1). As membership increased, so did Parliament's powers. Changes in the 1970s gave it shared responsibility with the Council of Ministers over the Community budget, meaning that—within certain limits—it could raise or lower Community spending, redistribute spending across different budget sectors, reject the annual budget altogether, and determine how the Commission spent money already approved for the budget.[3] Although this was the first instance of Parliament being given real legislative power, it was a 1980 Court of Justice decision that really helped expand the EP's legislative boundaries. In *SA Roquette Frères v. Council* (Case 138/79), a French company challenged a Council regulation limiting production of isoglucose (a starch-based sweetener used in a variety of food products), partly on the basis that it had been adopted without an opinion from Parliament. The Court agreed, thereby recognizing the right of Parliament to be consulted on draft legislation and giving Parliament standing to bring cases to the Court of Justice.[4]

Table 7.1 Growth of the European Parliament

Year	Membership	Details
1952	78	Common Assembly of the ECSC
1958	142	Parliamentary Assembly of the European Communities
1973	198	56 seats added for Britain, Denmark, and Ireland
1976	410	Membership increased in anticipation of first direct elections
1981	434	24 seats added for Greece
1986	518	84 seats added for Portugal and Spain
1994	567	Adjustments made to account for German reunification
1995	626	59 seats added for Austria, Finland, and Sweden
2004	732	Seat distribution reconfigured, and 162 seats added for Cyprus, Czech Republic, Estonia, Hungary, Latvia, Lithuania, Malta, Poland, Slovakia, and Slovenia
2007	785	Seats added for Bulgaria and Romania
2009	736	Reconfigured for 2009 elections
2011	754	Reconfigured under terms of Treaty of Lisbon
2013	766	Seats added for Croatia

Parliament took itself more seriously, and it was taken more seriously by other institutions (notably the Commission); it used parliamentary questions to hold these institutions more accountable and published reports that were designed to promote new legislative ideas. The Single European Act and the Maastricht treaty also gave Parliament more powers over a greater number of policy areas, and greater input into the lawmaking process generally. Under the SEA, for example, the consultation procedure (under which proposals for new laws were subject to a nonbinding opinion from Parliament) was joined by a cooperation procedure under which all laws relating to the single market had to be sent to the EP for two readings. With changes made under Maastricht and the Treaty of Amsterdam, a codecision procedure—now renamed the "ordinary legislative procedure" by the Treaty of Lisbon—was introduced and then widened, giving Parliament the effective right to veto new legislation (see later in this chapter).

The European Parliament today is thus considerably closer to being the main legislative body of the European Union. It has more powers over lawmaking, more powers over the budget, and more powers over the other institutions. Its credibility has increased in particular since the institution of direct elections, because it can claim to be the only EU institution with a direct mandate from EU citizens. However, until it can introduce new legislation, it will not have the kind of independence of action associated with national legislatures. And it still suffers from the lack of a strong psychological link with voters that would give it the credibility it needs to fully exploit its advantages.

STRUCTURE

The European Parliament is the only elected international assembly in the world, and the only directly elected body in the network of EU institutions. It consists of a single chamber, and its members are elected by universal suffrage for fixed, renewable five-year terms. It divides its time among three cities:

- The parliamentary chamber is situated in Strasbourg, France. This is where the EP holds its plenary sessions (meetings of the whole), but it meets there for just three or four days each month (except in August, when much of Europe goes on vacation). Plenaries achieve relatively little, can become bogged down in procedure, and can last late into the night. Accommodation in Strasbourg is also at a premium, often obliging MEPs and their staff to stay in distant hotels. As a result, plenaries are not well attended, and the sight of empty seats and the occasional dozing legislator does little to help the credibility of Parliament. But the siting in Strasbourg is less the fault of MEPs than of the French government (see Box 7.1).

- Parliamentary committees meet in Brussels for two weeks every month (except August). This is where most of the real bargaining and revising takes place, and since additional plenaries can be held in Brussels and a third week is set aside for meetings of political groups (cross-national groups of political parties; see chapter 10), committee meetings are relatively well attended, and MEPs spend most of their time in Brussels.

- The administrative Secretariat is in Luxembourg. This is where most of Parliament's 3,500 support staff work, more than one-third on translation and interpretation. Few MEPs need to visit or spend time here, so the Secretariat is relatively isolated.

Parliament has three main elements: the president, parliamentary committees, and the MEPs themselves.

The President. The European Parliament is overseen by a president, who must be an MEP and is elected by other MEPs for a renewable term of five years. He or she presides over debates during plenary sessions, signs the EU budget and all legislative proposals decided by the ordinary legislative procedure, passes proposals to committees, and represents Parliament in its relations with other institutions. The president also presides over meetings of the Conference of Presidents and the Bureau of the EP (see later in this chapter). To help deal with the many different political groups in Parliament, the president has fourteen vice presidents, who are also elected, for terms of two and a half years and can substitute for the president at meetings.

If Parliament had a majority political group, then the president would almost inevitably come from that group, but the absence of clear majorities has meant that presidents to date have been appointed as a result of inter-party bargaining and for only a half a term each (i.e., two and a half years). In 1989 the two largest political groups—the Socialists and the conservative European People's Party (EPP)—struck a deal whereby they would take turns holding the presidency, a pattern that has continued until today. This ongoing game of musical chairs makes it difficult for presidents (currently, Martin Schulz, a Social Democrat from Germany) to make a mark, and

Box 7.1 Parliament's Multisite Dilemma

The image problems suffered by the European Parliament are made worse by its rather absurd division among three sites, which not only forces a tiring and time-consuming travel schedule on MEPs but also encourages many to skip the Strasbourg plenary sessions because they are the least important. The division, moreover, inflates the parliamentary budget; an estimated $200 million (more than 10 percent of the EP budget) is spent each year moving MEPs, staff, and records back and forth, and it costs more than $25 million annually just to lease the EP building in Strasbourg for roughly sixty days of annual business. The absurdity of this "travelling circus" (as one MEP described it) reflects poorly on Parliament and is galling to the many MEPs who favor holding plenaries in Brussels.[5]

It would make sense to move Parliament to Brussels (not least because that is where most meetings of parliamentary committees are held), but Luxembourg has refused to surrender the Secretariat, and France has refused to give up the parliamentary chamber. The European Council decided in December 1992 that the EP Secretariat would remain in Luxembourg permanently and that the seat of the EP would remain in Strasbourg, but that additional plenaries could meet in Brussels. The EP responded by arguing that the decision was contrary to its right to determine its own working methods and to carry out its tasks in the most effective manner, and signed a lease on a new $1.2 billion Brussels building complex. Not to be outdone, the French built a new and larger $520 million home for the EP in Strasbourg, described by one British journalist as feeling "like a huge new airport, built by a third world government in the middle of a jungle, and totally pointless."[6] Finally, a protocol was added to the Amsterdam treaty confirming that the seat of Parliament would remain in Strasbourg.

Most MEPs are in favor of Parliament being given the right to decide the location of its seat and its meetings, but the governments of the member states have refused. Meanwhile, the extent to which governments can engage in petty territorial squabbles, and spend considerable money to defend those squabbles, is symbolized by the large and architecturally impressive—but usually almost empty—EP building in Strasbourg.[7]

Table 7.2 Recent Presidents of the European Parliament

Beginning of Term	Name	Member State	Political Group
July 1979	Simone Veil	France	Liberal Democrat
Jan. 1982	Pieter Dankert	Netherlands	Socialist
July 1984	Pierre Pflimlin	France	EPP
Jan. 1987	Sir Henry Plumb	UK	Conservative
July 1989	Enrique Barón Crespo	Spain	Socialist
Jan. 1992	Egon Klepsch	Germany	EPP
July 1994	Klaus Hänsch	Germany	Socialist
Jan. 1997	José Maria Gil-Robles	Spain	EPP
July 1999	Nicole Fontaine	France	EPP
Jan. 2002	Pat Cox	Ireland	Liberal Democrat
July 2004	Josep Borrell Fontelles	Spain	Socialist
Jan. 2007	Hans-Gert Poettering	Germany	EPP-ED
July 2009	Jerzy Buzek	Poland	EPP
Jan. 2012	Martin Schulz	Germany	Social Democrat

EPP=European People's Party ED=European Democrats

without a strong and well-known personality in the position, it is more difficult to draw public attention to the work of the EP.

There are parallels between the offices of the president of the European Parliament and the Speaker of the U.S. House of Representatives, but the comparisons go only so far. The lack of majorities in the EP means that the president is less political than the Speaker, who comes from the majority party and works to ensure that the party's political goals are met in the House. The Speaker also has a strong political role emanating from his or her relationship with the president of the United States; speakers either oversee presidential legislative programs (if the two people are from the same party) or act as the focus of opposition to the president (if they are from opposing parties). EP presidents have been known to be partisan, and even nationalistic, but they are limited by the need to build support across many different party groups. If and when majority parties or coalitions begin to emerge in the EP, the presidency could well be transformed: with the backing of a majority, the president could serve longer terms in office and could become a new force in the EP's dealings with other EU institutions, particularly the Council of Ministers.

Organizational matters in the EP are addressed by three groups:

- *Conference of Presidents.* Meeting bimonthly, this brings together the president and the heads of all of the political groups in Parliament. It decides the timetable and agenda for plenary sessions and manages the system of committees, establishing their size and their agendas.
- *Bureau of the EP.* Made up of the president of the EP and the vice presidents, this functions much like a governing council and is responsible for administrative, organizational, and staff issues, and for the EP budget.
- *Conference of Committee Chairs.* This meets monthly and brings together the chairs of parliamentary committees to discuss organizational issues and help draft plenary agendas. It keeps a close eye on the progress of proposals and brokers deals between the political groups regarding the parliamentary agenda.[8]

Parliamentary Committees. As with the U.S. Congress, most of the detailed work of the EP is done in a series of committees in which MEPs gather to discuss and amend legislative proposals. The number of standing (permanent) committees has grown in concert with the work and the size of the EP, and today totals twenty. The committees usually meet in Brussels, where they consider all new legislation relevant to their areas. The titles of the committees are a clue to the priorities of European integration: they include Foreign Affairs; International Trade; Economic and Monetary Affairs; the Environment, Public Health and Food Safety; Regional Development; Agriculture; and Women's Rights and Gender Equality (see Table 7.3). They range in size from twenty-eight to eighty-six members.

Just as in the U.S. Congress, there is strong competition among MEPs to win appointment to a committee, since some committees have a higher political status than others. Seats are divided on the basis of a balance of party affiliations, the seniority of MEPs, and national interests. (For example, member states such as Poland and Ireland have a particular interest in agriculture and less interest in foreign and defense issues.) Once appointed, committee members select their own bureaus (a chair and three vice chairs), who hold office for half a parliamentary term. In the U.S. Congress, committee leadership does not change much, committee chairs are appointed out of the majority party, and there is an unspoken rule that senior members will be considered first in appointments. In the EP the opposite is true: because there is no majority party, the chair positions are divided among political groups roughly in proportion to the size of their representation in Parliament, and there is more turnover.

In addition to the standing committees, Parliament also has a changing roster of temporary committees and committees of enquiry. Those formed

Table 7.3 Committees of the European Parliament

Agriculture and Rural Development

Budgetary Control

Budgets

Civil Liberties, Justice and Home Affairs

Constitutional Affairs

Culture and Education

Development

Economic and Monetary Affairs

Employment and Social Affairs

Environment, Public Health and Food Safety

Fisheries

Foreign Affairs

Industry, Research and Energy

Internal Market and Consumer Protection

International Trade

Legal Affairs

Petitions

Regional Development

Transport and Tourism

Women's Rights and Gender Equality

in recent years have looked at issues such as the foot and mouth disease crisis (2002), allegations of illegal CIA activities in Europe (2006–07), climate change (2007–08), the global economic crisis (2009), and organized crime, corruption, and money laundering (set up in 2012). Finally, there is the Conciliation Committee, in which representatives of the EP and the Council of Ministers meet to try to reach agreement whenever the two sides have disagreed on the wording of a legislative proposal. There are twenty-seven members from each side, and representatives of the Commission also attend.

Members of the European Parliament (MEPs). The European Parliament in 2013 had 754 elected members (see Table 7.4) (and 12 appointed members for Croatia, which will be added to the election cycle in 2014). Seats are distributed among the member states roughly on the basis of population, with the bigger states being underrepresented and the smaller states being overrepresented. Taking an average for the EU as a whole, there should be one MEP per 665,000 Europeans. But German, French, and British residents are all underrepresented (about 840,000 people per MEP), while Maltese and Luxembourgers are greatly overrepresented (with 80,000 to 83,000 people per MEP). A similar mathematical imbalance can be found in the United States, where the population per district in the U.S. House of Representatives averages 690,000 people, but there is a high of 1:967,000 in Montana and a low of 1:525,000 in Rhode Island. The imbalances are even greater in the U.S. Senate, where California's two senators share some 37 million constituents, while those from Rhode Island share just over 525,000.

In the past, MEPs were elected members of national parliaments who were also appointed to the EP, holding a so-called dual mandate. But as the workload of Parliament grew, the dual mandate became increasingly impractical; several member states (including Belgium and Spain) made it illegal, and it has been effectively eliminated. The result has been a weakening of the links between national legislatures and the EP, and greater independence and credibility for MEPs. Candidates for elections are chosen by their national parties, but once in office they have an independent mandate and cannot always be bound by those parties.[9] Turnover is fairly high—typically about half of the MEPs who win election to the EP are newcomers.[10] This stands in contrast to the case in the United States, where the advantages of incumbency are well-known, and more than 90 percent of members of Congress typically win reelection. MEPs are paid by their home governments and are paid the same salaries as members of their re-

Table 7.4 Distribution of Seats in the European Parliament 2013

Germany	99	Portugal	22	Lithuania	12
France	74	Czech Republic	22	Croatia	12
United Kingdom	73	Hungary	22	Latvia	9
Italy	73	Sweden	20	Slovenia	8
Spain	54	Austria	19	Estonia	6
Poland	51	Bulgaria	18	Cyprus	6
Romania	33	Slovakia	13	Luxembourg	6
Netherlands	26	Denmark	13	Malta	6
Greece	22	Finland	13		
Belgium	22	Ireland	12	**Total**	**766**

spective national parliaments. But salary levels vary significantly by member state, with the new Eastern European MEPs behind their Western European counterparts. In 2005 an agreement was reached that— in effect from the new parliamentary term in 2009—all MEPs will be paid the same.

By socioeconomic makeup, the EP is similar to most national legislatures in the member states; it is dominated by white, middle-aged, middle-class professional men from urban backgrounds. Nonetheless, women are increasingly better represented; the percentage has grown steadily from 16 percent in 1979 to 19 percent in 1989 to 35 percent today. This is below the average of the national legislatures of Scandinavian countries (37–47 percent), but is well above that of Britain (22 percent), more than double the figure of the United States (16 percent) and almost triple the figure of Russia (13 percent).[11]

Many MEPs already have political experience at the national level, but where Parliament was once seen as a haven for also-rans, the quality of candidates has improved, and the EP is no longer an easy option for people who have failed to win office in national elections or who have been temporarily sidelined in (or have retired from) national politics. The EP has counted among its members senior national leaders, including former German chancellor Willy Brandt, former French president Valéry Giscard d'Estaing, former Italian prime ministers Emilio Colombo and Silvio Berlusconi, and former Belgian prime minister Leo Tindemans. Emphasizing the increasing role of Parliament as a stepping-stone to office elsewhere, several MEPs have gone on to be appointed to the European

Commission, including presidents Jacques Delors and Jacques Santer and commissioners Ray MacSharry, Viviane Reding, Carlo Ripa de Meana, Karel van Miert, and Antonio Vitorino. Several MEPs have also gone on to high national office, including French prime minister Jean Pierre Raffarin, British defense minister Geoff Hoon, and Spanish foreign minister Ana Palacio.

How Parliament Works

Conventional democratic legislatures have a virtual monopoly on the introduction, amendment, and adoption of new laws (although final adoption is normally subject to signature by the executive or the head of state). This is not the case with the European Parliament, which—thanks to efforts by member states to preserve their powers in the Council of Ministers—has been left with a mix of formal and informal powers, ranging from the modest to the significant. These powers fall broadly into three main groups: those over legislation, those over the budget, and those over the other EU institutions.

Powers over Legislation. Although the Commission has a monopoly on the development of proposals for new laws, the EP has informal channels of influence open to it at this stage. For example, it can send representatives to the early development meetings held by the Commission, at which point it can encourage the Commission to address issues it thinks are important. It can also publish "own initiative" reports in which it draws attention to a problem, almost daring the Commission and the Council of Ministers to respond. The EP has been, for example, a legislative entrepreneur on a variety of environmental issues, sparking EU bans on imports of seal products from Canada, kangaroo products from Australia, old growth lumber from Canada, and the fur of animals caught using leghold traps in Russia and North America.[12] Generally, though, Parliament must wait until it receives a proposal from the Commission before it can really get down to work. At that point, it enters a process of give-and-take with the Council of Ministers that has taken on complex proportions.

Initially, Parliament was limited mainly to the consultation procedure, under which it can either accept or reject a proposal from the Council of Ministers or ask for amendments. If amendments are needed, they are made by the Commission, and the new proposal is sent back to the Council of Ministers, which then decides whether to accept or reject the proposal, to which it can make additional changes if it wishes. No limit is placed on how long Parliament can take to give its opinion, and so it has the power of delay—a traditional practice of opposition parties in many national legislatures. This power was given new significance with the 1980 isoglucose case; Parliament was subsequently able to drag its feet as a means of getting the Council to take its opinion seriously.[13] The consultation procedure is now rarely used.

The Single European Act increased the powers of Parliament, introducing a cooperation procedure under which Parliament was given the right to a second reading for certain laws adopted by the Council of Ministers, notably those relating to regional policy, the environment, and the European Social Fund. This meant that Parliament was now involved more directly in the legislative process and no longer had a purely consultative role.[14] Maastricht extended the procedure to cover a variety of new policy areas, but then it was all but eliminated by the Amsterdam treaty.

Maastricht further strengthened the powers of Parliament by introducing the codecision procedure, renamed the "ordinary legislative procedure" by Lisbon (see Box 7.2), which is now the usual approach to lawmaking. Initially, codecision meant that Parliament was given the right to a third reading on certain kinds of legislation, the list of which was then expanded to include laws relating to the single market, research and development, consumer protection, the environment, education, and culture, and then expanded again by Lisbon to include agriculture, fisheries, the structural funds, and transport. This has effectively given the EP equal powers with the Council of Ministers on decision making, making the two institutions into co-legislatures. At one time the Council of Ministers could still overrule a rejection by Parliament of a new proposal after a third reading, but this was ended by the Treaty of Amsterdam; as a result an EP–Council conciliation committee must now meet after the second reading to see if it can work out an agreeable joint text, which in most cases it does. The new text then goes to the EP and the Council for a third reading and a vote.

Finally, under the consent procedure Parliament has veto powers over the Council on the following: allowing new member states to join the EU and giving other countries associate status; the conclusion of international agreements; penalties the Council may choose to impose on a member state for serious and persistent violations of fundamental rights; any efforts to introduce a uniform electoral system for European elections; and the powers and tasks of the European Central Bank. Maastricht also extended Parliament's powers over foreign policy issues by obliging the presidency of the

BOX 7.2 THE ORDINARY LEGISLATIVE PROCEDURE

The tension between intergovernmental and supranational pressures in the EU has resulted in constant change in the decision-making procedure of the EP, leading to the current preferred arrangement, known as the "ordinary legislative procedure." The process by which the EP and the Council of Ministers interact on the debate over the adoption of new laws in most areas involves the following steps:

1. The Commission sends a proposal for a new law to Parliament and the Council of Ministers.

2. The relevant parliamentary standing committee looks it over and draws up a report (which may be seen and commented upon by other committees with an interest in the issue, by individual MEPs, and by political groups). Parliament then votes on the report in a plenary session. This is the *first reading*.

3. If no changes are suggested, or if the Council agrees with the EP's suggested changes, then the proposal is adopted. But if the Council disagrees with the suggested changes, it modifies them in a common position.

4. The common position is then sent to Parliament, which has three months to respond. If it approves the common position or fails to act by the deadline, the amended proposal is adopted. But the relevant parliamentary committee may reject the common position or propose amendments. Its recommendation is then discussed by Parliament in a *second reading*.

5. The changes are forwarded to the Commission, which gives its opinion. The proposal then goes to the Council, which can accept the changes—in which case the proposal is adopted—or reject them. In the latter case, the proposal is sent to a conciliation committee, which works to reconcile the differences.

6. If the committee cannot agree within six weeks, the proposal lapses. But in most cases, the committee reaches agreement and issues a joint text, which then goes to Parliament for approval. This is the *third reading*. If Parliament agrees with the joint text, the proposal is adopted, but if it rejects the joint text, the proposal lapses.

European Council to consult with the EP on the development of the Common Foreign and Security Policy. During the 1990s the EP used the assent procedure several times to delay agreements between the EU and third parties. For example, it held up an agreement with Russia in protest of Russian policy in Chechnya, with Kazakhstan in protest of that country's poor democratic record, and with Turkey in protest of human rights violations.[15]

The cumulative effect of all these changes has been to give the Council of Ministers and Parliament equal powers over the adoption of most new laws. In other words, the EU now has a bicameral legislature in all but name. The changes have also encouraged party groups in Parliament to work more closely together, and have made the EP a new target for lobbyists trying to influence the shape of new legislation (see chapter 10).

Powers over the Budget. Parliament has joint powers with the Council of the EU over confirming the EU budget, so that between them the two institutions are the budgetary authority of the EU. Parliament meets with the Council biannually to consider a draft developed by the Commission and to discuss possible amendments. It can ask for changes to the budget, it can ask for new appropriations for areas not covered (but it cannot make decisions on how to raise money), and ultimately—with a two-thirds majority—it can completely reject the budget, which it has done only three times so far (in 1979, 1982, and 1984). A draft budget is normally introduced by the Commission in April each year and—following meetings between the Council and the Commission—is adopted in July, then sent to the EP for two readings. Only when Parliament has adopted the budget (usually in December) and it has been signed by the president of the EP does it come into force.

Powers over Other EU Institutions. Parliament has several direct powers over other EU institutions, including the right to debate the annual legislative program of the Commission, a practice that was introduced by Jacques Delors during the mid-1980s and has since been used by the Commission to emphasize its accountability to Parliament.[16] It can also take the Commission or the Council of the EU to the Court of Justice over alleged infringements of the treaties and has had the power since 1994 to approve the appointment of the Commission president and all of the commissioners. Although it cannot vote on individual commissioners, concerns raised by the EP about individuals can lead to their appointment being blocked—this happened in 2005, for example, over Italian nominee Rocco Buttiglione (see chapter 5). The extension of the term of the College of Commissioners from four years to five (to coincide with the term of the EP) significantly altered the relationship between the two institutions.

The makeup of the College is not tied to the balance of party power in the EP (in the way that the membership of governments in parliamentary systems is a reflection of party numbers in the legislature), but the right of the EP to vote on the proposed membership of the College is a step closer to the day when there will be ideological and policy alignment between the two, and membership of the College will be directly affected by the balance of party power in the EP.

The most potentially disruptive of Parliament's powers over the Commission is its ability—under certain conditions and with an absolute majority of MEPs and a two-thirds majority of votes cast—to force the resignation of the entire College of Commissioners through a motion of censure. Much like a nuclear weapon, though, this power is mainly a deterrent; censure motions have been proposed, but they have all been defeated or withdrawn. As noted in chapter 5, the closest the EP has come to removing the College was during a vote in January 1999 over charges of fraud and corruption; 232 MEPs voted in favor of removing the College, but this was far less than the required two-thirds majority of 416. Nonetheless, the size of the negative vote shocked the Commission and led to the creation of a committee of inquiry, whose report ultimately brought down the College. The event has gone down as a watershed in the relationship between the EP and the Commission.

The EP also has a critical relationship with the Council of the EU. Apart from having equal powers with the Council over the adoption of most new laws, Parliament also closely monitors the work of the Council, regularly submitting oral and written questions on matters of policy. The two institutions work particularly closely together on policy issues such as the Common Foreign and Security Policy, judicial cooperation, asylum and immigration issues, and international crime. The president of the EP gives an address at the opening of every meeting of the European Council, expressing the views of Parliament on the Council agenda.

Parliament has also taken the initiative through the years to win new powers for itself over the work of EU institutions. For example, it introduced its own question time in 1973 and so can demand oral or written replies to questions from commissioners, helping to make them more accountable. It initiated the 1992 reconfiguration of the number of seats in Parliament, and it led the campaign for the creation of the Court of Auditors in 1993.

It can generate public debate on EU policies and can set up committees of inquiry, as it did during 1996 to look into the crisis set off by mad cow disease in Britain.

Questions to Consider

1. In terms of its power, how has the European Parliament evolved over the years, and what difference have such changes made to its relationships with other EU institutions?
2. In what ways is the EP similar to and different from other legislatures, such as the U.S. Congress? Should the EP be given the same powers as the U.S. Congress?
3. Why has the European Parliament failed to capture the imagination of EU voters (who have been turning out in declining numbers at EP elections)? What more could be done to address its lack of a strong psychological link with EU citizens?

Further Reading

Michael Shackleton and Richa Francis Jacobs. *The European Parliament*, 8th ed. (London: John Harper, 2011).
> The standard reference work on the EP, written by an MEP and two staff members and describing in some detail the powers and workings of Parliament.

David Judge, David Earnshaw, Neil Nugent, and William E. Paterson. *The European Parliament*, 2nd ed. (Basingstoke, UK: Palgrave Macmillan, 2008).
> A survey of the EP, including chapters on its history, its powers and organization, the party groups, and its role in EU decision making.

Bernard Steunenberg and Jacques Thomassen, eds. *The European Parliament: Moving Toward Democracy in the EU* (Lanham, MD: Rowman and Littlefield, 2002).
> An edited collection of studies of the changing role of the European Parliament.

Richard Corbett and Klaus Hansch. *The European Parliament's Role in Closer EU Integration* (Basingstoke, UK: Palgrave Macmillan, 2002).
> A study of the theory and practice of the EP's contribution to European integration.

Notes

1. John Gillingham, *Coal, Steel, and the Rebirth of Europe, 1945–55* (New York: Cambridge University Press, 1991), 282.

2. See discussion in Berthold Rittberger, *Building Europe's Parliament: Democratic Representation Beyond the Nation-State* (Oxford: Oxford University Press, 2005), chapter 3.

3. Richard Corbett, Francis Jacobs, and Michael Shackleton, *The European Parliament*, 6th ed. (London: John Harper, 2005), 240.

4. Renaud Dehousse, *The European Court of Justice* (New York: St. Martin's, 1998), 98.

5. Roy Perry, MEP, quoted in David Judge and David Earnshaw, *The European Parliament* (Basingstoke, UK: Palgrave Macmillan, 2003), 163.

6. Andrew Gimson, *Boris: The Rise of Boris Johnson* (London: Simon and Schuster, 2006), 108.

7. For more discussion on the multisite issue, see Judge and Earnshaw, *The European Parliament*, 158–63.

8. Corbett, Jacobs, and Shackleton, *The European Parliament*, 119.

9. Simon Hix and Christopher Lord, *Political Parties in the European Union* (New York: St. Martin's, 1997), 85–90.

10. Corbett, Jacobs, and Shackleton, *The European Parliament*, 48.

11. "Women in National Parliaments," *Inter-Parliamentary Union*, 2012, http://www.ipu.org/wmn-e/world.htm. Figures are for 2012, for lower or single chambers of national legislatures.

12. Christopher Pienning, "The EP Since 1994: Making Its Mark on the World Stage," in Juliet Lodge, ed., *The 1999 Elections to the European Parliament* (Basingstoke, UK: Palgrave Macmillan, 2001).

13. Corbett, Jacobs, and Shackleton, *The European Parliament*, 200.

14. John Fitzmaurice, "An Analysis of the European Community's Cooperation Procedure," *Journal of Common Market Studies* 26, no. 4 (June 1988): 389–400.

15. Pienning, "The EP Since 1994."

16. Clive Archer and Fiona Butler, *The European Community: Structure and Process*, 2nd ed. (London: Pinter, 1996), 47.

8

THE EUROPEAN COURT OF JUSTICE

CHAPTER OVERVIEW

- The least well-known of the EU institutions, the European Court of Justice is the judicial arm of the EU, responsible for interpreting the meaning of the treaties and for resolving disputes between the member states, EU institutions, and individuals affected by EU law.
- The Court consists of twenty-eight judges appointed for six-year renewable terms by common accord of the member states, headed by a president, assisted by eight advocates-general charged with reviewing cases as they come to the Court and delivering independent opinions. Below this, there is also the General Court, which serves as the first point of decision on less complicated cases and the EU Civil Service Tribunal, which rules on cases involving disputes between EU institutions and their employees.
- The Court can be considered the unsung hero of European integration: well-respected and uncontroversial, the Court has created a body of law that is uniformly interpreted and applied throughout

the EU and has issued judgments that, together, have greatly facilitated the integration process.

   The European Court of Justice (ECJ, and officially the Court of Justice of the European Union) is the judicial arm of the EU. Its charge is to rule on the "constitutionality" of all EU law, to rule on conformity with the treaties of any international agreement considered by the EU, to give rulings to national courts in cases in which there are questions about EU law, and to rule in disputes involving EU institutions, member states, individuals, and corporations. The Court is based in Luxembourg and consists of twenty-seven judges appointed for six-year renewable terms of office. As the workload of the Court has increased, so subsidiary courts have been created: a Court of First Instance (now called the General Court) was set up in 1989 to deal with less complicated cases, and the EU Civil Service Tribunal was set up in 2004 to deal with disputes involving EU institutions and their staff.

   The contribution of the Court to European integration has been critical, because without a body of law that can be uniformly interpreted and applied throughout the EU, the Union would have little authority, and its decisions and policies would be arbitrary and inconsistent. By working to build such a body of law, the Court of Justice—perhaps the most purely supranational of the major EU institutions—has been a key player in promoting integration.

   Unlike the U.S. Supreme Court, which bases its rulings on judicial review of the Constitution, the ECJ has so far had no constitution beyond the accumulated treaties and laws agreed to by the member states. But the treaties have needed interpretation and clarification, and just as the U.S. Supreme Court helped clarify its own powers with decisions such as *Marbury v. Madison* (the 1803 decision establishing the power of judicial review), so has the ECJ.[1] Its rulings have established that the Treaty of Rome is a constitutional instrument that imposes direct and common obligations on member states, established the primacy of EU law, and greatly simplified completion of the single market. Court decisions have had a significant impact on issues as varied as the free movement of people, money, goods, and services; the external relations of the EU; competition policy; human rights; gender equality; and external trade.

   Despite its critical contributions to the process and goals of European integration, the work of the Court has attracted surprisingly little political attention or analysis. As public interest has focused on the Commission and the Council of the EU, the Court has quietly gone about the business of interpreting EU law, its members remaining the least well-known of all the leading actors in the EU system. Unlike judgments of the U.S. Supreme Court, which often make national headlines and generate public debate, rulings by the Court of Justice attract little public attention.

EVOLUTION

The Court was established in 1952 as the Court of Justice of the ECSC and was intended to be a watchdog for the Treaty of Paris and to rule on the legality of decisions made by the ECSC High Authority in response to complaints submitted by either the member states or the national coal and steel industries; the Treaty of Paris was its primary source of authority. It made 137 decisions during its brief existence, many of which are still relevant to EU law today.[2]

The Treaties of Rome created separate courts for the EEC and the European Atomic Energy Community (Euratom), but a subsidiary agreement gave jurisdiction over the treaties to a common seven-member Court of Justice of the European Communities. Its members were appointed by the Council of Ministers on the recommendation of the member states; they heard cases involving disputes between Community institutions and member states, and their verdicts were final. Its power, reach, and significance grew as the work of the Community expanded, as its membership grew during the 1970s and 1980s, and as the Court issued more judgments against Community institutions and member states. Although decision making in the EU revolved around the axis of the Commission and the Council of Ministers, the Court made decisions that had far-reaching consequences for the process of European integration. Three of its most famous cases illustrate its contribution.

First, the principle of direct effect (EU law is directly and uniformly applicable in all member states) is a consequence of the 1963 *Van Gend en Loos* decision, one of the most important handed down by the ECJ. A Dutch transport company had brought an action against Dutch customs for increasing the duty it had to pay on a product imported from Germany. Its lawyers argued that this went against Article 12 of the EEC Treaty, which—in the interest of building the common market—prohibited new duties or increases in existing duties. The Dutch government argued that the Court had no power to decide whether the provisions of the EEC Treaty prevailed over Dutch law and that resolution fell exclusively within the jurisdiction of national courts. The ECJ disagreed, ruling that the treaties were more than international agreements and that EC law was "legally complete . . . and produces direct effects and creates individual rights which national courts must protect."[3]

Second, the principle of the supremacy of EU law (EU law trumps national law in policy areas where the EU has responsibility) was established with the 1964 decision *Flaminio Costa v. ENEL*. Costa was an Italian who had owned shares in Edison Volta, an electricity supply company. When the company was nationalized in 1962 and made part of the new National Electricity Board (ENEL), Costa refused to pay his electric bill (equivalent to about $1.50) because he claimed he had been hurt by nationalization, which he argued was contrary to the spirit of the Treaty of Rome. The local court in Milan asked the Court of Justice for a preliminary ruling, even though both the Italian government and ENEL argued that there were no grounds for taking the case to the European Court. The government further argued that a national court could not take a dispute over domestic law to the European Court.

The Court disagreed, arguing that by creating "a Community of unlimited duration, having its own institutions, its own personality, its own legal capacity . . . and real powers stemming from limitation of sovereignty or a transfer of powers from the States to the Community, the Member States have limited their sovereign rights, albeit within limited fields, and have thus created a body of law which binds both their nationals and themselves."[4]

Third, the issue of the supremacy of European law was confirmed—and the jurisdiction of the Community extended—with a dispute that broke in 1967 over the issue of human rights. The EEC Treaty had said nothing about human rights, a reflection once again of how little authority the member states were prepared to give up to the EEC and how focused they had been on economic integration. In October 1967 the German Constitutional Court argued that the EEC had no democratic basis because it lacked protection for human rights and that the Community could not deprive German citizens of the rights they had under German law.[5] The Court of Justice refuted this in *Nold v. Commission*, in which it established that "fundamental rights form an integral part of the general principles of law."[6] (See also Box 8.1.)

BOX 8.1 THE EU CHARTER OF FUNDAMENTAL RIGHTS

An example of the manner in which a Court ruling can have broader policy implications is offered by the issue of human rights. The European Convention on Human Rights was adopted in 1950 by the Council of Europe in order to protect human rights and basic freedoms. Although all EC/EU member states signed the convention, there was support for the idea of the EC/EU developing its own charter of human rights, the idea being not to change the list of rights so much as to make them more visible to Europeans.[7]

New impetus was offered in 1996 when the Court of Justice ruled that the treaties did not give the EU the power to accede to the convention. On German initiative, agreement was reached on the drawing up of the charter at the Cologne European Council in June 1999. A sixty-two-member Convention was established, consisting of representatives of the member states, the European Parliament, and national legislatures. It had its first meeting in December 1999 and produced a draft that was formally adopted in December 2000. Points raised in the charter include:

- Freedom of thought, conscience, religion, expression, and assembly.
- The right of all citizens to education (including the possibility of free compulsory education), property and asylum, equality before the law, access to social security and health care, freedom of movement within the EU, and a fair and public trial.
- The prohibition of the death penalty, torture, human cloning, slavery, and child labor.
- The right of workers to collective bargaining and action, and protection from unjustified dismissal.

The charter has been signed by all EU member states, but was more a "solemn declaration" than a legally binding document. It would have been incorporated into the European constitution, in spite of concerns from some EU member states that it would have created new legal obligations that would erode national sovereignty and that it was more appropriate to have some of the issues dealt with by elected political leaders rather than unelected judges.[8] However, it was not officially incorporated into the Lisbon Treaty but rather "solemnly proclaimed," albeit given the "same legal value as the treaties" according to Article 6.

STRUCTURE

The European Court of Justice is based in a cluster of buildings in the Centre Européen, a network of EU institutions situated on the Kirchberg Plateau above the city of Luxembourg. The land was bought by the Luxembourg government in 1961 as a site for the EC institutions, presumably in the hope that they would all eventually be moved there. The black steel and glass Palais de Justice was opened in 1973 and has since been expanded four times in response to EU enlargement and the growing workload of the Court. It is now part of a modest but not insubstantial complex that includes the Secretariat of the European Parliament, buildings for the Commission and the Council of Ministers, the seat of the Court of Auditors, and the headquarters of the European Investment Bank.[9]

The Court has five main elements: the judges, the president of the Court, the advocates general, the Court of First Instance, and the EU Civil Service Tribunal.

The Judges. The Court of Justice has twenty-eight judges, each appointed for a six-year renewable term of office. About half come up for renewal every three years, so terms are staggered. Theoretically, the judges have always been appointed by common accord of the member state governments, so there is no national quota and there are no "Spanish seat" or "Slovenian seat" on the Court. Judges do not even have to be EU citizens; as Court president Lord McKenzie Stuart quipped in 1988, it could be made up "entirely of Russians."[10] In practice, however, because every member state has the right to make one appointment, all judges are national appointees. The persistence of this practice emphasizes the role that national interests still play in EU decision making. However, Lisbon added a new layer to the appointment process by stipulating that before being appointed by the member states, candidates must first be vetted by a seven-member panel consisting of former members of the Court of Justice, members of national constitutional courts, and lawyers, of whom one is nominated by the European Parliament. The panel gives its opinion, leaving the states free to decide how to act.

In addition to being acceptable to all of the other member states, judges must be scrupulously independent and must avoid promoting the national interests of their home states. They must also be qualified lawyers, or as the Treaty of Paris so thoughtfully put it, they must "possess the qualifications required for appointment to the highest judicial offices in their respective countries or . . . be jurisconsults of recognized competence." (U.S.

Supreme Court justices do not have to be attorneys, although in practice they all have been.) Some European judges have come to the Court with experience as government ministers, some have held elective office, and others have had careers as lawyers and academics, but, since the Treaty of Rome, they have all been lawyers.[11]

Although most judges are renewed at least once, the Court has far more turnover than the U.S. Supreme Court, where appointments are for life. Life appointments have the benefit of encouraging independence and exploiting experience, but they also contribute to the highly charged political nature of U.S. Supreme Court appointments and reduce the injection of new thinking. Appointments to the European Court, by contrast, are both relatively frequent and nonpolitical. The European Court has had nearly sixty judges since it was created, about three times as many as the U.S. Supreme Court over the same period. The average age of European judges in 2003 was sixty-one (compared to sixty-nine for U.S. justices), and ten of the fifteen judges then sitting had served four years or less on the Court, while U.S. justices had been in their posts for an average of seventeen years. The 2004–07 enlargement of the EU brought twelve new judges into the Court (lowering the average age to fifty-nine), along with a significant body of new thinking, perspectives, and priorities (see Table 8.1 for the court's current composition).

European judges enjoy immunity from having suits brought against them while they are on the Court, and even after they have left they cannot be sued for their decisions. They are not allowed to hold administrative or political office while on the Court. They can resign, but they can be removed only by the other judges and the advocates general (not by member states or other EU institutions), and then only by unanimous agreement that they are no longer doing their job adequately.[12] Almost all the judges have been men. In 2012 there were just four women on the Court: Rosario Silva de Lapuerta from Spain, Camelia Toader from Romania, Maria Gerger from Austria, and Alexandra Prechal from the Netherlands.

All judges can sit together as a full court, but they do this only for the most important cases, while the rest are heard by chambers of five or seven judges, or by a Grand Chamber of thirteen judges. Chambers were once used for hearing only cases that did not need to be brought before the full Court, such as staff cases. Since the workload of the Court has increased, though, any case can now be assigned to a chamber, including preliminary rulings and actions brought by or against member states (unless a member state or an institution specifically asks for a hearing before the full Court, or unless the case is particularly important or complex).

Table 8.1 Judges of the European Court of Justice, 2012

Name	Member State	Year of Birth	Year of Appointment
Vassilios Skouris	Greece	1948	1999
José Rodrigues	Portugal	1940	2000
Allan Rosas	Finland	1948	2002
Rosario Silva de Lapuerta	Spain	1954	2003
Koen Lenaerts	Belgium	1954	2003
Konrad Schiemann	United Kingdom	1937	2004
Endre Juhász	Hungary	1944	2004
George Arestis	Cyprus	1945	2004
Anthony Barthet	Malta	1947	2004
Marko Ilešič	Slovenia	1947	2004
Jiří Malenovský	Czech Republic	1950	2004
Uno Lõhmus	Estonia	1952	2004
Egils Levits	Latvia	1955	2004
Aindrias Ó Caoimh	Ireland	1950	2004
Lars Bay Larsen	Denmark	1953	2006
Antonio Tizzano	Italy	1940	2006
Jean-Claude Bonichot	France	1955	2006
Thomas von Danwitz	Germany	1962	2006
Alexander Arabadjiev	Bulgaria	1949	2007
Camelia Toader	Romania	1963	2007
Jean-Jacques Kasel	Luxembourg	1946	2008
Marek Safjan	Poland	1949	2009
Daniel Šváby	Slovakia	1951	2009
Maria Berger	Austria	1956	2009
Alexandra Prechal	Netherlands	1959	2010
Egidijus Jarašiūnas	Lithuania	1952	2010
Carl Gustav Fernlund	Sweden	1950	2011

As this book went to press, the judge from Croatia had not yet been appointed.

Unlike all of the other EU institutions, in which English is slowly be-coming the working language, the Court mainly uses French, although a case can be heard in any of the official languages of the EU; when the de-fendant is a member state or a citizen of a member state, the case must be heard in the defendant's language. The Court has about 1,500 staff mem-bers, most of whom are bureaucrats or translators.

The President. While the chief justice in the United States is nominated by the president and must be confirmed by the U.S. Senate, the president of the European Court of Justice is elected by the judges from among their own number in a secret ballot by majority vote to serve a three-year renew-able term. The president presides over meetings of the Court and is respon-sible for technical issues such as assigning cases to chambers, appointing judge-rapporteurs (see later in this chapter), and deciding the dates for hearings. Presidents also have considerable influence over the political di-rection of the Court, like the chief justice of the U.S. Supreme Court, but their exact role is subject to much less public and political scrutiny.

The president elected in 2003 was Vassilios Skouris, a lawyer and pro-fessor of public law from Greece. First appointed to the Court in 1999, Skouris was educated in Germany, earning a doctorate in constitutional and administrative law from Hamburg University. He was then a professor of law for several years, and served twice in the Greek government as min-ister of internal affairs. He has made clear his views that the Court of Justice is not a political body: "The Commission . . . is a political body with the right of initiative. The Court of Justice has never been and could never be like that. We rule on the cases that are brought before us. . . . The im-portance of the role of the Court is a good subject for conferences and uni-versities but at the end of the day it's a court of justice that carries out a normal task for any court: to rule on the cases, and nothing more."[13] In October 2006 and October 2012, Skouris was reelected as president of the Court (see Table 8.2).

The Advocates General. Because it is based on the French legal model, the Court has eight advocates general who review each of the cases as they come in, study the arguments, and deliver preliminary opinions in court before the judges decide on what action should be taken and which EU laws apply. The judges are not obliged to agree with these opinions or even to refer to them, but they provide the main point of reference from which to reach a decision. In theory the advocates general are appointed (like judges) by common accord of the governments of the member states, but in practice one is appointed by each of the five biggest member states, and

Table 8.2 Presidents of the European Court of Justice

Term	Name	Member State
1958–1961	A. M. Donner	Netherlands
1961–1964	A. M. Donner	Netherlands
1964–1967	Charles Hammes	Luxembourg
1967–1970	Robert Lecourt	France
1970–1973	Robert Lecourt	France
1973–1976	Robert Lecourt	France
1976–1979	Hans Kutscher	West Germany
1979–1980	Hans Kutscher	West Germany
1980–1984	J. Mertens de Wilmars	Belgium
1984–1988	Lord McKenzie Stuart	United Kingdom
1988–1991	Ole Due	Denmark
1991–1994	Ole Due	Denmark
1994–1997	Gil Carlos Rodríguez Iglesias	Spain
1997–2000	Gil Carlos Rodríguez Iglesias	Spain
2000–2003	Gil Carlos Rodríguez Iglesias	Spain
2003–2006	Vassilios Skouris	Greece
2006–2009	Vassilios Skouris	Greece
2009–2012	Vassilios Skouris	Greece
2012–2015	Vassilios Skouris	Greece

the rest are appointed by the smaller states; one is appointed by his/her peers as First Advocate General on a one-year rotation. As with Court judges, most advocates general have been men, but the record on diversity is improving; three of the eight serving in 2012 were women.

The General Court. As European integration deepened and widened, the Court of Justice became busier: in the 1960s it was hearing about 50 cases per year and making 15 to 20 judgments; today it hears 400 to 550 new cases per year (about twice the volume of cases coming before the U.S. Supreme Court) and makes 400 to 700 judgments.[14] It was particularly busy after 1987, hearing cases and making preliminary rulings on issues relating to the single market in the lead-up to 1992. As the volume of work grew during the 1970s and 1980s, there were more delays, with the Court taking up to two years to reach a decision. To help clear the logjam, agreement was reached under the Single European Act to create a subsidiary Court of First Instance, renamed the General Court by the Treaty of Lisbon.

It is the first point of decision on some of the less complicated cases involving aspects of competition, actions brought against the Commission under the Treaty of Paris, and disputes between EU institutions and their staff (a job now done by the Civil Service Tribunal—see below). If the cases are lost at this level, the parties involved have the right to appeal to the Court of Justice, in much the same way as parties losing a case in a federal district court or circuit court of appeal in the United States can appeal to the Supreme Court.

One judge is appointed to the court from each of the member states for a total of twenty-seven, and although the court has its own rules of procedures, it operates in much the same way as the Court of Justice (although it has no advocates general). It can sit as a full court, as a Grand Chamber of thirteen judges, or in smaller chambers of five, three, or even single judges. A president is elected by the judges for three-year renewable terms: Judge Marc Jaeger of Luxembourg, a member of the court since 1996, was elected president in 2007.

The EU Civil Service Tribunal. This is one of the EU's newest institutions, set up in 2004 to take over from the Court of First Instance any cases involving disputes between the EU institutions and their staff. It began work in 2005, its membership consisting of seven judges appointed for six-year renewable terms and overseen by a president. Its decisions can be appealed on questions of law to the General Court, and in exceptional situations to the European Court of Justice.

SOURCES OF EUROPEAN UNION LAW

The foundations of the American legal system are provided by the constitutions of the United States and the states. The EU has no constitution in the sense that there is a single codified document that is the functional equivalent of the U.S. Constitution, but it does have treaties that have been regularly amended over time and collectively function as something like a constitution of the EU.[15] They include the Treaty of Paris (until it expired in July 2002), the Treaties of Rome, the Merger treaty, treaties of accession signed by new members, the Single European Act, Maastricht, Amsterdam, Nice, Lisbon, various other key EU agreements, and all related annexes and amendments. Collectively, they are the primary source of European law.[16] There are also secondary sources of EU law, so described because they come out of the primary sources. These consist of all the individual binding laws adopted by the EU (regulations, directives, and decisions—see Box 5.2), relevant international law (most of which is weak and vague but which the Court still often uses to create precedent), and the Court's own interpretation. Judgments by the ECJ have helped give EU law more focus and strength, making up for the weaknesses that have often arisen out of the compromises made to reach agreement on various laws. The Court not only gives technical interpretations but often goes a step further, filling in gaps and clarifying confusions.

As the European Union evolved, pressure grew for agreement on a constitution that would bring together all of the principles established by the treaties and case law. Federico Mancini, a former judge on the Court of Justice, argued in 1991 that the direction in which EU case law had moved since 1957 coincided with "the making of a constitution for Europe." He noted that the EU was created by a treaty (unlike the United States, which is founded on a constitution), that the EEC Treaty did not safeguard the fundamental rights of individuals or recognize a right to European citizenship, and that the main work of the Court had been to "constitutionalize" the EEC Treaty and "to fashion a constitutional framework for a quasi-federal structure in Europe."[17] Against this background, the publication of the 2003 draft constitutional treaty was inevitable, and its collapse unfortunate.

How the Court Works

The ECJ is the supreme legal body of the EU; its decisions are final, and it is the final court of appeal on all EU laws. As such, it has played a vital role in determining the character of the EU and in extending the reach of EU law. For example, when the Community slipped into a hiatus in the late 1970s and early 1980s, the Court kept alive the idea of the Community as something more than a customs union.[18] It has been particularly involved in cases relating to the single market, nowhere more so than in the *Cassis de Dijon* decision, establishing the principle of mutual recognition (see Box 8.2) that was at the heart of the Single European Act.[19]

The core goal of the Court is to help build a body of common law for the EU that is equally, fairly, and uniformly applied throughout the member states. It does this by interpreting EU treaties and laws and in some cases taking responsibility for directly applying those laws. EU law takes precedence over the national laws of member states when the two come into conflict, but only in areas in which the EU is active (that is, has "competence") and

Box 8.2 Liquor, Beer, and the Single Market

Of all the cases heard and rulings made by the Court regarding the single market, few were more fundamental than those establishing the principle of mutual recognition, under which a product made and sold legally in one member state cannot be barred from another member state.

The roots of the issue go back to a 1979 case arising out of a refusal by West Germany to allow imports of a French blackcurrant liquor, Cassis de Dijon, because its wine-spirit content (15–20 percent) was below the German minimum for fruit liqueurs (25 percent). The importer charged that this amounted to a "quantitative restriction on imports," which was prohibited under the Treaty of Rome. The Court of Justice agreed, ruling that alcoholic beverages lawfully produced and marketed in one member state could not be prohibited from sale in another on the grounds that they had a lower alcohol content.[20] Although this established the principle of mutual recognition, it did not prevent challenges from occurring.

The issue came up again in the 1984 case *Commission v. Federal Republic of Germany* over the question of beer imports into West Germany. Thanks to the *Reinheitsgebot* (a purity law passed in 1516 by the Duke of Bavaria), German beer is allowed to contain only malted barley, hops, yeast, and water. Germans drink more beer than anyone else in the world—an average of 38 gallons (173 liters) per person per year, compared with 24 gallons (110 liters) per person per year in the United States—and long refused to import foreign beer on the grounds that most such beer contained "additives" such as rice, maize, sorghum, flavoring, and coloring. The Commission took Germany to Court on the grounds that a 1952 German law effectively prevented any beer being imported or sold in Germany that did not meet the *Reinheitsgebot*, thereby infringing the Treaty of Rome.[21]

Germany argued that since the average German male relies on beer for a quarter of his daily nutritional intake, allowing imports of "impure" foreign beer would pose a risk to public health. The Court disagreed and ruled in 1987 that Germany could not use the public health argument to ban beer imports and had to accept foreign beer imports as long as brewers printed a list of ingredients on their labels. The Court decision simplified decisions on issues of trade between member states, and the precedent was used to open up domestic markets to food and drink imports.

the member states have given up powers to the EU. The Court, for example, does not have powers over criminal and family law; it has made most of its decisions on the kinds of economic issues in which the EU has been most actively involved, and has had less to do with policy areas in which the EU has been less active, such as education and health.

Court proceedings usually begin with a written application, which is filed by a lawyer with the court registrar and published in its *Official Journal*. This describes the dispute, explains the grounds on which the application is based, and gives the defendant a month to respond. The president then assigns the case to a judge-rapporteur (a judge of the Court who is charged with drawing up a preliminary report on the case), while the first advocate general appoints an advocate general to the case. The advocate general and judge-rapporteur make their recommendations to the Court, and the case is assigned to a chamber. The case is then argued by the parties involved at a public hearing before the chamber, the larger chambers being reserved for only the most important cases. At the end of the oral phase, the advocate general delivers an opinion, and once the chamber has reached a decision, it delivers judgment in open court.

The entire process can take as long as two years for preliminary rulings, although the average has fallen of late, as the workload has been shared among chambers and with the General Court and the Civil Service Tribunal. Court decisions are technically supposed to be unanimous, but votes are usually taken on a simple majority, as in the U.S. Supreme Court. Unlike the U.S. Supreme Court, however, all the votes of the European Court are secret, so it is never publicly known who—if anyone—dissented. Like its U.S. counterpart, the Court has no direct powers to enforce its judgments; implementation is mainly left up to national courts or the governments of the member states, with the Commission keeping a close watch. Maastricht gave the Court of Justice new powers by allowing it to impose fines, but the question of how the fines would be collected was left open.

The work of the Court falls into two main categories: preliminary rulings and direct actions.

Preliminary Rulings

These rulings make up the most important part of the Court's work and account for 40–60 percent of the cases it considers. Under the Treaty of Rome, a national court can (and sometimes must) ask the Court of Justice for a ruling on the interpretation or validity of an EU law that arises in a national court case. The issue of validity is particularly critical, because chaos would reign if national courts could declare EU laws invalid.[22] Members of EU institutions can also ask for preliminary rulings, but most are made on behalf of a national court and are binding on the court in the case concerned. (The word *preliminary* is misleading: the rulings are usually requested and given *during* a case, not before it opens; the term *concurrent rulings* might be more appropriate.)

The *Van Gend en Loos* and *Flaminio Costa* cases are classic examples of preliminary rulings, but another ruling that had crucial implications for individual rights came in 1989. During a vacation in France, a British citizen named Ian Cowan was mugged outside a subway station in Paris. Under French law, he could have claimed state compensation for damages, but the French courts held that he was not entitled to damages because he was neither a French national nor a resident. Cowan argued that this amounted to discrimination, and the Court of Justice was asked for a ruling. In *Cowan v. Le Tresor Public*, the Court ruled that because Cowan was a tourist and was receiving a service, he could invoke Article 7 of the Treaty of Rome, which prohibits discrimination between nationals of member states on the grounds of nationality.[23]

Direct Actions

These are cases in which an individual, corporation, member state, or EU institution brings proceedings directly before the Court of Justice (rather than a national court), usually with an EU institution or a member state as the defendant. They can take several forms.

Actions for Failure to Fulfill an Obligation. These are cases in which a member state has failed to meet its obligations under EU law, and they can be brought either by the Commission or by a member state. The defending member state is given two months to make restitution, so most of these cases are settled before they go to the ECJ. If a state fails to comply once proceedings have begun, the case goes to the Court, which investigates the problem and decides on the measures to be taken; these can involve a fine or suspension of EU payments to the state (under the European Regional Development Fund, for example).

The Commission has regularly taken member states to the Court on the grounds that they have not met their obligations under the Single European

Act. Although individuals cannot bring such cases, interest groups have also been known to report a member state to the Commission for failing to enforce an EU law, and the Commission then takes the member state to the Court. Private companies are also often involved, especially in issues involving competition and trade policy. Even companies based in the U.S., Japan, and other countries can take a case to the Court if they think a member state is discriminating against them or their products.

Actions for Annulment. These actions are aimed at ensuring that EU laws (even nonbinding opinions and recommendations) conform to the treaties, and they are brought in an attempt to cancel those that do not conform. If a member state, an individual, or one of the main EU institutions believes that an EU law is illegal (in whole or in part), they may ask for an annulment. The effect is to give the Court the power to review the legality of the acts of the EU institutions. The defendant is almost always the Commission or the Council of the EU, because proceedings are usually brought against an act one or the other has adopted.[24] One exception was Luxembourg's inconclusive attempt in 1981 to challenge a European Parliament resolution that all future plenary sessions of Parliament should be held in Strasbourg (Case 230/81).

Actions for Failure to Act. These actions relate to the failure of an EU institution to act in accordance with the terms of the treaties, and they can be brought by other institutions, member states, or individuals who are directly and personally involved. For example, the European Parliament brought such an action against the Council of Ministers in 1983 (Case 13/83), charging that the Council had failed to agree to a Common Transport Policy as required under the EEC Treaty. The Court ruled in 1985 that although there was an obligation, no timetable had been agreed to, so it was up to the member states to decide how to proceed.[25]

Actions for Damages. These are cases in which damages are claimed by third parties against EU institutions and their employees. A claim could be made that the institution was acting illegally, or an individual could claim his or her business was being hurt by a piece of EU law. Most of these cases are heard by the General Court.

Actions by Staff. These cases involve litigation brought by staff members against EU institutions as their employers, and they are the only cases in which a private individual can go directly to the Court. For example, someone who works for the European Parliament might ask the Court for a ruling on the application of a staff regulation, an instance of gender discrimination, a biased staff report, or a decision to hold a civil service exam on a religious holiday in their home country. Staff actions account for about one-third of the Court's overall workload, and since 2004 they have been dealt with by the EU Civil Service Tribunal.

Appeals. The Court of Justice may hear appeals on points of law regarding judgments made by the General Court.

The Court also has the right of opinion in cases in which a decision is needed on the compatibility of draft international agreements with the treaties. The Commission, the Council of Ministers, and member states can ask for a Court opinion, and if the Court gives an unfavorable ruling, the draft agreement must be changed accordingly before the EU can sign it. Finally, the Court can be called in to arbitrate both on contracts concluded by or on behalf of the EU (conditional proceedings) and in disputes between member states over issues relating to the treaties.

Questions to Consider

1. How does the U.S. Supreme Court's power of judicial review compare to the authority of the European Court of Justice?
2. Compare the selection process for the Supreme Court with that of the Court of Justice. Should judges for the Court of Justice be elected? If not, should they be subject to the same kind of hearings given Supreme Court nominees? Should the judges have lifetime appointments?
3. Is the Court of Justice a political body? If so, whose interests does it serve?

Further Reading

Anthony Arnull. *The European Union and Its Court of Justice*, 2nd ed. (Oxford: Oxford University Press, 2006).

> Although somewhat dated, this is still one of the more accessible general studies of the organization, jurisdiction, and procedure of the Court of Justice.

Gerard Conway. *The Limits of Legal Reasoning and the European Court of Justice* (Cambridge: Cambridge University Press, 2012).

> A critical analysis of the ECJ's dominant judicial philosophy. Conway argues that the court's approach to law is inconsistent with the constitutional values of the EU.

Allan Rosas, Egils Levits, and Yves Bot. *The Court of Justice and the Construction of Europe: Analyses and Perspectives on 60 Years of Case Law* (The Hague: T.M.C. Asser, 2013).

> Published by the ECJ to celebrate its sixtieth anniversary, this edited volume has contributions from legal experts throughout the EU on topics ranging from the structure and function of the ECJ and the EU's legal basis to rights of EU citizens.

Stephen Weatherill. *Cases and Materials on EU Law*, 9th ed. (Oxford: Oxford University Press, 2010). Margot Horspool and Matthew Humphreys. *European Union Law*, 6th ed. (Oxford: Oxford University Press, 2010). John Fairhurst. *Law of the European Union*, 9th ed. (Harlow, UK: Pearson, 2012).

> Just three of the many studies of EU law that have been published in recent years.

Notes

1. For a comparison of U.S. and EU law see R. Daniel Kelemen, *Eurolegalism: The Transformation of Law and Regulation in the European Union* (Cambridge, MA: Harvard University Press, 2011).

2. K. P. E. Lasok and D. Lasok, *Law and Institutions of the European Communities*, 7th ed. (London: Butterworths, 2001), 15.

3. *Van Gend en Loos v. Nederlandse Administratie Belastingen* (Case 26/62), in Court of Justice of the European Communities, *Reports of Cases Before the Court*, 1963.

4. *Flaminio Costa v. ENEL* (Case 6/64), in Court of Justice of the European Communities, *Reports of Cases Before the Court*, 1964.

5. G. Federico Mancini, "The Making of a Constitution for Europe," in Robert O. Keohane and Stanley Hoffmann, eds., *The New European Community: Decisionmaking and Institutional Change* (Boulder: Westview Press, 1991), 187.

6. *Nold, Kohlen-und Baustoffgrosshandlung v. Commission* (Case 4/73), in Court of Justice of the European Communities, *Reports of Cases Before the Court*, 1974.

7. Jonas Bering Liisberg, "Does the EU Charter of Fundamental Rights Threaten the Supremacy of Community Law?" working paper (New York: Jean Monnet Center, New York University School of Law, 2001).

8. See Steve Peers and Angela Ward, eds., *The EU Charter of Fundamental Rights: Politics, Law and Policy* (Oxford: Hart, 2004).

9. The European Court of Justice should not be confused with two other European-based international courts: the Strasbourg-based European Court

of Human Rights (which comes under the jurisdiction of the Council of Europe and promotes human rights issues in Europe) and the International Court of Justice (which is part of the United Nations system, is based in The Hague, and arbitrates on issues relating to UN activities).

10. L. Neville Brown and Tom Kennedy, *The Court of Justice of the European Communities*, 5th ed. (London: Sweet and Maxwell, 2000), 45.

11. Renaud Dehousse, *The European Court of Justice: The Politics of Judicial Integration* (New York: St. Martin's, 1998), 8.

12. K. P. E. Lasok, *European Court Practice and Procedure*, 3rd ed. (Haywards Heath, UK: Tottel, 2007), 7–8.

13. Vassilios Skouris, interview, *Financial Times* (London), 30 June 2004.

14. *Annual Report of the Court of Justice of the European Communities* (2006), http://curia.europa.eu/jcms/upload/docs/application/pdf/2008–09/06 _trib_stat_2008–09–29_13–32–40_772.pdf.

15. See David Phinnemore and Clive H. Church, *Understanding the European Union's Constitution* (London: Routledge, 2005), and Jean-Claude Piris, *The Constitution for Europe: A Legal Analysis* (Cambridge: Cambridge University Press, 2006).

16. Lasok and Lasok, *Law and Institutions of the European Communities*, chapter 4.

17. Mancini, "The Making of a Constitution for Europe," 177–79.

18. Martin Shapiro, "The European Court of Justice," in Alberta Sbragia, ed., *Euro-Politics: Institutions and Policymaking in the "New" European Community* (Washington, DC: Brookings Institution, 1992).

19. Dehousse, *The European Court of Justice*, 84–88.

20. *Rewe-Zentral AG v. Bundesmonopolverwaltung fur Branntwein* (Case 120/78), Court of Justice of the European Communities, *Reports of Cases Before the Court*, 1979.

21. *Commission of the European Communities v. Federal Republic of Germany* (Case 178/84), Court of Justice of the European Communities, *Reports of Cases Before the Court*, 1987.

22. Brown and Kennedy, *The Court of Justice of the European Communities*, 173–76.

23. *Cowan v. Le Tresor Public* (Case 186/87), in Court of Justice of the European Communities, *Reports of Cases Before the Court*, 1989.

24. Lasok, *European Court Practice and Procedure*, 323.

25. *European Parliament v. Council* (Case 13/83), in Court of Justice of the European Communities, *Reports of Cases Before the Court*, 1985.

9

THE EUROPEAN COUNCIL AND OTHER INSTITUTIONS

CHAPTER OVERVIEW

- The European Council is the meeting place of the leaders of the EU member states and acts as something like a board of directors for the European Union. Although the day-to-day management of EU business is still left with the Commission, the Council of the EU, and the European Parliament, the European Council sets the broad direction of policy.
- The European Central Bank, created in 1998 to oversee monetary policy for countries in the eurozone, has also become a powerful and important EU institution. It currently lacks some of the powers of the U.S. Federal Reserve Board but appears to have started to move in this direction in the wake of the European debt crisis.
- As the EU has grown, the work of more specialized agencies—such as the European Police Office (Europol) or the Committee of the Regions (CoR)—has also grown, so much so that the EU

is increasingly taking on the trappings of a federal administration for Europe.

The European Council is the meeting place for the leaders of the EU member states, their foreign ministers, and the president of the Commission. This group convenes periodically at short summit meetings and provides strategic policy direction for the EU. The Council is something like a steering committee or a board of directors for the EU; it sketches the broad picture and usually leaves it to the other institutions (particularly the Commission and the Council of the EU) to fill in the details. It was created in 1974 in response to a feeling among EC leaders that the Community needed stronger leadership to clear blockages in decision making and to give it a sense of direction. Its existence was given legal recognition with the Single European Act, and Maastricht confirmed that the Council would "provide the Union with the necessary impetus for its development and shall define the general political guidelines thereof." Since the Treaty of Lisbon it has had an appointed president.

The Council is intergovernmental at heart, but this does not mean that it ignores general European interests. It has been an important motor for integration, launching major new initiatives (including every new EU treaty), issuing key declarations on international crises, generating EU institutional changes, and giving new momentum to EU foreign policy. It has been argued that without Council summits, the Community would not have survived the economic problems of the 1970s, launched the single market program during the 1980s, or adjusted to changes in the international environment during the 1990s.[1] However, the Council has also had its failures, including its inability to speed up agricultural and budgetary reform and to reach agreement on common EU responses to the two Gulf wars, the Bosnian conflict, the crisis in Kosovo in 1998 and 1999, and in failing to respond more quickly and vigorously to the debt crisis in the eurozone.

While the Council takes the broad view on European issues, a growing family of other EU institutions and specialized agencies has been created through the years to deal with the narrower interests of the EU. Most prominent among these has been the European Central Bank, which is responsible for managing the euro and setting interest rates for the eurozone, and Europol, a criminal intelligence organization that oversees information exchange on problems such as terrorism and drug trafficking. Meanwhile, the Economic and Social Committee provides employers, workers, and other sectional interests with a forum in which they can meet and develop advice for the EU institutions, while the Committee of the Regions does much the same for local and regional governments. As the EU has become busier, the list of specialized agencies has grown to deal with everything from vocational training to occupational safety and health, fisheries control, disease prevention and control, environmental information, the monitoring of racism, and maritime and aviation safety.

EVOLUTION

The idea of holding formal high-level meetings among Community leaders traces its roots back to Charles de Gaulle's ideas about political union. In July 1960 he broached the idea of a European political union that would include periodic summit meetings of heads of state or government and foreign ministers.[2] Although his motives were distrusted by many of his EEC partners, the idea survived, and the first formal summits were held in 1961 (Paris in February, Bonn in July). At the Paris meeting, a committee was formed under the chairmanship of Christian Fouchet, French ambassador to Denmark, which produced a draft treaty for a "union of states," including a suggestion for a council of heads of government or foreign ministers that would meet every four months and make decisions on the basis of unanimity. But because the Fouchet plan was an attempt to build a Community dominated by France, it met with little support outside that country.[3]

No more summits were held until 1967 and 1969, by which time it was becoming increasingly obvious to many that the EC had no clear sense of direction, and that decision making had become blocked by struggles over national interests in the Council of Ministers. The end of the Bretton Woods system in 1971 emphasized Europe's inability to respond quickly and effectively to major external crises, as did the Community's halfhearted response to the 1973 energy crisis, which prompted French foreign minister Michel Jobert to declare that Europe was a "nonentity."[4] What was needed, Jean Monnet argued, was "a supreme body to steer Europe through the difficult transition from national to collective sovereignty"; he suggested calling it the "Provisional European Government."[5] Agreement was reached at a summit in Copenhagen in December 1973 to arrange more frequent meetings among heads of government.

Changes in leadership in Britain, France, and West Germany formed the background for the December 1974 summit of heads of government in Paris, where it was decided to formalize the links among them. Valéry Giscard d'Estaing and Helmut Schmidt argued for the need to bring leaders together regularly to provide policy direction and to clear logjams. A declaration was issued committing heads of government to meet at least three times annually and emphasizing the need for "an overall approach" to the challenges of integration and the importance of ensuring "progress and overall consistency in the activities of the Communities and in the work on political co-operation."[6]

The wording of the declaration was kept deliberately vague; it said nothing about the exact powers of the new body or its relationship to the other institutions, gave it no legal standing, and was careful not to allow the new body's creation to disturb or complicate the existing EC decision-making system. Concerns among the Benelux states that the summits would weaken the supranational qualities of the Community were offset in part by an agreement to hold direct elections to the European Parliament.[7] The new body even lacked a name until Giscard's announcement at a press conference at the close of the meeting that "the European summit is dead; long live the European Council."[8] Suggestions that a new secretariat be created for the Council were outweighed by desires not to expand the European bureaucracy or weaken the work of existing institutions. This is why the Council—which has been institutionalized to the extent that it exists and follows increasingly routine patterns of functioning—is the only branch of the EU without a secretariat or a large, salaried body of staff.

The first meeting of the Council was held in Dublin in March 1975 under the lumbering title "the Heads of Government Meeting as the Council of the Community and in Political Cooperation." It met more or less three times a year throughout the 1970s and 1980s, but a decision was made at the December 1985 summit to hold just two regular summits each year, in June and December, with additional extraordinary meetings as needed. Legal recognition of the Council finally came with the Single European Act, which confirmed the membership of the Council and reduced the number of annual meetings from three to two. The most recent round of changes came with the Treaty of Lisbon, under whose terms a president was appointed to manage meetings of the Council and move its members toward a consensus, and a new pattern of four regular annual meetings in Brussels was set.

STRUCTURE

The European Council brings together the heads of government of the EU member states (and the head of state in the cases of countries such as Cyprus and France), an accompanying minister of the member states (usually but not always the foreign minister), the president of the European Council, the president of the European Commission (and a deputy commissioner if needed), the High Representative of the Union for Foreign Affairs and Security Policy, and small retinues of staff and advisers, including Permanent Representatives. They convene at regular summits lasting no more than two days, under the direction of a full-time president.

According to Lisbon, the president's responsibilities include chairing the European Council and "driving forward its work," overseeing much of its preparatory work along with the president of the Commission and the General Affairs Council, and acting as an external representative for the EU. The president is elected by the Council using a qualified majority vote for a term of two and a half years, renewable once. He or she cannot also be a sitting leader of a member state but, like the Commission president, will almost certainly come from the ranks of existing or former national leaders. Although there was some sentiment for choosing a strong and highly visible personality for the initial president, European leaders ultimately choose Herman van Rompuy, a former Belgian prime minister known for his ability as a facilitator and negotiator. He assumed the position in November 2009.

European Council summits once took place either in the capital of the member state holding the presidency of the Council of Ministers or in a regional city or town, such as Cardiff, Venice, Strasbourg, or—in December 1991—Maastricht in the Netherlands, where the Treaty on European Union was agreed. In order to ensure less cost and greater efficiency, all European Council meetings are now held in Brussels.

The Council has multiple personalities. It can be seen as the decision maker of last resort, as a collective presidency in which sovereignty is pooled, as a body that parallels other EU institutions by dealing with issues outside their competence, or as a true "council" that can engineer broad package deals.[9] There are three keys to understanding the way the Council works and fits into the EU system:

- *Flexibility.* The relative lack of rules, regulations, and attendant bureaucrats gives the Council a level of freedom and independence enjoyed by none of the other EU institutions.
- *Informality.* European Council summits are built on advance preparation, but agendas are kept general, summits try to keep away from formal votes, and meetings are kept as small and informal as possible.

- *Delegation.* Any signs that the Council is becoming bogged down in the routine day-to-day business of the EU are usually resisted. The Council instead focuses on the big picture, leaves other institutions to work out the details, and acts as something like a court of appeal if attempts to reach agreement at a lower level fail.[10]

The major goal of each summit meeting is to agree to a set of formal conclusions, an advanced draft of which usually awaits the leaders at the beginning of the summit, and provides the focus for their discussions (see Box 9.1).

HOW THE COUNCIL WORKS

Preparation is the key to the success of European summits.[11] Officially, the Council has no set agenda, but some direction is needed. Before Lisbon, much of the preparatory work for the summits was done by the member state holding the presidency: senior officials from the presidency worked with the Council of Ministers to identify agenda items which were then channeled through the Antici Group to the Committee of Permanent Representatives. The monthly meetings of the foreign ministers under the General Affairs and External Relations Council would then try to resolve potential disagreements.[12] With the advent of a new president of the European Council much of this preparatory work has now fallen to it. According to Lisbon, however, the president works "in close cooperation" with the member state holding the rotating presidency in the Council of Ministers as well as the president of the Commission.

The items on the agenda depend on circumstances: national delegations normally have issues they want to raise, there has to be some continuity from previous summits, and leaders must often deal with a breaking problem or an emergency that requires a decision. Some issues (especially economic issues) are routinely discussed at every summit, the Commission may promote issues it would like to see discussed, and an active presidency in the Council of Ministers might use the summit to bring items of national or regional interest to the attention of the heads of government.[13] Summits may also occasionally launch or finalize a major policy initiative, such as the June 2012 summit, which put forward some major initiatives to deal with the eurozone crisis. Some summits are routine and result in general agreement among leaders; in others, deep differences of opinion arise, with some member states perhaps refusing to agree to a common set of conclusions.

BOX 9.1 EUROPEAN SUMMITS

Meetings of the European Council usually run for a period of two days; emergency or informal summits will normally last no more than a day. They begin with discussions over breakfast and move into the nuts and bolts at plenary sessions during the morning and afternoon. Overnight, officials will work on the draft set of conclusions, which are discussed at a second plenary on the morning of day two, and—if necessary—at a third in the afternoon. The summit then normally ends with a press conference and publication of the Conclusions.

During summit plenaries, the prime ministers of the member states (and the presidents of Cyprus and France) sit around a table with their foreign ministers and two officials from the Commission, including the president. To keep meetings as manageable as possible, few other people are allowed into the room; no more than one adviser per country, one from the Council of the EU Secretariat, and three from the Commission—but even this can result in a meeting with several hundred people present.

The Council makes its decisions on the basis of consensus (except where the treaties say otherwise), although some member states may want to attach conditions or reservations to the conclusions. In addition to the formal plenary sessions, summits usually break out into subsidiary meetings, including those of foreign ministers, and regular bilateral meetings of prime ministers over breakfast or coffee. This has become more common as membership in the EU has grown—it is sometimes easier to negotiate in smaller groups than in meetings of the whole.

The summits are often major media events, and great symbolism is often attached to the conclusions, which are assessed according to the extent to which they represent breakthroughs or show EU leaders to be bogged down in disagreement. The headline-making nature of the summits is sufficient to focus the minds of participants and to encourage them to agree. A "family photo" is also taken of the national leaders and the president of the Commission, symbolizing the process of European integration. The smiles on their faces would look shallow if major disagreements had not been resolved.

The exact role of the European Council has been kept deliberately ambiguous by its members, the early statements of EU leaders suggesting that the purpose of the Council was to exchange views, give political impetus to the development of the EU, guarantee policy consistency, and reach common positions on foreign policy matters.[14] The Treaty of Lisbon describes it mission as follows:

[to] provide the Union with the necessary impetus for its development and . . . define the general political direction and priorities thereof. It shall not exercise legislative functions.

More specifically, the Council makes the key decisions on the overall direction of political integration, internal economic matters, foreign policy issues, budget disputes, treaty revisions, new member applications, and institutional reforms. The summits achieve all this through a combination of brainstorming, intensive bilateral and multilateral discussions, and bargaining. The mechanics of decision making depend on a combination of the quality of organization and preparation, the leadership skills of the president, the ideological and personal agendas of the individual leaders, and the strength of their political bases at home. Also, most European governments are coalitions, meaning that national leaders have to please a broader constituency and are less able to follow the courage of their convictions. The interpersonal dynamics of the participants are also important:

- The political significance of the Franco-German axis has always been critical, given additional influence by the strong personal relations that have usually existed between the leaders of the two states (Brandt and Pompidou, Schmidt and Giscard, Kohl and Mitterrand, Schröder and Chirac, and Merkel and Sarkozy or Hollande).
- Leaders who have been in office for a relatively long time or who have a solid base of political support at home will be in different negotiating positions from those who have not. The June 2007 European Council suffered from something of a leadership and experience vacuum: the leaders of Austria, France, Germany, the Netherlands, and Sweden were all relatively new, and the leaders of several other countries—including Bulgaria, the Czech Republic, Finland, Poland, and Romania—governed in uneasy coalitions. Greece, Hungary, Ireland, Latvia, and Spain were among the few

EU countries at the time whose governments had both stable majorities and some longevity.

- Some leaders are respected and have strong credibility, while others
  do not. For example, German chancellor Helmut Kohl became a
  towering presence on the EU stage, holding on to office for sixteen
  years (1982–98) and becoming something of an elder statesman
  of European integration (helped, of course, by the dominating economic power of Germany). By 2002–03 there was no longer a single dominant leader on the European scene, although the tripartite
  relationship among Tony Blair, Jacques Chirac, and Gerhard
  Schröder was playing an influential role on several issues, notably
  defense matters and European foreign policy. As this book went
  to press, François Hollande and Angela Merkel were the prime
  candidates for taking up the mantle of leadership.

In addition to the regular summits, special meetings of European leaders
can also be convened to deal with a breaking issue or a persistent problem.
Examples include the November 1989 summit in Paris to discuss rapidly
changing events in Eastern Europe, the October 1992 summit in Birm-
ingham to discuss the crisis in the Exchange Rate Mechanism, the July
1994 summit convened to choose a successor to Jacques Delors, the March
1999 summit to negotiate reforms to the EU budget, and the February
2003 summit held to try to heal rifts among the member states over the
impending invasion of Iraq. There will also occasionally be informal meetings of EU leaders, held outside the confines of the European Council but
often designed to discuss matters of importance to the EU. Examples include
the October 2005 meeting at Hampton Court near London to discuss globalization, and the October 2006 meeting with Russian president Vladimir
Putin at Lahti in Finland.

SPECIALIZED AGENCIES

As the reach of the EU has broadened and deepened, the work of its
more specialized institutions—and the pressure for the creation of new
institutions—has grown. Some have been there since the early days, while
others have been set up more recently in response to new needs. As their
number and authority increases, so the EU increasingly takes on the trappings of a federal administration of Europe.

European Central Bank (ECB). Created in 1998, the ECB has become one of the most powerful and visible of EU institutions. Its job is to ensure price stability by setting interest rates and managing foreign reserves for the countries participating in the euro, now used officially by 330 million consumers in seventeen countries, and unofficially by millions more in many other countries. As the euro has become more familiar to governments, business, and consumers (and, frankly, as the eurozone crisis took off after 2008), so the ECB has grown in stature. David Howarth and Peter Loedel may be overstating the case when they describe it as a "leviathan" and "the most important institutional creation in Europe since the institutionalization of the nation state in the seventeenth century,"[15] but it is certainly symbolic of the extent to which national powers have been pooled at the European level. It does not yet have the global political and economic clout, nor play the more direct political role of the U.S. Federal Reserve, primarily because it lacks many of the Fed's powers over monetary policy, but its role has grown in the wake of the eurozone crisis.

First proposed in 1988, the framework of the Bank was described in the Maastricht Treaty, and its precursor—the European Monetary Institute (EMI)—was founded in 1994, charged with strengthening central bank cooperation and coordination of monetary policy in preparation for the creation of the euro. The ECB was formally established on June 1, 1998, replacing the EMI. Based in Frankfurt, Germany, the Bank works within two overlapping spheres: the European System of Central Banks (ESCB), of which all national banks in the EU are members, and the Eurosystem, which comprises only the national banks of those member states that have adopted the euro.

The Bank has three main organizational units. First, there is the Governing Council, consisting of the seventeen central bank governors from each state in the eurozone and the Bank's Executive Board. This meets twice-monthly to discuss monetary and economic developments in the eurozone and to make decisions on monetary policy. Second, there is the Executive Board, consisting of the president (currently, Mario Draghi), the vice president, and four other members, all of them appointed by "common accord" of the member state governments to serve nonrenewable terms of eight years. It manages the day-to-day business of the Bank and implements eurozone monetary policy in accordance with Governing Council decisions. Finally, the Bank has links to non-eurozone countries through the General Council, composed of the central bank governors of the EU member states. If and when all EU member states adopt the euro, the General Council will be dissolved.

The Bank got off to a shaky start, thanks to yet another of the farcical nationalistic squabbles that occasionally divert the work of EU institutions. Most governments were in favor of seeing Wim Duisenberg, the Dutch president of the EMI, confirmed as the first president of the ECB. The French government disagreed, preferring the governor of the Bank of France, Jean-Claude Trichet. After a twelve-hour debate at the May 1998 summit, convened to launch the euro, a messy compromise was reached whereby Duisenberg would serve half a term (1998–2002), then would "voluntarily" step down in favor of Trichet. In the event, Trichet's appointment was delayed because of a court case resulting from charges that he ignored financial mismanagement at the Credit Lyonnais bank while he was an official with the French Treasury. He was cleared in June 2003 and took over as ECB president for an eight-year term in November of that year. He was succeeded by Mario Draghi, governor of the Bank of Italy, in November 2011.

The Bank has significant policy-making powers and considerable autonomy, and it plays a major role in the direction of European integration.[16] It was based on the model of the German Bundesbank, famous for both its competence and its independence. The Bundesbank, created in 1957, was based on the model of the U.S. Federal Reserve.[17] So important was the Bundesbank model, indeed, that Chancellor Helmut Kohl's insistence that the Bank be headquartered in Frankfurt won out over French arguments that it should be based in France, which had a long history of political interference in monetary affairs.[18] The German role in both the design and the location of the Bank has ensured that the German model of central banking and monetary policy has been exported throughout the eurozone.

Despite its growing power and influence, however, the ECB has not been without its detractors, especially as the eurozone debt crisis unfolded. Critics have suggested, for example, that economic stimulus should become one of the bank's tasks, while others have argued that the continued autonomy of national banks to regulate their own banks and to step in and lend euros points to a fundamental design flaw of the current ECB.[19] The agreement reached at the June 2012 European Council meeting to provide a single, Europe-wide regulator for all member state banks would seem to point in just this direction. The prospects of a full banking union, under which the ECB will take over supervision of the EU's more than six thousand banks from the European Banking Authority, promise to give the

ECB yet more muscle, but there has been opposition to the details of this plan from some of the member states.

European Investment Bank (EIB). Based in Luxembourg, the EIB is an autonomous institution that was set up in 1958 under the terms of the Treaty of Rome to encourage "balanced and steady development" within the EEC by providing long-term finance for capital projects. It must give preference to projects that help the poorer regions of the EU and promote communications networks, environmental protection, energy conservation, and the modernization and improved competitiveness of EU industry; it can also make loans to non-EU members. Its funds come from borrowing on worldwide capital markets and from subscriptions by EU member states. It deals only in large loans, rarely lends more than half of the total investment cost of a project, and often co-finances projects with other banks. The Bank's major focus in recent years has been on projects that help promote the single market through the development of trans-European road, rail, and communications networks; its single biggest project was the Euro-tunnel between Britain and France, which opened in 1994 (and has operated at a loss ever since). It has also supported the Airbus project and France's high-speed train system (see chapter 12), financed projects that were aimed at helping Eastern European countries prepare for EU membership, and financed development projects in poorer non-European countries such as Lesotho and Chad.

The EIB is managed by a board of governors consisting of the finance ministers of the member states, who appoint a decision-making board of directors (twenty-seven members plus a representative from the European Commission) to five-year renewable terms, and a nine-person management committee to six-year renewable terms. Werner Hoyer of Germany was appointed president and chairman of the board of directors in 2012.

Court of Auditors. This is the EU's financial watchdog, based in Luxembourg and founded in 1977 to replace the separate auditing bodies for the EEC/Euratom and for the ECSC. The Court likes to call itself the "financial conscience" of the EU. It carries out annual audits of the accounts of all EU institutions to ensure that revenue has been raised and expenditure incurred in a lawful and regular manner and to monitor the Union's financial management. Its most important job relates to the EU budget, which it audits on the basis of both accounts supplied by the Commission by June each year and its own independent research. The Court reports back to the Commission, the Council of Ministers, and Parliament by the end of November each year. Parliament is supposed to approve the Court's report by the following April, but it can use the report to force changes in the Commission's spending and accounting habits.

The Court has issued often scathing criticisms of waste, mismanagement, and fraud in the EU's financial affairs. It has found everything from excessive expense claims by European commissioners to massive fraud in funds made available under the Common Agricultural Policy. It has been particularly critical in recent years of the inadequacy of steps taken by the Commission to keep an eye on how structural funds are used and managed. Although the nature of its work would seem to make it unpopular with the Commission, in fact the two bodies have a close working relationship. The Court also has a symbiotic relationship with Parliament; each has helped promote the powers and the profile of the other.

It is headed by one auditor appointed from each of the member states of the EU for a six-year renewable term. Nominations come from the national governments and must be approved unanimously by the Council of Ministers following nonbinding approval by Parliament (which the EP would like to upgrade to binding approval). The auditors then elect one of their number to serve as president for three-year renewable terms. The members of the Court must be members of an external audit body in their own country or have other appropriate qualifications, but they are expected to act in the interests of the EU and to be completely independent. Much like the Court of Justice, the members can sit in chambers of a few members each.

European Police Office (Europol). With the Single European Act opening up the borders between member states, some direction had to be given to the development of police cooperation; hence the creation of Europol. Based in The Hague, Europol is not a law enforcement body in the pattern of the FBI in the United States but a criminal intelligence organization more like Interpol, the international police organization founded in 1923 and headquartered in Lyon, France. Its job is to oversee an EU-wide system of information exchange targeted at combating terrorism, drug trafficking, vehicle smuggling, clandestine immigration networks, illegal nuclear material trafficking, money forging and laundering, and other serious forms of international crime. It coordinates operations among the national police forces of the EU, playing a supporting role to them. Some scholars see it as the forerunner of a European police force, but since there is no common penal code or police law in the EU, such a force is unlikely to emerge any time soon.[20]

Set up in 1994 as the Europol Drugs Unit, it operated in limbo thanks to a refusal by the British government to agree on questions about Europol's

Box 9.2 Specialized Agencies of the European Union

In addition to the institutions discussed in the body of the text, numerous agencies have been created by the EU to deal with specific aspects of its work. Listed in order of their year of creation, they include the following:

- *European Centre for the Development of Vocational Training* (CEDEFOP; Thessaloniki, Greece, 1975).
- *European Foundation for the Improvement of Living and Working Conditions* (EUROFOUND; Dublin, 1975).
- *European Satellite Center* (Madrid, 1992). Analyzes satellite information in support of EU foreign and security policy.
- *European Monitoring Centre for Drugs and Drug Addiction* (Lisbon, 1993). Provides information on drugs and drug addiction that can be used in anti-drug campaigns.
- *Translation Centre* (Luxembourg, 1994). A self-financing office that helps most of these specialized agencies with their translation needs.
- *European Agency for Safety and Health at Work* (EU-OSHA; Bilbao, Spain, 1994). Provides information in support of improvements in occupational safety and health.
- *Community Plant Variety Office* (Angers, France, 1995). An independent agency that is responsible for implementing EU plant variety rights.
- *Office for Harmonization in the Internal Market* (Alicante, Spain, 1996). Responsible for the registration and administration of EU trademarks and designs.
- *European Food Safety Authority* (Parma, Italy, 2002). Provides independent scientific advice on issues relating to food safety.
- *European Aviation Safety Agency* (Cologne, Germany, 2002). Promotes civil aviation safety in the EU.
- *European Maritime Safety Agency* (Lisbon, 2002). Promotes maritime safety and pollution prevention.
- *European Railway Agency* (Valenciennes/Lille, France, 2004). Promotes an integrated and competitive European rail network.
- *European Centre for Disease Prevention and Control* (Stockholm, 2005). Works to strengthen Europe's defenses against infectious disease.
- *European Chemicals Agency* (Helsinki, 2007). Manages the registration and evaluation of chemicals.
- *European Institute for Gender Equality* (Vilnius, Lithuania, 2010). Information clearinghouse.

job being interpreted by the European Court of Justice. Britain acquiesced when it was given an opt-out on Court rulings. The Europol Convention was signed at the European Council in Florence in June 1996, and Europol became fully operational in July 1999. It is overseen by a management board with one representative from each of the member states, and it is run by a directorate made up of a director appointed for five years (who can be renewed for a term of four years), and three deputies appointed for four-year terms, renewable once. The appointments are made by the Council of Ministers.

European Bank for Reconstruction and Development (EBRD). The EBRD is not an EU institution, but its work has an important impact on the economic policies of the EU. Much like the International Bank for Reconstruction and Development (the World Bank), the EBRD was founded to provide loans, encourage capital investment, and promote trade, but its specific focus is helping the countries of Eastern Europe make the transition to free-market economies. Suggested by French president François Mitterrand in 1989 and endorsed by the European Council, the EBRD began operations in March 1991 and quickly became the single largest investor in Eastern Europe and the former Soviet Union. While the World Bank lends mainly to governments, the EBRD (at the insistence of the United States) makes 60 percent of its loans to the private sector.

Based in London, it is an independent bank owned and operated by its sixty shareholder countries, together with the EU and the European Investment Bank; the largest shares are held by the United States, Britain, France, Germany, Italy, and Japan. It has a board of governors consisting of representatives from each shareholder country, typically the minister of finance. The board appoints a president who oversees the operations of the Bank; Sir Suma Chakrabarti of Britain was appointed the Bank's sixth president in 2012.

European Economic and Social Committee (EESC). Based in Brussels, the EESC is an advisory body set up under the Treaty of Rome to give employers, workers, and other sectional interests a forum in which they could meet, talk, and issue opinions to the Commission, the Council of Ministers, and—more recently—the European Parliament. It was modeled on parallel bodies that existed in five of the six founding members of the EEC (West Germany being the exception) and was created in part because of fears that the European Parliament would not represent sectional interests; the fears proved unfounded. The EESC has 344 members, drawn from the member states roughly in proportion to population size (see Table 9.1). They are

Table 9.1 Membership of the EESC and the CoR

Britain	24	Sweden	12
France	24	Croatia	9
Germany	24	Denmark	9
Italy	24	Finland	9
Spain	21	Ireland	9
Poland	21	Lithuania	9
Romania	15	Slovakia	9
Austria	12	Estonia	7
Belgium	12	Latvia	7
Bulgaria	12	Slovenia	7
Czech Republic	12	Cyprus	6
Greece	12	Luxembourg	6
Hungary	12	Malta	5
Netherlands	12		
Portugal	12	Total	353

proposed by national governments and appointed by the Council of Ministers for renewable four-year terms. There are three groups of members:

- Group I comes from industry, services, small businesses, chambers of commerce, banking, insurance, and similar areas.
- Group II is made up of representatives from labor unions.
- Group III represents more varied interests, such as agriculture, small businesses, consumer and environmental groups, and the professions.

A president is elected by the EESC for a two-year term and chairs two-day meetings of the Committee in Brussels about nine or ten times each year. The three groups hold separate meetings to discuss matters of common interest, breaking down into smaller sections to deal with specific issues such as agriculture, social policy, transport, energy, regional development, and the environment. Although questions have long been raised about its value, consultation of the EESC by the Commission is mandatory in several areas, including agriculture, the movement of workers, social policy, regional policy, and the environment.

The fundamental weakness of the EESC is that neither the Commission nor the Council of Ministers is obliged to act on its opinions or views. "Consultation" is an ambiguous concept, and although the Commission can "take note" of an EESC opinion and the Council of Ministers can recognize a "useful" opinion, this amounts to little. The influence of the EESC is further minimized by the fact that its members are unpaid part-time appointees (they can claim expenses for attending meetings) and are not officially recognized as representatives of the bodies to which they belong. Also, EU proposals are often sent to the EESC only after they have reached an advanced stage of agreement by the Council of Ministers and Parliament. The best that can be said of the EESC is that it is another forum for the representation of sectional interests, but as the European Parliament becomes stronger and the number of lobbyists in Brussels grows, the value of the Committee in its present form becomes more questionable.

Committee of the Regions (CoR). Disparities in wealth and income across Europe have always posed a handicap to the process of integration; there can never be balanced free trade, a true single market, or even meaningful economic and political union so long as some parts of the EU are richer or poorer than others. The problem was addressed by the creation of three entities: the European Regional Development Fund in 1975, the ad hoc Assembly of European Regions in 1985, and the Consultative Council of Regional and Local Authorities in 1988. The need for a stronger response led to the creation under the terms of Maastricht of the Committee of the Regions.

Based in Brussels, the CoR met for the first time in January 1994. It has the same membership structure as the EESC: 344 members chosen by the member states and appointed by the Council of Ministers for four-year renewable terms. Although Maastricht did not specify what qualifications Committee members should have (beyond saying they should be "representatives of regional and local bodies"), most are elected local government officials, including mayors and members of state, regional, district, provincial, and county councils. It meets in plenary session five times per year and has the same advisory role as the EESC. It must be consulted by the Commission and the Council of Ministers on issues relating to economic and social cohesion, trans-European networks (see chapter 12), public health, education, and culture, and provides the EU with a local and regional perspective on policy. However, it suffers from the same structural problems as the EESC.

Questions to Consider

1. What role does the European Council play in the politics of the EU? Could any of its functions be compared with U.S. institutions, and if so, which one(s)?
2. How does the European Central bank compare to that of the U.S. Federal Reserve? Should the ECB become more like the Fed? What are the advantages and disadvantages?
3. Of the other EU institutions or specialized agencies discussed in this chapter, which ones play the most significant roles?

Further Reading

Jan Werts. *The European Council* (London: John Harper, 2008).

This is the only book-length study of the European Council, which is surprising given the role that the Council has long played in the process of European integration.

David Howarth and Peter Loedel. *The European Central Bank: The New European Leviathan?* 2nd ed. (Basingstoke, UK: Palgrave Macmillan, 2005). Jakob de Haan and Helge Berger, eds. *The European Central Bank at Ten* (Heidelberg: Springer, 2010).

Two of the increasing number of studies that are being written on this emerging and critical actor in European politics and economics.

Martijn Groenleer. *The Autonomy of European Union Agencies: A Comparative Study of Institutional Development* (Delft, Netherlands: Eburon Academic, 2011).

A detailed study of six EU agencies, comparing how they operate and their power of autonomous decision-making.

John D. Occhipinti. *The Politics of EU Police Cooperation: Toward a European FBI?* (Boulder: Lynne Rienner, 2003).

A study of European police cooperation, focusing on Europol and the key events and actors in its development.

Notes

1. Desmond Dinan, *Ever Closer Union? An Introduction to European Integration*, 4th ed. (Boulder: Lynne Rienner, 2010), 235.

2. Annette Morgan, *From Summit to Council: Evolution in the EEC* (London: Chatham House, 1976), 9.

3. Mary Troy Johnston, *The European Council: Gatekeeper of the European Community* (Boulder: Westview Press, 1994), 2–4.

4. Philippe Moreau Defarges, "Twelve Years of European Council History (1974–1986): The Crystallizing Forum," in Jean-Marc Hoscheit and Wolfgang Wessels, eds., *The European Council 1974–1986: Evaluation and Prospects* (Maastricht: European Institute of Public Administration, 1988), 38–39.

5. Jean Monnet, *Memoirs* (Garden City, NY: Doubleday, 1978), 502–3.

6. Communiqué of the Meeting of Heads of Government of the Community (Paris, 10 December 1974), *Bulletin of the European Communities* 12 (December 1974): 7–12.

7. Johnston, *The European Council*, 14.

8. Morgan, *From Summit to Council*, 5.

9. Wolfgang Wessels, "The European Council: A Denaturing of the Community or Indispensable Decision-Making Body?" in Hoscheit and Wessels, eds., *The European Council 1974–1986*, 9–11.

10. Guy de Bassompierre, *Changing the Guard in Brussels: An Insider's View of the EC Presidency* (Westport, CT: Praeger, 1988), 78.

11. See de Bassompierre, *Changing the Guard in Brussels*, 80–87, for more detail on the organization and outcomes of the European Council.

12. See Johnston, *The European Council*, 27–31.

13. Uwe Puetter, "Europe's Deliberate Intergovernmentalism: The Role of the Council and the European Council in EU Economic Governance," *Journal of European Public Policy* 19, no. 2 (2012): 161–78.

14. Paris Declaration 1974, in European Parliament, Committee on Institutional Affairs, Selection of Texts Concerning Institutional Matters of the Community from 1950 to 1982 (Luxembourg: European Parliament, 1982); Statement of the European Council London 1977, in Commission of the EC, Bulletin 7 (1977); and Solemn Declaration of Stuttgart 1983, in Commission of the EC, Bulletin 6 (1983).

15. David Howarth and Peter Loedel, *The European Central Bank: The New European Leviathan?* 2nd ed. (Basingstoke, UK: Palgrave Macmillan, 2005), xi.

16. Jakob de Haan and Helge Berger, eds. *The European Central Bank at Ten* (Berlin/Heidelberg: Springer Verlag, 2010).

17. Karl Kaltenthaler, *Policy-Making in the European Central Bank: The Masters of Europe's Money* (Lanham, MD: Rowman and Littlefield, 2006), 165, 168–69.

18. Howarth and Loedel, *The European Central Bank*, 44.

19. Aaron Tornell and Frank Westermann, "Europe Needs a Federal Reserve," *New York Times*, 21 June 2012.

20. For a detailed study of Europol, see John D. Occhipinti, *The Politics of EU Police Cooperation: Toward a European FBI?* (Boulder: Lynne Rienner, 2003).

10

Representing Public Opinion

Chapter Overview

- Europeans have ambivalent attitudes about the EU. While most are generally strongly supportive of the European project and have a European identity above and beyond their national ones, others express skepticism about the Union's direction and have failed to develop a strong psychological attachment to the EU.
- Referendums are one way in which EU citizens can voice their opinions on the EU. However, the use of referendums in the EU has had several distinct disadvantages, not the least of which has been their capacity to make integration more difficult.
- Another important way that EU citizens can make their views about the EU known is through direct elections to the European Parliament. Although such elections remain the most visible of ways in which EU citizens can directly engage with the EU, turnout has fallen.
- In recent years, interest groups have directed more of their attention to Brussels as EU policy has had more impact on the lives of Eu-

ropeans. The work of interest groups has helped strengthen the legitimacy and responsiveness of the EU decision-making system.

As the powers and reach of the European Union have grown, and as it has taken on more of the conventional features of a political system, so more Europeans have become interested in trying to influence its work. Even as late as the 1980s, European affairs attracted relatively little public attention, but—particularly since the Single European Act, Maastricht, the failed attempt in 2004–05 to agree on a constitution for the EU, and the eurozone debt crisis—more people have come to realize that the EU affects their lives, and have taken an interest in EU politics. For some this has been a positive interest, driven by a belief that the EU institutions play an important role in European affairs. For others it is a negative interest, driven by perceptions that the EU institutions are undemocratic and too powerful.

While each of the individual member states of the EU has a well-developed civil society, the same cannot yet be said of the EU. Its institutions have long had a reputation among Europeans for being elitist and bureaucratic, and there is still a troubling distance between the EU and many of its citizens. But a European civil society is slowly emerging, thanks mainly to three developments. First, there is the psychological effect of elections to the European Parliament. National elections are still considered more important by voters and political leaders, and European elections are often fought on national issues and approached by voters as opportunities to comment on the performance of their national governments. Nonetheless, an increasingly consistent and active set of party groups has emerged in the EP, giving more focus to European electoral issues.

Second, referendums—used irregularly by different member states—offer voters the opportunity to express themselves on European matters and to periodically turn their attention to some of the big questions that face Europe. Some are votes on national policy (for example, joining the EU has been subject to confirmation in several countries, and in one country—Norway—majorities have twice voted against membership). Other referendums have had Europe-wide significance; for example, the ratification of the Maastricht and Nice treaties was delayed by negative votes in Denmark and Ireland, respectively, and the European constitution was stopped in its tracks by negative votes in France and the Netherlands. The *absence* of referendums in some countries has also been significant, heightening criticisms of the manner in which some of the most important decisions on Europe are made.

Finally, as EU policy has had more impact on the lives of Europeans, so interest groups have directed more of their attention to Brussels. Interest groups are invited to participate in the early planning stages of new legislative proposals, have developed often strong links with the Commission, are used by the Commission as a source of expertise and to report on the implementation of EU law by member states, and are generally seen as an increasingly effective channel for changing EU policy. Their work has helped strengthen the legitimacy and responsiveness of the EU decision-making system.

AN EMERGING EUROPEAN IDENTITY

One of the prerequisites for a successful political system is a strong civil society, consisting of all the voluntary and spontaneous forms of political association that evolve within a state and are not formally part of the state system, but show that citizens can operate independently of the state.[1] The EU is not a state, but it has institutions responsible for making decisions that affect the lives of the people who live within its borders, and in order for it to succeed, Europeans must feel that the EU matters and that they can engage with its work.

Unfortunately, Europeans are ambivalent about the EU. Some are supportive, believing that it serves a valuable purpose, and arguing that its member states—and individual Europeans—have benefited from its creation and development. Others, known most often as Euroskeptics, are less supportive of the EU, believing that it is a harmful development, and regretting the shift of sovereignty away from the member states to the EU institutions.[2] In between, many Europeans do not have strong feelings one way or the other, do not fully understand how the EU works or what impact it has had on their lives, and engage with its work only sporadically. In that sense, the EU is much like a national political system; the balance in the United States between those who are politically engaged, those who are not, and those who do not much care is not so different.

The work of the EU is compromised by the competing sense of affiliation that Europeans have toward their home states and toward the EU; most Europeans still feel closer to their home states, owe them their primary allegiance, and often think of the member states as competing with one another rather than being involved in a joint endeavor. About two in every three EU residents feels that they are citizens of the EU, with rates ranging from a high of 77–88 percent in Luxembourg, Slovakia, and Finland, to a low of 41–48 percent in Latvia, Greece, Bulgaria, and the UK (see Figure

10.1). Suggestions that Europe should be brought closer to its citizens were outlined in a 1975 report drawn up at the request of the European Council by Leo Tindemans, prime minister of Belgium. However, little was done until 1984, when attention turned briefly to the idea of a "people's Europe." Pietro Adonnino, a former Italian MEP, was appointed to chair a committee to make suggestions on closing the gap between the Community and its citizens. Its recommendations fell into three main parts:

1. It endorsed plans for a European passport and a European flag. All national passports—which came in different designs and colors— were replaced from 1986 by a burgundy-colored "European" passport bearing the words *European Union* in the appropriate national language, and the name and coat of arms of the holder's home state. These passports do not make their holders European citizens, but they do make sure that Europeans are given equal treatment by the customs and immigration authorities of other countries. Also, citizens of an EU member state finding themselves in need in a non-EU country where their home state has no diplomatic representation can receive protection from the embassy or consulate of any EU state that has a local office. Meanwhile, the Community adopted the flag that had been used by the Council of Europe since 1955—a circle of twelve gold stars on a blue background, which can now be seen flying on buildings throughout the EU.

2. Several Adonnino recommendations were adopted under the Single European Act (SEA), notably the easing of restrictions on the free movement of people and plans for the mutual recognition of professional qualifications. Despite the understanding that an open labor market would be essential to the single market, restrictions (albeit limited) still remain on the free movement of people within the EU (see chapter 12).

3. The EU has developed its own concept of European citizenship, although it is not the same as the citizenship we associate with states. According to the Treaty of Lisbon, "every person holding the nationality of a Member State shall be a citizen of the Union," but it also states that "citizenship of the Union shall be additional to and not replace national citizenship" (Article 20). In other words, EU citizenship is still not much more than a symbolic notion, and distinctions are made among Europeans on the basis of their national citizenship—distinctions which continue to have political

consequences. Thus while all EU citizens can now vote in and stand for local and European Parliament elections in whichever country they are living (subject to residency requirements), they remain citizens of their own states, identify with those states, and carry important exclusive prerogatives of that state—for example, EU "citizens" cannot vote in each other's national elections.

The changes that came out of the Adonnino committee had an important effect on the psychological relationship between Europeans and the EU institutions and helped make the EU more real to Europeans. Icons are an important element of belonging, and the European flag, for example, has played a vital role in giving the EU a personality that goes beyond the work of its bureaucrats. The same can be said of the euro: Europeans can now use it wherever they go in the eurozone, and the foreignness that came with different currencies—and reminded Europeans of their differences—is now, for the most part, gone.

But there is more to remind Europeans of what divides them than what unites them. For example, different parts of Europe have quite different histories, with which most other Europeans are not familiar. They have different social policies born from different political attitudes and political culture, such as differences in the recognition of same-sex unions.[3] Finally, there is also little sense of shared culture, a problem that the EU has tried to address, driven by the commitment under Maastricht that it should "contribute to the flowering of the culture of the Member States" with a view to promoting and protecting the European cultural heritage. It has subsidized architectural restoration, encouraged the translation of works by European authors, and supported cultural activities such as the European Youth Orchestra, the declaration of European Capitals of Culture (including Florence, Dublin, Lisbon, Stockholm, and Liverpool), and the establishment of a European Cultural Month in cities in nonmember states (such as Krakow, Basel, and St. Petersburg).

While the sentiments behind such projects are laudable, the development of a European identity can work only if it comes from Europeans themselves, which in turn demands that Europeans must see themselves as distinctive, as united by common interests and values, and as engaged in a shared endeavor. The stake that Europeans have in the EU will not be truly forged until (a) they can see clearly the impact that decisions made at the level of the EU have on their lives, and (b) they have meaningful channels through which they can influence those decisions. Some channels already

Figure 10.1 Identifying with the European Union

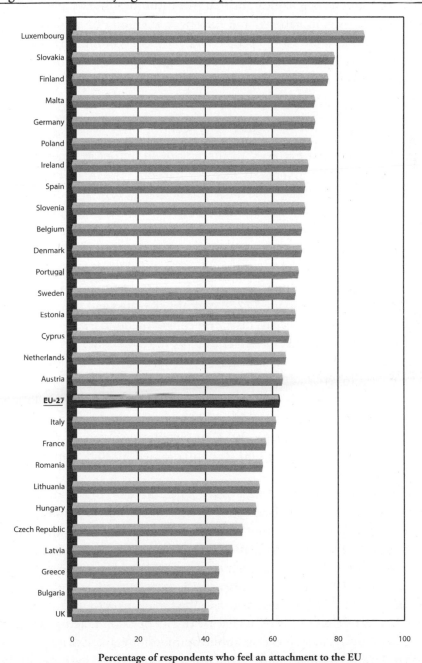

Percentage of respondents who feel an attachment to the EU

Source: European Commission, Eurobarometer 75, spring 2011

exist, and their significance is growing, but the stakes are not yet such that the need to participate is clear, or that most Europeans feel equally motivated to take part in national and European politics. For now, the most significant links between the people and the EU lie in four main arenas: referendums, elections to the European Parliament, the work of EP party groups, and the work of interest groups.

Referendums

European voters have expressed their opinions on European issues through national referendums. Not every member state offers them, they have only been used for selected issues, and the results of most have been unexceptional, but some have had conspicuous political effects with EU-wide implications and have occasionally stopped the process of integration in its tracks.

Most referendums have fallen into one of two major categories:

Whether or not to join the EU. These have been held only by newer members of the EU, beginning with the votes held in Denmark, Ireland, and Norway (but not Britain) in 1972. A majority of Danes and Irish approved, but a majority of Norwegians disapproved, saying no in a second referendum in 1994. Britain held a referendum in 1975 on continued membership in the Community following renegotiation of the terms, but its real purpose was to settle a division of opinion within its own government. All three countries that joined the EU in 1995 held referendums, as did nine of the twelve countries that joined in 2004. Croatia also held a referendum on EU membership, in January 2012, clearing its way to joining the Union. In contrast, when Bulgaria and Romania joined in 2007, neither used a referendum.

Whether or not to accept a new treaty. These have been used most often by Denmark, France, and Ireland, with sometimes surprising results. Denmark held a vote on the Single European Act in 1986, mainly to outmaneuver the Danish Parliament, which had voted against ratification. A majority of Danes said yes on that occasion, but a majority turned down Maastricht in 1992, and a majority of Irish voters turned down the Treaty of Nice in 2001. The negative votes resulted in changes to the treaties and also drew attention to the elitist nature of EU decision making, obliging European leaders to stop taking public opinion for granted. Referendums held in 1998 in Denmark and Ireland on the terms of the Amsterdam treaty were both positive. Most famously, referendums were held in France, Luxembourg, the Netherlands, and Spain in 2005 on the constitutional treaty, which French and Dutch voters turned down. Six other member states that had planned referendums put them on hold.

Ireland in particular has had headline-grabbing results with its referendums: constitutionally required to have a vote on a treaty whenever national sovereignty is at stake, Irish voters turned down the Treaty of Lisbon in 2009. A new referendum on Lisbon was held later that year, only after the Irish government negotiated written assurances from the EU on treaty provisions, and was passed successfully. More recently, a new fiscal compact negotiated by EU leaders during the debt crisis also was put to a vote in Ireland in May 2012. This time a second referendum was not necessary, as some 60 percent of Irish voters approved the new pact.

Although an argument can be, and has been, made that the use of referendums allows citizens more direct input into decision making, they have several distinct disadvantages. Because voters are almost always asked to vote up or down on a particular referendum question, the wording of the question can play a significant role in the outcome. The complexities and subtleties of treaties are, not surprisingly, largely lost in this process. Additionally, referendums often function as "second-order" elections, that is, voters' decisions are guided less by the issue at hand than by their judgment of national incumbent governments (see more on this below). Of course, holding repeated referendums on a single issue (as Ireland has a number of times) can get around these difficulties, but this has some public relations cost as it appears member states will repeat the process until they "get it right."

EUROPEAN ELECTIONS

Elections to the EP have been a fixture on the European political calendar since 1979. Held on a fixed five-year rotation, in years ending with a four or a nine, they give European voters a direct link with the work of the EU. The logistics of the elections are impressive: the electorate consists of some 380 million voters, many more than in the United States. Voters must be eighteen years old and citizens of one of the EU member states. At one time, member states restricted voting to their own citizens, but EU citizens have been allowed since Maastricht to vote in their country of residence, and even to run for the EP wherever they live, regardless of citizenship. They must make a declaration to the electoral authority of the member state in which they are living, and they must meet local qualifications if they want to vote, and qualifications in their home state if they want to run. Member states have different rules on the minimum age for candidates, which range from eighteen to twenty-five, and also have different rules on how candidates qualify; some do not allow independent candidates, some require candidates to pay deposits, others require them to collect signatures, and so on.

Voter turnout figures vary from one member state to another, but are generally lower than those at national elections and are not impressive (see Figure 10.2). Overall turnout fell steadily from 63 percent in 1979 to just under 57 percent in 1994, then took a relatively sharp fall to just over 43 percent in 2009. This brought the figures down into the same range as those for most recent presidential elections in the United States. Belgium and Luxembourg usually have the highest turnout (85–92 percent), and Italy and Greece hover in the range of 70–80 percent, but in almost all other countries fewer than half of all voters turn out. Results were particularly poor in 2004 among the new Eastern European members, which were taking part for the first time. Although large majorities turned out in Cyprus and Malta, less than 40 percent turned out in most other countries, and just 21 percent in Poland. Even those stalwarts of the European Union—France and Germany—have seen their turnout figures slide to just over 40 percent.[4]

The most compelling explanation for low voter turnout is the relative significance of "first-order" and "second-order" elections.[5] Because national elections determine who controls national executives and legislatures, which make the decisions that are seen as most immediate and relevant in the lives of citizens, they are seen as first-order elections by voters and parties alike. They attract more attention, they are more hard fought, and there is more direct interest among voters in their outcome—hence turnout at national elections is greater. By contrast, local and European elections are seen as second-order elections because there is less at stake.

There are several other explanations for low turnout:[6]

- Few European voters know what Parliament does or have developed strong psychological ties to Parliament, and they are either confused or badly informed about European issues.
- There is no change of leadership at stake, as there would be in a national election, so voters feel there is less to be lost or gained. The membership of the Commission bears no relation to the makeup of Parliament; if it did, voter turnout would almost certainly increase.

Figure 10.2 Turnout at European Parliament Elections, 2009

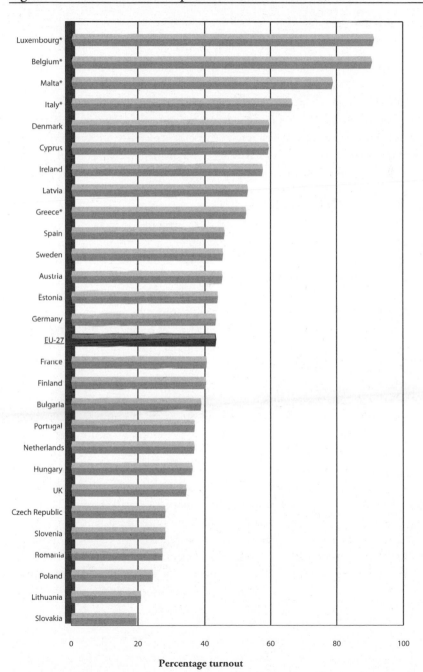

Percentage turnout

* States where voting is compulsory

Box 10.1 European Electoral Systems

Every EU member state uses variations on the theme of proportional representation (PR) for elections to the European Parliament. Where elections to the U.S. House of Representatives use the single-member plurality (SMP) system—each district is represented by one person, who is elected by winning more votes than anyone else, but not necessarily a majority—PR involves distributing seats among parties according to the share of the vote each receives. Typically, EP districts will have multiple representatives, and competing parties will publish lists of candidates for each district. The number of successful candidates on each list will depend on the percentage of votes each party receives.

SMP has the advantage of tying representatives to a particular district and making them responsible to a distinct group of voters. But it also has the disadvantage of not accurately reflecting support for different parties; those that have concentrated blocks of support will often win more seats than those whose support is more widely spread. Meanwhile, PR has the advantage of more accurately reflecting the proportion of the vote given to different parties, but voters are represented by a group of representatives from different parties, and constituents may never get to know or develop ties with an individual member. PR also spreads the distribution of seats widely among parties so that no one party has enough seats to form a majority. Although this encourages legislators from different parties to work together and reach compromises, it also makes it more difficult to get anything done and promotes government instability.

One of the recommendations made by the Adonnino committee was a uniform electoral procedure for European elections. The 1974 Paris summit of Community heads of government decided that the goal would be met if European elections were secret, direct, based on universal suffrage, and held on the same day, but this has not been the end of the story. The most obvious problem is that the member states use different forms of PR. Thus, while the majority of EU member states treat their entire territory as a single electoral district and parties publish national lists of candidates, four states (Belgium, France, Ireland, and the UK) divide themselves into three to twelve Euro-constituencies, and parties publish constituency lists of candidates.

- Turnover among MEPs has been so high—and the number of opportunities for MEPs to make a public reputation for themselves so low—that the EP generates few of the political personalities that will often spark voter interest in national elections.
- The media and national governments tend to downplay the significance of European elections. Where national elections receive headline coverage, ranging from the first political gossip about when an election might be called to the election campaign itself, EP elections receive minimal coverage and so generate less voter interest.
- A significant number of voters have little interest in the EU or are either skeptical about—or hostile to—the concept of integration, making them disinclined to take part in European elections.

Just as in the United States, opinion is divided on whether low turnout is a matter of concern or not. On the one hand, it means that not all opinions are represented and that results are determined by the kind of citizens who are most engaged in the political process. On the other hand, it might be argued that the right not to vote is just as much a part of the democratic process as the right to participate.

POLITICAL GROUPS

Members of the European Parliament (MEPs) do not sit in national blocs but sit together with MEPs from other member states with whom they share similar goals and values. Although these clusters are formally known as "political groups," they have roles and structures that are similar to national parties: they have common ideologies and policy preferences, they come together under a shared label in order to maximize their power and influence, and they tend to vote together on issues before the EP. The number and makeup of groups has changed through time, partly in response to enlargement and the arrival of MEPs from new member states, and partly in response to changed political circumstances and opportunities. Some groups are marriages of convenience, bringing together MEPs with different policies, but generally the groups have built more focus, and they cover a wide array of ideologies and policies, from left to right, from pro-European to anti-European.[7]

There are several rules relating to the formation of political groups, the most basic being that a group must have at least twenty-five members, who must be elected from at least one-quarter of member states. No party group has ever had enough seats to form a majority, so multipartisanship has been the order of business: groups must work together in order to achieve a majority. The balance of power is also affected by frequent changes in the number and makeup of party groups. Through all those changes, three groups have developed a particular consistency: the socialists (on the left), the liberals (on the center right), and the European People's Party (on the right) (see Figure 10.3).

Moving from left to right on the ideological spectrum, the party groups in 2012 were as follows:

European United Left–Nordic Green Left (GUE–NGL). The EUL is the main product of the game of musical chairs played on the left of Parliament since the mid-1980s. A Communist Group was formed in 1973, but the collapse of the Soviet Union in 1989 encouraged Italian and Spanish communists to form their own European United Left, while hard-line communists from France, Greece, and Portugal formed Left Unity. By 1994 only the EUL remained, made up mainly of Spanish, French, and Italian communists. In 1995 the label Nordic Green Left was added to account for the arrival of new MEPs from Finland and Sweden. In 2012 the group had members from thirteen EU states, the biggest national blocs coming from Germany, France, Portugal, and the Czech Republic.

Progressive Alliance of Socialists and Democrats (S&D). The S&D is the main left-wing group and was for many years the largest in Parliament, adding to the concerns of conservative Euroskeptics about the interventionist tendencies of the EU. The 1999 elections saw a rightward shift within the European electorate, however, and a reaction in Britain against the Labour Party. The result was that the group found itself losing more than forty seats and being pushed into second place in the EP, where it has remained since. The S&D has shades of opinion ranging from former communists on the left to more moderate social democrats toward the center, but has generally more ideological consistency than its key competitor, the EPP (see below). It has members from almost every EU member state, with those from Germany, Spain, and Italy forming the biggest national blocs.

The Greens–European Free Alliance (Greens–EFA). Usually associated with environmental issues, the Greens in fact pursue a wider variety of interests related to social justice and refuse to be placed on the traditional ideological spectrum. Once part of the Rainbow Group, the Greens formed their own group after doing well in the 1989 elections. In 1999 their numbers grew from twenty-seven to thirty-eight, which—when added to the

Figure 10.3 Party Balance in the European Parliament

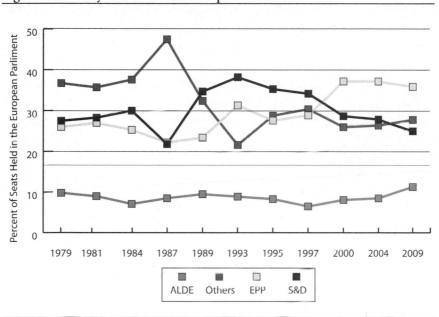

seven members of the European Free Alliance, a small cluster of regional parties—made the Greens-EFA the fourth biggest group in the EP. Their biggest national blocs in 2012 come from France and Germany.

Alliance of Liberals and Democrats for Europe (ALDE). Containing members from all but seven member states, the ALDE has consistently been the third largest group in the EP, but with just above 10 percent of the seats. It is difficult to pinpoint in ideological terms, most of its MEPs falling in or around the center and the group suffering over the years from defections to the EPP. The liberal democrats made headlines in 2002 when the conservatives and the socialists—unable to agree among themselves on whom to appoint as the new president of the EP—chose liberal democrat Pat Cox from Ireland as a compromise. Its biggest national delegations in 2012 came from Germany and the UK.

European People's Party (EPP). The EPP is the major party group on the political right and currently the biggest group in the EP, with members from every EU state except for the UK, whose Tories defected in 2009 to a new party group, the ECR (see below). It began life as a grouping of Christian Democratic parties from the six founding member states, and long stood for the mainstream Christian Democratic principles of social justice, liberal democracy, a mixed economy, and European federalism. The group's policies changed, however, as it incorporated center-right parties from other member states that subscribed neither to Christian Democracy nor to European federalism,[8] and in 1976 it changed its name to the European People's Party. Euroskeptic British and Danish conservatives remained sidelined as the European Democrats until 1992, when they joined forces with the EPP. The rightward shift continued in 2009, when the group won more than a third of the seats in the EP. Its biggest national blocs in 2012 came from Germany, Italy, France, Poland, and Spain.

European Conservatives and Reformists Group (ECR). The ECR was created before the 2009 EP elections by the UK's David Cameron and Mirek Topolanek, the leader of the Czech Civic Democratic Party and was later joined by the Polish Law and Justice Party. Euroskeptic, but not hostile to the EU, the ECR argues for a "flexible, open, and non-federalist agenda."[9]

Europe of Freedom and Democracy (EFD). The latest incarnation of a series of Euroskeptical political groups going back to the Europe of Nations party grouping of 1994, the EFD was formed in 2009 with thirty-two members from nine member states. At the heart of the new group were thirteen MEPs from the United Kingdom Independence Party (UKIP), which supports Britain's withdrawal from the EU. EFD "rejects the bureaucratization of Europe and the creation of a single centralized European superstate."[10] It has members from eleven states, with those from Britain and Italy making up nearly two-thirds of the group.

Non-Attached Members (NI). The EP has always had a number of MEPs who, for reasons of independence or failure to reach agreement with any established political group, operate outside the group structure of the EP. They have rarely numbered more than two to three dozen, with the number in 2012 standing at thirty.

Even though there is a distinctive political group system in the European Parliament, these groups are much less well-known to national voters than their constituent parties. They have not yet developed a habit of campaigning on a cross-European platform, which means that voters are still presented on election day with a choice among national parties rather than among European party groups (which is part of the reason why European elections are run more on national than on European issues). At the same time, though, the political groups have become more cohesive in spite of the sheer number of their constituent parties, and the distinctions across the ideological spectrum are clear.[11]

Table 10.1 Party Representation in the European Parliament, 2012

	EPP	S&D	ALDE	Greens-EFA	ECR	EUL-NGL	EFD	NI	Total
Germany	42	23	12	14	-	8	-	-	99
France	30	13	6	16	-	5	1	3	74
Italy	35	22	6	-	-	-	10	-	73
UK	-	13	12	5	26	1	10	6	73
Spain	25	23	2	2	-	1	-	1	54
Poland	29	7	-	-	11	-	4	-	51
Romania	14	11	5	-	-	-	-	3	33
Netherlands	5	3	6	3	1	2	1	5	26
Belgium	5	5	5	4	1	-	1	1	22
Czech Rep.	2	7	-	-	9	4	-	-	22
Greece	7	8	1	1	-	3	2	-	22
Hungary	14	4	-	-	1	-	-	3	22
Portugal	10	7	-	1	-	4	-	-	22
Sweden	5	6	4	4	-	1	-	-	20
Austria	6	5	-	2	-	-	-	6	19
Bulgaria	7	4	5	-	-	-	-	2	18
Denmark	1	4	3	2	1	1	1	-	13
Finland	4	2	4	2	-	-	1	-	13
Slovakia	6	5	1	-	-	-	1	-	13
Ireland	4	3	4	-	-	1	-	1	13
Lithuania	4	3	2	-	1	-	2	-	12
Latvia	4	1	1	1	1	1	-	-	9
Slovenia	4	2	2	-	-	-	-	-	8
Cyprus	2	2	-	-	-	2	-	-	6
Estonia	1	1	3	1	-	-	-	-	6
Luxembourg	3	1	1	1	-	-	-	-	6
Malta	2	4	-	-	-	-	-	-	6
EU-27	271	189	85	59	52	34	34	31	755

Note: Standing as of July 2012

INTEREST GROUPS

As vibrant democracies, every member state of the EU has a diverse and active community of interest groups that works to influence government on a wide variety of issues, using multiple methods. When policy was made primarily at the national or local level, these groups devoted most of their attention to trying to influence national and local governments. But as more decisions were made at the European level, more groups focused their efforts on European-level policy making, particularly in the European Commission and the European Parliament.[12] Many either opened offices in Brussels or became part of Brussels-based umbrella organizations; by 2006 there were thought to be more than 850 EU-level interest groups (or Eurogroups), mainly representing business interests, public interests, and the professions.[13]

Interest groups have provided an important counterbalance to the nationalist and intergovernmental inclinations of EU policy making, because they have often cut across national frontiers to promote the shared sectional interests of groups of people in multiple member states. The representation of interests at the European level has become more diversified and specialized, and Eurogroups are becoming protagonists—they now try to influence policy rather than simply monitor events, using increasingly sophisticated means to attract allegiance.[14] Something of a symbiotic relationship has developed between the Commission and interest groups, with the former actively supporting the work of many groups and giving them access to its advisory committee meetings, and the latter doing what they can to influence the content and development of policy and legislative proposals as they work their way through the Commission.

As the EU has become increasingly active in a broader variety of policy areas, so the number of special interest groups based in Brussels has increased, dealing with issues as diverse as the environment, agriculture, consumer protection, transport, trade, and social policy. Eurogroups use methods that are similar to those used by groups at the national or local level, such as promoting public awareness in support of their cause, building membership numbers in order to increase their influence and credibility, representing the views of their members, and forming networks with other interest groups. Relative to business groups, however, most special interest groups have critical handicaps:

- They tend to be relatively small and have neither the resources nor the professional expertise to compete with business federations.

- Their technical expertise does not always measure up to that of business groups, and they often lack the ability to discuss the costs and benefits of policy options in real terms. Much of the problem stems from their relative lack of resources; while the business lobby can often draw on the combined and substantial resources of some of the world's richest corporations, special interest groups can often do little more than employ outside experts as occasional consultants. They also often lack the grasp of technical issues needed to debate the business lobby.

- Brussels-based umbrella organizations are dependent for much of their support on their member organizations, most of which still focus more on trying to influence policy at the national rather than the European level. There is relatively little cross-national cooperation among special interest groups.

- The compartmentalized nature of policy making within the Commission requires that groups be able to monitor and respond to policy developments in multiple directorates-general. They need to go beyond the DG that deals most obviously with their policy area and work with other DGs as well, but they often lack the staff to be able to do so.

At the same time, groups have several important cards that they can play, and they have become better with time at exploiting their strengths, which include the following:

- The ability to influence the political agenda in Brussels by building pan-European coalitions and mustering the forces of the thousands of regional, national, and local groups active in the EU. Unlike business (which is often limited by narrow agendas and conflicts of interest), special interest groups are capable of taking a coordinated pan-European view of their long-term interests, providing a balance to the narrower views of the Commission.

- The ability to be of service by providing information. DGs are often overworked and understaffed, must rely on outside sources for expert technical information, and do not have the resources adequately to monitor compliance with EU law. National interest groups in particular can exert influence by actively assisting the Commission with the provision of technical information and by acting as watchdogs over compliance.[15]

Overall, the activities of interest groups have helped offset the problem of the democratic deficit (see Box 11.2) by offering Europeans channels outside the formal structure of EU institutions through which they can influence EU policy. They have also helped to focus the attention of interest group members on how the EU influences the policies that affect their lives, have helped to draw people more actively into the process by which the EU makes its decisions, and have encouraged them to bypass their national governments and to focus their attention on European responses to shared and common problems.

Questions to Consider

1. What are the major obstacles to developing a primary European identity, and can Europe be like the United States, where regional identities are trumped by an overarching American identity?
2. Should more states in the EU make use of referendums for questions concerning the EU as a way of improving the EU's democratic record, or are referendums harmful to the EU project?
3. What could the EU do to increase participation at EU elections? Should European leaders be worried about low turnout or can it be seen (as it sometimes is in the U.S.) as simply a consequence of a free society where citizens can choose to participate or not?

Further Reading

Justin Greenwood. *Interest Representation in the European Union*, 2nd revised ed. (Basingstoke, UK: Palgrave Macmillan, 2007).
> A survey of the work of interest groups at the national and European levels, with chapters on business, professional, labor, and public interest groups.

Bjorn Lindberg, Anne Rasmussen, and Andreas Warntjen, eds. *The Role of Political Parties in the European Union* (London: Routledge, 2009).
> An edited collection of studies on the mechanics and role of political parties in the European and national arenas.

Juliet Lodge, ed. *The 1999 Elections to the European Parliament* (New York: Palgrave Macmillan, 2001). Juliet Lodge, ed. *The 2004 Elections to the European Parliament* (Basingstoke, UK: Palgrave Macmillan, 2005).

Studies of two recent sets of elections to the European Parliament (the former including an overview of the EP and the EU electoral systems) and reviews of results in most of the member states.

Robin Pedler, ed. *European Union Lobbying: Changes in the Arena* (Basingstoke, UK: Palgrave Macmillan, 2002).

A series of case studies of lobbying campaigns directed at influencing EU policy on issues ranging from the environment to trade and enlargement.

Simon Hix, Abdul G. Noury, and Gérard Roland. *Democratic Politics in the European Parliament* (New York: Cambridge University Press, 2007).

A study of voting records in the EP over a period of twenty-five years, revealing the cohesiveness of party groups.

Notes

1. Michael Edwards, *Civil Society* (Cambridge: Polity, 2005).

2. For a review of Euroskepticism, see Paul Taggart and Aleks Sczerbiak, "Supporting the Union? Euroscepticism and the Politics of European Integration," in Maria Green Cowles and Desmond Dinan, eds., *Developments in the European Union* (Basingstoke, UK: Palgrave Macmillan, 2004). For an example of Euroskeptic thinking, see Christopher Booker and Richard North, *The Great Deception: Can the European Union Survive?* rev. ed. (London: Continuum, 2005).

3. Paul Geitner, "On Gay Marriage, Europe Strains to Square 27 Interests," *New York Times*, 26 July 2012, A3.

4. For an analysis of turnout, see Mark Franklin, "European Elections and the European Voter," in Jeremy Richardson, ed., *European Union: Power and Policy-Making*, 3rd ed. (New York: Routledge, 2006), 233–37.

5. See K. Reiff and H. Schmitt, "Nine Second-Order National Elections: A Conceptual Framework for the Analysis of European Election Results," *European Journal of Political Research* 8, no. 1 (1980): 3–44; and Simon Hix and Bjørn Høyland, *The Political System of the European Union*, 3rd ed. (Basingstoke, UK: Palgrave Macmillan, 2011), 190–94.

6. For discussion, see David Judge and David Earnshaw, *The European Parliament*, 2nd ed. (Basingstoke, UK: Palgrave Macmillan, 2008), 86–90.

7. For a history of EU party groups, see Luciano Bardi, "Transnational Trends: The Evolution of the European Party System," in Bernard Steunenberg and Jacques Thomassen, eds., *The European Parliament: Moving Toward*

Democracy in the EU (Lanham, MD: Rowman and Littlefield, 2002). For an overview of the groups, see Richard Corbett, Francis Jacobs, and Michael Shackleton, *The European Parliament*, 6th ed. (London: John Harper, 2005), chapter 5.

8. Judge and Earnshaw, *The European Parliament*, 133.

9. European Conservatives and Reformists Group, 2012, http://ecrgroup.eu /?page_id=954.

10. Europe of Freedom and Democracy in the European Parliament, 2012, http://www.efdgroup.eu/about-us/who-we-are/charter.html.

11. Simon Hix, Abdul G. Noury, and Gérard Roland, *Democratic Politics in the European Parliament* (New York: Cambridge University Press, 2007).

12. Sonia Mazey and Jeremy Richardson, "Interest Groups and the Brussels Bureaucracy," in Jack Hayward and Anand Menon, eds., *Governing Europe* (Oxford: Oxford University Press, 2003), and Sonia Mazey and Jeremy Richardson, "Interest Groups and EU Policy-Making," in Richardson, ed., *European Union*.

13. Richard Balme and Didier Chabanet, *European Governance and Democracy: Power and Protest in the EU* (Lanham, MD: Rowman and Littlefield, 2008).

14. Mark Aspinwall and Justin Greenwood, "Conceptualising Collective Action in the European Union: An Introduction," in Justin Greenwood and Mark Aspinwall, eds., *Collective Action in the European Union* (New York: Routledge, 1998).

15. For more details, see John McCormick, *Environmental Policy in the European Union* (Basingstoke, UK: Palgrave Macmillan, 2001), 111–22.

PART III
POLICIES

11

PUBLIC POLICY IN THE EU

CHAPTER OVERVIEW

- Most public policy within the EU continues to be made at the member-state level. However, in a growing number of areas—including various economic, foreign, and social policies—decisions are made at the EU level.
- The classical elements of the public policy cycle are agenda setting, formulation, legitimation, implementation, and evaluation. For a variety of reasons, all of these stages of the policy cycle are more complex within the EU than they are for normal states.
- The EU has its own budget, although this is far smaller than most national budgets and must be balanced each year. The major source of revenue for the EU is contributions from its member states; its major expenditures include development funds for poorer regions of the EU and agricultural subsidies for EU farmers.

Public policies are the courses of action that governments deliberately pursue (or avoid) when faced with the problems and needs of the societies they govern. When parties or candidates run for office, they publish a list of ideas and proposals for dealing with society's needs. Once elected, they supposedly set out to govern on the basis of those ideas and try to put the proposals into effect. The promises are sometimes lost in the mix, and governments change direction when faced with new problems, but their actions (or lack of action) collectively define their policies. Discussions of policy often include words such as *goals, programs, platforms, objectives, values*, and *needs*, and policies are usually expressed as laws, orders, regulations, and public statements. Put another way, if elections and public opinion are the inputs of politics in a democracy, then public policies are the outputs.

Debates have long raged about how policy is made and implemented at the national level in democracies, even though most have relatively stable, predictable, and institutionalized systems of government. Applied to the European Union, those debates are more complicated. Not only is its administrative structure quite different from those found in conventional states, but there is no agreement on how to characterize the EU, which is in a constant state of evolution: its rules change, its membership changes, its policy agenda changes, and its priorities are frequently redefined. Today's EU traces its origins back to the early 1950s, but its ultimate destination is still unclear, and it may never reach a state of stable equilibrium.[1] And because it is unique, much of the standard political science vocabulary—which is geared toward policy at the national level—does not help us understand how it works. The different policy areas in which the EU has been active have been studied in much depth, but our understanding of the overall EU policy process is still patchy.

In spite of all the questions about the sources and limits of EU power, there is no doubt that its authority has deepened and broadened. Where once European integration focused on coal and steel policy, the member states have transferred (or pooled) so much authority that the EU now has an impact on most aspects of European economic, foreign, and social policy, with national policies and governing structures being changed and brought into alignment by EU laws and policies. And yet the powers of the EU are often misunderstood and exaggerated; much of the authority for decision making still rests in the hands of the governments of the member states. And despite concerns about loss of sovereignty and complaints about the mythical powers of "Brussels," the EU still has no direct powers of enforcement and implementation, and it has only a small budget ($186 billion in 2011, equivalent to one-twentieth of the U.S. federal budget, or one-sixth the size of the British national budget). Against that background, this chapter looks at how EU policy is made and implemented, and discusses some of the principles of the EU policy process. It ends with an analysis of the structure and policy implications of the budget.

THE POLICY CYCLE

There are many different ways of approaching the study of public policy, but the most common method is to describe it in terms of a cycle. The problem with this approach is that it suggests that policy making is more logical and ordered than it really is—certainly more so than it is in the complex and often arcane world of European policy making.[2] But the approach has the advantage of imposing some order on a complex process. In the case of the EU, that cycle has six key steps: agenda setting, formulation, legitimation, adoption, implementation, and evaluation.

Agenda Setting. Before a policy choice can be made, the existence of a problem must be acknowledged, and the problem must be accepted as a legitimate concern of government and placed on the public agenda. The definition of the public agenda is affected by prevailing economic, social, and ideological values; by the nature and extent of government authority; and by changing levels of public and political interest. Some issues are almost perpetually on the agenda, some never make it to the agenda at all, some appear for a brief period of time then disappear, and yet others come and go. The broad or perpetual issues are those that tend to affect most people most of the time, such as economic questions, social issues, foreign policy, and the environment. Issues that rarely make it onto the EU agenda are those that are still mainly the responsibility of the member states, including welfare, health care, taxation, education, public safety, and crime.

It is important to appreciate that there is no single agenda in the EU, but many different agendas:

- The institutional agendas of the Commission, Parliament, and the Council of Ministers.
- The subinstitutional agendas of directorates-general within the Commission.
- Regional agendas pursued by groups of member states (poorer states will have different needs from richer states, agricultural states will have different needs from industrial states, and so on).

- National agendas pursued by individual member states.
- Cross-national agendas pursued by like-minded groups in multiple states, such as the environmental lobby, farmers, or multinational corporations.
- Social agendas pursued by groups or movements dealing with issues such as individual rights, transparency in government, education, and health care.

One key difference between agenda setting at the national and European levels lies in the relative roles of public accountability. Elected leaders at the national level often push issues onto the policy agenda in response to public opinion, ostensibly because they want to represent the public will but also because they want to be reelected. In that sense, agenda setting is voter driven. In the EU, however, most authority for agenda setting rests with the European Council and the Commission, neither of which is elected or directly accountable to an EU-wide constituency and thus is less subject to national voter influence. But mixed public opinion about European integration has combined with negative votes on key European initiatives (the Danish rejection of Maastricht in 1992, the Irish rejection of Nice in 2001, the Dutch and French rejection of the constitutional treaty in 2005) to encourage both bodies to pay more attention to public opinion.

A second difference lies in the extent to which easily identified solutions exist. At the national or subnational level, it is easier (but by no means easy) to identify problems and their causes and so to push the issue onto the policy agenda and formulate a response. At the EU level, the sheer complexity and variety of the needs, values, and priorities of the member states make it more difficult to be certain about the existence or the causes of problems or the potential effects of policy alternatives. Unemployment, for example, can have different root causes from one member state to another, tied to macroeconomic policies and different policies on education, job training, and unemployment benefits. This causes difficulty when making the case for placing an issue on the agenda.

While the European Council and the Commission are the primary agenda setters, they are subject to many different pressures and influences:

- Treaty obligations.
- Pressures to harmonize national laws and policies so as to avoid economic or social variation among the member states, and to remove obstacles to free trade.

- Policy evolution, in which policy responses are redefined as better understanding emerges about the causes and effects of problems.
- Legislative pressures, which cause new proposals for legislation to come out of requirements or assumptions built into existing laws.
- Pressures from EU institutions, including judgments by the Court of Justice, or pressure on the Commission from the European Parliament or the Council of Ministers to develop new laws or policies.
- Initiatives by individual national leaders or groups of leaders.
- Public opinion.
- Internal pressures, such as ongoing concerns about unemployment or the need to monitor the movement of criminals around the EU.
- External pressures, such as trade wars with the U.S., the fallout with the U.S. over Iraq, or heightening tensions between the EU and Russia in 2006–07.
- The requirements of international law many EU laws and policies have been responses to the requirements of international treaties that the EU has signed.
- Emergencies or crises, none of which have been so pressing or serious as the fallout from the crisis in the eurozone.

Agenda setting in the EU is based on a combination of (1) the extent to which national governments are prepared to allow the EU to have authority in different fields, (2) the extent to which economic, political, or technical pressures demand an EU response, and (3) the compromises reached in the process of resolving the often conflicting demands and needs of the member states. Different models have been developed to understand how EU agenda setting works (see Box 11.1), but the sheer size and complexity of the EU make it impossible to reach agreement on which offers the best explanation.

Formulation. Once a problem or a need has been recognized, a response must be formulated. This will typically involve the development of a plan or program, which may include agreeing on new laws and new spending, issuing instructions to bureaucrats, making a series of public statements designed to draw attention to a problem, or encouraging changes in patterns of behavior. On the other hand, policy makers might decide to ignore a problem or to deliberately take no action, perhaps because the problem is too complex, or because there is doubt about its causes and about the best response, or simply because it is politically expedient to push it aside. A

Box 11.1 Who Sets the European Agenda?

Most studies of public policy argue that agenda setting is determined in one of three ways, all of which are reflected in the EU:

- The *pluralist approach* argues that policy making is divided into separate arenas influenced by different groups and that government is ultimately the sum of all competing interests in a society. The most important of these groups in the EU system is the member states themselves, but pluralists usually think in terms of more specific interests. Thus farmers exert influence through their defense of the Common Agricultural Policy, and environmental interest groups have successfully lobbied the Commission and Parliament and have occasionally used the EU to bypass their own national governments.

- The *elitist approach* argues that decision making is dominated by a power elite consisting of those with the means to exert influence, whether it is money, status, charisma, or some other commodity. The EU is elitist in that important decisions are made by the leaders of the member states, the Council of Ministers, Coreper, and the unelected and only indirectly accountable European commissioners. The democratic deficit (see Box 11.2) comes largely from the fact that so few individuals in the EU power structure are elected and that so many of their meetings take place out of public view. The rise of interest group lobbying and the growing strength of the European Parliament have made the policy process more open and democratic.

- The *statecentric approach* argues that the major source of policies is the environment in which policy makers find themselves, and that the government itself, rather than external social interests, is the locus of agenda setting. The EU is statecentric in that the setting of the EU agenda has been determined in large part by the nature of integration. EU leaders made a conscious decision to sign the Single European Act, for example, which meant the EU had to become involved in a wide variety of new policy areas and to deepen its authority in policy areas in which it was already involved.

deliberate lack of action is just as much a part of public policy as a decision to act.

In an ideal world, some kind of methodical and rational policy analysis should be conducted in which the causes and dimensions of a problem are studied and all possible options and their relative costs and benefits considered before taking action. But this rarely happens; policy is often driven by incrementalism, intuition, opportunism, or responses to emergencies or changes in public opinion. One famous study by the American scholar Charles Lindblom argues that policy making is often simply a matter of "muddling through."[3] Several obstacles interfere with the orderly formulation of policy.

- People disagree over problems, their causes, and their urgency. What may seem logical, moral, or reasonable to one person may seem illogical, immoral, or unreasonable to another.
- Policy makers may not always have enough information to give them a clear understanding of a problem or its causes, and even when they do, they may not always agree on its interpretation. What, for example, causes poverty? Are people poor because they lack the will or ambition to improve their lives, because of their social environment, or because political and economic barriers make it impossible for them to improve their lives?
- Responses to problems are affected by personal, social, and ideological biases. A conservative Czech prime minister will see policy issues in a different light than his or her Spanish socialist or Swedish social democrat counterpart because of different ideological values, different worldviews, and the often different needs of their constituencies.
- It is frequently difficult or impossible to be sure about the outcomes of a policy or how that policy will work in practice. Even with the best intentions and the finest research and planning, policies can have unintended or unanticipated consequences.
- The distribution of power in any system of government is often ambiguous, partly because constitutions are subject to different interpretations and partly because the process of government is determined by *implied* powers, by the values and personalities of officeholders, and by the varied ways in which officeholders use the powers of the same office. For example, the role of the European

Figure 11.1 The European Union Policy Process

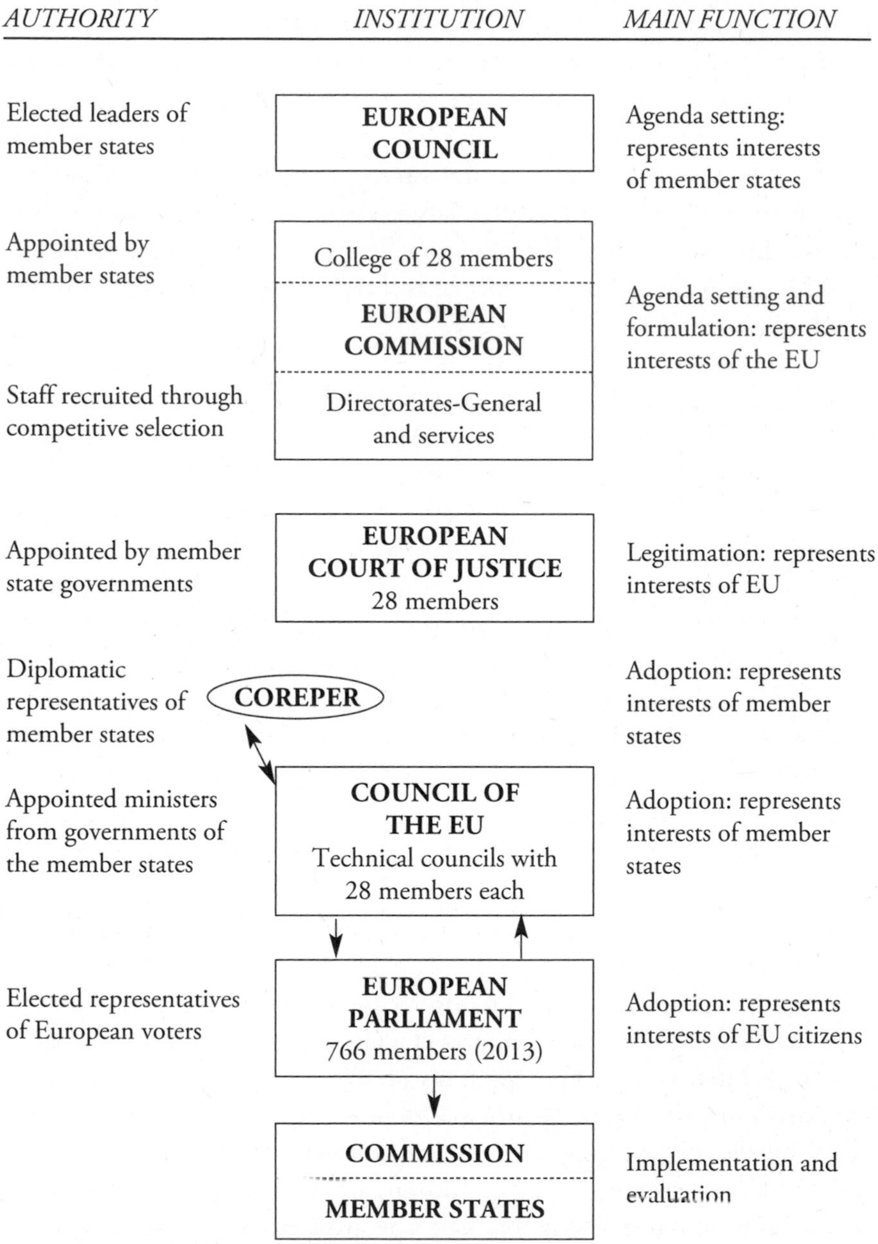

AUTHORITY	INSTITUTION	MAIN FUNCTION
Elected leaders of member states	**EUROPEAN COUNCIL**	Agenda setting: represents interests of member states
Appointed by member states	College of 28 members **EUROPEAN COMMISSION**	Agenda setting and formulation: represents interests of the EU
Staff recruited through competitive selection	Directorates-General and services	
Appointed by member state governments	**EUROPEAN COURT OF JUSTICE** 28 members	Legitimation: represents interests of EU
Diplomatic representatives of member states	**COREPER**	Adoption: represents interests of member states
Appointed ministers from governments of the member states	**COUNCIL OF THE EU** Technical councils with 28 members each	Adoption: represents interests of member states
Elected representatives of European voters	**EUROPEAN PARLIAMENT** 766 members (2013)	Adoption: represents interests of EU citizens
	COMMISSION **MEMBER STATES**	Implementation and evaluation

Commission in the policy process has depended less on the terms of the president's job than on the president's personality.

The major focus of policy formulation in the EU is the Commission, which has the sole power to initiate new legislation, is responsible for protecting the treaties and ensuring that their spirit is expressed in specific laws and policies, and is charged with overseeing the EU budget. However, the Commission does not work in a vacuum: it listens to national governments, public opinion, interest groups, corporations, and policy think tanks, and is often influenced by the ideological, social, or national biases that its own staff bring to their analysis of a problem. The European Council will often also have an impact on policy formulation, since it decides not just what to do but sometimes how to do it. Commission proposals are also routinely changed as a result of lobbying and as they are discussed by the Council of Ministers and the European Parliament.

Legitimation. In a democratic system, few policies are likely to be able to succeed unless, at a minimum, they are based on legal authority and win public recognition. *Legitimacy* is a concept that describes the extent of the belief of citizens that the government under which they live has the authority to govern and make laws, and also describes the extent to which the actions of government are regarded as proper and acceptable. *Legitimation* is the process by which a government gives legitimacy to its actions; in other words, its policies must be converted into generally acceptable means for achieving its objectives. Legitimation in the EU is achieved through one of four main channels: the treaties, legislation, decisions by the European Court of Justice, and public opinion.

Leon Lindberg has argued that "the essence of a political community . . . is the existence of a legitimate system for the resolution of conflict, for the making of authoritative decisions for the group as a whole."[4] The less legitimacy such a community enjoys, the less it will be able to achieve by democratic means. In political systems founded on the rule of law (government based on a mutually agreed set of rules and laws, to which all residents are equally subject), there are usually few questions regarding the authority of government to make and implement policies. With the EU, however, the authority and powers of EU institutions have long been bones of contention.

Among the EU's fundamental handicaps is the authority gap—the difference between what EU institutions would like to be able to do and what EU citizens and governments allow them to do. That gap is wide, but it has slowly been narrowing, helped by direct elections to the European Parliament: despite its weaknesses and despite low voter turnout, Parliament is still the only institution in the EU system that is directly accountable to the citizens. Voting in fair, regular, and competitive elections is one of the foundations of political legitimacy, and direct elections to Parliament have helped to build the credibility and legitimacy of the EU. Its legitimacy has also grown simply with the passage of time: EU citizens are learning to live with the effects of integration, and the EU is becoming more real, more permanent, and more acceptable.

Adoption. Once a new law or policy has been formulated, it must be adopted. Responsibility for this is shared between the Council of Ministers (particularly Coreper) and the European Parliament. Adoption has become more complex and time-consuming as the EP has won new powers relative to the Council, and particularly since the introduction of the codecision procedure (now the ordinary legislative procedure). The EP has become more forceful in offering amendments to proposals from the Commission, to some extent making up for the relatively limited role that it has in the formulation phase.

The adoption of a new proposal is driven by the negotiating styles of the representatives of each member state, which will be influenced by tradition, by the attitude of the home government toward European integration, and by the extent to which a member state depends on EU law. For example, while British governments have long had a reputation for running hot and cold on the idea of European integration, British civil servants are widely regarded as among the most efficient and effective at the EU level, and Britain has a reputation for taking its obligations under EU law seriously and working hard to negotiate an agreement with which it can live. Italy and Greece take their obligations less seriously, which is why they have been taken to the Court of Justice more often than any other EU member states for failure to meet their obligations.

Implementation. Policies are only words or ideas until they are implemented and enforced. In the case of the EU this means monitoring the application of new laws and regulations, arguably the most difficult step in the policy cycle. To assume that once the EU has made a decision it will automatically be enforced is delusory; policies can be reinterpreted and redefined even at this stage.[5] Many different problems can arise: a lack of political agreement or political will; the inefficiency of the institutions responsible for implementation; a lack of cooperation from the subjects of policy (people, corporations, public agencies, and governments); inadequate funding; a lack of workable or realistic goals; a redefinition of priorities as a result of changed circumstances or new data; a lack of agreement on underlying goals and the best methods of implementation; conflicting interpretations; a lack of public support; inefficiency, stagnation, or conflicting interests within bureaucracies; and unanticipated structural problems or side effects.

Responsibility for overseeing implementation lies with the Commission, although it must work through the bureaucracies of member states to ensure that governments turn EU laws and policies into practical change on the ground. The Commission also relies on individuals and interest groups to review the progress of implementation, and on the Court of Justice to ensure that laws are uniformly interpreted and applied and that disputes are resolved. Implementation has also been made easier by the creation of specialized agencies such as Europol and the European Central Bank, with responsibilities in focused policy areas.

Evaluation. The final stage in the policy cycle is determining whether a law or policy has worked. This is difficult unless specific goals were set from the beginning and unless member states can be trusted to report accurately to the Commission on the results of policies. In many cases it is almost impossible to know which actions resulted in which consequences, particularly in the more complex areas of policy, such as economic management. Assuming, however, that the outcomes of policies can be identified and measured (in whole or in part), policies can be continued, adjusted, or abandoned. Evaluation in the EU is carried out by a combination of the Commission, the Council of Ministers, the European Council, the European Parliament, and reports from member states, interest groups, and individuals.

FEATURES OF THE POLICY PROCESS

Writing about the policy process in the United States, Guy Peters argues that "American government has a number of structures but no real organization." He notes the lack of effective coordination and control, which he argues was intentional, given the concern of the framers of the U.S. Constitution about the potential for tyranny by a powerful central executive.[6] In many respects, the same can be said about policy making in the EU. There is no real organization, in large part owing to ubiquitous concerns about loss of sovereignty. The result has been a policy process driven not just by the usual pressures of compromise and opportunism, but also by some features that are unique to the European experience.

Compromise and bargaining. Except in dictatorships, all politics is a matter of compromise (a reality that many lawmakers in the U.S. Congress seem lately to have forgotten). Individuals cannot always have it their own way, because there are always others who will disagree with their analyses of problems, their suggested prescriptions, and their priorities. The fewest compromises are needed in unitary systems of government with a history of majoritarian political parties (such as Britain and Spain), where the focus of political power rests with a national government usually made up of a single political party. More compromises are needed in federal systems such as Belgium and Germany, where there is a division of powers between national and subnational government, or in member states governed by coalitions (such as Austria, Ireland, or Portugal).

Political games. Politics is driven by struggles for power and influence, with one person or group trying to press its views on others. Such struggles are magnified in the EU by the extent to which member states and institutions compete with each other. Peters describes three sets of interconnected games in the EU: a national game among member states, which are trying to extract as much as possible from the EU while giving up as little as possible; a game played out among EU institutions, which are trying to win more power relative to one another; and a bureaucratic game in which the directorates-general in the Commission are developing their own organizational cultures and competing for policy space.[7] Peters argues that policy making has become fragmented as institutional and policy goals have parted company and different policy communities have emerged.[8]

Incrementalism. Owing to concerns about the loss of national sovereignty, the absence of a consensus on the wisdom of European integration, and the need for constant compromise, EU policy making is generally slow and cautious. The EU occasionally has agreed on relatively dramatic policy initiatives (such as the Single European Act, Maastricht, the launch of the euro, and eastern enlargement), but most EU policy making is based on gradual and incremental change. Since there are so many counterweights and counterbalances in the policy process, member states and EU institutions can rarely take the initiative without conferring first with other member states or EU institutions. The process has sometimes slowed to the point where critics of integration have complained about inertia, but the achievements have been substantial. None, however, came out of the ether; all emerged incrementally from a combination of opportunity and need.

Multispeed integration. In the United States—even though different states have different policies with regard to capital punishment, speed limits, voting procedures, and rates of taxation, for example—the country is generally moving at the same pace in most key policy areas. In other words, different states do not opt in or out of different federal policy areas according to local political preferences. In the EU, by contrast, not all member states have adopted exactly the same sets of common policies, and so they are moving at different speeds. There has been universal adoption of laws and policies on the single market and agricultural policy, for example, but only seventeen of the twenty-seven member states have adopted the euro.

Subsidiarity. One of the key principles of European integration has been the requirement that, except in those policy areas that fall exclusively within the competence of the EU (such as competition, customs, trade, and fiscal policy in the eurozone), the EU should take action only in those areas or on those problems in which it makes more sense to take joint action than to leave it to the member states. In other words, the EU should do only what it does best, and the member states should do everything else. There are no hard rules regarding the best division of responsibilities, which are shared in almost every field of policy. But it has come to be understood that certain issues are best dealt with jointly (such as the single market and external trade negotiations), and there is political resistance to the EU becoming involved in policy areas that are still seen as the preserve of member states, such as education, health care, policing, criminal justice, and taxation. One result has been to cause the procedures for making policy to vary from one policy area to another.

Europeanization. In thinking about the way the European Community would make decisions, Jean Monnet thought that national policies would simply be replaced with European policies. Otherwise known as the Community method,[9] this was the earliest, simplest, and purest of the different models of European policy making, but it was also the most difficult to achieve because it assumed wholesale agreement on switching authority from the member states to the EU. What has instead happened, according to many who study the EU, has been a process of Europeanization, in which laws and policies in the member states have been brought into alignment with EU law and policy through a process of harmonization, or perhaps even of homogenization.[10] This is a process that has not yet been studied in great depth, and opinion is divided on just how far it has gone, or just how useful it is as a means of understanding the EU policy process.[11] It is also unclear just how far the pressures that have led to policy change have been clearly European, as opposed to coming out of the member states or out of international pressures such as globalization.

Spillover. Critics of the EU (like critics of the U.S. federal government) have often charged that it has tried to become involved in too many policy areas, but often it has had little choice: the launch of a new initiative can reveal or create new problems that in turn can lead to a demand for additional supporting initiatives. As Aaron Wildavsky put it, policy can become its own cause.[12] Spillover has been an ongoing feature of policy making in the EU, the prime example coming from efforts to complete the single market. The task of removing barriers to the free movement of people, money, and goods and services could not be achieved either easily or quickly, and it involved making many adjustments—anticipated or not—that opened up the European market. This meant moving into new areas of policy that were never anticipated by the founding treaties, including social issues, working conditions, and the environment.

THE BUDGET

Arguably the biggest influence on policy at any level of government is the budget. The amount of money a government has available—and how and where it decides to raise and spend that money—affects both its policy choices and the true effectiveness of policy implementation. It is often less a question of *how much* is raised and spent than of *how* and *where* that money is raised and spent. Controversies swirl in the United States over budget deficits, the national debt, wasted spending, and the billions that are spent on defense instead of on education, health care, and infrastructure. The EU budget, too, is controversial, but less for how EU funds are spent than for how they are raised. The depth of the debate is surprising given the small amount involved: €142 billion ($186 billion) in 2011—less than the U.S. federal government spent to service interest on the national debt.

The EU budget has two notable features:

- Unlike almost any national budget, it must be balanced. This means that there is no EU debt, so the EU is spared the problems that normally accompany debts (such as interest payments). In this regard the EU stands in stark contrast to the U.S., which has had a budget surplus in only eleven years since 1945, and by 2012 was in the red to the tune of about $15 trillion.
- The sources and the quantity of EU revenues have been at the heart of the conflicts that have emerged during the evolution of the EU.

BOX 11.2 THE DEMOCRATIC DEFICIT

The lack of institutional openness and accountability has been a recurring theme in studies of the EU. The European Parliament is the only directly elected EU body, but most of the power lies with the Commission and the Council of Ministers, neither of which has much direct public accountability. As one Member of the European Parliament once quipped, if the EC were a state and applied for Community membership, it would be turned down on the grounds that it was not a democracy.[13] At the heart of the problem is the democratic deficit, or the gap between the powers transferred to the EU institutions and the ability of European citizens to influence the decisions they make. Several problems contribute to the deficit:

- Meetings of the European Council, the Council of Ministers, Coreper, and the College of Commissioners are typically closed to the public, despite the fact that they make important decisions on law and policy.
- The citizens of Europe have no direct input into the process by which the president of the Commission or members of the College of Commissioners are chosen, and Parliament lacks the power of confirmation over individual commissioners or over judges in the Court of Justice.
- The governments of the member states often make key decisions (such as changes to the treaties) without a national vote.

But does the deficit really exist? Some have argued that the EU does not need the same democratic processes as national democracies because—if it is a confederation—it is a system in which governments interact, not people and governments. The governments of the member states are given legitimacy by the democratic processes in which their citizens participate and are in turn given a mandate to negotiate on behalf of those citizens. The political scientist Andrew Moravcsik, for one, challenges the idea that the EU lacks democratic legitimacy. He argues that the EU is a weak and dependent state structure, that EU institutions are under direct or indirect democratic control, that the Council of Ministers is democratically accountable, and that commissioners and judges on the Court of Justice are named by directly elected national governments.[14]

The biggest battles have been over the balance between national contributions (which give member states leverage over the EU) and the EU's own sources of revenue. The greater the latter, the greater independence the EU would have, and the greater the concerns about loss of national sovereignty by the member states.[15]

Revenues. While the European Coal and Steel Community had its own income, raised by a levy on producers, the EEC and Euratom—like most international organizations—were originally funded by national contributions. The contributions to the EEC were calculated roughly on the basis of size; thus France, Germany, and Italy each contributed 28 percent, Belgium and the Netherlands 7.9 percent, and Luxembourg 0.2 percent. In an attempt to win more independence, the Commission in 1965 proposed that the revenue from tariffs placed on imports from outside the EC should go directly to the Community, thereby providing the EC with its own resources. At the same time, Parliament began pushing for more control over the budget as a means of gaining more influence over policy. Charles de Gaulle thought the Commission had too much power already, and it was these proposals (combined with France's opposition to reform of the Common Agricultural Policy) that led to the 1965 empty chair crisis.

Pressure for budgetary reform persisted regardless, and changes between 1970 and 1975 led gradually to an increase in the proportion of revenues derived from the EC's own resources: customs duties, levies on agricultural imports, and a proportion (no more than 1 percent) of value-added tax (VAT). Two problems with this formula emerged. First, it took no account of the relative size of member-state economies. This became a particular problem for Britain, which paid much more into the EU coffers than it received. Second, the amounts involved were insufficient to meet the needs of the Community, which was not allowed to run a deficit or to borrow to meet shortfalls. The EC's freedom of action was reduced further by the fact that two-thirds of spending went to agricultural price supports, which grew as European farmers produced more crops (see chapter 13). At the same time, revenue from customs duties fell because the Community's external tariffs were reduced, revenue from agricultural levies fell as the EC's self-sufficiency in food production grew, and income from VAT failed to grow quickly enough because consumption was falling as a percentage of the Community's GDP.[16] The problem was compounded by the unwillingness of some member states to raise the limit on the EC's own resources.

Figure 11.2   The European Union Budget

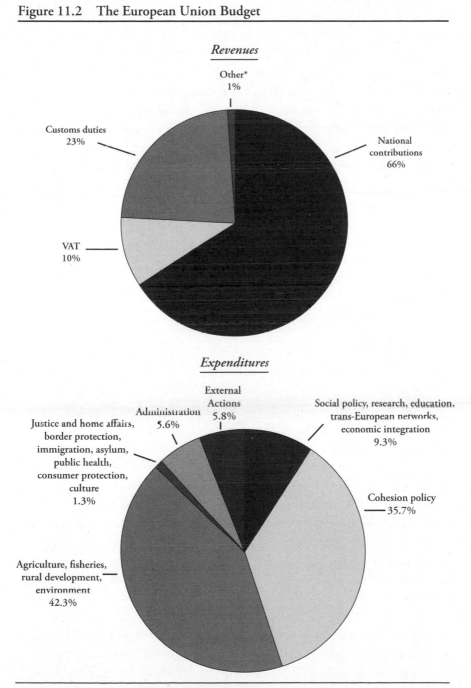

Source: European Commission. Figures are for 2012.

* Includes taxes on EU staff salaries, contributions from non-EU countries to selected programs, and fines on companies for breaching EU competition laws.

By the early 1980s the Community was on the brink of insolvency, and it was obvious that either revenues had to be increased or expenditures had to be restructured or cut. The issue of budget reform was brought to a head by Margaret Thatcher's insistence on a recalculation of the British contribution; at her first European Council appearance in 1979 she bluntly told her Community partners, "I want my money back"; a complex deal was eventually reached in 1984 by which Britain was given a rebate and its contribution was cut, and the Community's own resources were increased with the setting of a new ceiling of 1.4 percent from VAT. More reforms agreed to at an extraordinary meeting of the European Council in Brussels in February 1988 resulted in the current system of revenue raising:

- The budget cannot be greater than 1.23 percent of the combined GNP of the member states.
- About 66 percent of revenues in 2012 came from national contributions based on national GNP levels (up from 43 percent of revenues in 2003). Each member state pays a set amount in proportion to its GNP.
- Revenues from VAT accounted for just 10 percent of revenues in 2012, down from 38 percent in 2003.
- About 23 percent of revenues in 2012 came from customs duties on imports from nonmember states and from agricultural levies.
- This formula produces a system in which the richer states make the biggest net contributions, while the poorer states have the biggest net receipts.

Expenditures. As with almost any budget, EU expenses consist of a combination of mandatory payments in which it has little or no choice (such as agricultural price supports) and discretionary payments (such as spending on regional or energy policy), regarding which there is more flexibility. EU spending is about equally divided between the two and in 2012 was committed as follows.

- About 46 percent of spending ($67.5 billion) went to sustainable growth, the largest share of which is the cohesion funds (the old structural funds, or development spending on poorer regions of the EU, amounting to about $41 billion), but also including competitiveness funds, supporting projects and activities on entrepreneurship, innovation, information, and similar areas.

- About 41 percent (or $60 billion) went to natural resources, including rural development funds and agricultural subsidies and supports to fisheries. These still soak up a large share of the EU budget. However, because of reforms in agricultural policy (see chapter 13), the proportion of EU spending that goes to agriculture has fallen substantially from its peak during the 1970s, when it accounted for nearly 75 percent of the budget.
- A small percentage is also budgeted for citizenship, freedom, and security (1.4 percent), targeting "vulnerable returnees" (refugees who face uncertainty and instability when they return to their home states or regions) as well as for projects to enhance and promote a common EU citizenship.
- Another 6.4 percent of the budget is earmarked for the EU to use as a global player, including pre-accession funds (for prospective EU states), humanitarian aid, and development cooperation and other funds tied to the Common Foreign and Security Policy.
- Finally, only about 5.6 percent (nearly $10 billion) went to administrative costs for the EU institutions. As an indication of how much misunderstanding there is about those institutions—particularly the Commission—public opinion polls routinely find that most Europeans think that administration is one of the major costs of the EU.

Questions to Consider

1. What distinctive features of public policy making in the EU make this more challenging than in conventional states?
2. How does the EU compare with the U.S. federal government in terms of its taxing authority? Should the EU have greater independence in this, say by having its own income tax?
3. What do the various categories of expenditures from the EU budget say about policy priorities within the EU?

Further Reading

Sebastiaan Princen. *Agenda-Setting in the European Union* (New York: Palgrave Macmillan, 2009).

A study of what policy areas get put on the EU agenda, with comparative case studies in environmental and health policy in the U.S. and the EU.

Helen Wallace, Mark Pollack, and Alasdair Young, eds. *Policy-Making in the European Union*, 6th ed. (Oxford: Oxford University Press, 2010).
An edited collection focusing on specific policy areas, including agriculture, the single market, competition, and social policy.

Simona Milio. *From Policy to Implementation in the European Union: The Challenge of a Multi-Level Governance System* (London: Tauris Academic, 2010).
An examination of the deficiencies of EU policy implementation at the member state level, with Italy, Spain, and Poland as case studies.

Johannes Lindner. *Conflict and Change in EU Budgetary Politics* (Abingdon: Routledge, 2006).
One of the surprisingly few full-length studies of the EU budget.

Notes

1. See the discussion in Brigid Laffan, Rory O'Donnell, and Michael Smith, *Europe's Experimental Union: Rethinking Integration* (London: Routledge, 2000), and Sonia Mazey, "European Integration: Unfinished Journey or Journey Without End?" in Jeremy Richardson, ed., *European Union: Power and Policy-Making*, 2nd ed. (New York: Routledge, 2001).

2. For a portrait of the complexity, see Jeremy Richardson, "Policy-Making in the EU: Interests, Ideas and Garbage Cans of Primeval Soup," in Jeremy Richardson, ed., *European Union: Power and Policy-Making*, 2nd ed. (New York: Routledge, 2001); see also Sebastiaan Princen, *Agenda-Setting in the European Union* (New York: Palgrave Macmillan, 2009).

3. Charles Lindblom, "The Science of 'Muddling Through,'" *Public Administration Review* 19, no. 2 (1959): 79–88.

4. Leon N. Lindberg, *The Political Dynamics of European Economic Integration* (Stanford: Stanford University Press, 1963), vii.

5. See Simona Milio, *From Policy to Implementation in the European Union: The Challenge of a Multi-Level Governance System* (London: Tauris Academic, 2010), and Christoph Knill, "Implementation," in Richardson, ed., *European Union*.

6. B. Guy Peters, *American Public Policy: Promise and Performance*, 7th ed. (Washington, DC: CQ Press, 2007), 25.

7. B. Guy Peters, "Bureaucratic Politics and the Institutions of the European Community," in Alberta Sbragia, ed., *Euro-Politics: Institutions and Policymaking*

in the "New" European Community (Washington, DC: Brookings Institution, 1992), 106–7.

8. Peters, "Bureaucratic Politics and the Institutions of the European Community," 115–21.

9. See Leon N. Lindberg and Stuart A. Scheingold, *Europe's Would-Be Polity: Patterns of Change in the European Community* (Englewood Cliffs, NJ: Prentice Hall, 1970).

10. Edward C. Page, "Europeanization and the Persistence of Administrative Systems," in Jack Hayward and Anand Menon, eds., *Governing Europe* (Oxford: Oxford University Press, 2003).

11. See Page, "Europeanization and the Persistence of Administrative Systems," and Paolo Graziano and Maarten P. Vink, eds., *Europeanization: New Research Agendas* (Basingstoke, UK: Palgrave Macmillan, 2007).

12. Aaron Wildavsky, ed., *Speaking Truth to Power: The Art and Craft of Policy Analysis* (Boston: Little, Brown, 1979), 62–85.

13. David Martin, quoted in Vernon Bogdanor and Geoffrey Woodcock, "The European Community and Sovereignty," *Parliamentary Affairs* 44, no. 4 (October 1991): 481–92.

14. Andrew Moravcsik, "Democracy and Constitutionalism in the European Union," *ECSA Review* 13, no. 2 (spring 2000): 2–7.

15. For a brief survey of EU budgetary battles, see Brigid Laffan and Johannes Lindner, "The Budget: Who Gets What, When and How?" in Helen Wallace, Mark A. Pollack, and Alasdair R. Young, eds., *Policy-Making in the European Union*, 6th ed. (Oxford: Oxford University Press, 2010).

16. Michael Shackleton, *Financing the European Community* (New York: Council on Foreign Relations Press, 1990), 10–11.

12

ECONOMIC AND MONETARY POLICY

CHAPTER OVERVIEW

- European integration has always been a function of economic integration. Intended to promote peace and prosperity in the early years of the EU, in the last two decades significant progress has been made in completing the single market and breaking down remaining physical, fiscal, and technical barriers to integration.
- As part of the expansion and logic of the single market, the area of justice and home affairs has moved over the course of the last two decades from being a peripheral area of loose intergovernmental cooperation to an issue area requiring more robust integration of policies, laws, and approaches.
- One of the most visible emblems of the single market has been the euro, now used by seventeen countries in the EU. Created in 1999 as a result of Maastricht, the euro has been a singular achievement and a boon for consumers and business. But the rules and mechanisms governing the euro have been found wanting, and have been

at the heart of a eurozone debt crisis that has shaken the EU to its core.

What we now know as the European Union began life as the European Economic Community, and therein lies a fundamental clue to how the process of European integration has evolved: it was launched as a limited experiment in economic cooperation, was broadened during the 1960s to become a customs union, wrestled during the 1970s with attempts to build common economic policies and exchange rate stability, launched a new initiative in the late 1980s to complete the single market, and then agreed on the steps that have led in 1999 to the adoption of a single currency across the seventeen countries of the eurozone. The changes wrought have not just affected the lives of Europeans—they have been felt on a global scale: the EU is now the wealthiest marketplace and biggest trading power in the world, and with the euro (assuming its problems can be resolved) it has one of the world's three leading international currencies.

The EU has made progress in other policy areas too (such as agriculture, the environment, regional development, and foreign policy), but the engine of integration has ultimately been the economy. Economic integration was intended to promote peace and prosperity by generating the wealth and opportunity that would allow Europe to recover from the ravages of war. By no means was the process plain sailing, and while most of Western Europe prospered during the 1950s, by the 1960s and 1970s it was facing numerous problems, including faltering economic growth, market fragmentation, competition from the Americans and the Japanese, energy crises, and exchange rate instability. By the 1980s there were widespread worries about Eurosclerosis: the combination of high unemployment, low growth in productivity, and economic stagnation that seemed to plague much of Europe.

But since the 1990s much has changed. The near-completion of the single market has helped boost productivity and wealth, European corporations have become bigger and more competitive, trade and foreign investment have grown, and inflation has stabilized. The news has not all been good, to be sure, with slow economic growth, the impact of demographic change on supporting an aging population, and the debt crisis, among other things, all of great concern. Recognizing that more sustained action was needed, the EU in 2000 adopted the Lisbon Strategy with the ambitious goal of modernizing the European economy so as to make it "the most competitive and the most dynamic knowledge-based economy in the world" within ten years. It proved a disappointment, was rechristened the "Europe 2020" strategy, and moved the deadline for Lisbon's changes to 2020 with the goals of increased innovation, sustainable growth, and job creation.

THE SINGLE MARKET AND EUROPE 2020

Whatever has been said and done regarding the many different facets of European integration, the fundamental goal of the Treaty of Rome—and of much that was later done in its name—was the completion of a single European market in which there would be free movement of people, money, and goods and services. Early progress was uneven, leading eventually to the idea of "relaunching" Europe, which was to be the foundation of the Single European Act. Its core objective was to finally remove the remaining barriers to the single market, which took three main forms:

- *Physical barriers.* Internal customs and border checks persisted because national governments wanted to control the movement of people (especially illegal immigrants), collect taxes and excises on traded goods, and enforce different health standards. These barriers not only reminded Europeans of their differences, but were also a significant economic constraint. The checks were removed in stages during the late 1980s and early 1990s, member states agreeing at the same time to work toward police cooperation (to which end they created Europol in 1999) and toward common measures on visas, immigration, extradition, and political asylum.
- *Fiscal barriers.* Indirect taxation caused distortions of competition and artificial price differences among the member states and thus was a barrier to the single market. A particular problem was posed by different rates of value-added tax (VAT, a consumption tax assessed on the value that is added to goods and services) and of excise duties on items such as tobacco and alcohol. Agreement was reached first on a minimum rate of 15 percent VAT, then on minimum rates for excise duties, and then on an EU wide VAT system under which tax is collected only in the country of origin.
- *Technical barriers.* There was a persistence of different technical regulations and standards, most based on concerns about safety, health, and environmental and consumer protection. The Community had tried to develop EC-wide standards, but this was a time-consuming task that did little to discourage the common im-

age of interfering Eurocrats. Three breakthroughs helped simplify the process: the 1979 *Cassis de Dijon* decision (see chapter 8, Box 8.2) confirmed the principle of mutual recognition, a 1983 law required member states to tell the Commission and other member states if they planned new domestic technical regulations, and the Cockfield White Paper included a new approach to technical regulation. This meant that instead of having the Commission work out agreements on every rule and regulation, the Council of Ministers would agree on laws that had general objectives, and detailed specifications could then be drawn up by private standards institutes.

Although there was much progress along the way during this time, there was also less progress than champions of the single market would have liked, and there were calls in the late 1990s—led by British prime minister Tony Blair and Spanish prime minister José María Aznar—for a new focus on modernizing the European economy. As a result, the European Council meeting in Lisbon in March 2000 set the goal of making the changes needed to finally complete the single market and bring the EU up to the levels of competitiveness and dynamism that are features of the U.S. economy. The Lisbon Strategy called on EU governments to make a wide range of changes, including integration and liberalization of the telecommunications market, liberalization of the natural gas and electricity markets, rationalized road tax and air traffic control systems, lowering unemployment, movement toward harmonization of EU corporate tax, and more progress toward making the EU a digital, knowledge-based economy.[1] However, it was already clear by 2004 that the Lisbon Strategy was not working because too few EU governments had been prepared to make the necessary reforms. Consequently, the strategy was reformulated as Europe 2020 with a new emphasis on innovation, education, sustainable growth, a low-carbon economy, and job creation, all to be completed by 2020.

With many, although not all, of the obstacles removed, the single market has made accelerated progress, and the effects on the lives of Europeans have been many, varied, and often substantial. The EU is still not a full-fledged single market like the United States, where there is unlimited free movement, but the restrictions of even a generation ago are mostly gone, and the member states of the EU are now better understood as one large multinational marketplace rather than as a cluster of individual national marketplaces. The effects are illustrated by progress in five areas of policy: rights of residence, the development of European transport and energy networks, corporate mergers and acquisitions, competition policy, and justice and home affairs.

Rights of residence. All citizens or legal residents of an EU member state now have the right to enter and live in any other EU member state, although restrictions can be imposed for security or public health reasons. (Temporary restrictions placed on the movement of Eastern Europeans into Western Europe following enlargement in 2004–07—symbolized by the image of a "Polish plumber" as cheap labor undercutting native British and French workers—have now expired.) Indeed, within the Schengen area (see Box 12.1) there are almost no restrictions and no identification checks at internal borders; border posts have been removed, and the only indication that a road traveler is moving from one country to another is a sign announcing that they are entering a different country.

Nationals of one member state are entitled to health care in all other member states if needed, and can buy almost any goods or services for personal use and take them home. They have the right to work, study, settle, or retire in any other member state, and to be enrolled at an educational institution, subject only to the proviso that they have sufficient resources to sustain themselves. Migrants can take all their personal possessions with them without paying duties or taxes, but road vehicles moved from one country to another must be registered and taxed in the new country; EU driver's licenses are valid throughout the EU. Migrant workers can also move all their financial assets with them and receive the same social security and health-care benefits as local workers, as long as they make contributions. Once they retire, they are allowed to stay in the country in which they were working, with the same access to retirement benefits as local nationals. Meanwhile, they can vote or run for office in local elections (without losing the right to vote in equivalent elections at home) and can also vote or run in European Parliament elections (but in one country at a time).

Transport and energy networks. Markets are only as close as the ties that bind them, and one of the priorities of economic policy in the EU has been to build a system of trans-European networks (TENs) aimed at integrating the transport, energy supply, and telecommunications systems of the member states, thereby pulling the EU together and promoting mobility. The TENs policy was given a legal base with Maastricht, and since then a list of priority projects has been developed and work is underway on many of them.

For example, the rail industry has been revitalized as a cost-efficient and environmentally friendly alternative to road and air transport. A Europe-wide

Box 12.1 The Schengen Agreement

Frustrated by the lack of progress on opening borders, representatives from France, Germany, and the Benelux states met in June 1985 near the Luxembourg town of Schengen and signed an agreement allowing for free movement of people among signatory states. A second agreement was signed in 1990, and borders were opened in 1995. Twenty-six European countries are now fully participating members of the agreement: all EU member states except Britain, Bulgaria, Cyprus, Ireland, and Romania, along with Iceland, Liechtenstein, Norway, and Switzerland. Britain has claimed concerns about the difficulty that an island state faces in controlling illegal immigration (although skeptics feel it is more a question of Britain's traditional lukewarm attitude to integration), while Ireland has stayed out mainly because it has a passport union with Britain. Travel between Britain and Ireland and the rest of "Schengenland" is virtually unrestricted, but is subject to stronger controls if needed, and new receiving areas have been created to scrutinize travelers between Schengen and non-Schengen states.

The agreement has resulted not only in passport-free travel for EU citizens (and the requirement of only a single visa for noncitizens), but also the end of all but security checks at airports for flights among signatory states, the drawing up of rules for asylum seekers, cross-border rights of surveillance and hot pursuit for police forces, the strengthening of legal cooperation, and the creation of the Schengen Information System, which provides police and customs officials with a database of undesirables whose entry into Schengenland they want to control. Schengen countries are allowed to reimpose border patrols for short periods in cases of particular need, as Portugal did during the 2004 European Football Championship and as France did in the wake of the terrorist bombings of July 2005 in London.

Border controls among the eastern states, and between them and the western states, will not come down quite so easily. Travel requires a passport or identity card, and internal border controls will be removed only after all parties are assured that free movement of undesirables has been brought under control. Given concerns about the western states acting as an economic magnet for workers from the east, and about the security of external borders in the east, this is likely to take some time.

rail network is under development, including thirty "priority axes" such as the Paris-Brussels-Cologne-Amsterdam-London high-speed rail system, high-speed rail links through southwest and eastern Europe, and a Athens-Sofia-Budapest-Vienna-Prague-Nuremburg rail link. The EU has also invested considerable capital in developing a twenty-two-thousand-mile high-speed train network connecting Europe's major cities; the 1994 opening of the Eurotunnel under the channel between Britain and France and the 1998 opening of a bridge between Sjaelland and Fyn in Denmark were important steps.

Investments have been made in developing a European highway system, aimed at connecting the existing motorways of Britain, autobahns of Austria and Germany, autoroutes of Belgium and France, autopistas of Spain, and autostrada of Italy, and at filling in critical gaps, mainly in the poorer peripheral regions of the EU. In Eastern Europe, ten "corridors" connecting major cities and ports have been identified as priorities for the development and improvement of transport networks, with the prospect of eventually being combined with the Western European TENs.

Meanwhile, Europeans are also hoping to develop independence from American technology by working on a European Navigation Satellite System known as Galileo, designed to be an alternative to the U.S.-operated Global Positioning System (GPS). GPS was developed by the U.S. Department of Defense mainly for military purposes, and because the U.S. reserves the right to limit its signal strength, or to close public GPS access completely during times of conflict, there are clear incentives for the EU to develop an alternative. Several non-EU countries have joined the project, including China and India, and there has been talk of several others joining in the future, including Australia, Brazil, Canada, Japan, Mexico, and Russia. Developmental problems have delayed the launch of Galileo, with the launch of the thirty necessary satellites now projected to be completed in 2019.

Corporate mergers and acquisitions. Before World War II many of the world's biggest corporations were European. They were more global in scope than their American counterparts, benefiting from the preferential markets created by colonialism. But after World War II European companies steadily lost markets at home and abroad to competition, first from the United States and then from Japan. U.S. and Japanese corporations were more dynamic, invested more in research and development, and had access to large home markets. European business, meanwhile, was handicapped in its attempts to move across borders into neighboring states, facing merger and capital gains taxes, double taxation on company profits, different legal systems, differences in regulations and standards, and limits on the movement of goods and services. The growth of the European single market changed the rules and increased the opportunities for Europe-wide corporate operations and larger-scale production, but progress was slow, and most mergers and joint ventures in Western Europe were still either national (among companies in the same country) or international (among European and foreign corporations), and there was relatively little intra-Community activity (among companies in different EEC states).

With the revival of competitiveness being pushed to the top of the EC agenda, the Commission became involved in trying to overcome market fragmentation and the emphasis placed by national governments on promoting the interests of often state-owned "national champions." Barriers to cross-border mergers were removed by changes in company laws and regulations, and the single market increased the pressures and the opportunities for the development of pan-European corporations, as well as the number of consumers they could reach. Community programs aimed at encouraging research in information technology, advanced communications, and industrial technologies also helped. As a result, there has been an unprecedented surge of takeovers and mergers involving European companies since the mid-1980s, notably in the chemicals, pharmaceuticals, and electronics industries. In 1984–85 there were 208 mergers and acquisitions in the EC; in 1989–90 there were 622, and—for the first time—the number of intra-EC mergers overtook the number of national mergers.[2] In 1996 the value of cross-border mergers reached a record of more than $250 billion, and the European mergers and acquisitions market is now bigger than that of the United States. Notable recent examples include:

- The aggressive program of takeovers pursued by the British cell phone company Vodaphone, which merged in 1999 with the U.S. company AirTouch, then with Bell Atlantic, and in 2000 took over the much bigger German company Mannesmann.
- The 2000 mergers of British company Shire Pharmaceuticals and the Canadian company BioChem Pharma, and of British companies Glaxo Wellcome and SmithKline Beecham (itself the result of the 1989 merger of SmithKline of the United States and Britain's Beecham Group) to become GlaxoSmithKline.
- Two large mergers in 2006 in the energy market (E.ON of Germany bought Endesa of Spain, and Suez of France bought Gaz de France), and the hostile takeover that year by Spain's Ferrovial of

Britain's BAA. The latter runs five major British airports and at one time had management contracts at four U.S. airports: Baltimore-Washington, Boston Logan, Pittsburgh, and Indianapolis.

- The growth of the Bank of Scotland, which by 2005 had become the sixth biggest bank in the world.
- The rise of ING, a Dutch company, to become the biggest commercial and savings bank in the world by 2009.

Competition policy. While corporate mergers and acquisitions can further the functioning of the single market, they can also lead to market distortions. Although there can never be such a thing as a perfectly free and open market, distortions caused from monopolies and cartels (or even government subsidies to business) can give unfair advantages to one competitor in the market over another. Consequently, the EU—and the institution charged specifically with overseeing this, the Commission—has long been engaged in identifying and addressing such market distortions through a competition policy aimed at promoting liberalization of the market by preventing abuses (such as price fixing), monitoring state subsidies to corporations, and guarding against abuses of dominant position by bigger companies.[3] An EU regulation adopted in 1989 allows the European Commission to scrutinize all large mergers. So, for example, it changed the terms of a 2006 merger between French oil companies TotalFina and Elf Aquitaine and blocked the proposed takeover in 2007 by low-cost airline Ryanair of the Irish national airline Aer Lingus. The Commission can even try to block mergers involving companies based outside the EU, as it did unsuccessfully in the case of Boeing and McDonnell Douglas in 1997, and successfully in the case of the planned takeover of Honeywell by General Electric in 2001. The latter would have been the biggest merger in history and was approved by the U.S. government, but the Commission argued that it would have created dominant positions in the markets for the supply of avionics and non-avionics equipment, particularly jet engines. There was an angry response from U.S. politicians and media, but the takeover was shelved nonetheless.[4]

JUSTICE AND HOME AFFAIRS

As the EU has moved from being overwhelmingly an association promoting narrow economic integration before the 1980s to one in which political and social integration have now assumed more prominent positions, cooperation in the area of law enforcement—including the monitoring and control of terrorism, drugs, and organized crime—has also grown. Although by the mid-1970s member states had begun to exchange information and undertake limited cooperation, there was no reference to justice and home affairs (JHA) in the Treaty of Rome and hence no institutionalization of JHA concerns. As the idea of completion of the single market was pushed forward by SEA and by Maastricht, it was clear that a more focused, structured, and integrated approach to JHA by the EU was also needed.

Under Maastricht, police and judicial cooperation was made one of the three "pillars" of the EU (the Common Foreign and Security Policy and the European Economic Community being the other two), and a new European Police Office (Europol) was established to help coordinate cross-border police actions. However, since the kinds of security issues addressed by JHA are central to many issues deeply entrenched in national political and judicial systems, all of which relate strongly to national sovereignty,[5] differences of opinion quickly emerged as to how JHA issues were to be tackled. Consequently, as part of the pillar system of Maastricht, JHA issues were reserved for intergovernmentalism (that is, unanimity), hindering a truly integrated European approach.

The Treaty of Amsterdam—reflecting general dissatisfaction with intergovernmentalism—gave JHA added importance by creating an "area of freedom, security and justice" within the EU. As a result of Amsterdam, Schengen countries were brought into the common *acquis* (excepting Britain, Denmark, and Ireland, which received opt-outs), and asylum, immigration, and judicial cooperation were made EU responsibilities. JHA moved closer to the top of the EU agenda following the 2001 terrorist attacks in the United States.[6] In 2004 the European Council adopted the Hague Programme, which aimed to create a comprehensive asylum policy, the provision of crime "threat assessments," and a strengthening of information gathering and sharing within the Schengen area.

The Treaty of Lisbon underscored the evolution of JHA by abolishing the pillar system and moving JHA into the mainstream of EU decision making (rather than having it left as a stand-alone, intergovernmental area, as continues to be the case for the Common Foreign and Security Policy). Special opt-outs for the non-Schengen states (Denmark, Ireland, and the UK) continue, of course; many issues will continue to be decided by unanimity; and community action is complicated by the involvement of non-EU members Iceland, Liechtenstein, Norway, and Switzerland in Schengenland. However, JHA has evolved from a rather loose cooperative arrangement to one more closely resembling other policy fields within the EU, and there are several areas within JHA where the normal procedure of QMV will now operate.

THE EURO

Even if most Americans do not know much about the European Union, none of those who have traveled to the EU can ignore one of the most visible effects: the euro. And the recent crisis in the eurozone—which has threatened even to undermine the shaky economic recovery in the United States—has drawn even more American attention to the story of European integration. A total of seventeen EU member states now use the single currency, which was created in 1999 and finally replaced national currencies in the eurozone in early 2002. Its introduction was a momentous event: never before in history had a group of sovereign nations voluntarily given up their national currencies and adopted a common currency. Although it was primarily an economic achievement, in that it represented the final realization of the goal of European economic and monetary union, it was also a political achievement, in that its creation involved the surrender of significant national sovereignty by eurozone governments. It also had global economic implications, offering Europe a world-class currency that would sit alongside the U.S. dollar and the Japanese yen and that posed the first serious threat to the global leadership of the U.S. dollar since the latter had taken over from the British pound in the 1950s (see Box 12.2).

Stable exchange rates had been considered by European leaders to be central to the building of a single market, but the postwar system of fixed exchange rates took care of most of their concerns. It was only when this system came to an end with the U.S. decision in 1971 to break the link between gold and the U.S. dollar that European leaders paid more attention to the idea of monetary union. The earliest steps were derailed by international currency turbulence in the wake of the energy crises of the 1970s (see chapter 4). The European Monetary System (EMS) followed in 1979 with the goals of creating a zone of exchange rate stability and keeping inflation under control. Although several member states had difficulty meeting its terms, the EMS contributed to exchange rate stability and to the longest period of sustained economic expansion since World War II.

New attention was focused on monetary union by the Delors Plan in 1989, the basic principles of which were affirmed by Maastricht. It was agreed that EU member states wanting to take part in the single currency had to meet four "convergence criteria":

- A national budget deficit of 3 percent or less of GDP (the average deficit in the member states fell from 6.1 percent of GDP in 1993 to 2.4 percent in 1997).
- A public debt of less than 60 percent of GDP.
- A consumer inflation rate within 1.5 percent of the average in the three countries with the lowest rates.
- A long-term interest rate within 2 percent of the average in the three countries with the lowest rates.

EU leaders decided in 1995 to call the new currency the "euro" and to introduce it in three stages. The first of those came in May 1998 when a decision was made on which countries were ready. All member states had met the budget deficit goal, but Greece had not been able to reduce its interest rates sufficiently; Germany and Ireland had not met the inflation reduction target; and only seven member states had met the debt target.[7] However, Maastricht allowed countries to qualify if their debt to GDP ratio was "sufficiently diminishing and approaching the reference value at a satisfactory pace," so all but Britain, Denmark, Greece, and Sweden were given the green light. This raised questions in the minds of Euroskeptics about the seriousness with which the convergence criteria were being treated (a criticism which has now gained even more traction in the light of the Greek debt crisis).

The second stage began on January 1, 1999, when (1) the euro became available as an electronic currency, (2) participating countries fixed the exchange rates of their national currencies against one another and against the euro, and (3) the new European Central Bank began overseeing the single monetary policy. All the Bank's dealings with commercial banks and all its foreign exchange activities were transacted in euros, which was quoted against the yen and the U.S. dollar. But more doubts were created by opinion polls that found public opinion in many EU countries hostile to the euro; a majority of Swedes were opposed, opposition in Britain ran three to one, and—in a national referendum in September 2000—Danes voted against adopting the euro. Even the Germans were doubtful; they saw little advantage in monetary union and signed on only because they saw a need to reaffirm their commitment to Europe in the wake of German reunification.[8]

The final stage began in January 2002 when euro coins and notes began to replace national currencies in all the EU–15 member states except Britain, Denmark, and Sweden. Europeans were initially given up to six months

Map 12.1 The Eurozone

to make the transition, but it went so smoothly that it was over by the end of February. In January 2007, Slovenia became the first new country to adopt the euro, followed by Cyprus and Malta in January 2008, Slovakia in 2009, Estonia in 2011, and Latvia poised to adopt the euro in 2014.

The most immediate advantage of the new single currency to consumers, of course, was that they no longer needed to exchange currencies when moving from one eurozone country to another or pay fees charged by banks and *bureaux de change*. There is today also greater transparency in that consumers can immediately see how much goods and services cost without having to convert prices back into their home currency. One of the effects has been to allow them to compare the costs of living in different countries more easily. The euro also helps businesses, whose transactions are now easier to undertake and who do not have to be concerned about fluctuations in exchange rates.

For some critics of the euro, the biggest concern with its introduction was loss of sovereignty. Where national governments were once able to make largely independent decisions on interest rates, for example, those decisions are now made on behalf of the seventeen eurozone countries by the European Central Bank. Different countries have different economic cycles, economic structures, and levels of wealth and poverty, and having separate currencies allowed them to devalue, borrow, and adjust interest rates in response to changed economic circumstances. Now they must, in theory at least, try and move in concert with all their neighbors. The costs of this became almost immediately evident with the effects of the stability and growth pact (SGP) signed in 1997 among the eurozone states at the insistence of Germany and have become even more apparent as the European debt crisis has deepened.[9]

For other critics (as discussed in chapter 4), the central problem of the euro has always been less about a loss of sovereignty per se than the lack of the EU's power to effectively manage fiscal policy. Thus while eurozone members all use the same currency and share the same monetary policy, they have continued to set their own fiscal policies, leading in the worst cases (Greece) to overspending and a subsequent debt trap whereby states cannot manage their deficits and loss of competitiveness by devaluing their currencies. Meanwhile the SGP was criticized on the one hand as too lenient (allowing some fudging of the rules of the SGP) and on the other as too inflexible in that it made no distinctions among countries with different economic bases. Indeed, Commission president Romano Prodi was even moved in October 2002 to abandon the usual language of diplomacy and to describe attempts to enforce the pact without taking heed of changing circumstances as "stupid."

By the second half of 2003 the European Central Bank was warning that most eurozone countries were in danger of failing to meet the target on budget deficits, thereby damaging prospects for economic growth. In November

2003 the two biggest eurozone economies—France and Germany—both went over the limits and prevented other EU finance ministers from imposing large fines on the two countries. Its ministers, along with their British counterpart, argued that the rules of the pact were too rigid and needed to be applied more flexibly if they were to work. By December the pact had all but collapsed, and in 2005 the rules were relaxed in order to make it more achievable and enforceable. However, the world economic crisis that broke in 2007 made budget deficit limits much more difficult for members to achieve, and Greece soon became emblematic of the challenges of using the SGP to coordinate fiscal policy. Then came the eurozone crisis (see Box 12.2).

Box 12.2 The Euro Crisis

The U.S. economic crisis originating in massive problems in the sub-prime mortgage industry in the United States triggered a global financial crisis in late 2007. Although some European countries, such as Germany, appeared to have initially weathered the crisis, other countries (such as Ireland) were hit hard and by 2010 all of the EU states were feeling the full effects, none more so than Greece. Greece's main industries were especially vulnerable to a severe economic downturn, and as the government attempted to help shore up the economy its debt rose dramatically. Moreover, as the Greek government sought financial help from the EU it was revealed that Greece had for years under-reported its debt load, fudging its balance sheet even as it entered the eurozone. In the spring of 2010 the country's sovereign rating was downgraded to junk status and the country began a slide toward financial insolvency.

The EU's initial response to the growing crisis was a series of half-measures. Germany took a hard line, arguing that any financial assistance to Greece from the EU would be contingent upon the Greek government slashing its budget, cutting government spending dramatically, and agreeing to strict oversight from the EU as it reformed bloated and inefficient financial policies.[10] Not unexpectedly, this policy of forced austerity proved deeply unpopular in Greece. The government fell, political turmoil ensued, and only the last in a series of elections in the late spring of 2012 staved off the prospect of a radical-left led Greek government abrogating its financial assistance agreement with the EU and leaving the eurozone (the so-called "Grexit").

Yet Greece soon showed that this was only the tip of the iceberg, with Spain being the next country to experience severe crisis. Unlike Greece, Spain is one of the major economic players in the EU's economy; it had seen dramatic economic growth in recent years and had a debt load at the time the economic crisis hit at about the same level as Germany. But the economic crisis in Spain led to the bursting of a housing bubble—as in Ireland and the U.S. before it—that had ripple effects throughout the Spanish economy, threatening to engulf its banking industry. Unemployment soared to almost a quarter of the population (with over 50 percent of young Spaniards unemployed); Spanish government debt rose and its borrowing costs skyrocketed. Spain threatened to descend into a debt spiral: in debt but unable to borrow money on world markets, the government would be forced to undertake draconian cuts, which would further weaken the economy and further discourage international investors who would continue to raise Spain's borrowing costs.[11]

Measures taken by the EU in June of 2012 to address the sovereign debt crisis (see below) seemed to stem the tide in Spain: while unemployment remained high, Spain's borrowing costs stabilized. Even so, Spain's economy remained fragile, and vulnerable to other shocks in the eurozone, such as the markets' reaction to political turmoil in Italy, and the continued deterioration of the economy there. Thus whether these measures by the EU will prove to be decisive enough to address underlying economic and debt problems throughout the eurozone still remains an open question.

As discussed in chapter 4, although the global financial crisis affected all of the EU to one degree or another, it was the Greek crisis that precipitated a larger crisis in the eurozone, with Spain experiencing an explosion in its sovereign debt as investors began to doubt the economic viability of Spain, raising its borrowing costs to an untenable level. The EU's response, in an IGC in June 2012, agreed on a plan to recapitalize troubled banks directly through the EU (rather than lending money to the Spanish government to do this itself, as Germany had originally argued), as well as an EU regulator (through the ECB) who would oversee all banks within the member states as part of a future EU banking union. Although the rescue fund—the European Stability Mechanism (ESM)—encountered few problems, the EU regulator for banking quickly came up against several objections. For one, the EU regulation plan failed to make clear whether there would also be some kind of institution with the authority to restructure or liquidate failed banks. Simple oversight might prevent banks from failing, but it would do little to provide a solution for banks that had already failed. Second, in order to reassure investors the EU would need to provide some kind of deposit guarantees, much like the FDIC (Federal Deposit Insurance Corporation) does in the United States. Finally, in order for the proposed banking union to work, there would have to be agreement on what to do with the members of the EU who are not (or not yet) members of the eurozone.[12] In December 2012 the EU agreed on the basic framework of EU banking regulation: it established the ECB as the single supervisor responsible for bank oversight for around 150 banks throughout the EU, including at least three banks from each member state as well as any bank having assets greater than €30 billion ($39 billion). However, at the time this book went to press, the deposit guarantee plan was still under discussion and the exact resolution mechanism for liquidating troubled banks was yet to be worked out.

Beyond these initial measures, there was much discussion on future institutional and policy changes in the wake of the crisis. Despite German resistance to both EU-wide treasury bonds (the so-called Eurobonds) and, initially, to the form of the ESM and banking regulator, Angela Merkel has repeatedly called for "more Europe" or "political union" as a more encompassing solution. What this means in practice is unclear, but a meeting of EU foreign ministers in mid-September 2012 (under the name "The Future of Europe Group") gives some idea. In the economic area, the document issued by the foreign ministers calls for more EU oversight over national budgets and more powers for the EP in budget oversight at the national and EU level. It also suggested that the new eurozone bailout fund should become something of a "European Monetary Fund" much like the International Monetary Fund.[13] An elected president of the EU, a new EU finance minister, and a more powerful European foreign minister are other ideas making the rounds.[14] Obviously, the feasibility of all these proposed changes has not been studied in any detail. Just as obviously, and as with all such radical change in the EU, the prospect of any of these proposals becoming reality soon is unlikely.

Questions to Consider

1. NAFTA (discussed briefly in chapter 1) and the EU remain very different entities. What kinds of physical, fiscal, and technical barriers would need to be overcome to achieve something like a single market made up of the U.S., Canada, and Mexico?

2. Which areas/issues that could be covered within JHA might lend themselves more easily to intergovernmentalism and which ones to a more tightly integrated approach? Why?
3. Why do most East European countries remain enthusiastic about membership in the eurozone? What are some of the benefits it might bring them? The costs?

Further Reading

Larry Neal. *The Economics of Europe and the European Union* (Cambridge: Cambridge University Press, 2007).
> The best single-author survey of economic policy in the EU, including chapters on the economies of key member states.

Frank McDonald and Stephen Dearden, eds. *European Economic Integration*, 4th ed. (New York: Financial Times, 2005).
> A useful introduction to EU economic integration, with separate chapters on related policy areas from agriculture to the environment.

Michelle Cini and Lee McGowan. *Competition Policy in the European Union*, 2d ed. (Basingstoke, UK: Palgrave Macmillan, 2009).
> A useful survey of EU competition policy, with chapters on its development, the responsible policy actors, and key activities.

Michelle Chang. *Monetary Integration in the European Union* (Basingstoke, UK: Palgrave Macmillan, 2008).
> A textbook survey of the history behind the euro, monetary policy making in the EU, and the effects of the euro.

David Marsh. *The Euro: The Politics of the New Global Currency* (New Haven, CT: Yale University Press, 2010).
> One of the many new studies of the euro and its problems.

Notes

1. Anthony Wallace, "Completing the Single Market: The Lisbon Strategy," in Maria Green Cowles and Desmond Dinan, eds., *Developments in the European Union 2*, 2nd ed. (New York: Palgrave Macmillan, 2004).

2. European Commission figures quoted in Loukas Tsoukalis, *The New European Economy Revisited: The Politics and Economics of Integration*, 3rd ed. (Oxford: Oxford University Press, 1997), 110.

3. Michelle Cini and Lee McGowan, *Competition Policy in the European Union* (London: Macmillan Press, 1998); Stephen Wilks, "Competition Policy:

Towards an Economic Constitution," in Helen Wallace, Mark A. Pollack, and Alasdair R. Young, eds., *Policy-Making in the European Union*, 6th ed. (New York: Oxford University Press, 2010), 133–56.

4. See T. R. Reid, *The United States of Europe: The New Superpower and the End of American Supremacy* (New York: Penguin, 2004), 88–91, 94–105.

5. Sandra Lavenex, "Justice and Home Affairs: Communitarization with Hesitation," in Wallace, Pollack, and Young, eds., *Policy-Making in the European Union*, 457–80.

6. John D. Occhipinti, "Police and Judicial Cooperation," in Cowles and Dinan, eds., *Developments in the European Union 2.*

7. The Economist, "An Awfully Big Adventure," 11 April 1998.

8. Loukas Tsoukalis, "Monetary Policy and the Euro," in Jack Hayward and Anand Menon, eds., *Governing Europe* (Oxford: Oxford University Press, 2003), 334–35.

9. For a discussion about the implications of the stability and growth pact, see Madeleine O. Hosli, *The Euro: A Concise Introduction to European Monetary Integration* (Boulder: Lynne Rienner, 2005), 67–69.

10. On Germany's position on the euro crisis see for example Hans-Werner Sinn, "Why Berlin Is Balking on a Bailout," *New York Times*, 13 June 2012, A23; also see Nicholas Kulish, "Germany Is Open to Pooling Debt, with Conditions," *New York Times*, 5 June 2012, A1.

11. See *Economist*, "Going to Extra Time," 16 June, 2012, 26–28.

12. On this, see *Economist*, "Eurobankingfragilistic," 8 September 2012, 53.

13. Stephen Castle, "Foreign Ministers Call for Stronger Ties within Europe," *New York Times*, 19 September 2012, A6.

14. See *Economist*, "SimEurope," 22 September 2012, 64.

13

COHESION AND
OTHER INTERNAL POLICIES

CHAPTER OVERVIEW

- "Cohesion policy" is the name given to a number of EU policies and funds designed to provide more balanced economic and social development and thus offset some of the distortions and inequalities of the free market.
- More controversial among some member states, EU social policy aims toward providing one avenue to balanced development by setting standards for the improvement of working and living conditions, worker rights, and gender equality, among other things.
- EU education policies can also be seen as tools for reducing structural inequalities throughout the union by increasing the portability of educational opportunities and qualifications.

Balanced economic and social development—or "cohesion" in EU jargon—is difficult as long as there are large differences in levels of wealth, income, and opportunity. Most economists agree that the free market unavoidably contains or promotes social and economic inequalities that have so far defied attempts to remove them, and that equality is more an ideal than an achievable objective. Nonetheless, there is strong support among Europeans for public programs aimed at redistributing wealth and providing safety nets for those who find themselves at a disadvantage. With European integration, national programs have been joined by a series of Europe-wide efforts to address regional disparities. Included under this are educational programs aimed at maximizing the portability of educational qualifications, given that regional disparities in economic opportunity are in part a function of different levels of attainment and quality of education. Furthermore, all of these policies can be seen as an attempt not only to ameliorate disparities but to create greater economic opportunities for those in the poorer states and regions of the EU.

The Treaty of Rome noted the need for an improved standard of living in Europe, but economic expansion and profit were at the heart of the single market program, and less attention was paid to the quality of life. By the early 1970s, however, there was a new focus on encouraging an equitable distribution of the benefits of integration. The 1973 enlargement accelerated the process by widening the gap between the richest and poorest parts of the Community and drawing new attention to the importance of removing social differences. Issues such as employment, working conditions, social security, labor relations, education, training, housing, and health all moved up the agenda at this time. Today, cohesion policy is the second biggest item on the EU budget at almost 36 percent in 2012, and—even bigger if social policy and education (listed as separate budget items) are factored in.

At its core, cohesion policy focuses on the reduction of disparities in regional wealth and income through investments in decaying industrial areas and poorer rural areas, promoting employment and equal opportunities, and improving living and working conditions. The wealthier member states have long had their own domestic programs of regional economic development, aimed at encouraging new investment in poorer areas, at offsetting the effects of rural decline, and at trying to revive old industrial areas and the centers of large cities. Indeed, EU regional spending is not intended to replace national spending, which has continued regardless, with individual EU member states trying to deal with their own internal problems in different ways. Britain, for example, has designated special Development Areas and has given industry incentives to invest in those areas and to relocate factories. Italy created the Fund for the South to help provide infrastructure and encourage investment in the Mezzogiorno—everywhere south of Rome, including areas so riddled with corruption and so heavily controlled by organized crime that they are effectively independent subgovernments. All the major industrialized states have also tried to address the problem of urban decline in different ways, reflected in the renaissance of many once-troubled cities such as Manchester, Glasgow, Hamburg, Rotterdam, and Barcelona. But while these programs have addressed economic disparities *within* member states, there is a limit to how much they can deal with such disparities *among* member states. Hence the need for an EU-wide regional policy.

Meanwhile, EU social policy addresses problems relating to employment, including job creation, the free movement of labor, improved living and working conditions, and protecting the rights and benefits of workers. It was all but ignored until the 1970s, when a series of social action programs provided new focus, to be followed in 1989 by the controversial Social Charter, which pushed the EU further toward protecting the rights of workers. The linchpins of EU social policy today are the European Employment Strategy, aimed at addressing the worryingly high and curiously persistent unemployment rates in parts of the EU, and the Social Agenda, aimed at providing jobs, fighting poverty, reforming pensions and health care, and addressing inequality and discrimination.

BUILDING A LEVEL PLAYING FIELD

The European Union may be one of the wealthiest regions in the world, but—as in the United States—levels of wealth and opportunity are unequal. Not only are there significant economic and social disparities within most of its member states, but there are also disparities from one state to another. The scale of the problem has grown with eastern enlargement, which brought into the EU new member states suffering the effects of decades of underinvestment and state economic control. The differences are clearly revealed by using the comparative measure of per capita GDP adjusted for purchasing power parity (PPP, or the purchasing power of each member state currency). Expressing the average for the EU as 100, the differences in 2011 within the EU–27 ranged from 274 in Luxembourg to 45 in Bulgaria (see Figure 13.1). The contrasts are even greater when the 268 regions within the member states are considered: at one end of the scale stand inner London (343) and Luxembourg (280), and at the other stand Severozapaden, Bulgaria, (28), and Nord-Est Romania (25).[1]

Generally speaking, the wealthiest parts of the EU are in the north central area, particularly in and around the "golden triangle" between London, Dortmund, and Milan, while the poorest parts are the eastern, southern, and western peripheries, from the Baltic states down to Cyprus and Greece, and across southern Italy to Spain, Portugal, and up to western Ireland and western Scotland. The EU's marginal areas are relatively poor for different reasons: some are depressed agricultural areas with little industry and high unemployment; some are declining industrial areas with outdated plants; some are geographically isolated from the prosperity and opportunity offered by bigger markets; and most suffer relatively low levels of education and health care and have underdeveloped infrastructure, especially roads and utilities.

One of the core goals of cohesion policy has been to address the persistence of a multispeed Europe and to bring the poorer member states closer to the level of their wealthier partners. In addition to the obvious economic benefits of spreading the largesse, there is an important psychological element to this: investments made by the EU in the poorer parts of the member states can help the citizens of those states more clearly see some of the benefits of EU membership, as well as capitalizing on the opportunities provided to wealthier states by building new markets.[2] Cohesion policy is built around three main financial instruments which go under the name "structural funds"

- The European Regional Development Fund (ERDF), which directs funds to the poorest parts of the EU, invests in support for underdeveloped areas and inner cities, financing infrastructure, job creation, and aid for small firms.
- The European Social Fund (ESF), designed to promote employment and worker mobility, combats long-term unemployment and helps workers adapt to technological changes.
- The Cohesion Fund was set up in 1992 under the terms of Maastricht to compensate poorer states (in practice, Greece, Ireland, Portugal, and Spain) for the costs of tightening environmental regulations and to provide financial assistance for transport projects. Cyprus, Malta, and the ten Eastern European members have been added to the list of eligible countries, while Spain is being phased out.

The EU also has four other funds that are more specifically focused on particular problems or market areas:

Figure 13.1 Differences in Economic Wealth

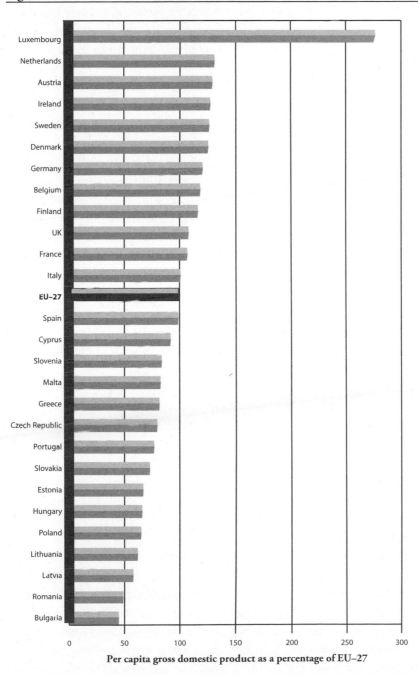

Per capita gross domestic product as a percentage of EU–27

Source: Eurostat, 2012. Figures are for 2011.

- The European Agricultural Fund for Rural Development, created in 2006, was set up to help modernize farming, diversify rural economies and develop rural areas, foster a higher level of food quality, and help to offset the costs of EU policies in the agricultural sector.
- The European Fisheries Fund (formerly the Financial Instrument for Fisheries Guidance) fosters sustainable development of coastal fishing areas and helps fishermen affected by EU policies designed to control overfishing.
- The Solidarity Fund, created in 2002 in response to serious floods in Austria, the Czech Republic, France, and Germany, supports the EU in its efforts to respond quickly to natural disasters by helping with the costs of restoring infrastructure, providing temporary shelter, funding rescue services, and protecting the EU's cultural heritage.
- The Globalization Adjustment Fund, created in 2007, is designed to provide support for workers in the competitive global job market and to help businesses affected by globalization to restructure and rebuild their competitiveness. The fund has been particularly targeted at those in the automobile, mobile phone, furniture, and textile and clothing industries.

Economies, of course, are complex entities that even economists do not fully understand, so the effects of these kinds of investments are not always certain, and reducing the differentials is as much a function of sensible economic policies, changes in the wider economic environment, and the attitudes of individuals toward the creation and accumulation of wealth as it is of the redistribution of wealth. And it is often impossible to be sure which actions have resulted in particular effects. The story of Ireland's remarkable economic transformation prior to the eurozone crisis was often touted as an example of the possibilities of EU cohesion policy, but EU investments were only part of the formula (see Box 13.1). The prospects of similar investments bringing change to Greece were undermined there by the failure of the government to reduce its stake in major utilities, by inefficient bureaucratic procedures that discouraged the creation of new business, and by job protection policies that handicapped women and younger workers, something that became even more apparent as Greece slid into its debt crisis.[3] If Eastern Europe is to benefit fully from EU regional policy, then

Box 13.1 Ireland:
From Expansion to Contraction

Nowhere have the possibilities (as well as the limitations) of cohesion policy been illustrated more clearly than in Ireland, which was once a member of the relatively poor and underdeveloped periphery of the EU but by 2008 had come to be ranked as the fifth wealthiest country (by per capita GDP) in the world by the OECD. It saw double-digit annual economic growth through much of the 1990s (peaking in 2000 at a remarkable 11.5 percent), unemployment fell to a record low, and taxpayers were given substantial cuts in income tax. Foreign investment boomed, much of it (chiefly from the United States) going into the high technology and financial sectors. The resulting job creation helped Ireland move into the league of the EU's richest countries, and—after decades during which the Irish left Ireland to seek jobs in Britain and the United States—many started to return to Ireland, which also attracted immigrants from other countries. Borrowing language from the growth of Southeast Asian "tiger" economies, the media described Ireland as the "Celtic tiger."

There was no simple explanation for Ireland's economic success from the mid-1990s to 2007, and partial credit must be given to the general upturn in economic growth that came to most capitalist economies during the 1990s, and to the economic policies of the Irish government. At the same time, membership in the EU was a boon for Ireland, not only because of the substantial flow of investments under the various structural funds, but also because of the opportunities provided by the single market. The Irish economy would no doubt have grown without the EU, but not at the same rate.

Unfortunately, the global financial crisis landed hard on Ireland, bringing the country into recession and raising unemployment. Easy credit meant that more people borrowed to buy property, leaving Irish banks over-exposed and leading to lay-offs and the imposition of austerity measures that led to strikes and industrial unrest. Interventions by the EU and the International Monetary Fund were unable to allay short-term fears, and emigration began to grow again.

a change in domestic political and economic attitudes is just as important as investment from the wealthier EU states.

The spending priorities of these funds—who gets what and how much—were once based on dividing the regions of the EU into three categories known as Objectives 1, 2, and 3. These now have different names, even if the goals are largely the same.

- The Convergence Objective (formerly Objective 1) targets regions with a per capita GDP of 75 percent or less of the EU average that are suffering from low levels of investment, higher than average unemployment rates, a lack of services for businesses and individuals, and poor basic infrastructure. Before eastern enlargement, they were mainly on the margins of the EU–15: Greece, southern Italy, Sardinia and Corsica, Spain, Portugal, Ireland, western Scotland, northern Finland, and eastern Germany. But except for a few sparsely populated areas in Scandinavia, the Convergence Objective has now moved east, where almost the entire area of the ten Eastern European countries qualifies, with the region accounting for about 80 percent of spending for all of the funds. In addition to these criteria, this fund also highlights innovation and adaptability to economic and social change.
- The Regional Competitiveness and Employment Objective (formerly Objective 2) focuses on areas suffering from high unemployment, job losses, and industrial decline—mainly in older industrial regions undergoing economic change, rural areas facing a decline in traditional activities, and coastal areas with falling income from fisheries. This objective targets economically and socially troubled regions whose GDP exceeds 75% of the EU average, and tries to strengthen the attractiveness of these areas to investment (and thus employment).
- The Territorial Cooperation Objective (formerly Objective 3) attempts to encourage cooperation between European regions and the finding of common solutions to common development issues. This objective accounts for only a fraction of the total structural funds spent by the EU.

Whether the structural funds make much of a difference in reducing regional disparities is an open question. An independent report commissioned by the Prodi Commission and published in 2003 concluded that there was little hard evidence that the structural funds had made a significant difference in closing regional disparities.[4] Although the Commission itself disagreed, the focus of regional policy was changed to the current structure of funds and objectives. On the other hand, some have argued that although there has clearly been some waste and duplication of EU resources, the structural funds have helped reduce the income gap between rich and poor states.[5]

SOCIAL POLICY

Cohesion in the EU has meant investments not only in agriculture, industry, and services but also in social matters such as the rights of workers and women, and improved working and living conditions. Social policies are a logical outcome of the long histories of welfare promotion in individual Western European states and an important part of the drive toward building a single market by ensuring equal opportunities and working conditions. At the same time, they have been controversial and have led to some of the most bruising ideological battles the EU has witnessed since its foundation. Generally speaking, social policies are favored by national labor unions, the Commission, and Parliament (at least when it was dominated by social democratic parties) and are opposed by business interests and conservative political parties, which argue that social policy threatens to make European companies less competitive in the global market.[6]

Even though worker mobility and the expansion of a skilled labor force were important parts of the idea of building a common market, the Treaty of Rome was ultimately based on the naive assumption that the benefits of the single market would improve life for all European workers. This was true to the extent that it helped increase wages and improved the quality of life for many farmers, but market forces failed to deal with gender and age discrimination, disparities in wage levels, different levels of unemployment, and safety and health in the workplace. Although the treaty made it the Community's business to address working conditions, equal pay for equal work, and social security for migrant workers, and to set the goal of creating the European Social Fund (ESF) to help promote worker mobility, social questions moved down the Community agenda as it concentrated on completing the single market and resolving battles over agricultural policy; the movement of workers was meanwhile heavily restricted.

The widened economic gap brought on by enlargement in 1973 pushed social issues back up the agenda, and the first in a series of four-year Social

Action Programs was launched in 1974, aimed at developing a plan of action to achieve full employment, improved living and working conditions, and gender equality. A combination of recession and ideological resistance from several European leaders ensured that the words failed to be translated into deeds, although there was increased spending under the ESF, aimed at helping to combat long-term unemployment and creating jobs and training schemes for young people. ESF spending since the mid-1980s has accounted for 7–9 percent of the annual EU budget: the current budget cycle (2007–2013) of the ESF (under the title "Investing in People") is €75—representing some 10 percent of the EU's budget—and is targeted at, among other things, increasing the adaptability of individuals and firms in the global marketplace and improving access to employment opportunities.[7]

The Single European Act underlined the importance of social policy by raising questions about the mobility of workers and bringing up concerns about "social dumping" (money, services, and businesses moving to those parts of the EU with the lowest wages and social security costs). The Commission began promoting social policy more actively, trying to focus the attention of national governments on the "social dimension" of the single market. However, economic recession ensured that the SEA initially lacked a social dimension, which encouraged Commission president Jacques Delors—a moderate socialist—to launch an attempt in 1988 to draw more attention to the social consequences of the single market.

The idea of a charter of basic social rights had been introduced by the Belgian presidency of the Council of Ministers in 1987, modeled on Belgium's new national charter. The concept was taken up by Delors in 1989 and was helped by the determination of the socialist government of François Mitterrand in France to promote social policy during its presidency of the EC. Germany was also in favor—even though it was led by the moderate conservative government of Helmut Kohl—as were states with socialist governments, such as Greece and Spain. By contrast, the conservative Margaret Thatcher was enthusiastically opposed; she considered it "quite inappropriate" for laws on working regulations and welfare benefits to be set at the Community level and saw the Charter of the Fundamental Social Rights of Workers (the Social Charter) as "a socialist charter—devised by socialists in the Commission and favored predominantly by socialist member states."[8] In the event, the Social Charter was adopted at the 1989 Strasbourg summit by eleven of the twelve member states—all but Britain.

The Social Charter brought together all of the social policy goals that had been mentioned throughout the life of the Community, including freedom of movement, improved living and working conditions, vocational training, gender equality, and protection for children, the elderly, and people with disabilities, but it was heavy on general goals and light on specifics. An action program listed forty-seven measures that needed to be taken, but the challenge of reaching unanimity in the Council of Ministers meant that little progress was made. Britain was regularly painted as the major opponent of the Social Charter, but there was heated debate involving several other member states over working hours, maternity leave, and employment benefits for part-time workers.

There were plans to incorporate the Social Charter into Maastricht, but the government of John Major in Britain again refused to go along, so a compromise was reached whereby the Charter was attached to Maastricht as a protocol and Britain was excluded from voting in the Council on social issues while the other member states formed their own ad hoc Social Community. This all changed in 1997, when the incoming government of Tony Blair committed Britain to the goals of the social protocol, and it was incorporated into the treaties by the Treaty of Amsterdam.

Despite all the rhetoric about social matters, the focus of most attention since 1991 has been on just one problem: the failure of the EU to ease unemployment, the persistence of which was once described as equivalent to the persistence of poverty in the United States.[8] The single market has been unable to generate enough jobs for Europeans, so that while unemployment in late 1998 hovered around 5 percent in the United States and 4 percent in Japan, it ranged between 4–6 percent in the Netherlands, Britain, and Sweden, 11–12 percent in Germany, France, and Italy, and a high of nearly 19 percent in Spain.[9] By 2007 the figures had improved slightly but were still not impressive: Poland and Belgium were in double digits, France and Germany were at 8–9 percent, and the eurozone was running at 7.1 percent, compared to a healthy 4.5 percent in the United States.

The reasons unemployment rates were so high even before the global economic and European debt crisis are debatable, but at least part of this is attributable to the role of unions and a less flexible labor market than in the United States. Another factor is the size of the black market, which is all but institutionalized in southern Italy, where it overlaps with the destructive power of organized crime. Also, while millions of new jobs were created in the EU prior to the global economic crisis, nearly half were temporary or part-time jobs, and many were in the service sector. Because men and women new to the job market were filling many of these jobs, their creation did little to help ease long-term unemployment. The EU has launched a host of retraining programs and is shifting resources to the poorer parts of the EU through various regional and social programs, but with mixed results. Robert Geyer and Beverly Springer argue that EU employment policy has had "high visibility but little focus" and that the search for solutions is hampered by a lack of support among member states, which have traditionally been responsible for employment policy. They also note that the EU faces the problem of trying to create jobs through increased competitiveness while preserving the traditional rights of employees.[10]

The Amsterdam treaty introduced a new employment chapter that—while leaving competence for employment policy in the hands of member states—called on them to work toward a coordinated strategy for employment. Amsterdam also maintained the commitment to a high level of employment, emphasized that employment was a matter of "common concern" to member states, contained the principle of "mainstreaming" employment policy (account should be taken of the employment impact of all EU policies), and set up a system under which information on the employment policies of the member states could be shared. It also obliged the EU and member states to work toward a coordinated strategy on employment; to promote a skilled, trained, and adaptable workforce; and to encourage labor markets that were responsive to economic change. In November 1997 the European Council met in Luxembourg with employment as the sole item on its agenda and launched the European Employment Strategy, agreeing to common guidelines on employment policy, including fresh starts for the young and the long-term unemployed and simplified rules for small and medium-sized enterprises. The long-term goal of the Strategy was to raise the overall EU employment rate to 70 percent by 2010 and the employment rate among women to 60 percent.

The global financial and eurozone crises put an end to these plans, at least over the short-term. Then came the Greek debt crisis, the bursting of the housing bubbles in Ireland and Spain, and the long-term effects of anemic economic growth in Italy, which combined to lead to a significant surge of unemployment in some EU member states (although initially not in others, such as Austria, Belgium, and Germany, where the rates have actually declined since 2007). Spain and Greece were by 2012 suffering the worst at around 25 percent and 22 percent unemployment respectively. Over the course of a sixteen-month period from the spring of 2011 to the fall of 2012, unemployment increased by some 2 million persons across the EU, with the unemployment rate rising a percentage point, to 11 percent, and female unemployment also rising (see Figure 13.2). Unemployment

Figure 13.2   Unemployment in the EU

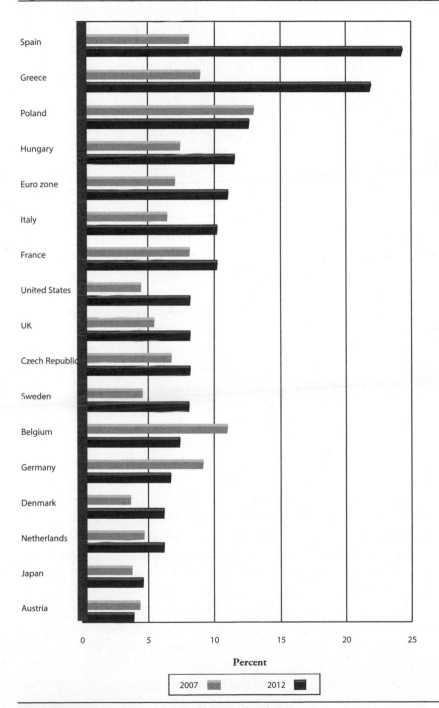

Percent

2007   2012

was even more pronounced in the eurozone than in the non-eurozone countries. Perhaps most dramatically, youth unemployment in the EU climbed to almost 23 percent, with the biggest surges in Greece and Spain, but also in countries less dramatically affected by the eurozone crisis, such as the U.K. The possible success of the EU's long-term unemployment strategy remains an open question; but in the short term, the solution seems to be fairly simple, if still bedeviling: economic growth, most especially in Greece and Spain.

EDUCATION AND LANGUAGES

It had been understood as early as the signing of the Treaty of Rome that an open labor market was an essential part of the creation of a true single market, and although every citizen of the Community was given the right to "move and reside freely" within the territory of the member states, this was subject "to limitations justified on grounds of public policy, public security or public health." The movement of workers was initially seen mainly in economic terms, so the emphasis was placed on removing the barriers for those EU citizens who were economically active. Migration was limited, at first because governments wanted to discourage skilled workers from leaving for other countries and subsequently because of the lack of opportunities in the target states.[11]

Today, as noted in chapter 12, there is virtually unlimited movement for all legal EU–15 citizens, and greater ease of movement than before for citizens of Cyprus, Malta, and the Eastern European member states. There is no question that Europeans have become more mobile in the last generation, and the numbers of nonnationals living in member states have multiplied. Precise figures are unavailable because of the growing openness of borders, but the total is certainly well into the millions. Although the flow of immigration was initially from the south to the north, and consisted largely of workers from Mediterranean states seeking employment and then bringing their families with them, immigration flows in recent years have become much more complex, and there has been an increase in the movement of professionals and managers.[12] In other words, there has been a tendency away from economically motivated migration toward voluntary migration by people wanting to move to a different environment for a variety of reasons.

In a labor market such as the United States, which has a standardized educational system in which qualifications are fully portable and a common language is almost universally used, there are few technical barriers to the free movement of people: if Americans want to move to a different part of the country in search of better jobs or a different lifestyle, or if they are transferred by their employer from one office to another, their educational qualifications are recognized, and most people speak the same language. But the same has not been true in the EU. Apart from the obvious problem of almost every state speaking a different language, the educational systems of almost every state are different, and deciding the equivalency of qualifications has been difficult.

As a result, member states have made concerted efforts—particularly since Maastricht—to encourage educational exchanges and to ease the portability of educational qualifications. At the core of these efforts is the Lifelong Learning Program (LLP), running from 2007 to 2013 and replacing an earlier program called Socrates. The LLP has four subprograms:

- Comenius is aimed at preschool through secondary education and supports school partnerships, the training of staff, and the building of networks. Recent projects have included intercultural education aimed at combating violence, racism, and xenophobia; the creation of a network to examine the meaning of European citizenship; and the promotion of environmental education.
- Erasmus is aimed at higher education and encourages student and faculty exchanges among colleges and universities and greater cooperation among institutions of higher education. As many as three million students will have taken advantage of Erasmus (launched in 1987) by 2012 and something of an "Erasmus generation" (see Box 13.2) has been created.
- Leonardo da Vinci is aimed at vocational education. (Grundtvig is aimed at the world of adult education; both have similar goals of promoting mobility and cooperation.)
- Grundtvig (named for a nineteenth-century Danish theologian) is an adult education/retraining program which promotes cross-border mobility and cooperation.

The direction of EU education policy has been shaped profoundly by the Lisbon Strategy (see chapter 4) and Europe 2020, (see chapter 12) which have provided encouragement for greater mobility and retraining, with their focus on EU competitiveness in a global marketplace. Meanwhile, the portability of qualifications has been a particular priority, encouraged

BOX 13.2 THE ERASMUS GENERATION

The idea that international education is critical to future success has gained wide currency among Europe's younger generation. Since the launch of Erasmus, the number of students studying and gaining degrees outside of their country of origin has increased dramatically. And as the Single European Act, the Maastricht treaty, and the Schengen agreement have enabled people to move freely across borders within the EU, the number of younger people who have stayed on to work in their new home or who have sought career opportunities throughout the EU has also increased. This generation—the cosmopolitan young who study and work outside their country of origin, are highly mobile, multilingual, make friends across borders, and sometimes marry citizens of other member states—has been dubbed the "Erasmus Generation." The name is, of course, that of a loose sociological category, not a fixed institution. Nevertheless, the Erasmus Generation does have its own organizations, such as the Erasmus Student Network,[13] (an interdisciplinary student association which works to improve the accessibility of student mobility in higher education and has chapters in thirty-five countries) and garagErasmus[14] (the first foundation focused on the Erasmus generation, attempting to promote professional mobility and contacts through commercial partnerships with public and private institutions).

Although it would be too much to suggest that this is a generation completely without borders, it is nevertheless true that younger, educated Europeans are almost equally at home in their adopted countries as they are in their home country. And they appear to share something of a common culture. As the journalist T. R. Reid has noted, the Erasmus generation tends to "read the same books, wear the same clothes, watch the same shows . . . and drink the same cocktails."[15] More importantly, the Erasmus Generation has a much stronger sense of a common European identity, premised on support for democracy, environmental concerns, and the use of more soft power than hard power (see chapter 15) in foreign policy. Eurobarometer polls have shown that 65 percent of people under twenty-five feel at least as much European as they do their own national identity (compared to only 45 percent of those older than fifty-five),[16] Could this portend the creation of a truly European identity? Despite the current rise of national tensions brought about by the eurozone crisis, if a common European identity takes root it could mean that national wrangling in the EU might be a lot less sharp and intense than it has been heretofore.

since 1999 by what is known as the Bologna Process, the goals of which are to establish a European higher education area within which university education is compatible, comparable, and transferable, and to make European higher education more attractive and internationally competitive. So instead of students being restricted to attending college or university in their home state, they are now able to look at options in different member states and transfer credits from one country to another in much the same way as American students can transfer credits across U.S. states.

Under Bologna, there is a European Credit Transfer and Accumulation System (ECTS) under which study at any university in the EU is translated into a common credit system, with one academic year of study equal to 60 ECTS credits. A bachelor's degree or its equivalent requires 180 to 240 ECTS credits, and a master's degree or equivalent requires 90 to 120 ECTS credits. Degrees can still retain their different names, but most EU member states have switched to a common bachelor's degree system: so, for example, Italy has converted its four- to six-year *laurea* into a three-year undergraduate *laurea triennale* and a two-year postgraduate *laurea magistrale*, and Austria's *Magister* and *Diplom* have been replaced with a *Bakkalaureus*. All EU member states have signed on to the process, along with Turkey, Russia, and almost every other European country. The United States is also affected, thanks to the transatlantic flow of students looking to transfer their educational achievements when they enroll in American universities.

Language training is another key facet of worker mobility: the inability to speak more than one language not only discourages migration but can also pose a handicap to multinational businesses by making it more difficult to build exports. There is also an important psychological effect: the inability to speak more than one language reminds Europeans of their differences and makes it more difficult to gain insight into the way other European societies think and work. Unlike the United States, which has a common language (but is increasingly having to plan for the growth in the number of Spanish-speaking immigrants), the EU is home to many different languages. In addition to twenty-four official languages (Bulgarian, Croatian, Czech, Danish, Dutch, English, Estonian, Finnish, French, Gaelic, German, Greek, Hungarian, Italian, Latvian, Lithuanian, Maltese, Polish, Portuguese, Romanian, Slovak, Slovenian, Spanish, and Swedish), there are many local languages (including Basque, Catalan, Occitan, Corsican, and Welsh), dozens of dialects, and other languages spoken by non-EU European countries.

Learning a second language is compulsory in lower secondary education in every EU member state, although requirements tail off in upper secondary education. English is by far the preferred language of study, being the preference of students in every EU member state for which there are data (except Britain and Ireland, of course). German is a popular second choice (eight countries), followed by French (six countries). In spite of the historic place of the Franco-German relationship at the center of Europe, only 13 percent of German adults claim to have a knowledge of French (compared to 56 percent who are familiar with English) and only 9 percent of French adults know German (compared to 44 percent who claim to know English).[17]

The issue of language cuts to the core of cultural pride and particularly upsets the French, who have done everything they can to stop the perfidious spread of "franglais"—the common use of English words in French, such as *le jumbo jet* (officially *le gros porteur*) and *le fast food* (officially *pret-à-manger*). Despite the number of EU employees who work as translators, the publication of every key EU document in all official languages, and the attempts by France to stave off the inroads made by English and Anglo-American culture, almost all EU business today is conducted in English or French. Germany has been eager to ensure that German is not forgotten, and one of the consequences of the 2004 enlargement was an increase in the number of Europeans who spoke German, thus altering the linguistic balance of power. But it is inevitable that English—powered by its use as the global language of commerce and entertainment—will continue its trend toward becoming the common language of Europe, presenting the French with, so to speak, a *fait accompli*.

Questions to Consider

1. What is the purpose of having a cohesion policy? Does it make economic or political sense or would the EU be better off using its resources for other purposes?
2. Why has EU social policy been controversial?
3. What might the effects of the Erasmus generation be on European integration and a European identity?

Further Reading

Willem Molle. *European Cohesion Policy* (London: Routledge, 2007).
    A weighty survey of the whole range of activities undertaken by the EU to promote cohesion.

Linda Hantrais. *Social Policy in the European Union*, 3rd ed. (Basingstoke, UK: Palgrave Macmillan, 2007).

> A look at social policy in the EU, its role in setting a European social policy agenda, and its impact on national welfare systems.

Pierre Pestieau. *The Welfare State in the European Union: Economic and Social Perspectives* (New York: Oxford University Press, 2006).

> A review of the functioning, the successes, and the failures of the welfare state in the European Union.

Jeremy Rifkin. *The European Dream: How Europe's Vision of the Future Is Quietly Eclipsing the American Dream* (New York: Tarcher, 2004).

> A controversial assessment by an American economist and writer of the contrasting European and American social models.

James W. Russell. *Double Standard: Social Policy in Europe and the United States*, 2nd ed. (Lanham, MD: Rowman and Littlefield, 2010).

> Compares the comprehensive Western European welfare model with the minimalist American model, assessing their responses to a variety of social problems.

Notes

1. Eurostat, 2011, http://epp.eurostat.ec.europa.eu/portal/page/portal /eurostat/home/.

2. For a detailed review of the structure and effects of cohesion policy, see European Commission, *Growing Regions, Growing Europe: Fourth Report on Economic and Social Cohesion* (Luxembourg: Office for Official Publications of the European Communities, 2007).

3. OECD, *Economic Survey of Greece 2005*, 7 July 2005, http://www.oecd .org/greece/economicsurveyofgreece2005.htm.

4. André Sapir et al., *An Agenda for a Growing Europe: Making the EU Economic System Deliver* (Oxford: Oxford University Press, 2004).

5. Robert A. Pastor, *Toward a North American Community* (Washington, D.C.: Institute for International Economics, 2001), 59–62.

6. Robert Geyer and Beverly Springer, "EU Social Policy after Maastricht: The Works Directive and the British Opt-Out," in Pierre-Henri Laurent and Marc Maresceau, eds., *The State of the European Union, vol. 4: Deepening and Widening* (Boulder: Lynne Rienner, 1998), 208.

7. European Commission, "The European Social Fund: Investing in People" (statistical factsheet), 2013, http://ec.europa.eu/employment_social/esf/docs

/facts_figures_en.pdf. For an analysis of the impact of the ESF, see Jacqueline Brine, *The European Social Fund and the EU: Flexibility, Growth, Stability* (London: Continuum, 2002).

8. Ralf Dahrendorf, *The Modern Social Conflict* (London: Weidenfeld and Nicholson, 1988), 149.

9. *The Economist*, multiple issues, late 1998.

10. Geyer and Springer, "EU Social Policy after Maastricht," 208.

11. Ian Barnes and Pamela M. Barnes, *The Enlarged European Union* (London: Longman, 1995), 108.

12. Anna Triandafyllidou and Ruby Gropas, *European Immigration: A Sourcebook* (Aldershot: Ashgate, 2007).

13. See the Erasmus Student Network website, www.esn.org, for more information.

14. See the garagErasmus website, http://www.garagerasmus.org/, for more information.

15. T. R. Reid, *The United States of Europe. The New Superpower and the End of American Supremacy* (Penguin Books: New York, 2004), 200.

16. European Commission, Public Opinion, http://ec.europa.eu/public _opinion/archives/eb/eb44/chap2_en.htm.

17. Lene Mejer, Sadiq Kwesi Boateng, and Paolo Turchetti, "Population and Social Conditions," Eurostat, Statistics in *Focus* 49/2010 (Brussels: European Commission, 2010), http://epp.eurostat.ec.europa.eu/cache/ITY _OFFPUB/KS-SF-10-049/EN/KS-SF-10-049-EN.PDF.

14

AGRICULTURAL AND
ENVIRONMENTAL POLICY

CHAPTER OVERVIEW

- The EU is one of the world's export powerhouses when it comes to agricultural products despite having only a small proportion of its population engaged in farming.
- The EU's approach to agriculture is defined by its Common Agricultural Policy, or CAP. For decades CAP was essentially a system of expensive, wasteful, protectionist, and controversial subsidies to farmers. Since the late 1990s, however, CAP has been fundamentally reformed, the results being significantly fewer EU funds spent on agriculture and more sustainable farming practices.
- EU environmental policy has not only been widely welcomed and supported by the public, but also assumed a much more prominent position within the EU. The EU has become a world leader in the abatement of waste, the regulation of chemicals, and the reduction of greenhouse gases.

Except for those dealing with developing countries, textbooks on national politics rarely make much mention of agriculture. While important, to be sure (because we all need nutrition), in most liberal democracies agriculture plays only a small part in economic activity and is rarely a lead story, if only because so few people are employed in farming. But the situation was for many years quite different in the EU. Agriculture used to be a prominent issue—perhaps the most important issue—in the European Union. Agriculture today employs just under 5 percent of the population in Western Europe and accounts for less than 3 percent of the GDP of the EU–15, and yet, traditionally, agricultural policy dominated the agenda of European integration.

There were two main reasons for this. First, it was expensive: for decades agriculture—in the form of the EU's Common Agricultural Policy (CAP)—topped the EU budget (it still swallowed about $53 billion/€43 billion in spending in 2012). Second, it was controversial: instead of being based on the principles of competition and free trade, it was protectionist, interventionist, and anti-market, insulating a critical economic sector from competitive forces. This drew criticism not only from the member states but also from the EU's major trading partners, such as the United States. The *Economist* was once moved to describe EU agricultural policy as "the single most idiotic system of economic mismanagement" ever devised by rich Western countries.[1] In the last decade, however, much has changed in the EU. Although CAP still soaks up a healthy chunk of the EU budget, enlargement, global trade agreements, and rising costs have led to a series of fundamental reforms in the way in which CAP operates.

In contrast to agriculture, EU initiatives on environmental policy have been both popular and relatively small in budget terms. Since the 1980s, environmental policy has assumed a more prominent position on the EU agenda and is a policy area that most Europeans agree is best addressed at the EU rather than the national level. The Treaty of Rome made ambiguous reference to promoting "harmonious development" and to raising living standards, but national governments in the 1950s were barely aware of the need to include environmental planning in their calculations. It was only in the 1970s, when Western public opinion became increasingly critical of what was widely seen as uncaring affluence, and when science rang alarm bells about the effects of consumer society on the environment, that wider attention began to be drawn to problems such as air and water pollution and to the damage done to the environment by chemical pesticides and herbicides.

Environmental issues have since climbed up the EU agenda. Attention to environmental quality was driven at first by concerns over the extent to which different standards distorted competition and complicated progress on the building of a common market. A series of environmental action programs provided more policy consistency and direction, and the Single European Act gave the environment legal status as a policy concern of the Community. Maastricht, Amsterdam, and Lisbon placed further emphasis on sustainable development and environmental protection as part of "harmonious and balanced" economic growth, and institutional changes gave public opinion (through the European Parliament) a stronger voice in designing environmental policy and introduced QMV on most environmental law and policy. Most recently, the urgency of effective environmental policies has been emphasized with new public concerns about climate change.

AGRICULTURAL POLICY

At the time the Treaties of Rome were being negotiated, agriculture sat high on the domestic policy agendas of Western European governments. Not only were the disruptions of war and the memories of postwar food shortages and rationing still fresh in their minds, but agriculture still accounted for about 12 percent of the GNP of the Six and for the employment of about 20 percent of the workforce.[2] Agriculture long had a special place on the EU policy agenda, for several reasons.

First, agriculture was a key element in the tradeoff between France and Germany when the EEC was first discussed.[3] France was concerned that the single market would benefit German industry while providing the French economy with relatively few advantages, a possibility that was reflected in the statistics: agriculture accounted for 12 percent of GNP in France (compared with 8 percent in West Germany) and employed nearly 25 percent of the workforce (compared with 15 percent in West Germany).[4] Concerns that the single market would not provide enough benefits to its farmers encouraged the French government to insist on a protectionist system.

Second, agricultural prices are more subject to fluctuation than are prices for most other goods, and since Europeans spend about one-quarter of their incomes on food, those fluctuations can have effects throughout the economy. Price increases can contribute to inflation, while price decreases can force farmers to go deeper into debt, perhaps leading to bankruptcies and unemployment. The problem of maintaining minimum incomes has been exacerbated by mechanization, which has led to fewer Europeans working in farming. Thus it was argued in the 1950s that subsidies would help encourage people to stay in the rural areas and discourage them from moving to towns and cities and perhaps adding to unemployment problems.

Third, self-sufficiency in food has been a primary factor in determining the direction of agricultural policy. World War II made Europeans aware of how much they depended on imported food and how prone those imports were to disruption in the event of war and other crises. Before the war, for example, Britain imported about 70 percent of its food, including wheat from the United States and Canada, beef from Argentina, and sugar-cane from the Caribbean. Thanks in part to a massive program of agricultural intensification launched after the war, Britain now imports less than one-third of its food. The pattern has been similar across the EU, which has experienced a large decline in agricultural imports from outside the EU and a growth in trade among the member states.

Fourth, the EU is an agricultural export powerhouse, with exports in 2011 worth €105 billion, placing it neck and neck with the U.S.[5] With so much wealth and profit at stake, it is no surprise that European farmers are anxious to continue to protect their opportunities.

Finally, although the farm vote in the EU is generally much smaller than it was during the mid-1960s, it is not insubstantial, and its balance initially changed with the 2004 enlargement. In the EU–15, the number of people employed in agriculture has fallen from about 25 percent of the population in 1950 to less than 5 percent today, but there are variations across countries: from 9–12 percent in Greece, Portugal, and Ireland, to 5–7 percent in Austria, Finland, and Spain, to less than 2 percent in Britain and Belgium. For many of the newer members of the EU, meanwhile, the percentage of the population engaged in agriculture is higher than in Western Europe but has fallen dramatically in recent years (with the exception of Romania, where it remains at a high level, about 29 percent).[6]

Farmers are an essential part of the rural fabric of most EU states and support a substantial number of people and services in small towns, villages, and rural areas. These populations add up to a sizable proportion of the vote (20 percent in France alone), which no political party can afford to ignore, especially because there is little organized resistance to the agricultural or rural lobbies at either the national or the EU level. Farmers in the richer EU states have also traditionally had strong unions working for them; in addition to national unions, more than 150 EU-wide agricultural organizations have been formed, many of which directly lobby the EU.

No discussion of EU agricultural policy would be complete without mentioning the special case of France. The farming population there fell between

1950 and 2000 from 31 percent of the total population to just 1.8 percent,[7] yet farmers have long had strong influence over the French government, which has lobbied on their behalf in the halls and corridors of Brussels. French farmers have been keen on European agricultural subsidies and have developed a reputation for taking to the streets when they feel that their interests are threatened. They have used tactics such as letting cattle loose in local government buildings, blocking main highways with tractors, dumping farm waste on Parisian avenues, blocking the Eurotunnel to Britain (as part of a protest in 2000 against rising fuel prices), and even ransacking a McDonald's restaurant in protest against U.S. duties on French cheeses (imposed after the EU banned imports of American hormone-treated beef).

The influence of the farm lobby in French domestic politics is explained by the fact that more than 20 percent of agricultural production in the EU–15 comes from France, which is the world's second largest exporter of food after the United States. The role of the farm lobby must also be seen in the context of the French national psyche. Even though three of every four French citizens live in towns or cities, the rural ideal still has a nostalgic hold on the sentiments of many, as does the idea that France is still a great power. Even urban voters are prepared to defend the rural ideal, to which any attempts to reform European agricultural policy are seen as a threat. Recent developments suggest that the influence of farmers on domestic politics—and on EU agricultural policy—is declining. Many small farmers are living in poverty, thousands leave the land every year to look for other work, and the farm lobby has been unable to stop reforms to EU agricultural policy.

The core of the EU's approach toward agriculture is the Common Agricultural Policy (CAP). Until just recently, CAP was essentially a system of agricultural subsidies, its goals as outlined in the Treaty of Rome being increased agricultural productivity, a "fair standard of living" for the farming community, stable markets, regular supplies, and "reasonable" prices for consumers. The details of how these goals would be achieved were discussed at a landmark conference convened in Stresa, Italy, in July 1958, which agreed on three principles: a single market in agricultural produce, "Community preference" (a polite term for protectionism aimed at giving EU produce priority over imported produce), and joint financing (the costs of CAP would be met by the Community rather than by individual member states). In practice, CAP guaranteed farmers throughout the EU the same minimum price for their produce, regardless of volume and prevailing levels of supply and demand, and all member states shared the financial burden for making this possible.

BOX 14.1 THE COMMON FISHERIES POLICY

In addition to CAP, the EU also has a Common Fisheries Policy (CFP), the main goal of which has been to help support and sustain the fishing industry in the member states by preventing overfishing, fostering sustainable fishing practices, and ensuring a sufficient quality and quantity for European consumers. Reforms over the years have promoted sustainability and attempted to minimize the impact of fishing on marine ecosystems by setting national quotas for catches and setting rules on the type of fishing equipment used.

Fisheries policy was never quite as controversial nor as headline-grabbing as agriculture, and the fishing industry employs only about 400,000 people.[8] However, the health of the fishing industry is a key part of life in coastal communities all around the EU; not only does the EU have the world's largest maritime territory, but coastal areas are home to 60 percent of its population, and they account for more than 40 percent of EU gross domestic product. Hence the issue has important economic implications for some of Europe's poorer regions.

Disputes over fishing grounds in European waters have occasionally led to bitter confrontations among Europe's neighbors. There were, for example, the infamous cod wars of the 1960s between Britain and Iceland over access to fisheries in the North Atlantic. Similarly, in 1984 French patrol boats fired on Spanish trawlers operating inside the Community's two-hundred-mile limit, and more than two dozen Spanish trawlers were intercepted off the coast of Ireland. Spain's fishing fleet was bigger than that of the entire EC fleet at the time, and fishing rights were a major issue in Spain's negotiations to join the EC. Spanish fishing boats became an issue in domestic British politics in 1994 when Euroskeptics in the governing Conservative Party used the Spanish presence in traditional British waters to complain about the effects of British membership in the EU.

Efforts to resolve competing claims to fishing grounds and develop an equitable management plan for Community fisheries resulted in agreement on the CFP in 1983, which has since been modified several times. Among other measures, the CFP has attempted to regulate fisheries by imposing national quotas (Total Allowable Catches, or TACs) on the take of Atlantic and North Sea fish and by regulating fishing areas and equipment. Problems with the enforcement of the CFP led to the creation in 2005 of the Fisheries Control Agency, set up to pool EU and national fisheries control systems and resources. However, there were always serious problems with CFP's quota system. For one thing, it has led to particularly distasteful and wasteful practices such as "discards," whereby (dead) fish are thrown back into the sea to avoid exceeding the quota, with some estimates suggesting that the discard in some EU fisheries approaches 70 percent of the total recorded catch![9] The CFP's shortcomings prompted Maritime and Fisheries Commissioner Maria Damanaki to recently declare CFP a "failure."[10] In response, the Commission has proposed a new way of calculating quotas as well as giving more decision making on fishing policies to member states.

This arrangement became increasingly expensive as technological developments helped European farmers produce more food from less land, exceeding consumer demand for commodities such as butter, cereals, beef, and sugar. The EU tried to discourage production by subsidizing exports and by paying farmers not to produce food. But the real problem with CAP was the artificially high levels at which prices were set.

Costs have been borne by the European Agricultural Guidance and Guarantee Fund (EAGGF), which was created in 1962 and until recently was the single biggest item in the EU budget; reforms to CAP brought the proportion of agricultural spending in the EC/EU budget down from about 75 percent in 1970 to just 33 percent in 2007 and today to about 32 percent. The bulk of funds are spent in the Guarantee Section, which protects markets and prices by buying and storing surplus produce and encouraging agricultural exports. Most of the money goes to producers of dairy products (the EU accounts for 60 percent of global dairy production) and to producers of cereals, oils and fats, beef, veal, and sugar. The Guidance Section is one of the elements that make up the EU's structural funds (see chapter 13), and it is used to improve agriculture by investing in new equipment and technology and helping those working in agriculture with pensions, illness benefits, and other support.

In terms of increasing productivity, stabilizing markets, securing supplies, and protecting European farmers from the fluctuations in market prices, CAP has been a success. Encouraged by guaranteed prices, and helped by intensification and the increased use of fertilizers (EU farmers use nearly 2.5 times as much fertilizer per acre of land as U.S. farmers), European agriculture has grown in leaps and bounds:

- European farmers have produced as much as possible from their land, with the result that production has gone up in virtually every area.
- The EU is self-sufficient in almost every product it can grow or produce in its climate (including wheat, barley, wine, meat, vegetables, and dairy products) and produces far more butter, cereals, beef, and sugar than it needs. The EU has become the world's largest exporter of sugar, eggs, poultry, and dairy products, accounting for nearly 12 percent of world food exports (compared with the U.S. share of 13 percent).
- Duplication has been reduced as member states have specialized in different products. Thus most of the permanent cropland is now found in the southern states, and most livestock is raised in the northern states.
- CAP has helped make farmers wealthier and their livelihoods more predictable and stable; farm incomes have grown at roughly the same rate as those in other economic sectors.

However, as noted above, CAP also created numerous problems: EU farmers produced much more than the market could bear, so that excess production once had to be stockpiled in warehouses across the Community (the so-called butter mountains and wine lakes); much of the excess was sold cheaply to developing countries, undercutting farmers there and distorting the international marketplace; stories of fraud and the abuse of CAP funds were rife, with rules encouraging farmers and suppliers to inflate production figures and even to claim subsidies for nonexistent stocks of food[11]; the income gap between rich and poor farmers in the EU was not reduced, and bigger, richer farms or agribusiness seemed to benefit the most; it upset consumers forced to pay inflated prices for food, despite production that was often surplus to needs (leading in turn to greater skepticism about European integration); and environmentalists were unhappy about the way CAP encouraged the increased use of chemical fertilizers and herbicides and encouraged farmers in wasteful practices.

Under the circumstances, the case for reform was clear, but most suggestions came up against the resistance of farming lobbies and the governments over which they had the most influence.[12] Early efforts at reforming CAP included the Mansholt Plan of 1968, named for the incumbent European agriculture commissioner. Its main suggestion was that small farmers be encouraged to leave the land and farms be amalgamated into bigger and more efficient units, notions that were both vehemently opposed by small farmers in France and Germany. Reform then slipped down the agenda as currency problems pushed economic and monetary issues to the fore, but Margaret Thatcher brought new pressures for change during the early 1980s, although she was concerned less with reforming CAP than with renegotiating British contributions to the Community budget. Her campaign to win a British rebate drew new attention to the problem of agricultural overproduction, and by the late 1980s there was a general agreement on the need for reform.

Pressure for reform was increased by the international criticism leveled at CAP as the Community negotiated tariff reductions under the Uruguay Round of GATT (which finally concluded in late 1993) and by the trade embargo imposed by the EC on Iraq during 1990–91 (which caused a drop in export prices). In 1991 Agriculture Commissioner Ray MacSharry warned of the rising volume of stored agricultural produce and proposed replacing guaranteed prices with a system of direct payments to farmers if prices fell below a certain level, and encouraging farmers to take land out of production (the "set aside" system, whereby farmers would be compensated for subsidy reductions only if they took 15 percent of their land out of production).[13] In spite of the opposition of many farmers and their unions, the proposals were approved in 1992. But the pressures for change continued, fueled in particular by the prospect of increased CAP spending in new Eastern European member states and continued pressure from major trading partners, particularly the United States.

Proposals were introduced in 1998 by Agriculture Commissioner Franz Fischler that involved a shift away from compensating farmers when prices fell below a certain level and toward subsidizing them for certain kinds of production. He proposed price cuts on beef, cereals, and milk, the end of set-aside schemes, more environmental management conditions to be attached to payments to farmers, and more investment in rural development generally. The core idea behind the Fischler reforms was "decoupling," or breaking the link between subsidies and production, with the goal of encouraging farmers to produce for the market rather than for EU subsidies. A new set of reforms agreed on in 2003 went further toward achieving the goals of the critics of CAP, promising to leave it, in the rhetoric of Fischler, "virtually unrecognizable from the days of old."[14]

Since 2005, the link between subsidies to farmers and the amount they produce has been broken, and farmers instead receive a single payment (although individual member states are allowed a limited reversion to the old system if there is a danger of significant job losses). Intervention prices on milk powder, butter, and other products have been reduced and direct payments for bigger farms cut. At the same time, member states such as Britain that want to move ahead with more radical reforms have been allowed to do so. Fischler argued that the reforms would make CAP less trade distorting and more market oriented, that they would offer more opportunities for farmers to diversify, and that they would give the EU a stronger hand in negotiations within the World Trade Organization. Critics were not so sure, arguing that it would be several years before the long-term effects became clear.

The implications of eastward enlargement were high on the agricultural agenda for several years, with concerns about the small size of farms and the generally low productivity of much of Eastern Europe. For example, nearly one in five Poles work in agriculture, but half of them produce only enough to feed their families and contribute nothing to the broader market.[15] For the twelve new members to have been given immediate and unlimited access to CAP funding would likely have bankrupted the EU. At the same time, special efforts needed to be made to ensure that Eastern European governments and their farmers did not feel that they were being treated as second-class citizens. The compromise ultimately agreed on—and not met with great enthusiasm—was to allow Eastern European farmers a small but growing proportion of agricultural payments. Coming on top of the €22 billion ($31 billion) spent in 2000–06 under a program called SAPARD (the Special Accession Program for Agriculture and Rural Development, designed to help applicant countries prepare for CAP), a package worth €5.1 billion ($7.2 billion) was made available for 2004–06, and agreement was reached that direct aid would be phased in over ten years, starting at 25 percent in 2004 and moving up in annual increments of 5 percent.

In 2008, the EU undertook a review of agricultural policy (the so-called health check) and made additional significant changes (such as abolishing milk quotas) as well as simplifying the new CAP system and decoupling CAP even more from compensation for production. This has had the result that direct payments to farmers have now fallen and guaranteed prices are now used only when prices for agricultural goods become unsustainable. Additionally, there has been a new focus on quality, rather than just quantity, in EU food production, as well as a strong emphasis on sustainability—things the EU consumer has come to value. The current funding for CAP will expire in 2013 and the EU has put forward a new set of reform proposals that emphasize further sustainable farming practices as well as the modernization of farms among the newer EU member states. In addition, the EU has proposed eliminating export subsidies, as well as a reduction in import duties for such goods, in the last (Doha) round of international trade talks.[16] The process of reforming EU agricultural policy is far from over.

ENVIRONMENTAL POLICY

After decades in which the EU has quietly built an impressive body of policies and laws on the environment that have drawn relatively little public or political attention, all has now changed with the explosion of international attention being paid to a single issue: climate change (see Box 14.2). Scientists outlined the mechanics of the problem in the 1980s and, together with environmental interest groups, tried to draw the attention of political leaders. But it was only in the early years of the twenty-first century that it became a headline issue.

Climate change has been described as the ultimate global environmental issue, and the ability of environmental problems to cross national frontiers is well-known, leading since the mid-1970s to a new emphasis on international responses to such problems as air pollution and the management of shared rivers. However, national governments have been reluctant to take unilateral action for fear of losing comparative economic advantage, and unwilling to give significant powers to international organizations, such as the United Nations Environment Program, and to commit to ambitious goals under the terms of international environmental treaties.

Regional integration offers a solution to both dilemmas. As states become more dependent on trade and foreign investment, and more inclined to reduce the barriers to trade, so they will be more inclined to eliminate any differences in environmental standards that may cause trade distortions, particularly if they know that neighbors are moving in the same direction. International negotiations and treaties are useful in this regard, but regional integration is a more compelling influence, because participating states know they are involved in a joint endeavor with shared costs and benefits.

There was no specific mention of the environment in the Treaty of Rome, although the ambiguous goal of "an accelerated raising of the standard of living" could be interpreted as opening the door to the environmental initiatives that came later. The Community agreed on several pieces of environmental law during the late 1950s and 1960s, dealing with issues such as the protection of workers from radiation and the management of dangerous chemicals. But these laws were prompted by the drive to build a single market and were incidental to the Community's overriding economic goals.[17] It was only during the 1970s that the EEC began to think about a broader environmental policy, encouraged by new public and political interest in the environment, arising in turn out of a combination of improved scientific understanding, several headline-making environmental disasters, new affluence among Western middle classes, and growing concern about quality-of-life issues.[18]

Changes in public and political opinion culminated in the landmark 1972 United Nations Conference on the Human Environment in Stockholm, which drew broader political and public attention to the problems of the environment for the first time, prompting the creation of national environmental agencies and a growth in the volume of national environmental law. In October 1972, just three months after Stockholm, the EEC heads of government meeting in Paris agreed to the need for an environmental policy, as a result of which the Commission adopted its first Environmental Action Program (EAP) in late 1973. Subsequent EAPs came into force in 1977, 1982, 1987, 1993, and 2002, the most recent (the seventh) running until 2020.

The first two EAPs were based on taking preventive action and guarding against allowing different national policies to become barriers to building a common market. The Court of Justice made an important contribution in 1980 when—in response to a refusal by Italy to meet the deadline set by a directive on the biodegradability of detergents, on the grounds that the environment was not part of the policy competence of the Community—it argued that competition could be "appreciably distorted" without harmonization of environmental regulations.[19] States with weaker pollution laws, for example, had less of a financial and regulatory burden than those with stronger laws and might attract corporations wanting to build new factories with a minimum of built-in environmental safeguards.

The third EAP marked a sea change, with a switch to a focus on environmental management as the basis of economic and social development. For the first time, environmental considerations were consciously factored into other policy areas—notably agriculture, industry, energy, and transport—and were no longer subordinate to the goal of building a common market.[20] But these changes took place without amendments to the Treaty of Rome, so Community environmental policy lacked a clear legal basis and was technically unauthorized by the member states.[21] Additional complications came with enlargement to Greece, Portugal, and Spain, whose industries

BOX 14.2 THE CLIMATE CHANGE CONTROVERSY

One environmental policy problem that has attracted much public and political attention is climate change. The EU has been keen to see international action taken to reduce emissions of greenhouse gases such as carbon dioxide (CO_2), to which end it championed the signature of the 1992 UN Framework Convention on Climate Change and a protocol to the convention, signed in Kyoto, Japan, in 1997, designed to give the convention some substance. In 2000 the Commission launched the European Climate Change Program, which identified measures that could be taken to reduce emissions, and in 2002 the EU–15 ratified the Kyoto Protocol, committing them to cutting CO_2 emissions by 8 percent on 1990 levels by 2008–12. At the heart of EU efforts is the EU Emissions Trading Scheme, launched in 2005, under which member states set a national cap on CO_2 emissions from industries, which are issued with emission allowances. Those that use less than their allotted number of allowances can sell them to companies having trouble meeting the limits.

The results have been mixed. By 2004 the EU–25 had reduced their CO_2 emissions by 7.3 percent, compared to a rise in U.S. emissions of 15.8 percent.[22] But seven member states—Austria, Belgium, Denmark, Ireland, Italy, Portugal, and Spain—have projected that they will exceed their emission limits. In March 2007, the EU announced a long-term strategy aimed at making sure that by 2020 (a) at least 20 percent of its energy comes from renewable sources, (b) at least 10 percent of the fuels used in transport will be biofuels (fuel made from plant matter such as corn and sugarcane), and (c) CO_2 emissions will be cut by 20 percent below 1990 levels—or 30 percent if the U.S., China, India, and Russia follow the EU lead. The agreement included all twenty-seven member states and was intended to be a bargaining position as preparations were made for a replacement to the Kyoto Protocol, which expired in 2012.

A follow-up meeting to the March 2007 agreement was held in December 2009, with signatories to Kyoto meeting in Copenhagen to try and strengthen the Kyoto agreement. The failure in Copenhagen to arrive at a binding agreement, rather than more vague commitments, demonstrated how difficult it was to move decisively forward on this issue. Still, the leadership and commitment of the EU in trying to address the most pressing of all environmental problems stands in marked contrast to the U.S. and the other main players in climate change, India and China.

were relatively underdeveloped and whose environmental standards were relatively weak.

The accumulating problems were finally addressed by the SEA, which gave a legal basis to Community environmental policy and made environmental protection a required component of all EC policies. Maastricht provided further clarification by making "sustainable and non-inflationary growth respecting the environment" a fundamental goal of the EU, introducing QMV in the Council of Ministers on most environmental issues, and making environmental laws subject to codecisions by the European Parliament. Amsterdam built on these changes by listing sustainable development (economic development that takes place within the carrying capacity of the environment) as one of the general goals of European integration.

Additional support for EU action has come from public opinion; Eurobarometer polls have found that more than two-thirds of Europeans believe that decisions on the environment should be taken at the EU level rather than at the national level and that pollution is an urgent and immediate problem. Public interest in the environment has also been reflected in the election of members of Green political parties to the national legislatures of most member states, including Austria, Belgium, Finland, Germany, Greece, Ireland, Italy, Luxembourg, Portugal, and Sweden. Greens have also become members of coalition governments in several countries, including Belgium, Finland, France, Germany, and Italy, and have been elected to the European Parliament from more than a dozen EU states.

EU environmental policy has not covered the full range of issues usually dealt with by national-level policy (for example, it is barely active in land use management or forestry), but it has been active on the following:

- *Water quality.* The initial focus of EU policy was on public health and the setting of water quality standards for drinking and bathing water. Concerns about the aquatic environment were then added to the list with controls on the discharge of dangerous substances into inland and coastal waters. More recently there has been a strategic approach to water management, combining the different uses for which water needs to be protected.
- *Waste control.* Waste production from agriculture, mining, industry, and domestic households has prompted the EU to work to reduce the amount produced, to encourage recycling and reuse, to improve

controls on waste disposal, and to control the transport of wastes across national borders.

- *Air quality.* Air pollution was a latecomer to the agenda, with most key EU laws dating only from the late 1980s and based on setting uniform air quality standards or on controlling emissions from vehicles or industrial plants. EU laws now deal with controls on sulfur dioxide, lead, fine particles, nitrogen dioxide, benzene, carbon monoxide, and heavy metals.
- *Chemicals.* The control of dangerous chemicals and other substances has been at the heart of the single biggest body of EU environmental law, focusing on the handling of new chemicals, accidents at chemical plants, pesticides, and trade in dangerous chemicals.
- *Biodiversity.* EU policy on the protection of wildlife and natural habitats has come mainly in response to the terms of international treaties, particularly those dealing with trade in endangered species and the protection of migratory species.
- *Noise pollution.* It is debatable whether or not noise is really an environmental issue, but this has not discouraged the EU from developing a large body of law aimed at making Europe a quieter place, and limiting noise from road vehicles, aircraft, compressors, tower cranes, welding generators, power generators, and concrete breakers.
- *Genetically modified organisms (GMOs).* European consumers have been far more concerned than Americans about the genetic modification of plant-based food, an issue that has brought the EU into conflict with the United States. Genetic modification is widely used in this country (creating what critics like to call "Frankenfood"), and their potential export to the EU has become an issue in transatlantic trade discussions.

Much has been achieved by the EU, and policy in the EU is now driven more by the needs and effects of regional integration than by the priorities of the individual member states. But the results remain patchy, with continued concerns over issues such as air quality in the cities (particularly in Eastern Europe), mostly from heavy and growing concentrations of road traffic; the effects of intensive agriculture on natural habitats; the pollution of freshwater sources by sewage, pesticides, and industrial waste; and the lack of significant progress in the development of waste disposal policies.

At the heart of the EU approach to environmental policy is the concept of sustainable development.[23] Typically defined as development that "meets the needs of the present without compromising the ability of future generations to meet their own needs,"[24] its role in EU environmental planning has grown. The SEA defined one of the Community's environmental objectives as the "prudent and rational utilization of natural resources"; Maastricht called explicitly for "sustainable and non-inflationary growth respecting the environment"; and the Treaty of Amsterdam spoke of the need for "balanced and sustainable development of economic activities." Amsterdam made sustainable development one of the core objectives of the EU, so that it now applies to everything the EU does. The sixth EAP (now in effect) highlights this core objective by, among other things, encouraging business and consumers to become more environmentally conscious of land use, consumption patterns, and sustainable production.

In giving the principle so much emphasis, the EU also stands in contrast to the United States. For U.S. policy makers, "conservation" (which means much the same as sustainable development) was at the heart of early approaches to the management of land, waterways, and forests, and the management of public land has been guided since 1960 by the Multiple-Use Sustained-Yield Act, which requires that it be used for different purposes and in a sustainable manner. But sustainable development has yet to be adopted as part of a generalized policy on the environment in the U.S., and consumption has long been at the heart of American consumer approaches to natural resources, encouraged by the sense that the United States is so big and so well-endowed that limits are unlikely to be reached. The differences are revealed in the statistics: per capita, Americans use four times as much water as Europeans, use more than twice as much energy, and generate one and a half times as much municipal waste.[25]

Questions to Consider

1. Why has agriculture been of particular importance to the EU?
2. What were the essential elements of the Common Agricultural Policy before 2000? What caused it to change and in what ways?
3. Why did it take so long for environmental policy to assume a prominent place in the EU? What can be considered the successes of EU environmental policy? Failures?

Further Reading

Berkeley Hill. *Understanding the Common Agricultural Policy* (Abingdon: Earthscan, 2011). Johann Swinnen. *The Perfect Storm: The Political Economy of the Fischler Reforms of the Common Agricultural Policy* (Brussels: Centre for European Policy Studies, 2009).

> Two recent studies of CAP, the former focusing on the policy process and the latter on the effects of recent reforms to policy.

Antonio Piccinini and Margaret Loseby. *Agricultural Policies in Europe and the USA* (Basingstoke, UK: Palgrave Macmillan, 2001).

> A study of the establishment and development of CAP, comparing it to policies in the United States and discussing its implications for Eastern Europe and developing countries.

Andrew Jordan. *Environmental Policy in the EU: Actors, Institutions and Processes*, 2nd ed. (London: Earthscan, 2005). Andrew Jordan and Duncan Liefferink, eds. *Environmental Policy in Europe: The Europeanization of National Environmental Policy* (Abigdon: Routledge, 2006).

> Two studies of environmental policy in the EU, the latter focusing on how policy approaches have been Europeanized.

Paul G. Harris, ed. *Europe and Global Climate Change: Politics, Foreign Policy and Regional Cooperation* (Cheltenham: Edward Elgar, 2007).

> An edited collection of studies of how the political debate over climate change has evolved in Europe.

Norman J. Vig and Michael G. Faure, eds. *Green Giants? Environmental Policies of the United States and the European Union* (Cambridge, MA: MIT, 2004).

> A collection of studies arguing that the U.S. has been losing its historical role as a leader in environmental regulation and that the EU is catching up.

Notes

1. *The Economist*, 29 September 1990.

2. European Commission, *The Agricultural Situation in the Community*, 1993 Report (Luxembourg: Office for Official Publications, 1994), Table 3.5.1.3.

3. Wyn Grant, *The Common Agricultural Policy* (New York: St. Martin's, 1997), 71–72.

4. H. von der Groeben, *The European Community, the Formative Years: The Struggle to Establish the Common Market and the Political Union (1958–1966)* (Brussels: European Commission, 1987), 71–72.

5. World Trade Organization, International Trade Statistics 2006, https://www.wto.org/english/res_e/statis_e/its2006_e/its06_toc_e.htm; European Commission: Monitoring Agri-Trade Policy (DG Agriculture and Rural Development), Agricultural Trade in 2011: The EU and the World, 2012, http://ec.europa.eu/agriculture/publi/map/01_12_en.pdf..

6. Data from the World Bank, "Agriculture and Rural Development," 2012, http://data.worldbank.org/topic/agriculture-and-rural-development.

7. Christilla Roederer-Rynning, "Agricultural Policy: The Fortress Challenged," in Helen Wallace, Mark A. Pollack, and Alasdair R. Young, eds., *Policy-Making in the European Union*, 6th ed. (Oxford: Oxford University Press, 2010), 163.

8. Christian Lequesne, "Fisheries Policy: Letting the Little Ones Go?" in Wallace, Wallace, and Pollack, eds., *Policy-Making in the European Union*.

9. Annalisa Barbieri, "Discard This Common Fisheries Policy and Stop the Waste," *Guardian*, 2 March 2011, http://www.guardian.co.uk/comment isfree/2011/mar/02/discard-common-fisheries-policy-waste-eu.

10. "EU Revamps Fishing Policy to Save Depleted Stocks," BBC News Europe, 13 July 2011, http://www.bbc.co.uk/news/science-environment-14133913.

11. Brigid Laffan, *The Finances of the European Union* (New York: St. Martin's, 1997), 207–10.

12. See Desmond Dinan and Marios Camhis, "The Common Agricultural Policy and Cohesion," in Maria Green Cowles and Desmond Dinan, eds., *Developments in the European Union 2*, 2nd ed. (Basingstoke, UK: Palgrave Macmillan, 2004).

13. David P. Lewis, *The Road to Europe: History, Institutions and Prospects of European Integration 1945–1993* (New York: Peter Lang, 1993), 337.

14. Franz Fischler, speech before the First European Parliamentary Symposium on Agriculture, Brussels, 16 October 2003.

15. James Arnold, "Down on the Farm," BBC News Online, 3 December 2002, http://news.bbc.co.uk/2/hi/business/2514705.stm.

16. 1 European Union, "Agriculture: Not Just Farming . . . ," 2012, http://europa.eu/pol/agr/index_en.htm.

17. Philipp M. Hildebrand, "The European Community's Environmental Policy, 1957 to 1992: From Incidental Measures to an International Regime?" in David Judge, ed., *A Green Dimension for the European Community: Political Issues and Processes* (London: Frank Cass, 1993).

18. See chapter 3 in John McCormick, *The Global Environmental Movement*, 2nd ed. (London: John Wiley, 1995).

19. *Commission v. Italy* (Case 91/79), Court of Justice of the European Communities, *Reports of Cases Before the Court*, 1980.

20. Hildebrand, "The European Community's Environmental Policy, 1957 to 1992."

21. Eckard Rehbinder and Richard Steward, eds., *Environmental Protection Policy*, vol. 2: Integration through Law: Europe and the American Federal Experience (Florence: European University Institute, 1985), 19.

22. United Nations Framework Convention on Climate Change, 2007, http://unfccc.int.

23. See Susan Baker and John McCormick, "Sustainable Development: Comparative Understandings and Responses," in Norman J. Vig and Michael G. Faure, eds., *Green Giants: Environmental Policy of the United States and the European Union* (Cambridge, MA: MIT, 2004).

24. World Commission on Environment and Development, *Our Common Future* (Oxford: Oxford University Press, 1987), 8.

25. Figures are from 2012; OECD, occd.org and from World Bank, world bank.org.

15

EXTERNAL RELATIONS

CHAPTER OVERVIEW

- Launched by the Maastricht treaty and since that time modified and strengthened, the Common Foreign and Security Policy (CFSP) is at the heart of EU foreign policy.
- Despite institutional changes making it easier for the EU to speak with one voice in foreign policy matters, there is a gap between the potential influence of the EU and its actual performance, at least in terms of its hard power. Combined, the EU has one of the largest militaries in the world in terms of both personnel and military equipment (albeit still significantly smaller than the United States'), yet the EU has not been able to project a unified front in security matters and therefore act decisively in military matters on the world stage.
- Compared to its relatively undersized role in security and lack of hard power, the EU's soft power in the global arena is beyond a doubt: among other things, the EU is the world's largest trading

power and the biggest source of foreign investment and official development assistance in the world. Because of this, the EU is both a benefactor of as well as a competitor to many countries in the world.

For those who question the merits and achievements of European integration, one of the clearest examples of the gap between promise and achievement lies in the field of foreign policy. The EU is clearly an economic and trading powerhouse, and yet its critics argue that it is punching below its weight when it comes to turning its wealth into global political influence. Attempts to explain the contradiction have been many and varied, but at the heart of the issue lie three problems.

First, military power dominates most analyses of international influence. The claim, for example, that the United States is the world's last remaining superpower rests mainly on the size, reach, and technological prowess of the U.S. military. The fact that the EU has not built a common military or developed a common security policy is seen by most critics as undermining Europe's claims to global power. Second, the EU has not yet been able always to project a united front on the most troubling international problems, or to make its voice heard. It has been building a common foreign and security policy, and has developed common positions and strategies on a wide range of issues, but it has also been left with much egg on its face by disagreements over how to respond to problems in the Middle East, the Balkans, and, most recently, in the Arab world, such as in Libya and Syria. Third, more public attention has been drawn to the EU's short-term policy failures than to its longer-term successes. Much of what the EU has achieved in foreign policy has been a result of steady investments of time, diplomacy, and encouragement, little of which attracts headlines in the same way—for example—as its public failure to agree over whether or not to support the U.S.-led invasion of Iraq.

Paradoxically, most of the criticism of the EU stems from the fact that more is now *expected* of it as an international actor. It is not that the EU has failed to provide leadership, but rather that its failures are at odds with expectations for an economic superpower. The lessons have not been lost on European leaders, for whom the divisions over the 1990–91 Gulf War and the 1991–95 crises in the Balkans were wake-up calls and the divisions over Iraq reminders of how much more work needed to be done. Not only were Europe's leaders in disagreement with each other over Iraq, but also those in favor of the invasion were at odds with their own publics: polls found that large majorities in every EU country—even prospective Eastern European member states—were opposed to the war, and several governments that supported the war (notably in Spain, Italy, and Britain) paid the price through loss of public support.

On several fronts there is now growing evidence of the EU playing a more assertive international role, even if this is not always immediately clear or if the EU does not receive as much credit for its achievements as it deserves. Its real strengths lie not in its military credentials but in its impact as a new kind of civilian superpower. It has been more adept at employing soft power (incentives and influence through economic and cultural power) rather than hard power (threats, coercion, and force tied to military power) to achieve change (see Box 15.1), a quality that places it at an advantage in a world where globalization, economic investment, and international cooperation are the emerging norms.

TOWARD A COMMON FOREIGN POLICY

Foreign policy was a latecomer to the agenda of European integration. It was not mentioned in the Treaty of Rome, and the Community focused most of its attention during the 1950s and 1960s on internal economic matters. Modest progress began to be made with the agreement in 1970 of European Political Cooperation (EPC), a loose and voluntary foreign policy process that revolved around regular meetings of the Community foreign ministers. EPC helped European leaders learn to negotiate shared positions, a habit formally recognized when it was agreed under the Single European Act that member states would "endeavour jointly to formulate and implement a European foreign policy." But the problems of a "mixed system" remained: instead of developing a common overall policy—or even a set of common targeted policies—the Community was driven by a combination of national and common policies.[1]

The resulting difficulties were exposed by events in the 1990s. First came the Gulf War of 1990–91, when the United States responded quickly to the August 1990 Iraqi invasion of Kuwait, orchestrated a multinational air war against Iraq, and launched a four-day ground war in February 1991. Britain provided strong support and placed a large military contingent under U.S. operational command; France also made a large military commitment but placed more emphasis on a diplomatic resolution in order to maintain good relations with Arab oil producers and protect its weapons markets; and Germany was constrained by a postwar tradition of pacifism

Box 15.1 Europe's Soft Power Advantage

Recent debates about international relations have drawn new attention to the differences between hard power and soft power.[2] All great powers have hard and soft power tools available to them, but there has been a tendency in recent years to associate hard power with the U.S. and soft power with the EU. The U.S. has a long history of effectively using diplomacy, political support, and economic investment to bring change, but critics of U.S. foreign policy point to Iraq as the latest example of a U.S. tendency to rely heavily on its military power to achieve its objectives. Those same critics argue that hard power is counterproductive, rarely brings about permanent positive change, and actually heightens tensions by making the U.S. appear to be a threat to world peace. Rather than being a leader for change, the United States has become something of a "rogue nation"[3] and has lost much of its ability to persuade.

Meanwhile, claims of European global power are dismissed by cynics mainly on the basis that the EU does not have a large, combined military or much desire to use what it has, except for peacekeeping. But there is evidence to suggest that the EU's preference for soft power may actually be its trump card. The idea of encouraging a change in behavior through incentives rather than threats, through opportunities and negotiation rather than through violence and intimidation, carries considerable weight in the era of globalization. A growing number of analysts argue that rather than shirking on defense, the EU is instead expanding the set of tools it applies to post–Cold War security and defense problems, relying less on defense than on economics, diplomacy, and engagement by negotiation.[4]

If the definition of power is expanded to include its political, economic, moral, and cultural aspects, then the idea of the United States as the world's only superpower loses some of its luster. Rather than an international system based on military unipolarity, we may actually be living in a bipolar world in which two superpowers—the United States and the European Union—share influence and resources with a growing network of emerging regional powers in Asia and Latin America, such as Brazil, China, and India. All of these have the potential to become superpowers, raising the prospects of a new multipolar international order, but for now the two most important poles in the international system are the U.S. and the EU, and they offer two contrasting notions of how power might be used.

and constitutional limits on the deployment of German troops outside the NATO area. An abashed Luxembourg foreign minister, Jacques Poos, admitted that the Community's response illustrated "the political insignificance of Europe." For Belgian foreign minister Mark Eyskens, it showed that the EC was "an economic giant, a political dwarf, and a military worm."[5]

The Community's shortcomings were revealed again in the Balkans, where the end of the Cold War released the ethnic, religious, and nationalist tensions that had been kept in check by the Tito regime (1944–80). When Croatia and Slovenia unilaterally declared independence in June 1991, the Yugoslav federal army responded with force, throwing down a challenge for the Community to intervene. There was early promise in an EU-brokered peace conference, and a buoyant Jacques Poos declared, "This is the hour of Europe, not of the United States."[6] But when the Community recognized Croatia and Slovenia in January 1992, it lost its credibility as a neutral arbiter, and it was left eventually to the United States to broker the 1995 Dayton Peace Accords. Then, when ethnic Albanians in Kosovo tried to break away from Yugoslavia in 1997–98, it was left to NATO—again under U.S. leadership—to organize the bombing campaign against Serbia in March–June 1999. This was to be the catalyst that finally encouraged the EU to take action on building a military capability.[7]

Progress was made with Maastricht, by which the EU agreed on a Common Foreign and Security Policy (CFSP) that represented a stronger commitment to a common foreign policy: joint action could be initiated and implemented by QMV in the Council (although unanimity was still the norm on the biggest questions), security issues were fully included, and the CFSP was part of the institutional structure of the EU.[8] The CFSP brought a convergence of positions among the member states on key international issues, helped by improved links among the foreign ministers and by the EU's development of joint actions and of common strategies and positions.

Although the Treaty of Lisbon clarified some of the initial confusion on institutional roles within the CFSP (see Box 15.2) difficulties remain, mostly stemming from policy differences among the governments of the member states. Some have national agendas that they want to pursue (Britain and France, for example, have special interests in their former colonies, while Austria, Finland, Ireland, and Sweden want to maintain their neutrality[9]), but there is also a more fundamental strategic division: Atlanticists such as Britain, the Netherlands, Portugal, and several Eastern European states favor

BOX 15.2 WHO SPEAKS FOR EUROPE?

One of the persistent problems with the development of a European foreign policy has been a lack of focus and leadership. This is not an issue in the United States, where the president and the secretary of state between them clearly represent national policy. But in the EU, the presidency of the Council of Ministers changes every six months, and for many years there was no one in the EU institutions who could act as an authoritative focal point for discussions with other countries. This presented a problem for any non-EU governments that wanted to negotiate or do business with the EU, summed up nicely in the (sadly apocryphal) question credited to former U.S. secretary of state Henry Kissinger, "When I want to speak to Europe, whom do I call?"

The division of external relations portfolios in the Commission ended with the creation in 1999 of a single external relations portfolio, but the waters were muddied when a second position was created at the same time in the form of the High Representative (HR) for the CFSP, who was intended to be the spokesperson on foreign affairs. The first officeholder was Javier Solana, former secretary-general of NATO, who was appointed in 1999 for an initial five-year term, renewed in 2004.

The Treaty of Lisbon brought significant change as well as some clarity, combining the post of external relations commissioner with the HR in the new position of the High Representative for CFSP and External Relations. The High Representative is charged under Lisbon with "conducting" the CFSP, chairing the Foreign Affairs Council in the Council of Ministers, and serving as a vice-president in the Commission, giving the EU's external policies more consistency among its various institutions. At the same time, the new post of president of the European Council as well as the president of the Commission still "speak for Europe" in their own capacities. Still, although Kissinger's question cannot quite be said to have been definitively answered, Lisbon has brought more clarity to how the EU handles its external relations—and who is ultimately responsible for it.

a close foreign policy association with the United States, while Europeanists such as France and Germany prefer greater European independence. When the European Security and Defense Identity (ESDI) was launched in 1994 in an attempt to underpin the CFSP by developing a separate European initiative on security matters, Atlanticists felt that it should be tied closely to NATO, while Europeanists saw it as an opportunity to develop some real independence from the United States.

TOWARD A COMMON SECURITY POLICY

Security issues have been the most troubling element of attempts to build a common European foreign policy, having been repeatedly sidetracked by debates over the place of NATO. Although Western European forces have always made up the bulk of NATO's military capability in Europe, NATO has always been politically dominated by the United States, and most Europeans (France excepted) have been content with the security blanket provided by the Americans. But since the end of the Cold War, there has been pressure to redefine the mission of NATO, the key question being the tripartite relationship between the United States, the EU, and NATO.

Added together, the military resources of the EU are substantial; in 2010–11, the EU member states collectively spent about $230 billion on defense, and while this was less than half the US total, it was more than the combined spending of Japan and the four BRIC states (Brazil, Russia, India, and China) combined. Together they have more active personnel (about 1.7 million) than the United States, and bigger navies and air forces than China and India combined.[10] Under a joint command system the EU military would be the second biggest in the world after the United States. But general cooperation among EU member states on military matters has been slow in coming.

For a while, one way out of the dilemma was offered by the Western European Union (WEU), an organization founded in 1954 in the wake of the collapse of the European Defense Community, which committed its members to much stronger joint defense obligations than NATO. But it was never elevated to the same status as NATO and found itself stretched beyond its limits by the 1990–91 Gulf War. Following a 1992 meeting of WEU foreign and defense ministers at Petersberg, near Bonn, a declaration was issued that limited the WEU to the Petersberg tasks: humanitarian, rescue, peacekeeping, and other crisis management operations, including peacemaking. Meanwhile, an attempt had been made outside formal Community structures to address the lack of a joint military force with the creation in 1991 of an experimental Franco-German brigade. In May 1992 this was converted into Eurocorps, a joint military force that has been operational since November 1995, consisting of up to sixty thousand troops from Belgium, France, Germany, Luxembourg, and Spain. It has sent missions to Bosnia (1998), Kosovo (2000), and Afghanistan (2004 to the present).

In 1997 the Amsterdam treaty resulted in a closer association between the WEU and the EU, and the Petersberg tasks were incorporated into the EU treaties. That same year, Tony Blair became British prime minister and signaled his willingness to see Britain play a more central role in EU defense matters. He and French president Jacques Chirac began to more fully explore the potential of the Anglo-French axis in European security matters, and—after a December 1998 meeting in St. Malo, France—the two leaders declared that the EU should be in a position to play a full role in international affairs and "must have the capacity for autonomous action, backed up by credible military forces, the means to decide to use them, and the readiness to do so." They suggested the creation of a European Rapid Reaction Force (RRF), which was later endorsed by German chancellor Gerhard Schröder.[11]

In 1999 the EU launched the European Security and Defense Policy (ESDP). An integral part of the CFSP, this was to consist of two key components: the Petersberg tasks and a sixty-thousand-member RRF that could be deployed at sixty days' notice, be sustained for at least one year, and carry out these tasks. The plan was to have it ready by the end of 2003, but while it was declared partly operational in December 2002 and launched its first mission—a peacekeeping operation in Macedonia—in March 2003, it took longer to finalize than initially estimated. ESDP was renamed the Common Security and Defense Policy (CSDP) by the Lisbon treaty. Although CSDP continues to operate under the principle of unanimity, Lisbon provided the possibility for "enhanced cooperation," whereby member states with more robust military capabilities are allowed, with the EU's blessing, to create a limited but more structured cooperative arrangement for peacekeeping, disarmament, and other military operations.

In December 2003, the European Council adopted the European Security Strategy, the first ever declaration by EU member states of their strategic goals. The Strategy declared that the EU was "inevitably a global player" and "should be ready to share in the responsibility for global security."

It listed the key threats facing the EU as terrorism, weapons of mass destruction, regional conflicts, failing states, and organized crime. In May 2004, EU defense ministers agreed on the formation of several battle groups that could be deployed more quickly and for shorter periods than the RRF, be used in support of UN operations, and be capable of anything up to full-scale combat situations. The groups would consist of 1,500 troops each, could be committed within 15 days, and could be sustainable for between 30 and 120 days.

It is important to note that in spite of all the political disagreements, the EU has achieved more on security cooperation than most people think, driven by a desire to decrease its reliance on the U.S.[12] It has, for example, taken part in many military actions.[13] In 2003, it deployed peacekeeping troops in Macedonia (Operation Concordia) and the Democratic Republic of Congo (Operation Artemis), and in December 2004 it launched its biggest peacekeeping mission when seven thousand troops (many coming from outside the EU, it is true) took over from NATO in Bosnia. By 2006, the EU was contributing 50 percent of the peacekeeping forces in Bosnia (where the Office of High Representative in charge of implementation of the Dayton Peace Accords has always been held by an EU national), and 70 percent of the forces in Kosovo.

The EU has also had police and other missions in West and Central Africa, Chad, Indonesia, and most significantly, Afghanistan, where it accounts for some 40 percent of forces. National military interventions have also continued, including Britain's operation in Sierra Leone in 2001 (establishing order after a UN force had failed) and France's operations in Côte d'Ivoire in 2002 and in Mali in 2013.

Europeanists such as France continue to want to develop an independent EU capability. The United States is content to see the Europeans taking responsibility for those tasks from which NATO should best keep its distance, but it insists that there should be no overlap or rivalry in the event of the creation of a separate European institution. Meanwhile, Atlanticists such as Britain continue to feel nervous about undermining the U.S. commitment to Europe, while realizing that the commitment may eventually wane, regardless.[14] The debate remains open, and it is unclear how the different views will be resolved. A new element was added to the debate in 2004, when seven Eastern European states—whose governments mainly hold Atlanticist views—joined both NATO and the EU (see Table 15.1).

Table 15.1 Membership of NATO

Albania (2009)	Greece (1952)	Portugal
Belgium	Hungary (1999)	Romania (2004)
Bulgaria (2004)	**Iceland**	Slovakia (2004)
Canada	Italy	Slovenia (2004)
Croatia (2009)	Latvia (2004)	Spain (1982)
Czech Republic (1999)	Lithuania (2004)	**Turkey** (1952)
Denmark	Luxembourg	United Kingdom
Estonia (2004)	Netherlands	**United States**
France	**Norway**	
Germany (1955)	Poland (1999)	

Note: Founding members unless otherwise indicated by year of membership. EU member states that are not members of NATO are Austria, Cyprus, Finland, Ireland, Malta, and Sweden. Boldface = non-EU member states.

TRADE POLICY

Whatever the doubts and questions about the EU's military power and global political influence, its massive economic presence is uncontested:

- It is the wealthiest capitalist marketplace in the world, still far larger than the BRIC economies combined, accounting for nearly one-third of global economic output (see Figure 15.1).
- It is the world's biggest trading power, accounting for about 20 percent of trade in merchandise and commercial services (see Figure 15.2).
- Its currency, the euro, sits alongside the U.S. dollar and the Japanese yen as one of the three most important currencies in the world.
- It is the biggest source of foreign direct investment in the world, accounting in 2010 for about a quarter of the world's inward flow of foreign direct investment and around 32 percent of all outward flow.[15]
- It is the biggest market in the world for mergers and acquisitions; European multinationals have grown rapidly in strength and reach, reclaiming some of the dominant positions they held before the rise of competition from the United States and Japan.

Figure 15.1 The EU in the Global Economy

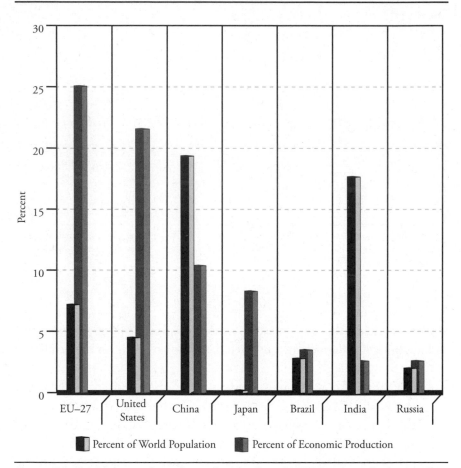

Source: Calculated from population figures for 2010 from the UN Population Division, website at http://www.un.org/esa/population, and GDP figures for 2011 from the World Bank, website at http://data.worldbank.org.

These developments have made the EU an economic superpower, willing and able to exert its economic influence on a global scale. In perhaps no other area has the impact of European integration been more substantial than in the field of trade, where—in contrast to its difficulties in agreeing on a common foreign and security policy—the EU has built common positions and wielded them to great effect. The basis of its success is the Common Commercial Policy (CCP), contained in the Treaty of Rome. Aimed officially at contributing "to the harmonious development of world trade, the progressive abolition of restrictions on international trade, and the lowering of customs barriers," the CCP has in fact been designed to protect the EU's trading interests. It was not finally put in place until the completion of the single market, but along the way it helped establish strong EU positions on global trade negotiations and protected the EU's balance of trade; in 2012 it had a balance of trade deficit of $207.7 billion (€159.6) compared to a U.S. deficit of $559.9 billion.[16] The EU share of global trade has also grown in the past half-decade, while that of the United States has fallen.

The growing confidence of the EU on trade matters is reflected in the number of times it has been involved in cases brought before the World Trade Organization (WTO). If a country adopts a trade policy measure or takes an action that is considered to be a breach of a WTO agreement, the dispute can be taken to the WTO, which investigates and issues a judgment that is binding upon member states. Not surprisingly—given that they are the world's two biggest trading powers—the EU and the United States have brought more cases before the WTO than anyone else, and in many instances the disputes have been between the EU and the U.S. (see chapter 16).

The EU has not always been able to have its way on trade negotiations, and at least one analysis finds a mismatch between the institutional unity of the EU on trade issues and its external bargaining power.[17] But the statistics make a compelling case, and whatever doubts may be cast on the internal economic policies of the EU—regarding low productivity, high unemployment, and an aging population (see chapter 12)—the global economic presence of the EU is clear. Military power is still needed to deal with the most serious security problems, but in a world of globalization, new technology, and greater market freedom, the power of economic opportunity has many advantages over the power of violence, and—on the economic front at least—the EU is in a commanding position.

DEVELOPMENTS IN THE NEIGHBORHOOD:
EASTERN EUROPE AND RUSSIA

Nowhere are Europe's soft power advantages more clearly on display than in the EU's relationship with countries in its neighborhood. Within three months of taking office in January 1989, U.S. president George H. W. Bush was presciently describing Western Europe as an economic magnet that could pull Eastern Europe toward a new commonwealth of free nations, and the United States encouraged the Community to take responsibility for coordinating Western economic aid to the East. From those beginnings, the EU has evolved into an economic club to which almost all its neighbors

Figure 15.2 The EU Share of World Trade

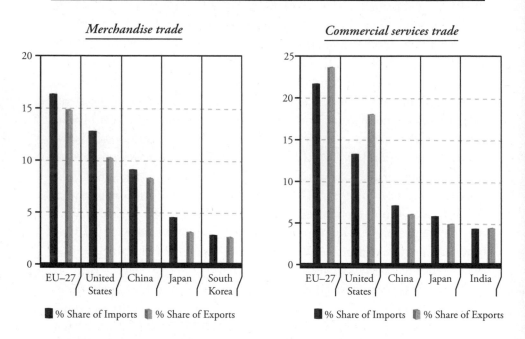

Merchandise trade

Commercial services trade

■ % Share of Imports   ▌ % Share of Exports   ■ % Share of Imports   ▌ % Share of Exports

Source: World Trade Organization, *International Trade Statistics 2011*, at http://www.wto.org (retrieved July 2012). Figures are for trade in 2010, and they exclude intra-EU trade.

want access, either as fully paid-up members or through preferential access agreements. The impact on the promotion of democracy and capitalism throughout the region has been profound.[18]

The foundations were laid by trade and cooperation agreements between the Community and almost all Eastern European states, the provision of several billion dollars in loans through the European Investment Bank, the launching of several programs to help Eastern European social reform, and the creation in 1990 of the European Bank for Reconstruction and Development. Talk of the expansion of Community membership to the east followed in short order, leading to association agreements that allowed for the gradual expansion of free trade, provided for foreign policy coordination and cultural exchanges, and encouraged preparations for eventual EU membership.[19]

The expansion to twelve new member states in 2004–07 was the logical conclusion to all these developments, but something of an "enlargement fatigue" has since set in among existing EU members, driven by concerns about the economic costs of integrating poorer member states and about absorbing new members into an EU whose decision-making procedures have reached their capacity. Polls find that Europeans are now about equally divided for and against more enlargement. A total of sixteen countries could theoretically qualify for membership in the EU: Albania, Armenia, Azerbaijan, Belarus, Bosnia, Georgia, Iceland, Kosovo, Macedonia, Moldova, Montenegro, Norway, Serbia, Switzerland, Turkey, and Ukraine. Five of these—Iceland, Macedonia, Montenegro, Serbia, and Turkey—have been formally accepted as "candidate countries," meaning that membership has been agreed in principle and negotiations on terms have begun.

Whatever the prospects for more enlargement, the EU has been conscious of the need to reach out to its neighbors and to create a "circle of friends." In 1995 the Euro-Mediterranean Partnership—otherwise known as the Barcelona Process—was launched, aimed at strengthening political, economic, and social ties between the EU and twelve neighboring countries. In 2004, the European Neighborhood Policy was launched, targeted at the EU's sixteen closest neighbors: Algeria, Armenia, Azerbaijan, Belarus, Egypt, Georgia, Israel, Jordan, Lebanon, Libya, Moldova, Morocco, the Palestinian Authority, Syria, Tunisia, and Ukraine. (Russia is the subject of a separate set of agreements—see below). The policy promotes a relationship that the EU describes as "privileged," with the goal of promoting democracy, human rights, the rule of law, good governance, and market economics.[20]

The most controversial application for EU membership to date has been that from Turkey. The Community agreed as long ago as 1963 that Turkish membership was possible, but Turkey has a weak record on human rights, and it is big, poor, and predominantly Muslim, which raises troubling economic and social questions. There has also been a side debate about whether it is really European; since Europe ends at the Bosporus Strait, only a small part of Turkey is actually in Europe. (Geography, however, did not pose a barrier to Cyprus joining in 2004.) Turkey has been an associate member since 1963 and applied for full membership in 1987; a customs union between the EU and Turkey came into force in December 1995; and Turkey was formally recognized in 2002 as an applicant country. Negotiations on Turkish membership in the EU opened in 2005 but were almost immediately tripped up by Turkey's refusal to open its ports to Greek Cyprus, human rights concerns, its slow progress on changing its laws to fit with EU law. All of these contributed to a near freezing of negotiations over entry

Map 15.1   The EU and Its Neighborhood

 Potential EU Members

Countries without prospects of EU
membership, but which have special
links with the EU

into the EU. Nevertheless, the dynamic between the EU and Turkey has begun to change, largely because while the EU continues to suffer economic problems, Turkey has recorded a very solid GDP growth of about 5.2 percent over the last decade. Thus France's recent announcement that it would reopen talks on one chapter (policy area) that all potential EU members must complete, as well as recent talks between Angela Merkel and Turkish prime minister Recep Tayyip Erdogan on moving Turkey's application forward have raised the prospect that Turkish membership—still believed to be a number of years away, of course—could happen much sooner than was earlier thought.

Uncertainties also shadow the EU's relationship with Russia.[21] As its closest big neighbor, the security and economic stability of Russia is viewed by the EU as crucial, and—despite EU criticism of Russian policy on the breakaway province of Chechnya—links between the two sides improved during the 1990s: Russia sought the respectability and economic opportunities that would come from a good relationship with the EU, while the EU looked for Russian support for eastern enlargement. In the event, enlargement was not met with enthusiasm in Russia, particularly as it included three former Soviet republics (Estonia, Latvia, and Lithuania); Russians worried about a new economic rift between a wealthy Europe and a relatively poor Russia and about the impact of enlargement on Russian exports to Eastern Europe. Russia was also displeased by the role of the EU in the outcome of the 2004 election in Ukraine.

The relationship today is deeply troubled, with both sides needing each other but not entirely trusting the other's motives. They have a common land border of 1,400 miles (2,250 kilometers), and the EU is deeply conscious of its reliance on Russia for energy supplies—about one-fifth of the EU's oil and one-quarter of its natural gas come from Russia. Problems were heightened in 2006, when a dispute over gas prices between Russia and Ukraine disrupted supplies of natural gas to the EU. The EU is also conscious of its need to balance criticism of policy in Chechnya with its need to encourage Russia as a partner in the war on terrorism. For its part, Russia is conscious that the EU now accounts for 70 percent of its exports and that the EU is the biggest source of foreign investment in Russian industry and infrastructure. Curiously, polls indicate that 60 percent of Russians would like to go so far as to join the EU,[22] and yet most Russians still give more weight to their country's relations with the U.S., perhaps because of a holdover from the Cold War.

Relations with a Rising Power: EU–China Relations

In recent years China has emerged as a major global player, the object of much speculation and fascination. Over the centuries, Europe and China have had a long relationship, even if it has not always been a particularly good one. Contacts between the EU and China were thin before the 1980s (the first visit to China by a European Commissioner was in 1975) and the relationship was set back by the events of Tiananmen Square in 1989. But relations improved in the mid-1990s, with a series of EU–China summits held between 1998 and 2002. Today, the EU is China's largest trading partner, and China is the EU's second largest trading partner after the United States, with significant increases in the volume of trade between China and the EU occurring in just the last few years.

However, the EU–China dynamic in the post–Cold War era has been especially colored by the tripartite relations between the U.S., China, and the EU. Europe (unlike the United States) has no military presence in East Asia; Taiwan is not an issue for the EU (as it is for the U.S.); and China does not see the EU as quite the rival the U.S. is. On the other hand, the EU—like the U.S.—is critical of China's human rights record, has serious concerns about China's authoritarian system, has accorded diplomatic contacts with individuals China sees as enemies (such as the Dalai Lama or other high-profile Chinese dissidents), and has seen eye-to-eye with the U.S. on issues of human rights and state sovereignty, such as military intervention and peacekeeping in Kosovo, actively supporting rebellion in Libya, humanitarian intervention in Sudan, and other issues which China sees as encroaching upon state sovereignty (thus threatening policies China deems as "internal matters"). Undoubtedly China would like to use the EU as something of a counter to the U.S., but most often (although not always, see chapter 16) the EU sides with the U.S. on the most important international issues. Moreover, even in the economic sphere, China has had tensions with the EU. For example, it has been angered at protectionist measures against its exports to Europe and the EU's long-standing opposition to China's membership in the WTO (which China joined in 2002).

Development Cooperation

The long history of European colonialism has left behind a heritage of strong political and economic ties between EU states and their former colonies. EU priorities are driven by a combination of moral concerns about underdevelopment, poverty, and hunger, and by altruism: the developing world accounts for about 12 percent of EU exports[23] and is the source of most of the EU's supply of key raw materials such as oil, rubber, copper, and uranium. But while claiming to be concerned about the plight of developing countries, the EU has avoided taking a lead on many of the security problems in its former colonies (such as Somalia and Rwanda), and its policies toward the developing world have not always had the desired results.[24]

Development aid is at the heart of the relationship.[25] The EU has become the biggest source of official development assistance in the world, with its member states together accounting for nearly 54 percent of the total of $134 billion given by the major donor countries in 2011.[26] In addition to bilateral aid, the EU channels assistance through the European Development Fund (EDF), which provides grants and low-interest loans to seventy-nine countries under the African, Caribbean, and Pacific (ACP) program. Support from the EDF goes mainly to educational development, the building of infrastructure, the development and diversification of production, humanitarian aid, and long-term projects aimed at reducing poverty and protecting the environment. Money is not everything though; the real impact of aid depends on how resources are used and how well they are used. And in spite of being the world's largest source of aid, the EU still does not have as much influence on international development debates as the U.S., the World Bank, or the International Monetary Fund.

The EU has also negotiated a series of cooperative agreements with selected former colonies, mainly the non-Asian former colonies of Britain and France. These began with the Yaoundé Conventions (named for the capital of Cameroon, where they were signed), which gave eighteen former colonies of the original six EEC member states preferential access to Community markets between 1963 and 1975. In return, the eighteen states allowed the Community limited duty-free or quota-free access to their markets. The accession of Britain to the Community in 1973 brought many former British colonies into the equation, so the Lomé Convention (named for the capital of Togo) was signed in 1975, raising the number of ACP states to forty-six and allowing ACP countries to export almost anything to the EU duty free.

Lomé III (1985–90) shifted the focus of aid away from the promotion of industrial development and more toward self-sufficiency and food security. Lomé IV (1990–2000) included an attempt to push EU policy in new directions by adding a structural adjustment element to ACP aid; in other words, it encouraged economic diversification in the ACP states rather than simply providing project aid. This made the EU more like the International Monetary Fund or the World Bank as a significant financial actor in international economic relations.[27] Lomé IV also banned exports of toxic wastes between the EU and ACP countries, and it included clauses aimed at promoting human rights and protecting tropical forests in ACP countries.

The ACP program may have resulted in the building of closer commercial ties between the EU and the ACP states—there was an overall increase in ACP exports to Europe—but there were many problems as well: few ACP countries saw economic growth (and in some, economic prospects actually worsened); imports to the EU from other parts of the world grew more quickly than those from ACP states; EDF funds took too long to be disbursed and were relatively small when divided up seventy-nine ways; too little attention was paid to the environmental implications of the focus on cash crops for export; and the program neither helped address the ACP debt crisis nor really changed the relationship between the EU and the ACP states.

In 1996 an intensive review of the ACP program was launched,[28] and negotiations opened in 1998 between the EU and the ACP states aimed at replacing the Lomé Convention with a more flexible structure based on a series of interregional free trade agreements between groups of ACP countries and the EU. The result was the Cotonou Agreement (named for the capital of Benin), which was signed in 2000 to cover a period of twenty years. Critics charge that it is based on an abandonment of preferential trade agreements, that it is less innovative and based more on following global trends, and that EU development aid policy today is less the model that it once was and has become more symbolic.[29]

Questions to Consider

1. What are the chief obstacles preventing the EU from projecting a more robust military capability? Is hard power still that important in today's world?

2. In which concrete ways does the EU's global economic power translate into political influence around the world?

3. What have been the significant achievements of EU aid to the developing world? Has the EU done this to genuinely help economic development in the developing world or is its foreign aid simply a way to increase its economic foothold in many countries?

Further Reading

Strangely enough for an area in which critics charge that the EU has not lived up to expectations, there are numerous published studies on different aspects of the EU's foreign and security policy. The following is just a small selection.

Charlotte Bretherton and John Vogler. *The European Union as a Global Actor*, 2nd ed. (London: Routledge, 2006).
> Offers a new theoretical approach to trying to understand the EU in the international system.

Karen E. Smith. *European Union Foreign Policy in a Changing World* (Cambridge: Polity, 2008).
> An assessment of the EU's foreign policy objectives, its foreign policy instruments, and its record in the fields of human rights and other issues.

Christopher Hill and Michael Smith, eds. *International Relations and the European Union*, 2nd ed. (Oxford: Oxford University Press, 2011).
> An edited collection with chapters on goals, institutions, processes, and specific activities and impacts.

Janet Adamski, Mary Troy Johnson, and Christina M. Schweiss, eds. *Old Europe, New Security: Evolution for a Complex World* (Aldershot: Ashgate, 2006).
> Responds to criticisms that the EU is not pulling its weight by arguing that—instead of relying on military means—it is developing a variety of economic and diplomatic tools to respond to security problems.

Steve March and Hans Mackenstein. *The International Relations of the EU* (New York: Longman, 2004).
> A survey of the economic and security dimensions of the EU's international relations, assessing their strengths and weaknesses.

Notes

1. Jean Groux and Philippe Manin, *The European Communities in the International Order* (Brussels: Commission of the European Communities, 1985).

2. See Klaus Knorr, *Power and Wealth: The Political Economy of International Power* (New York: Basic Books, 1973), 3–4. Joseph S. Nye, *Bound to Lead: The Changing Nature of American Power* (New York: Basic Books, 1991), and *Soft Power: The Means to Success in World Politics* (New York: PublicAffairs, 2004).

3. For further discussion, see Clyde Prestowitz, *Rogue Nation: American Unilateralism and the Failure of Good Intentions* (New York: Basic Books, 2003).

4. See Janet Adamski, Mary Troy Johnson, and Christina M. Schweiss, eds., *Old Europe, New Security: Evolution for a Complex World* (Aldershot: Ashgate, 2006).

5. Craig R. Whitney, "War in the Gulf: Europe; Gulf Fighting Shatters Europeans' Fragile Unity," *New York Times*, 25 January 1991, http://www.nytimes .com/1991/01/25/world/war-in-the-gulf-europe-gulf-fighting-shatters -europeans-fragile-unity.html.

6. Quoted in Alan Riding, "Conflict in Yugoslavia: Europeans Send High-Level Team," *New York Times*, 29 June 1991, http://www.nytimes.com/1991 /06/29/world/conflict-in-yugoslavia-europeans-send-high-level-team.html.

7. J. Bryan Collester, "How Defense 'Spilled Over' into the CFSP: Western European Union (WEU) and the European Security and Defense Identity (ESDI)," in Maria Green Cowles and Michael Smith, eds., *The State of the European Union: Risks, Reform, Resistance, and Revival* (Oxford: Oxford University Press, 2000).

8. Michael Smith, "What's Wrong with the CFSP? The Politics of Institutional Reform," in Pierre-Henri Laurent and Marc Maresceau, eds., *The State of the European Union, vol. 4: Deepening and Widening* (Boulder: Lynne Rienner, 1998).

9. There have been recent signs, however, that Sweden and Finland may be prepared to take stronger positions on foreign policy, prompted by concerns about Russia. See *The Economist*, "New Boots for NATO?" 30 June 2007.

10. International Institute for Strategic Studies, *The Military Balance 2011*. 111, no. 1. The executive summary is available at http://www.iiss.org /publications/military-balance/the-military-balance-2011/press-statement/.

11. For more details, see Collester, "How Defense 'Spilled Over' into the CFSP."

12. Seth G. Jones, *The Rise of European Security Cooperation* (Cambridge: Cambridge University Press, 2007).

13. Bastian Giegerich and William Wallace, "Not Such a Soft Power: The External Deployment of European Forces," *Survival* 46, no. 2 (January 2004): 163–82.

14. Paul Reynolds, "Defence: Atlantic or European?" BBC News Online, 1 December 2003, http://news.bbc.co.uk/2/hi/europe/3253724.stm.

15. European Commission, DG for Trade, 2012, http://trade.ec.europa.eu /doclib/docs/2006/september/tradoc_122531.pdf.

16. Eurostat, epp.eurostat.ec.europe.eu/portal/page/portal/eurostat/home; U.S. Census Bureau, "U.S. Internation Trade in Goods and Services Highlights," 2013, http://www.census.gov/indicator/www/ustrade.html.

17. Sophie Meunier, *Trading Voices: The European Union in International Commercial Negotiations* (Princeton, NJ: Princeton University Press, 2005).

18. On the EU's efforts at democracy promotion, see Richard Youngs, ed., *The European Union and Democracy Promotion* (Baltimore, MD: Johns Hopkins University Press, 2010).

19. For details, see Graham Avery and Fraser Cameron, *The Enlargement of the European Union* (Sheffield: Sheffield Academic Press, 1998).

20. On the EU's "neighborhood policy," see Richard G. G. Whitman and Stefan Wolff, eds., *The European Neighbourhood Policy in Perspective* (New York: Palgrave Macmillan, 2010).

21. Oksana Antonenko and Kathryn Pinnick, eds., *Russia and the European Union* (London: Routledge, 2005).

22. David Allen and Michael Smith, "External Policy Developments," in Geoffrey Edwards and Georg Wiessala, eds., *The European Union: Annual Review of the EU 2001/2002* (Oxford: Blackwell, 2002).

23. Calculated from European Commission, 2011, http://trade.ec.europa.eu /doclib/docs/2006/september/tradoc_111499.pdf, and World Trade Organization, 2011, http://www.wto.org/english/rcs_e/statis_e/its2012_e/its12 _appendix_e.htm.

24. Yves Bourdet, Joakim Gullstrand, and Karin Olofsdotter, eds., *The European Union and Developing Countries: Trade, Aid and Growth in an Integrating World* (Cheltenham: Edward Elgar, 2007).

25. On EU development aid and cooperation, see Paul Hoebink, *European Development Cooperation: In Between the Local and the Global* (Amsterdam: Amsterdam University Press, 2010).

26. Figures from the OECD (DAC Members' Net Official Development Assistance in 2011, 2007, http://www.oecd.org/general/searchresults/?q=dac %20members%20net%20official%20development&cx=01243260174851139 1518:xzeadub0b0a&cof=FORID:11&ie=UTF-8.

27. Carol Cosgrove and Pierre-Henri Laurent, "The Unique Relationship: The European Community and the ACP," in John Redmond, ed., *The External Relations of the European Community* (New York: St. Martin's, 1992).

28. For details, see Martin Holland, "Resisting Reform or Risking Revival? Renegotiating the Lomé Convention," in Cowles and Smith, eds., *The State of the European Union.*

29. Karin Arts and Anna K. Dickson, *EU Development Cooperation: From Model to Symbol* (Manchester: Manchester University Press, 2004).

16

The EU and the United States

Chapter Overview

- The relationship between the United States and the European Union is the most important in the world, but it has not always been an easy one: wary of each other before World War II, the Cold War forged a relationship of both common democratic values and mutual security needs. Since the end of the Cold War, the differences between the two have become more clear, a result of diverging sets of values and goals.
- Most of the time, the United States and the EU agree on policy, and the relationship between the two sides is close and productive. But they have also disagreed on such things as the role and scope of the United Nations, the gravity and proper response to the threat of climate change, and the role and powers of the International Criminal Court.
- Americans and Europeans have some fundamentally different attitudes about such things as the role of government, patriotism

and national identity, religion, and moral issues (such as abortion). These differences help to shape American and European attitudes on international relations generally and on specific policy areas, and they explain the sometimes uneasy relationship between the two allies.

The relationship between the United States and the European Union is the most important in the world. They are both economic superpowers, they have the most powerful military forces in the world, and they have used their economic and military leadership to achieve global political influence (the U.S. much more so than the EU). They dominate global culture—their corporations spearheading a communications and technology revolution that has given new meaning to the global impact of "the West." Their residents are the wealthiest, healthiest, and best-educated people in the world; their leaders agree on the promotion of democracy and capitalism; and what one says and does matters a great deal not only to the other but to much of the rest of the world.

And yet the relationship has not always been an easy one. Before World War II, Americans were suspicious of European values, wary of being pulled in to European conflicts, and critical of European colonialism. Meanwhile, Europeans cast nervous glances at the rising political, economic, and cultural influence of the United States. After World War II, Europeans fell into an often reluctant subservience to American leadership, worrying about U.S. foreign policy priorities but admitting their need for American economic investment and security guarantees. Privately, European governments might have criticized U.S. policy, but publicly they went along. As Europe recovered from the war, however, Europeans became more self-reliant and more conscious of their differences with the United States. They differed not just over policy issues, but over political and social norms and values.

The 2003 crisis over Iraq was a watershed in the transatlantic relationship. For the first time since 1945, several European governments—notably Germany and France—openly opposed U.S. policy. American critics accused the EU of dithering and of trying to appease the regime of Saddam Hussein. U.S. defense secretary Donald Rumsfeld dismissed Germany and France as "problems" and as "Old Europe," while arguing that the center of gravity had shifted eastward to "New Europe." Europeans responded by using unflattering Wild West metaphors to describe President George W. Bush.

The fallout over Iraq was the most serious crisis in modern transatlantic relations, and while much has been done to repair the cracks, many wonder if the U.S.–EU relationship will ever be the same again. Certainly the inauguration of President Barack Obama was widely welcomed in Europe (perhaps not least because of his symbolism as the "anti-Bush") and led to an improvement in transatlantic relations. However, personalities and even some normal dissent on strategic interests aside, Europe and the U.S. no longer have quite the same relationship they enjoyed during the Cold War. Buoyed by their economic power and new political influence over the last decade, Europeans have become more assertive and more willing to pursue their own interpretation of the most pressing international problems, and more aware of how they differ with the U.S. on the solutions. Optimists argue that the transatlantic relationship is vital, that both sides need each other, and that cooperation is far preferable to disagreement. But pessimists wonder if the two sides can really agree on the critical issues, given their different values and their often contrasting views about the most serious international problems, their causes, and their most likely solutions.

THE CHANGING INTERNATIONAL SYSTEM

Throughout the Cold War (approximately 1945 to 1991), the most important international relationship in the world was that between the United States and the Soviet Union. Both countries were superpowers, meaning that they had the ability and willingness to project their power on a global level.[1] The tensions between the two dominated the international system, and the key foreign and security policy choices made by one were driven by the other and by the other's attempts to contain and limit the one's relative influence. This bipolar system was dominated by competition in the development of weapons, the cultivation of military alliances, the drive for political and economic influence, the promotion of ideological values, the use of covert methods for gathering intelligence and undermining each other's influence, and the fighting of proxy wars between client states. The relationship was driven heavily by security matters, with economic issues entering the equation only in relation to the ideological struggle between capitalism and communism.[2]

Since the end of the Cold War and the breakup of the Soviet Union, majority opinion holds that we have moved into a new unipolar international era in which there is only one remaining superpower: the United States. Samuel Huntington wrote in 1999 of the U.S. as the "lonely superpower," existing in a world in which there were no significant other powers and it could resolve important international issues alone, with no combination of other states having the power to prevent it.[3] John Ikenberry later argued that the preeminence of American power was unprecedented in modern history: "We live in a one-superpower world, and there is no serious competitor in sight."[4] Former French foreign minister Hubert Védrine went further, claiming that the United States was a hyperpower, enjoying a level of global influence unprecedented in history.[5] The United States has been described as a global hegemon, with interests throughout the world, ownership of a surplus of usable power, and the ability to defy all challengers.[6] Some have even described it as a new kind of empire, upon which the world has come to rely for the promotion of peace, order, the rule of law, and stable fiscal and monetary policies.[7]

Most of the claims about U.S. power are based on its military dominance, and certainly the statistics are impressive: as noted in chapter 15, the U.S. has the world's biggest and most technologically advanced military, and a defense budget that is almost bigger than that of the rest of the world combined.[8] But military might is not always what it seems. The examples of Vietnam and Iraq show that there are limits to what even the U.S. can achieve, and some argue that military power may make the world less secure by encouraging hostility from states that feel threatened by U.S. power.[9]

More broadly, the realities of the international system have changed since the end of the Cold War, the ideological competition of the superpowers having been replaced by a complex set of threats and challenges in which military options play a minimal role: these include trade and economic competition, the pressures of globalization, and a host of issues ranging from environmental decline to public health, communications, human rights, migration, and population issues. Even international terrorism, the most alarming of current threats to personal and national security, cannot—in the views of many—effectively be resolved by military responses. This is certainly the view among most Europeans, and—as we saw in chapter 15—the EU has responded to changed international circumstances by deploying a broader set of nonmilitary tools.

Within this wider landscape, the relationship between the EU and the U.S. has changed, not just because of how the two sides see and relate to each other, but also because of how they each see and relate to the rest of the world. They are both deeply invested in each other, and both continue to look to each other for support and reassurance on critical international problems, but the balance of the relationship has changed. During the Cold War, Western Europe mainly followed the American lead, but it still played a critical role in American geostrategic policy, as both the location of many

Cold War confrontations and the primary U.S. ally in competition with the Soviet Union. Since the end of the Cold War, however, Europeans have become more confident and assertive, and less willing to follow the American lead. The EU may lack a large military and a common security policy, but its economic power is something that the U.S. cannot ignore. It is an enormously complex relationship currently undergoing changes whose effects are not yet clear.

THE TRANSATLANTIC RELATIONSHIP

As we saw in earlier chapters, the United States has played a critical role in the development of the EU, through both intentional policy and unintentional effects. Intentionally, the United States made a signal contribution to the birth of the EU by supporting the economic reconstruction of post-war Western Europe through the Marshall Plan and by encouraging Europeans to work together in the Organization for European Economic Cooperation. Meanwhile, through NATO, the United States also provided a security umbrella that allowed Western Europe to concentrate its energy and resources on internal reorganization and reconstruction instead of external threats. American administrations also generally gave their blessing to European integration, understanding that it played an important role in building European peace and stability, strengthening the foundations of Western Europe so it could become a marketplace for American exports, reinforcing its abilities to resist and offset Soviet power, and encouraging it as a political and economic partner of the United States.

At the same time, the U.S. has contributed unintentionally to European integration, in two main ways. First, it has pursued policies that have helped unite Europeans either in support of U.S. policy or in opposition, for example concerning the Soviet threat during the Cold War, the war in Vietnam, or U.S. policy in the 1980s toward Central America. All of this reached a watershed with the controversial 2003 invasion of Iraq. Second, U.S. policy initiatives have helped Europeans identify their weaknesses. For example, it was the feeble European responses to the crises in the Balkans in the 1990s that encouraged Europeans to work harder at developing common security policies.

Anti-Americanism (or, more accurately, opposition to American policy) grew in Western Europe during the 1960s despite the money, personnel, and resources the United States was still committing to its security, and despite the growth in transatlantic economic interdependence. The Nixon administration declared 1973 to be the "Year of Europe" in U.S. foreign policy, calling for a new "Atlantic Charter" in which Western Europeans committed themselves to a bigger contribution to the common defense of Western interests and reciprocity on matters of trade. But in June of that year—without consulting the Europeans—Nixon signed an agreement with the USSR on the prevention of nuclear war and the promotion of dé-tente (an easing of strained relations). Given that they had the most to lose in the event of a possible reduction in the number of U.S. troops based in Western Europe, Community governments were not pleased.[10]

The outbreak of another Arab–Israeli War (the "Yom Kippur" war) in October 1973 further emphasized the different views of Americans and Europeans, with Europeans more ready than Americans to criticize the fail-ure of Israel to return land it had illegally occupied since the 1967 Arab–Israeli War. Europeans grew suspicious of U.S. foreign policy, while Americans felt that Europeans could not be trusted to provide support where they felt it was needed. U.S. Community relations were further strained in the late 1970s and early 1980s by tensions with the Soviet bloc. The Community was slow to criticize the 1979 Soviet invasion of Af-ghanistan; West Germany was the only EC member state to support the U.S.-led boycott of the 1980 Moscow Olympics; and when the Reagan administration deployed new nuclear missiles in Europe, there was a revival of the Western European antinuclear movement, which attracted a level of popular support not seen since the late 1950s.

The end of the Cold War saw a number of diplomatic initiatives reflecting the recognition by the United States of the new importance of the EU and the relative decline of the central role of NATO. In a December 1989 speech, U.S. secretary of state James Baker spoke of the need for stronger economic and political ties and for stronger institutional and consultative links.[11] Ne-gotiations were opened, leading to the November 1990 signature of the first bilateral agreement between the two, the Transatlantic Declaration. This committed the two sides to regular high-level contacts and called for coop-eration in a variety of policy areas, including combating terrorism, drug trafficking, international crime, and preventing the spread of weapons of mass destruction.[12] Similarly, in late 1995 the New Transatlantic Agenda was signed, under which the two sides agreed to move from consultation to joint action aimed at promoting peace and democracy around the world, contributing to the expansion of world trade, and improving transatlantic ties. NATO was described in the Agenda as the "centerpiece of transatlantic security," and there was also a call for a New Transatlantic Marketplace.

Yet the end of the Cold War also created new difficulties. The United States hoped for a peace dividend in the form of a reduced need to finance and staff its security efforts, but soon found that new risks and dangers had replaced the old tensions of the Cold War, demanding a new set of approaches and structures. Any hopes among American leaders that the Community could take more of the responsibility for dealing with international crises were dashed by the divided European response to the 1990–91 Gulf War and the absence of Community leadership in the Balkans. Economic matters now also achieved a new significance with the European single market program and the growth of economic competition from the Community (see Box 16.1).

The terrorist attacks of September 2001 redefined the transatlantic relationship, injecting new elements into the definition of security policy on both sides of the Atlantic: terrorism (especially when it involved suicide attacks) (a) could not be met with conventional military responses, (b) transcended national borders, (c) showed that U.S. military power, while impressive, was not a guarantor of success in itself, and (d) revealed that Americans and Europeans had different definitions of both the causes of terrorism and the most effective responses. President Bush liked to argue that the terrorists had attacked the U.S. because they "hated" America and were envious of its democratic record, and that violence should be met with force. Europeans were more inclined to look at the root causes of militant resentment—including U.S. policy on the Arab–Israeli problem and the stationing of U.S. troops in Saudi Arabia—and to design policy accordingly.

The attacks prompted a massive outpouring of political and public sympathy in the EU, and European leaders hoped that the tragedy would herald a new era in U.S. foreign policy, with an emphasis on multilateralism and diplomacy. Within months, however, it was clear that the Bush administration planned to pursue unilateral responses to terrorism. President Bush drew particular European criticism for his reference in January 2002 to the "axis of evil," meaning Iran, Iraq, and North Korea—a characterization that was dismissed by the French foreign minister as "simplistic." Meanwhile, EU external affairs commissioner Chris Patten dismissed U.S. unilateralism as "ultimately ineffective and self-defeating."

Critics charged that the Bush administration had failed to provide global leadership at a time when a strong international stand was needed to combat terrorism. But while the easy knee-jerk reaction was to focus on the policies of a particular administration, others began to ask whether there were long-term structural differences in play and whether it would in fact

Box 16.1 Transatlantic Economic Ties

The North Atlantic is the wealthiest and most important two-way economic street in the world. The EU and the U.S. economies account together for just under half of world GDP and nearly a third of world trade flows. Indeed, whatever analysts claim about the rising economic power of China, it pales by comparison to the size and productivity of the EU–U.S. nexus. Total US investment in the EU is three times higher than in all of Asia, and EU investment in the U.S. is eight times more than that of India and China together.[13] The EU and U.S. also control two of the key international currencies, the dollar and the euro, and lead the world in the development of new technology. Consider, too, the following realities:

- The EU and the U.S. account for about one-fifth of each other's bilateral trade, and they are each other's biggest sources of foreign direct investment. In 2011 EU investment flows to the U.S. totaled €110.7 billion ($148 billion) while U.S. investment in the EU was €114.8 billion ($154 billion).
- While millions of Europeans work for U.S.-owned corporations, the reverse has become true as well. Already by 2004 about as many Americans (nearly 4.4 million) worked for European companies as vice versa.[14] "Our multinationals are so thoroughly intertwined," said EU trade commissioner Pascal Lamy in 2003, "that some of them have forgotten whether their origins are European or American." In his view, the size and significance of the relationship had become such that it defined "the shape of the global economy as a whole."[15]

Throughout the Cold War, the balance was firmly in favor of the United States, which was the world's dominating economic superpower. But the rise of the European single market—together with all its related economic effects—has changed the balance. Tellingly, the U.S. has a large trade deficit with the EU—around $99 billion in 2011.[16]

have made any difference who was in the White House. This point has been vindicated to some degree by the election of Barack Obama. Although immediately before and after his election Obama enjoyed huge popularity in Europe, his administration's foreign policy proved a disappointment to many Europeans, who had hoped that he might take a more active approach to the Arab–Israeli problem and to dealing with climate change. President Obama has even stepped up the extremely controversial policy of targeted killings of suspected terrorists (most via drone strike) started under the Bush administration.

In short, the problem (for Europeans) was never so much the Bush administration as a United States that remains still influenced by Cold War definitions of the structure of the international system and by a heavy reliance on the views and priorities of President Eisenhower's famous military-industrial complex. After long assuming that they were on the same page when it came to universal issues such as democracy and capitalism, Americans and Europeans were now motivated to look more closely at the transatlantic relationship, and what they saw surprised them.

A LITANY OF DISPUTES

Most of the time, the United States and the EU agree on policy, and the relationship between the two is close and productive. But they have also often disagreed, and the disputes they have had are indicative not just of Europeans' increasing willingness to resist following the American lead when the two disagree, but also of the extent to which the two bring different sets of values and goals to bear on their interpretations of the priorities of international relations.[17] Consider the following examples.

The United Nations. When the United Nations was created in 1945, it was with U.S. support and involvement, and an insistence by the Roosevelt administration that the mistakes made in the design and execution of the European-dominated League of Nations after World War I be avoided. It is all the more ironic, then, that while Europeans have been active supporters of the UN, and champions of the Security Council as a forum for the resolution of disputes, the United States— particularly since the 1980s—has kept its distance. Not only is majority public opinion in the United States hostile to the UN (whose work is misunderstood by most Americans), but the United States for several years refused even to pay its membership dues, at one point owing nearly $1.7 billion. The United States is the only major country that refuses to allow its troops to operate under UN command. European states have few such qualms.

The banana wars. Growing out of the ongoing transatlantic dispute over agricultural subsidies, the United States was for many years critical of EU policy that favored imports of bananas from its former Caribbean colonies over those from Latin America, which were distributed mainly by U.S. corporations. The United States brought the matter before GATT, which ruled against the EU but was unable to take action because of the dispute resolution procedures used by GATT. Its successor—the World Trade Organization—also ruled against the EU and gave it until January 1999 to take action. The United States meanwhile threatened to impose 100 percent duties on a wide selection of imports from the EU unless it respected the WTO ruling. In a landmark ruling in April 1999 the WTO authorized the United States to impose the sanctions, which it did. The dispute was finally settled in April 2001, to the benefit of the United States.[18]

Climate change. The first major dispute between the EU and the Bush administration came in 2001 over the signature of a protocol to the 1992 Convention on Climate Change. The goal of the convention was to reduce the carbon dioxide emissions implicated in climate change. The United States is the source of about 22 percent of global emissions, and the EU of about 16 percent, so the two played a major role in the negotiations. In 1997 a meeting of signatories to the convention took place in Kyoto, Japan, with the goal of reaching agreement on specific reductions in emissions of CO_2 and other greenhouse gases by 2008–12. The EU pushed for a 15 percent reduction by 2010 (on 1990 levels), but the United States wanted only a return to 1990 levels by 2010 and objected to the fact that China and India were to be exempted. The final agreement was for different reductions for different countries, including 8 percent for the EU and 7 percent for the United States.[19] Shortly after coming to office, however, President Bush announced that his administration would not sign the protocol, angering the EU as much for the decision as for the abrupt and unilateral manner in which it was announced.

The International Criminal Court. In 1998 a treaty was signed in Rome establishing a new International Criminal Court, designed to prosecute and bring to justice individuals responsible for genocide, crimes against humanity, and war crimes. Following the required number of national ratifications, the court was established in The Hague in 2002. First conceived during the Nuremburg trials of Nazi leaders after World War II, the court is independent of the United Nations, and—unlike the International Court of Justice that is part of the UN and rules on disputes between governments— it can prosecute individuals. All EU states have now ratified the Rome treaty, and there had been little to no public or political discussion about the merits of the Court in the EU. Britain, France, and Germany became its biggest sources of funds.

By contrast, the United States has been both wary and critical of the Court, and has informed the Court that it does not intend to become a party to the document (placing it in the company of other non-signatories, such as China, Iraq, Iran, Israel, and Sudan). President Clinton argued that U.S. soldiers might be subject to politically motivated or frivolous prose-cutions, but—in one of his final acts before leaving office—he signed the treaty. The Bush administration took a different view, stating its opposition to the Court and emphasizing concerns about the potential prosecution of American military personnel, a position which has not changed under Pres-ident Obama. The United States also negotiated bilateral agreements with individual governments under which they have agreed not to surrender U.S. nationals to the Court. It also accused several EU member states of lobbying these governments in an effort to keep them from signing the agreements with the United States.[20]

The Arab–Israeli problem. Europeans and Americans have been at odds over the issue of the territories illegally occupied by Israel almost from the time that the occupation began, following the 1967 Arab–Israeli War. Two of the territories—the West Bank and the Gaza Strip—are seen as a potential future Palestinian state, but rather than work actively to achieve that state, successive Israeli administrations have encouraged Jewish settlement in the territories and have often refused to negotiate with Palestinian leaders. Israel has also built a security wall to keep Palestinians out, but instead of following the original border has pushed into significant areas of the West Bank. While successive U.S. administrations have been strong in their support of Israel, and have tended to focus much of their criticism of the Arab–Israeli dispute on the Palestinians, the EU has been more critical of Israeli policy. In the lead-up to the 2003 Gulf War, several EU leaders argued that a settlement of the Arab–Israeli problem should precede an invasion of Iraq.

EXPLAINING THE DIFFERENCES

While there was little question about the closeness and complexity of the transatlantic relationship during the Cold War, the mutual interest of the United States and the EU in containing the Soviet threat papered over a number of important disagreements. With that threat now gone, and the EU established as an economic superpower, the differences have become more obvious. They became particularly clear once George W. Bush moved into the White House and his advisors promoted policies and goals that clearly were at odds with many of those being pursued by the EU: while Bush favored unilateralism, the EU favored multilateralism; while Bush favored use of the military as a tool of foreign policy, the EU kept its military in reserve; while Bush was less concerned with working through international organizations such as the UN, Europeans were champions of multilateralism and of resolving international disputes through diplomacy and the use of international organizations. And although the translatlantic relationship markedly improved with the election of Barack Obama, significant differences still remain.

How can the differences be explained? One approach is to take the long view and to appreciate that Americans and Europeans alike see themselves as exceptional groups of people, with distinctive views of the world and a degree of superiority toward other societies. The notion of American exceptionalism is usually credited to the French philosopher Alexis de Tocqueville, who argued in his study *Democracy in America* that "the position of the Americans is . . . quite exceptional, and it may be believed that no democratic people will ever be placed in a similar one."[21] But it is a strand that runs through American history, connecting a comment made in 1630 by John Winthrop, governor of Massachusetts Bay Colony—"[W]e must consider that we shall be as a City upon a hill. The eyes of all people are upon us"—to Ronald Reagan's attempts to revitalize the national psyche after Vietnam and Watergate,[22] to Bill Clinton's suggestion that the United States is "the indispensable nation" and the only country that could make the difference between war and peace, between freedom and repression, and between hope and fear,[23] to claims by George W. Bush that the U.S. was targeted on September 11 because it is "the brightest beacon for freedom and opportunity in the world."

Europeans, too, have a history of thinking of themselves as exceptional; thus the suggestion by the late Czech president Václav Havel that most Europeans never actually thought about the idea of being European and were taken by surprise when asked by opinion pollsters to declare their European affiliation. He felt that this could be explained by a sense of superiority and a long-held belief among Europeans that they did not need to define themselves in relation to others.[24] European confidence suffered a string of blows with World War I, World War II, and its division during the Cold War. But with the end of the Cold War and the removal of the iron curtain, a new sense of European identity is emerging, much of it based on a new awareness that Europeans have views about politics, economics, society, and international problems that regularly put them at odds with Americans. Consider the following examples.

- *Contrasting attitudes toward patriotism and nationalism.* Minxin Pei considers the United States "one of the most nationalist countries in the world," a belief which he concludes is based not on notions of ethnic superiority but on a belief in the ideals of American democracy.[25] Where most Americans are delighted to wear their patriotism on their sleeves, Europeans tend to be more wary about pride in country, in large part because they have had to live for so long with the war and conflict that can arise out of aggressive nationalism. The 2008 Pew Global Attitudes Project found that 78 percent of Americans were "very proud" to be American, compared to 44 percent of Spaniards, 42 percent of the British, 39 percent of the French, and 34 percent of Germans.[26]

- *Church and state.* There are significant transatlantic differences in views on the connection between church and state, based on different beliefs about organized religion. The same Pew poll in 2010 showed that 28 percent of Americans attended church services at least once a week, compared to only 16 percent of Spaniards, 11 percent of the British, 6 percent of the French, and 9 percent of Germans. Meanwhile, 70 percent of Americans claimed to believe in God, compared to just 22–24 percent of Germans, Britons, and French; and while nearly two-thirds of Americans held that religion is important in their lives, less than one in five Germans, Britons, Spaniards, or French felt the same way.[27] Moreover, well over half of all Americans believed that it is necessary to believe in God to have morals/good values, while only 20 percent of the British, 19 percent of Spaniards, and 15 percent of the French thought this.[28] Not surprisingly then, religion plays a prominent role in the public and private lives of Americans, as reflected in attitudes toward a wide range of issues, from abortion to the teaching of evolution to doctor-assisted suicide, and the expectation that presidential candidates must make public declarations of faith. Europe, by contrast, is a predominantly secular society in which religion plays only a marginal role (except in the case of the recent debate about the place of Islam in European society).

- *The role of government.* Americans and Europeans have different views about the role that government should play in their lives. Where the majority of Americans feel that it is more important for government to provide them with the freedom to pursue other goals, a strong majority of Europeans feel that it is more important for government to guarantee that no one is in need.[29] The effects can be seen in attitudes toward welfare: Americans use it (more often than most realize) and value it, but Europeans make it more widely available and are more willing to be taxed at higher rates in order to receive more services. Tellingly, the United States is the only liberal democracy in the world that does not have universal health care, a concept that is taken for granted in every European state.

- *Capital punishment.* While capital punishment is legal in most American states, and the United States is one of the few countries that allows it even for minors, it is illegal in the EU. The Charter of Fundamental Rights of the EU says that "no-one shall be condemned to the death penalty, or executed," and no country that uses capital punishment qualifies for EU membership. In preparation for its hoped-for eventual membership in the EU, for example, Turkey abolished capital punishment in 2004.

- *Homosexuality.* Although attitudes are changing rapidly even in the U.S., when asked in 2011 if homosexuality should be accepted by society, some 60 percent of Americans agreed compared to more than 80 percent of Germans, French, Britons, Swedes, and Spaniards.[30] Same-sex marriages are allowed in Belgium, Denmark, France, Iceland, the Netherlands, Portugal, Spain, and Sweden, and same-sex civil unions or partnerships are allowed in Britain, Denmark, Germany, Hungary, Ireland, the Netherlands, Poland, and Switzerland. But while half of Americans support the creation of a "separate but equal" legal status for same-sex couples, only nine states and the District of Columbia currently recognize same-sex marriages and thirty states have passed constitutional amendments against same-sex marriage.

There has been no time in modern history when so many questions have been raised about the future of the transatlantic relationship. Much was taken for granted during the Cold War about how Western Europeans

BOX 16.2 ARE AMERICANS FROM MARS, AND EUROPEANS FROM VENUS?

The debate about the state of transatlantic relations was given a controversial twist in 2002 with the publication of an essay by Robert Kagan, an American neoconservative political commentator.[31] Kagan argued that Europeans and Americans no longer share a common view of the world, and that while Europe has moved into a world of laws, rules, and international cooperation, the United States believes that security and defense depend on the possession and use of military power. On major strategic and international questions, he wrote, "Americans are from Mars and Europeans are from Venus." This is not a transitory state of affairs, he concludes—it is likely to endure. Most European intellectuals feel that the two no longer share a "strategic culture" and that the United States is dominated by a "culture of death." They argue that the United States is less patient with diplomacy and sees the world as divided between good and evil, friends and enemies. Meanwhile, Europeans see a more complex global system and are more tolerant of failure, more patient, and prefer to negotiate and persuade rather than to coerce.

Kagan went on to argue that the differences do not arise naturally out of the character of Europeans and Americans, but are instead a reflection of the relative positions of the two actors in the world; their attitudes have been reversed as their roles have been reversed. When European states were the key global powers in the eighteenth and nineteenth centuries, and when nationalism colored their views of one another, they were more ready to use violence to achieve their goals. But now that Europeans and Americans have traded places, they have also traded perspectives. When the United States was weak, argues Kagan, it used the strategies of the weak, but now that it is strong, it uses the strategies of power.

Kagan's arguments had a mixed response, with the majority seeing them as an accurate summary of the state of play, but with a minority suggesting otherwise. One response argued that Europeans had not stumbled upon a new approach to international relations in which force played only a limited role, but that Europeans have deliberately chosen to be militarily weak; Europe is not a continent of pacifists, but one where the "just" causes of war are actively debated and where there are different opinions about the role of military force.[32] Whatever the opinions about Kagan's thesis, however, it had the important effect of sparking a vigorous debate about the character and future of the transatlantic relationship.

would mainly follow the U.S. lead, limiting their opposition and criticism to private diplomatic meetings. The majority view today holds that the U.S. is still the dominant partner in the relationship, but the volume of disagreement with this view is growing. Reality today dictates three possible futures for the relationship:

- Continued American dominance. Certainly there are many Americans who believe this is the best and most likely option, arguing that only the United States has the resources to be able to deal with the most serious security problems and that there is little on the horizon to challenge U.S. economic power.
- A more equal relationship between the two sides. Numerous analyses hold that Europeans and Americans can and must continue to work together in their mutual interests, and that a more secure and prosperous world requires a division of labor, drawing on the best features of American and European approaches to international relations; in other words, the world needs European saloonkeepers as much as it needs American sheriffs.[33]
- Isolationism. Some worry that the U.S. might react to more disagreements by reverting to isolationism. But U.S. isolationism has always been exaggerated, and today it is less viable than ever before—the United States is simply far too invested in the global economy to make isolationism either possible or desirable.

There is little doubt that Americans and Europeans are diverging on a growing number of important issues, and that the nature of the transatlantic alliance is changing. The two sides continue to have much in common and many shared interests, but the growing unilateralism of the United States has combined with the growing confidence of the European Union to raise many questions about the future of the relationship. The disagreements about Iraq not only brought out the very different American and European perceptions of the world but also provided further encouragement for Europeans to back up their economic might with a unified military. Many Europeans—notably British political leaders—still want to keep the United States engaged in a positive manner with the international community, but many more now subscribe to the Franco-German view that the EU should develop a more independent voice in the world. Transatlantic relations are clearly at a new and critical point in their evolution.

President Obama's recent call for a free-trade agreement between the United States and the European Union is an indication that both sides are aware of this crucial juncture in the transatlantic relationship.[34] Entrenched interests in agriculture, pharmaceuticals, and other sectors of the two economies will no doubt fight to maintain their protected status, and other issues—such as European consumers' rejection of genetically modified food already well accepted in the U.S.—will prove thorny. Nevertheless, even a modest trade agreement between the U.S. and EU could stimulate economic growth (by getting rid of costly tariffs) and lower prices on goods in America and Europe. And just as importantly, it could do much to dampen tensions between the two partners and thus help to revive the transatlantic political relationship as well.

Questions to Consider

1. Did the end of the Cold War signal a decisive shift in U.S.–European relations? If so, why?
2. What factors might explain the U.S.'s and Europe's different views on the International Criminal Court? On climate change legislation?
3. Americans and Europeans differ on what they see as the proper role of government. What historical factors might help explain this difference in political culture?

Further Reading

Jussi Hanhimaki, Benedikt Schoenborn, and Barbara Zanchetta. *Transatlantic Relations since 1945: An Introduction* (Abingdon: Routledge, 2012).
    A good survey of the evolution of U.S.–European relations since the end of World War II.
Robert Kagan. *Of Paradise and Power: America and Europe in the New World* (New York: Knopf, 2003).
    A controversial analysis by an American neoconservative, who argues that American and European views of the world are diverging, that they agree on little, and that they understand each other less and less.
Peter Baldwin. *The Narcissism of Minor Differences: How America and Europe Are Alike* (New York: Oxford University Press, 2009).
    An assessment that runs counter to popular perceptions and argues that Europe and the U.S. are more similar than they think.

Stefan Fröhlich. *The New Geopolitics of Transatlantic Relations: Coordinated Responses to Common Dangers* (Baltimore, MD: Johns Hopkins University Press, 2012).

A new assessment of transatlantic relations, looking at the similarities and differences in economic aims, political habits, and cultural history.

Notes

1. For more discussion, see John McCormick, *The European Superpower* (Basingstoke, UK: Palgrave Macmillan, 2006), 17–20.

2. For an accessible history of the Cold War, see John Lewis Gaddis, *The Cold War: A New History* (New York: Penguin, 2007).

3. See, for example, Samuel Huntington, "The Lonely Superpower," *Foreign Affairs* 78, no. 2 (March–April 1999).

4. G. John Ikenberry, "Introduction," in G. John Ikenberry, ed., *America Unrivaled: The Future of the Balance of Power* (Ithaca: Cornell University Press, 2002), 1.

5. Hubert Védrine, with Dominique Moïsi, *France in an Age of Globalization* (Washington, DC: Brookings Institution, 2001), 2.

6. Josef Joffe, "Defying History and Theory: The United States as the 'Last Remaining Superpower,'" in Ikenberry, ed., *America Unrivaled*.

7. Niall Ferguson, *Colossus: The Price of America's Empire* (New York: Penguin, 2004), 2.

8. See International Institute for Strategic Studies, *The Military Balance 2011* 111, no. 1. The executive summary is available at http://www.iiss.org /publications/military-balance/the-military-balance-2011/press-statement/.

9. See discussion in Chalmers Johnson, *Blowback: The Costs and Consequences of American Empire* (New York: Metropolitan, 2000).

10. Mark Gilbert, *Surpassing Realism: The Politics of European Integration Since 1945* (Lanham, MD: Rowman and Littlefield, 2003), 133–34.

11. *New York Times*, "Upheaval in the East," 13 December 1989.

12. European Commission, *Transatlantic Declaration on EC–US Relations*, 23 November 1990 (Brussels: European Commission, 1991).

13. All figures cited from the European Commission, 2012, http://ec .europa.eu/trade/creating-opportunities/bilateral-relations/countries/united -states/.

14. Figures quoted by Raymond J. Ahearn, *US–European Union Trade Relations: Issues and Policy Challenges* (Washington, DC: Congressional Research Service, 2005).

15. Pascal Lamy, speech before Congressional Economic Leadership Institute, Washington, DC, 4 March 2003.

16. Figure cited from U.S. Census Bureau, "Trade in Goods with European Union," 2012, http://www.census.gov/foreign-trade/balance/c0003.html.

17. For an overview of some of the major foreign policy issues dividing the U.S. and EU, see Münevver Cebeci, *Issues in EU and US Foreign Policy* (New York: Lexington Books, 2011).

18. See Robert Read, "The 'Banana Split': The EU–US Banana Trade Dispute and the Effects of EU Market Liberalisation," in Nicholas Perdikis and Robert Read, eds., *The WTO and the Regulation of International Trade: Recent Trade Disputes Between the European Union and the United States* (Cheltenham: Edward Elgar, 2005).

19. For details, see John McCormick, *Environmental Policy in the European Union* (Basingstoke, UK: Palgrave Macmillan, 2001), 280–90.

20. For more details, see "Q&A: International Criminal Court," BBC News Online, 13 July 2002, http://news.bbc.co.uk/2/hi/europe/1923555.stm, and the International Criminal Court, http://www.icc-cpi.int.

21. Alexis de Tocqueville, *Democracy in America*, vol. 2 (New York: Penguin, 2003), book 1, chapter 9. For a thought-provoking analysis of American exceptionalism, see the survey "A Nation Apart," *Economist*, 8–14 November 2003.

22. Trevor B. McCrisken, *American Exceptionalism and the Legacy of Vietnam: US Foreign Policy Since 1974* (Basingstoke, UK: Palgrave Macmillan, 2003), chapter 5.

23. William J. Clinton, speech at George Washington University, 5 August 1996.

24. Václav Havel, address to the European Parliament, Strasbourg, 16 February 2000.

25. Minxin Pei, "The Paradoxes of American Nationalism," *Foreign Policy* 136 (May/June 2003): 30–37.

26. Pew Global Attitudes Project, 2008, http://www.pewglobal.org/question-search/?qid=436&cntIDs=&stdIDs=.

27. Associated Press/Ipsos poll, "Religious Fervor in U.S. Surpasses Faith in Many Other Highly Industrial Countries," 6 June 2005, http://www.ipsos-na.com/news-polls/pressrelease.aspx?id=2694.

28. Pew Global Attitudes Project, 2011, http://www.pewglobal.org/question-search/?qid=1126&cntIDs=&stdIDs=.

29. Figures on patriotism, religion, and government are from Allensbach Opinion Research Institute, National Opinion Research Center, and Pew Research Center, quoted in "A Nation Apart," 42.

30. Pew Global Attitudes Project, 2011, http://www.pewglobal.org /question-search/?qid=1125&cntIDs=&stdIDs=.

31. Robert Kagan, *Of Paradise and Power: America and Europe in the New World* (New York: Knopf, 2003). This is an extended version of the original essay published in the journal *Policy Review* (June–July 2002).

32. Anand Menon, Kalypso Nicolaidis, and Jennifer Welsh, "In Defence of Europe: A Response to Kagan," *Journal of European Affairs* 2, no. 3 (August 2004): 5–14.

33. Menon, Nicolaidis, and Welsh, "In Defence of Europe."

34. On this, see *The Economist*, "Come on, TTIP," 16 February 2013, 6.

CONCLUSIONS

The EU is facing what many would consider to be the gravest crisis in its history. To be sure, pessimism has always colored the musings of those who keep an eye on European affairs. Even before the ink had dried on the Treaty of Paris, ranks of doubting Thomases wondered if the European experiment was viable. There was too much complicated history to resolve, they said, and keeping the French and the Germans at peace was too tall an order. Following Paris (signed by disappointingly few countries—six), skeptics took heart at the collapse of the European Defense Community and the European Political Community. Following Rome (signed by the same few countries), there was de Gaulle's veto of further enlargement, then the empty chair crisis, and then Western Europe was stung by the collapse of Bretton Woods and the energy crises of the 1970s.

Thereafter, Europe's trials and tribulations followed one upon another, chipping away at the foundations of European cooperation and fulfilling the warnings of the pessimists. There were the squabbles over the budget in the 1980s, the ongoing arguments over CAP, the divisions over the 1990–91 Gulf War and the Balkans, the ERM crisis, the Danish rejection of Maastricht, the resignation of the Commission, the Irish rejection of Nice, the Danish and Swedish rejection of the euro, and the French and Dutch rejection of the constitutional treaty. For Euroskeptics, the breakdown of this treaty especially cast a heavier pall over the entire future direction, confirmed the general collapse of confidence in Europe, and threatened to lead to strategic and institutional paralysis.

Writing in 1993, somewhere between the signing of the Maastricht treaty and completion of the single market, Stanley Hoffman—one of the leading American scholars of the European Union—found little to celebrate in the state of European affairs. Maastricht, he lamented, had "marked the beginning of a serious crisis" for Europe; every Western European economy was stagnant, European governments had turned inward, troubling questions were being asked about the relationship between the EU and its member states, there was little progress on the single currency, Italian politics faced an "apocalyptic crisis," Britain was still in decline, Yugoslavia had been a "disastrous tragedy," and Europe's ambitious plans were "now falling apart." Disheartened by what he saw, Hoffman concluded that it might be time to say "goodbye to a united Europe."[1]

Although with time Hoffman's specific assessments were shown to have been wrong, it is nevertheless true that the current crisis in the eurozone is testing the EU like no other before it. Dramatic economic problems in not only Greece but in Spain as well, the possible departure of one or more countries from the common currency, a collapse of confidence in the economic outlooks for many EU countries, and even a collapse of the euro would have been unthinkable just a few years ago. The European public is nervous, national tensions have surfaced, and Euroskeptics feel vindicated.

Yet as with so many crises before, the current crisis in the EU has also brought into more sharp relief the options facing the EU—the paths that might be taken. There seem to be three possible scenarios:

The end of the current eurozone. This most dire scenario would, of course, signal the departure of Greece, but could certainly also mean Spain and Italy—and perhaps many other states (such as Cyprus) as well. The eurozone would either then completely collapse or be shrunk to a core of relatively (economically) well-performing countries. Although some critics have suggested that this is the only realistic (and perhaps desirable) option given the current crisis, a collapse or shrinking of the eurozone would be disastrous for Spain, Greece, and others. Any possible gains they might reap from the reintroduction of a (devalued) currency would be more than offset by enormous economic dislocation, with its attendant bank runs and other capital flight.

It would also be disastrous for the more economically sound countries, such as Germany, as its exports (calculated in euros) would now be far too expensive for the average Greek or Spanish consumer. The subsequent loss of this export market would most likely induce a very sharp recession across Europe that would far eclipse today's present economic situation. It would also have grave political consequences, with a probable sharp rise in national tensions and a resulting loss of confidence in the EU project that probably could not be overcome. This scenario presumes nothing about the intentions of all the major actors. Indeed, although only those most skeptical of Greece's ability to pull itself out of its hole actively wish for a "Grexit," the implosion of the euro is more likely to happen from *inaction* on the part of the EU rather than from any plan to actively reshape the EU itself.

"Muddling through." The EU could work through the crisis while continuing to move slowly toward more economic and political integration. The EU has already moved in this direction, with the European Stability Mechanism—a kind of permanent rescue fund for troubled EU countries to recapitalize their banks and to slow down or reverse negative trends in sovereign debt—having cleared some early hurdles (such as the challenge to its constitutionality heard by the German high court, which did affirm this). As has happened so often in the past, a mutual concession on the part of the member states was required for progress, in this case the establishment of the ESM, which is, at bottom, a greater mutualization of risk in exchange for more central control. A banking union with a EU banking regulator has also been approved. Still, as the latter shows, the devil is truly in the details. The plan has drawn fire from some quarters because, it is said, there are too many banks in the eurozone for the European Central Bank to properly supervise. As Germany's Angela Merkel has argued, "It is not acceptable if every bank is to be controlled, but not every bank can be controlled."[2] Moreover, the UK has expressed fear that a new banking union and greater centralization will negatively impact London, Europe's biggest financial center. Above all, some doubt that these measures alone will be sufficient to reverse the weakness of the eurozone and its most vulnerable members. "Muddling through" may be the only realistic scenario and may also provide enough institutional change to stem the crisis. However, it could also mean a slow erosion of the eurozone (and the EU as a whole in turn), rather than a quick death as events continue to race ahead of the EU's ability and willingness to respond.

A quantum leap toward much closer integration. Closer integration would mean a thoroughgoing Europeaniziation of various institutions and policy areas still left in national hands, most especially greater control over national economic and fiscal policy in exchange for a greater degree of effective action. France and Germany remain the crucial players here, even if other countries (such as those backing Germany and its harder line, the Netherlands and Finland) also will play their own role. Angela Merkel and Guido

Westerwelle, Germany's foreign minister, have both made a series of public statements affirming their commitment to Greece, to solving the problems of the eurozone, and to solutions that would lead to "more Europe." The open question here is whether the Germans (or Dutch, or Finns, or others) will match their rhetorical commitments with a plan to preserve the eurozone that is both far-sighted and workable.

Although the first scenario seems to be the least likely of these three by far, it is still too early to tell whether the EU will continue to take small, but important steps in an attempt to resolve the crisis or whether a new bold agenda for addressing the fundamental problems plaguing the EU will emerge.

Having said that, we should not lose perspective on what the EU has already achieved. Europe has enjoyed the longest spell of general peace in its recorded history, European democracy is stronger than ever before, and the divisions of the Cold War have all but faded into the mists of history. As of 2013, the EU has twenty-eight members (with more waiting politely in line to join), nearly four out of every five Europeans are now "citizens" of the EU, Europe is the biggest capitalist marketplace in the world, and there is virtually unlimited movement of people across most European borders. Moreover, the EU has transformed the lives of Europeans. It has meant freedom of movement, improved living and working conditions, increased multilingualism and protection of minority languages, more productive farmers, the end of currency exchange in most of Europe, more corporate competition, deregulation and the breakup of national monopolies, more investment in the poorer parts of Europe, stronger protection of human rights, regional cooperation on crime and immigration control, the end of the death penalty in Europe, more foreign study for students, cheaper and easier travel, an explosion of tourism, heightened consumer protection, European peacekeeping forces, improved food safety, cleaner air and rivers, greater protection for wildlife, and much more.

Of course, even beyond the successful resolution of the crisis in the eurozone much still remains to be done. European leaders have much to do in working out a common foreign policy, troublesome barriers remain to the single market, the EU must still rely on the security guarantee that only the United States can offer, and the member states continue to squabble with one another on a host of issues. Meanwhile, the merits of European integration remain a harder sell than ever, with large numbers of Europeans—even large majorities in several member states—unconvinced by what their leaders do in their collective name, and often badly informed about how

"Europe" works and what it means to the average citizen. In the wake of the crisis, nationalism has enjoyed a resurgence in much of the continent, translating in some quarters into worrying levels of xenophobia. Traditional suspicions of neighboring countries remain, and the majority of Europeans still do not think of themselves as Europeans.

Finally, work also needs to be done to bridge the gap between Europeans and the EU institutions. The democratic deficit remains a potent psychological barrier to the efficiency of the EU, in part because it denies Europeans adequate involvement in European policy making—other than through the intermediary of their national governments—and in part because it discourages Europeans from taking an interest in European issues. EU decision making also continues to suffer from a reputation for elitism, and several governments repeatedly refuse to hold national referendums on critical issues because they fear that their people will say no. Europeans make matters worse by failing to make effective use of the channels of participation already available to them or to demand greater access to those channels currently monopolized by their governments.

Nevertheless, despite its many longstanding problems and its severe current crisis—indeed in spite of any future challenges it will face—it can still be said that the construction of the European Union has been a unique achievement, and it has helped make Europeans safer, happier, healthier, and wealthier. Even now, it is less realistic to think of European states in isolation than to think of them as elements in a growing European Union. It is harder to find the distinctions between "Europe" and the European Union. Where the journey will end is hard to say, and even though the future promises many more surprises, crises, and dramas, there is no going back.

Notes

1. Stanley Hoffman, "Goodbye to a United Europe?" *New York Review of Books*, 27 May 1993, reprinted in Hoffman, *The European Sisyphus: Essays on Europe 1964–1994* (Boulder: Westview Press, 1995).

2. James Kanter and Stephen Castle, "Weary of Crisis, but Wary of Change," *New York Times*, 13 September, 2012, B1–2.

GLOSSARY

Acquis communitaire. The collective laws and regulations adopted by the EU.

Assent procedure. The legislative process under which no new member state can join the EU without the support of a majority in the European Parliament.

Atlanticism. The belief of some European states that a close transatlantic relationship—particularly with regard to security matters—is preferable to the independent European foreign policy that others prefer.

Authority gap. The difference between what EU institutions would like to be able to do and what EU citizens and governments allow them to do.

Benelux. A collective term for Belgium, the Netherlands, and Luxembourg.

Bretton Woods system. A plan worked out at a 1944 meeting in Bretton Woods, New Hampshire, among representatives of forty-four countries. Based on U.S. leadership, it was aimed at establishing international management of the global economy, free trade, exchange rate stability, low tariffs, and aid to war-damaged economies.

Cohesion. The goal of ensuring that the development of the European Union reduces the social and economic differences between its poorer and richer regions.

Common Agricultural Policy. An agricultural price support system incorporated into the Treaty of Rome that originally supported guaranteed prices to Community farmers for their produce but has since been reformed with a view to reducing payments.

Common Foreign and Security Policy. The process introduced by Maastricht under which the EU works toward agreeing on common foreign and defense policy positions.

Common market. See **Single market**.

Competence. A word that describes the authority of the EU in different policy areas. Thus it has competence (authority) in the fields of agricultural and trade policy but not in tax policy or criminal justice matters.

Confederalism. An administrative system in which independent political units cooperate and pool authority on issues of mutual interest while retaining independence, sovereignty, and control of their own affairs.

Convergence. The progressive movement of the policies of EU member states toward a common position.

Convergence criteria. The four requirements that EU member states must meet before being allowed to join the euro: controls on national deficits, public debt, consumer inflation, and interest rates.

Customs union. An arrangement under which a group of states agrees on a common external tariff on all goods entering the group from outside.

Deepening. The argument that the EU should focus on consolidating integration among existing members before allowing new members to join. Although this seems to contradict arguments in favor of enlargement (see **Widening**), the two are now seen less as alternatives and more as two sides of the same coin.

Democratic deficit. The gap between the powers of EU institutions and the ability of EU citizens to influence those institutions. In short, the public's perception of there being too little of a democratic nature in the way the officials of EU institutions (other than the European Parliament) are appointed, and too little direct accountability and sense of public responsibility among those institutions.

Economic and monetary union. The process by which the EU worked toward the goals of establishing fixed exchange rates and common monetary policies before adopting the single currency.

Eurocrat. A nickname for EU bureaucrats, particularly those working in the European Commission.

Europeanization. The process by which national policies and government structures in the member states have been changed and brought into alignment by European laws and policies.

European Monetary System. A process launched in 1979 under which attempts were made to encourage exchange rate stability and to control inflation within the Community.

European Stability Mechanism. The EU's emergency bailout fund for troubled member states, established in September 2012.

Eurosclerosis. A term used to describe the combination of slow economic growth, unemployment, and low rates of job creation in the EU.

Euroskeptic. Someone who is either opposed to European integration or critical of the nature, speed, or progress of integration.

Eurozone. The group of EU member states that have adopted the euro.

Exchange Rate Mechanism. An arrangement under the European Monetary System by which EU member states agreed to keep the value of their currencies relatively stable against those of the other EU member states.

Federalism. An administrative arrangement in which two or more levels of government with independent powers over specified policy areas coexist. Each level is directly accountable to its citizens.

Free trade. An arrangement by which the barriers to trade between two or more states are either reduced or removed.

Functionalism. The theory that if states cooperate in selected functional areas (such as the management of coal and steel), the ties they build will compel them to cooperate in other areas as well.

Governance. An arrangement in which laws and policies are made and implemented without the existence of a formally acknowledged set of governing institutions, but instead as a result of interactions involving states, institutions, interest groups, and other sources of influence.

Government. The exercise of influence and authority over a group of people, either through law or coercion. Also used to describe the body of officials and institutions that exercise that power.

Grexit. The slang term give to the possibility of Greece leaving the eurozone and readopting its old currency, the drachma.

Gross national product. The total value of all goods and services produced by a state, including the value of its overseas operations. (Gross domestic product is a measure that excludes the latter.) The basic measure of the absolute wealth of a state.

Harmonization. The goal of standardizing national legislation in EU member states in the interest of promoting competition and free trade. Involves removing legal and fiscal barriers to competition and free trade.

Intergovernmental conference. A summit meeting at which representatives of EU member states discuss and decide upon issues of broad strategic interest.

Intergovernmentalism. The phenomenon by which decisions are reached as a result of negotiation between or among governments. Usually applied to the work of the Council of Ministers and the European Council. Contrast with **Supranationalism**.

Internal market. See **Single market**.

Legitimation. The process by which a government converts its policies into generally acceptable means for achieving its objectives.

Liberal intergovernmentalism. The theory that regional integration proceeds mainly as a result of agreements and bargains among the participating governments, moved by the pressures of domestic politics.

Luxembourg Compromise. An arrangement worked out in 1966 following a crisis set off by Charles de Gaulle's concerns about the accumulation of powers by the European Commission. The "compromise" allowed member states to veto proposals when they believed their national interests were at stake.

Multilevel governance. A system in which power is shared among the different levels of government in the EU (supranational, national, subnational, and local) with considerable interaction among the levels.

Mutual recognition. An agreement that if a product or service can be lawfully produced and marketed in one EU member state, it must be allowed to be marketed in any other member state.

Nationalism. A belief that a state should be focused on a nation, and that national identity should be promoted through political action.

Neofunctionalism. A variation on the theme of functionalism, which argues that states are encouraged to cooperate by nonstate actors and that regional integration takes place through a process of spillover: cooperation in one area creates pressures that lead to integration in others.

Ordinary legislative procedure. Formerly known as the "codecision procedure," this is the legislative process under which the Council of Ministers cannot make a final decision on new laws without giving the European Parliament the opportunity for a third reading. Under the Treaty of Lisbon it was extended to almost all policy areas, making the European Parliament a co-legislature with the Council of Ministers.

People's Europe. A program aimed at making the EU more real and accessible to its citizens.

Petersberg tasks. A commitment by EU member states to focus the work of their military on humanitarian, rescue, peacekeeping, and other crisis management operations, including peacemaking.

Preliminary ruling. A ruling by the European Court of Justice on the interpretation or validity of an EU law that arises in a national court case in one of the member states.

Qualified majority voting. A system used with most votes taken in the Council of Ministers, whereby—instead of having one vote each—member states have different numbers of votes (based roughly on their population size). Under the Lisbon Treaty, decisions need the support of 55 percent of member states representing 65 percent of the EU's population.

Realism. A theory often described as the "traditional" approach to the study of international relations; it dominated the study of that field from the 1940s to the 1960s. It argues that states are the key actors in the world system, that world politics is driven by a struggle for power among states, and that states place national interests, security, and autonomy at the top of their agendas.

Regional integration. The process by which states voluntarily transfer authority to joint institutions, creating a common body of law and pooling responsibility in selected policy areas.

Schuman Plan. The plan developed by Jean Monnet and Robert Schuman to coordinate the coal and steel industries of Europe. Announced to the public on May 9, 1950, it led to the creation of the European Coal and Steel Community.

Single market. An area within which there is free movement of people, money, goods, and services. Also known as a "common market" or "internal market." The term can be applied to a single state (such as the United States) or to a group of states that have removed the necessary barriers (such as the EU).

Social Charter. The Charter of Fundamental Rights for Workers, agreed on in 1988 and promoting free movement of workers, fair pay, better living and working conditions, and related matters.

Sovereignty. The right to own and control. In relation to states, the term is usually used to connote jurisdiction over a territory, but it can also refer to the rights of one person or group relative to those of another (for example, the sovereignty of the people over government).

Spillover. An element of neofunctional theory that suggests that if states integrate in one area, the economic, technical, social, and political pressures for them to integrate in other areas will increase.

Stability and growth pact. An attempt launched in 1997 to encourage members of the eurozone to control borrowing and budget deficits.

State. A community of individuals living within recognized frontiers, adhering to a common body of law, and coming under the jurisdiction of a common government. Also used to describe collectively the officials, laws, and powers of that government.

Structural funds. Funds made available by the EU to promote regional development and economic and social cohesion. They include the European Regional Development Fund, the European Social Fund, the guidance element of the European Agricultural Guidance and Guarantee Fund, and the Cohesion Fund.

Subsidiarity. The principle whereby the EU agrees to take action only in those policy areas that are best dealt with at the EU level rather than at the national or local level.

Supranationalism. A view that emphasizes the common good or goals of the EU, as opposed to the separate interests of the member states. Decisions are made by a process or an institution that is independent of national governments. Often used to describe the work of the European Commission and the European Court of Justice. Contrast with **Intergovernmentalism**.

Trans-European networks. Transport, energy, telecommunications, and other networks designed to integrate the EU and promote the mobility of its residents.

Transparency. The process by which the documents, decisions, and decision-making processes of the EU are made more accessible and understandable to EU citizens.

Value-added tax. A form of consumption tax used in European states and applied to any product whose form has been changed through manufacturing, thereby adding value (for example, steel used to construct a car).

Widening. The argument that EU membership should be extended to other European states. Sometimes also used to describe the expansion of EU powers or policy interests. Can be contrasted with **Deepening**.

Appendix 1: Chronology of European Integration

1944	July	Bretton Woods conference to plan postwar global economy
1945	May	Germany surrenders; World War II ends in Europe
	October	Creation of United Nations
1946	March	Winston Churchill makes "iron curtain" speech in Fulton, Missouri
	September	Churchill makes "United States of Europe" speech in Zurich
1947	March	Announcement of Truman Doctrine
	June	U.S. Secretary of State George Marshall offers Europe aid for economic recovery
	October	General Agreement on Tariffs and Trade launched in Geneva
1948	January	Benelux customs union enters into force; GATT enters into force
	March	Treaty of Brussels signed by Britain, France, and Benelux states, creating Western Union
	April	Organization for European Economic Cooperation founded
	May	Congress of Europe held in The Hague
	June	Soviet blockade sparks eleven-month Berlin airlift
1949	April	North Atlantic Treaty signed in Washington, DC

	May	Treaty of London signed, creating Council of Europe; formalization of division of Germany
1950	May	Schuman Declaration
	June	Opening of IGC to plan European Coal and Steel Community
	October	Publication of plan outlining European Defense Community
1951	April	Treaty of Paris signed, creating ECSC
1952	March	Nordic Council founded
	May	Six ECSC members sign draft treaty creating European Defense Community
	July	Treaty of Paris comes into force
1953	March	Plans announced for European Political Community
1954	May	French defeat in Indochina
	August	Collapse of plans for European Defense Community and European Political Community
	October	Protocol to Treaty of Brussels signed, creating Western European Union
	December	European Court of Justice issues its first ruling
1955	May	Western European Union comes into operation, headquartered in London; creation of Warsaw Pact
	June	Opening of IGC in Messina to discuss the next step in European integration
	December	Council of Europe adopts flag with twelve gold stars on blue background
1956	June	Negotiations open on creation of EEC and Euratom
	October	Soviet invasion of Hungary
	October– December	Suez crisis
1957	March	Treaties of Rome signed, creating Euratom and EEC
1958	January	Treaties of Rome come into force
	February	Treaty creating Benelux Economic Union signed in The Hague
	July	Conference in Stresa, Italy, works out details of Common Agricultural Policy
1960	January	Seven countries sign European Free Trade Association Convention in Stockholm
	May	EFTA comes into force

	November	Benelux Economic Union comes into force
	December	OEEC becomes Organization for Economic Cooperation and Development
1961	February	First summit of EEC heads of government
	July	Ireland applies for EEC membership
	August	Britain and Denmark apply for EEC membership; construction begins on Berlin Wall
1962	April	Norway applies for EEC membership
	October	Cuban missile crisis
1963	January	De Gaulle vetoes British membership of EEC; France and Germany sign Treaty of Friendship and Cooperation
	July	Yaoundé Convention signed between EEC and eighteen African countries
	September	Death of Robert Schuman
1965	April	Merger Treaty signed, establishing a single Commission and Council for the three European Communities
	July	France begins boycott of Community institutions (the empty chair crisis)
1966	January	Empty chair crisis ends with Luxembourg Compromise
1967	May	Second application for EEC membership from Britain, Denmark, and Ireland, followed by Norway in July
	June	Arab–Israeli War
	July	Merger treaty comes into force
	November	Second veto by de Gaulle of British membership of EEC
1968	July	Agreement on a common external tariff completes creation of EEC customs union
1969	April	Resignation of Charles de Gaulle
	December	EEC leaders meeting in The Hague agree on principle of economic and monetary union
1970	June	Membership negotiations with Britain, Denmark, Ireland, and Norway resume; concluded January 1972
1971	August	United States abandons gold standard; end of Bretton Woods system of fixed exchange rates
1972	April	Launch of the European exchange rate stabilization system (the "snake")
	May	European Social Fund becomes operational; Irish referendum approves EEC membership
	September	Norwegian referendum rejects EEC membership
	October	Danish referendum approves EEC membership

1973	January	Britain, Denmark, and Ireland join Community, bringing membership to nine
	October	Yom Kippur War
1974	December	Community leaders decide to form European Council
1975	February	First Lomé Convention signed between EEC and forty-six ACP states
	March	First meeting of European Council in Dublin; creation of European Regional Development Fund
	June	British referendum on continued EC membership; Greece applies to join Community; negotiations open July 1976
1977	March	Portugal applies to join Community; negotiations open June 1978
	July	Spain applies to join Community; negotiations open February 1979
	October	Court of Auditors holds its first meeting
1978	December	European Council establishes European Monetary System
1979	February	Court of Justice issues *Cassis de Dijon* ruling
	March	European Monetary System comes into operation; death of Jean Monnet
	June	First direct elections to European Parliament
1981	January	Greece joins Community, bringing membership to ten
1982	February	Greenland votes to leave the EEC; finally leaves February 1985
1983	December	Agreement on Common Fisheries Policy
1984	January	Free trade area established between EFTA and the Community
	June	Second direct elections to European Parliament; European Council resolves British budget problem
1985	January	Jacques Delors begins first term as Commission president; introduction of European passports
	June	Publication of Commission white paper on the single market; signing of the Schengen Agreement
	September	Opening of IGC on the single market
	December	European Council agrees to drawing up of Single European Act
1986	January	Portugal and Spain join Community, bringing membership to twelve

	February	Single European Act signed in Luxembourg
	May	Flag of EC flown for the first time
1987	April	Turkey applies to join Community; negotiations do not open until 2005
	July	Single European Act comes into force
1988	October	Court of First Instance created
1989	April	Delors report on economic and monetary union
	June	Third direct elections to European Parliament
	July	Austria applies to join Community
	September–December	Collapse of communist governments in Eastern Europe; fall of Berlin Wall
	December	Adoption of the Social Charter by eleven EC member states
1990	June	Schengen Agreement signed by Benelux states, France, and Germany; negotiations open on creation of European Economic Area
	July	Cyprus and Malta apply to join Community
	August	Iraqi invasion of Kuwait
	October	German reunification brings former East Germany into Community
	December	Opening of IGCs on economic and monetary union and on political union
1991	January	U.S.-led invasion expels Iraq from Kuwait
	April	European Bank for Reconstruction and Development opens in London
	June	Outbreak of war in Yugoslavia
	July	Sweden applies to join Community
	December	Maastricht European Council agrees on draft Treaty on European Union; breakup of USSR
1992	February	Treaty on European Union signed in Maastricht
	March	Finland applies to join EU
	May	France and Germany announce creation of 35,000-member Eurocorps; Switzerland signs EEA membership agreement and applies to join EU
	June	Danish referendum rejects terms of Maastricht
	September	ERM crisis; Britain and Italy suspend membership
	November	Norway applies again to join EU
	December	Swiss referendum rejects membership of EEA; Swiss application for EU membership suspended

1993	January	Single European market comes into force
	February	Membership negotiations open with Austria, Finland, and Sweden (and with Norway in April)
	May	Second Danish referendum accepts terms of Maastricht
	November	Treaty on European Union comes into force; European Community becomes one of three "pillars" of a new European Union
1994	January	European Economic Area enters into force
	March	Inaugural session of Committee of the Regions; Hungary applies to join the EU
	April	Poland applies to join the EU
	May	Opening of channel tunnel linking Britain and France
	June	Fourth direct elections to European Parliament; referendum in Austria favors EU membership
	October	Finnish referendum accepts EU membership
	November	Swedish referendum accepts EU membership; Norwegians again reject membership
1995	January	Austria, Finland, and Sweden join EU, bringing membership to fifteen; GATT replaced by the World Trade Organization
	March	Schengen Agreement comes into force
	June	Romania and Slovakia apply to join EU
	July	Europol Convention signed
	October–December	Bulgaria, Estonia, Latvia, and Lithuania apply to join EU
	December	Dayton peace accords end war in Yugoslavia; European Council decides to call single currency the "euro"
1996	January	Czech Republic applies to join EU
	June	Slovenia applies to join EU
	December	Agreement on stability and growth pact
1997	June	European Council agrees on Treaty of Amsterdam
	July	Launch of Agenda 2000
	October	Treaty of Amsterdam signed
1998	March	Negotiations on EU membership opened with Cyprus, Czech Republic, Estonia, Hungary, Poland, and Slovenia
	June	Establishment of European Central Bank
1999	January	Official launch of the euro in eleven member states, which fix currency exchange rates relative to one another and to the euro

	March	Resignation of College of Commissioners following publication of report alleging fraud, mismanagement, and nepotism in Commission
	March–April	NATO air attacks on Kosovo
	May	Treaty of Amsterdam comes into force
	June	Fifth direct elections to European Parliament—record low voter turnout
2000	January	Negotiations on EU membership open with Bulgaria, Latvia, Lithuania, Malta, Romania, and Slovakia
	March	Launch of Lisbon Strategy
	June	Cotonou Convention signed between EU and ACP states
	September	Danish referendum rejects adoption of euro
	December	European Council agrees on Treaty of Nice
2001	February	Treaty of Nice signed
	March	Swiss referendum rejects EU membership
	June	Irish referendum rejects Treaty of Nice
	September	Terrorist attacks on the World Trade Center in New York and the Pentagon in Washington, DC
	December	Laeken European Council agrees to launch Convention on the Future of Europe
2002	January–March	Euro coins and notes begin circulating in twelve member states
	February	Opening of Convention on the Future of Europe
	July	Treaty of Paris expires
	October	Second Irish referendum accepts Treaty of Nice
2003	February	Treaty of Nice comes into force
	March	United States launches attack on Iraq despite French and German opposition
	July	Publication of draft treaty establishing a constitution for Europe
	March–September	Referendums in Czech Republic, Estonia, Hungary, Poland, Latvia, Lithuania, Malta, Slovakia, and Slovenia all approve EU membership
		Swedish referendum rejects adoption of euro
	October	IGC opens on the draft European constitutional treaty
	December	European Council fails to reach agreement on constitutional treaty
2004	March	Terrorist bombings in Madrid

	May	Ten countries, mainly Eastern European, join the EU, bringing membership to twenty-five
	June	Sixth direct elections to European Parliament; European Council reaches agreement on constitutional treaty
	October	European leaders sign treaty on the European constitution
	November	Lithuania is first member state to endorse constitution
2005	February	Spain is first member state to hold referendum on constitution; approves constitution
	May	France rejects constitution in national referendum
	June	Netherlands rejects constitution in national referendum
	July	Terrorist bombings in London
	October	Negotiations on EU membership open with Croatia and Turkey
2007	January	Bulgaria and Romania join the EU, bringing membership to twenty-seven; Slovenia becomes the thirteenth country to adopt the euro
	March	Berlin Declaration marking fiftieth anniversary of the signing of Treaties of Rome
	August	Global economic crisis begins, with slowly evolving consequences for EU member states
	October	European Council agrees on new Lisbon Treaty to replace defunct constitutional treaty
2008	January	Cyprus and Malta adopt the euro
	June	Irish referendum rejects Lisbon treaty
2009	January	Slovakia adopts the euro
	February	Spain enters into economic recession
	October	New Irish referendum on Lisbon passes
	November	Lisbon treaty comes into force
2010	April	The downgrading of Greek government bonds to junk status prompts fears of the collapse of the Greek economy; the EU and IMF agree on a €110 billion ($147 billion) bailout of Greece
2011	January	Estonia adopts the euro
	October	Second bailout package, of €130 billion ($175 billion), from the EU for Greece; Spain's economic outlook worsens and international ratings agencies downgrade its credit rating

2012	March	Treaty on Stability, Coordination and Governance in the Economic and Monetary Union (Fiscal Compact) signed by all EU states except the UK and the Czech Republic; member states begin the ratification process
	June	European Council agrees to bank recapitalization through ESM, a €120 billion ($160 billion) "European Growth Pact," and a plan for an EU-wide banking union.
	October	The European Council agrees to set a timetable for the set-up and legal foundations for a new eurozone bank regulator as part of the proposed EU Banking union
2013	February	EU leaders agree on budget package for 2014–20
	July	Croatia becomes the EU's twenty-eighth member state

APPENDIX 2:
SOURCES OF INFORMATION

For researchers on the EU, shortage of information is not a problem. Publishing on the EU has become a growth industry, and the flow of new books and journal articles matches both the EU's increasing powers and reach and its growing impact on global politics, economics, and public opinion. The challenge for the researcher lies less in finding material than in making sense of it all and in keeping up with rapidly changing developments. Rather than provide a lengthy bibliography that would quickly go out of date, this appendix provides a selective list of sources of information, which can be used as the foundation for a broader search.

Online Sources

There are literally thousands of websites dealing with the European Union, the most useful of which include the following:

Official EU Websites

- Europa: http://europa.eu. The official website of the EU, with multiple links to many kinds of official EU information.
- European Union Law: http://eur-lex.europa.eu/en/index.htm. The website for EUR-Lex, the authoritative source on all EU laws.

- European Commission: http://ec.europa.eu/index.htm
- Council of Ministers: http://www.consilium.europa.eu
- European Parliament: http://www.europarl.europa.eu
- Political Groups Online: http://www.europarl.europa.eu/about parliament/en/007f2537e0/Political-groups.html
- European Court of Justice: http://curia.europa.eu
- European Central Bank: http://www.ecb.int
- Delegation of the European Commission to the USA: http://www.eurunion.org
- Delegation of the European Commission-Canada: http://eeas.europa.eu/delegations/canada/index_en.htm

Academic Organizations for the Study of the EU

- Council for European Studies: http://www.councilforeuropean studies.org
- European Union Studies Association: http://www.eustudies.org
- University Association for Contemporary European Studies: http://www.uaccs.org

Sources of News on the EU

- *The Economist*. A weekly British news magazine that has news and statistics on world politics, including a section on Europe (and occasional special supplements on the EU): http://www.economist.com.
- *European Voice*. A weekly newspaper published in Brussels by the *Economist*; the best single source of print news and features on the latest developments in the EU: http://www.europeanvoice.com
- BBC News Online: http://www.bbc.co.uk/news
- EUBusiness: http://www.eubusiness.com
- EUObserver: http://euobserver.com
- EurActiv: http://www.euractiv.com
- *E!Sharp*: http://www.peoplepowerprocess.com

Publishers

The publishers that have developed the most comprehensive lists of books on the EU include Lynne Rienner, Oxford University Press, Palgrave

Macmillan, Routledge, and Rowman and Littlefield. A search of their websites will reveal many useful sources on the EU.

Academic Journals

There are numerous political science, comparative politics, international relations, and area studies journals that deal with EU issues, among the most consistently useful of which are the following:

- *Common Market Law Review*
- *Comparative European Politics*
- *European Foreign Affairs Review*
- *European Journal of International Relations*
- *European Journal of Political Research*
- *European Union Politics*
- *Foreign Affairs*
- *International Organization*
- *Journal of Common Market Studies*
- *Journal of European Integration*
- *Journal of European Public Policy*
- *Journal of European Social Policy*
- *Journal of Transatlantic Studies*
- *Parliamentary Affairs*
- *West European Politics*

EU Information Centers in North America

Most major university and college libraries in the United States and Canada carry general information on the EU, but some also contain more specialized resources. Some are EU Depository Libraries and receive a wide range of EU publications. Others are EU Centers of Excellence and offer a wider selection of services and activities. For a complete listing, visit the websites of the European Commission offices in Washington, DC, and Ottawa (see above, under Official EU Websites).

INDEX

Acheson, Dean, 64
ACP program, 313–314
Acquis communitaire, 81, 247
Adenauer, Konrad, 40, 50, 65,
  120
Adonnino committee, 198, 204
Agenda 2000, 87
Agricultural policy, 60, 61, 63,
  65, 113, 186, 222, 229, 232,
  235, 265, 277–287
  See also Common Agricultural
  Policy
Airbus, 185
Alliance of Liberals and
  Democrats for Europe, 207
American exceptionalism,
  329–330
Amsterdam, Treaty of, 6, 71, 83,
  112, 140, 142, 149, 165,
  200, 247, 267, 268, 279,
  290, 292, 303
Anti-Americanism, 322

Antici Group, 125, 179
Arab-Israeli problem, 323–328
Assent procedure, 151
Atlanticism, 300, 302, 304
Attlee, Clement, 40
Austria, 5, 28, 64, 81, 86, 105,
  181, 228, 262, 268, 273,
  280, 289, 290, 300, 305
  Accession, 67, 99
Authority gap, 225
Aznar, Jose Maria, 241

Baker, James, 323
Balkans, 84, 86, 297, 300,
  322–324, 338
Banking Union. *See* European
  banking union
Barcelona Process, 309
Barroso, José Manuel, 105, 106,
  107, 116
Battle groups, 304
Behavioralism, 27

Belgium, 5, 28, 40, 204, 228, 232, 267, 268, 289, 303, 331

Benelux countries, 40–41, 44–45, 47, 50–51, 57, 120, 177, 243

Bentham, Jeremy, 38, 49

Berlaymont building, 100, 123

Berlin airlift, 44

Berlin wall, 62, 76–77, 79

Berlusconi, Silvio, 147

Blair, Tony, 82, 106, 182, 241, 267, 303

Bologna Process, 273,

Brandt, Willy, 147, 181

Bretton Woods conference/ system, 36–37, 41, 68, 176, 338

Britain
  and agricultural policy, 280, 282, 286
  and CFSP, 300, 303
  and ECSC, 47–51
  and EEC membership, 63–65, 70
  and ERM, 68–69
  and EU budget, 232–234
  and EU Civil Service, 226
  and euro, 80, 82, 249
  and European integration, 64–65
  and minorities, 18
  and security, 44, 45, 86
  and social charter, 266–267
  and Suez crisis, 46–47, 52
  and postwar situation, 39–42, 55
  and Schengen, 243, 247

Brussels, Treaty of, 44, 45

Budget. *See* European Union, budget

Bulgaria, 87–88, 103, 181, 200, 243

Bush, George W., 86, 106, 307, 319, 328, 329
  and Kyoto Protocol, 327
  Bush Doctrine, 324

Buttiglione, Rocco, 101, 151

Canada, and federalism, 28

Capital punishment, 229, 331

Cassis de Dijon case, 166–167, 241

Charlemagne, 38

Charter of Fundamental Rights of the European Union, 83, 90, 159, 331

Charter of Fundamental Social Rights for Workers. *See* Social Charter

China, 2, 9, 62, 244, 289, 302, 312, 325, 327, 328

Chirac, Jacques, 181, 182, 303

Churchill, Sir Winston, 47, 51, 63
  and European unity, 49
  iron curtain speech, 44

Citizenship. *See* European citizenship

Civil Service Tribunal, 155–156, 160, 165, 168, 171

Civil society, 195–196

Climate change, 10, 128, 146, 279, 287–289, 326, 328

Clinton, Bill, 328, 239

Cockfield, Lord, 69, 241

Codecision procedure. *See* Ordinary Legislative Procedure

Cohesion Fund, 72, 234, 260

Cohesion policy, 257–270

Cold War, 3, 7, 9–10, 37, 44,
47, 76–77, 88, 300, 302,
318–326
College of Commissioners. *See*
European Commission
Colombo, Emilio, 147
Comenius, 271
Comitology, 110
Committee of Permanent
Representatives, 119,
124–125, 126, 129–130,
222, 226, 231
Committee of the Regions, 174,
176, 190–191
Common Agricultural Policy, 61,
65, 113, 186, 222, 232,
277–287
achievements of, 283–284
origins, 60
problems created by, 284
reform of, 278, 284–287
Common Commercial Policy,
60, 63, 306–307
Common Fisheries Policy,
282–283
Common Foreign and Security
Policy, 5, 79, 119, 239, 235,
247, 296–297, 300
and European Parliament, 151,
152
and Treaty of Lisbon, 300–302
High Representative, 90,
118–119, 126, 129, 178,
301, 304
Common positions, 340
Common strategies, 340
Community Plant Variety
Office, 213
Comparative politics and the EU,
16, 27

Competition policy, 156, 242,
246
Confederalism, 29, 30, 31
and European Union, 30–31
defined, 29
Congress of Europe, 47
Consent procedure, 133, 149
Constitution. *See* European
constitution
Consultation procedure, 133,
140, 148, 149
Convergence criteria. *See* Euro
Convergence Object, 264
Cooperation procedure, 140, 149
Copenhagen climate change
conference, 289
Copenhagen conditions, 81
Coreper. *See* Committee of
Permanent Representatives
Corporate mergers. *See* Mergers
and acquisitions
Council of Europe, 20, 47, 48,
51, 159, 197
Council of Ministers. *See*
Council of the European
Union
Council of the European Union
7, 51, 61, 118–120
and European Parliament, 70,
136–139
evolution, 56–59, 120–122
General Secretariat, 129
how it works, 129–133
meetings of, 132
presidency of, 125–128
structure, 123–129
technical councils, 123–124
and the treaties, 70, 83, 90
Court of Auditors, 13, 152, 160,
185

Court of First Instance, 70, 83, 156, 160, 165
Cox, Pat, 143, 207
Crespo, Enrique Barón, 143
Croatia, 79, 137, 146, 300
  accession of, 5, 88, 200
Cuban missile crisis, 62
Culture/cultural policy, 226
Cyprus, 67, 78, 82, 177, 243, 250, 270
  and eurozone crisis, 78, 91, 339
  accession, 87, 88, 309
Czech Republic, 86, 87–88, 181, 262

Davignon, Etienne, 78
Day, Catherine, 110
Dayton peace accords, 300, 304
Decisions (EU), 112
Defense policy. *See* Security policy
Dehaene, Jean-Luc, 117, 119
Delors, Jacques, 68, 104, 105, 107, 110, 148, 151, 182
  and economic and monetary union, 68, 248
  and single market, 266
Democratic deficit, 212, 222, 231
Denmark, 65
  and EEC membership, 5, 56–57, 63–65
  and EU law, 127
  and EU Presidency, 128
  and euro, 80, 82, 249
  and NATO, 45
  and Schengen, 247
  postwar situation, 41–42
  rejection of Maastricht, 195, 200

Development cooperation, 235, 312–314
Dien Bien Phu, 46
Directives (EU), 112
Directorates-general. *See* European Commission
Duisenberg, Wim, 184

ECB. *See* European Central Bank
Economic and Financial Affairs Council, 123
Economic and monetary union, 63, 67–69
Economic policy, 238–240
Eden, Anthony, 45
Education policy, 271–274
Eisenhower, Dwight D., 326
Elections. *See* European elections
Employment policy, 268
  See also Social policy
Empty chair crisis, 60–61, 99, 232, 338
Enlargement, 5, 74–78, 84, 92–93, 100–102, 304, 351
Environmental Action Programs, 279, 288–290
Environmental interest groups, 222, 287
Environmental policy, 277–278, 287–292
EPP. *See* European People's Party
Erasmus, 271
Erasmus generation, 272
Estonia, 82, 87–88, 250, 311
Euratom. *See* European Atomic Energy Community
Euro, 80, 83, 248–254
  convergence criteria, 69
  creation, 80–83
  stability and growth pact, 251

Eurobonds, 91, 254
Eurocorps, 339
Europe 2020. *See* Lisbon Strategy
Europe of Freedom and
    Democracy, 208
European Agency for Safety and
    Health at Work, 187
European Agricultural Fund for
    Rural Development, 262
European Agricultural Guidance
    and Guarantee Fund, 283
European Anti-Fraud Office, 108
European Atomic Energy
    Community, 5, 58, 157
European Aviation Safety
    Agency, 187
European Bank for
    Reconstruction and
    Development, 188, 308
European Banking Union, 92,
    184, 254, 340
European Central Bank, 69,
    80, 124, 173, 174–175,
    183–185, 227, 249, 251,
    253–254
    and eurozone crisis, 91, 340
European Centre for the
    Development of Vocational
    Training, 187
European Centre for Disease
    Prevention and Control, 187
European Chemicals Agency, 187
European citizenship, 28, 31, 80,
    166, 197, 271
European Coal and Steel
    Community, 3, 57–58, 64,
    71, 99, 120, 124, 138, 157,
    185, 232
    creation, 5, 37, 38, 50, 57
    structure, 50–51, 59

European Commission, 5, 6, 23,
    29, 46, 61, 87, 97–98, 185,
    210
    and Council of the EU, 178
    and EU external relations, 114
    and policy formulation,
        110–111, 222, 225, 246
    and policy implementation,
        111–113
    and Lisbon Treaty, 85, 100
    cabinets, 104
    College of Commissioners, 97,
        101–104
    Committees, 110
    directorates-general, 107–109
    evolution, 99–100
    how it works, 110–115
    managing EU finances,
        113–114
    president of, 104–107
    Secretariat-General, 109–110
    structure, 100–110
European Conservatives and
    Reformists Group, 208
European constitution, 77, 79,
    84, 106, 159
    and EU law, 7, 79, 156,
        165–166, 223
    failure of, 6, 85, 100, 128,
        130, 195, 200, 220, 338
European Convention on
    Human Rights, 130
European Council, 7, 30, 60, 70,
    79, 81, 84, 90, 100, 128,
    174–175
    and agenda setting, 111
    and Council of Ministers, 119,
        121
    and policy formation, 220, 225
    evolution, 176–177

European Council *(continued)*
how it works, 179–182
meetings, 178, 179–182
president of, 85, 125, 177–178,
301
structure, 177–179
European Court of Justice, 7, 29,
70, 77, 113, 155–156
advocates general, 163–164
cases
*Commission v. Federal
Republic of Germany*
(178/84), 167
Cowan v. Le Tresor Public
(186/87), 169
Flaminio Costa v. ENEL
(6/64), 158, 169
*Nold, Kohlen-und
Baustoffgrosshandlung v.
Commission* (4/73), 158
SA Roquette Frères v. Council
(138/79), 139
*Van Gend en Loos v.
Nederlandse Administratie
Belastingen* (26/62),
157–158, 169
chambers, 161
direct actions, 169–171
evolution, 157–160
how it works, 166–171
judges, 160–163
preliminary rulings, 168–169
president, 163
structure, 160–163
European Credit Transfer and
Accumulation System, 273
European currency unit, 68
European Defense Community,
51, 60, 302, 338
European Development Fund, 313

European Economic and Social
Committee, 190
European Economic Area, 81
European Economic
Community, 16, 22, 76–77
becomes European
Community, 76–77
becomes European Union, 79,
239
creation, 58–59
early years, 57–58
structure, 59
European elections, 79, 137–149,
195, 208
electoral systems, 2149, 204
voter turnout, 202–205
European Employment Strategy,
259, 268
European Fisheries Fund, 262
European Food Safety Authority,
187
European Foundation for the
Improvement of Living and
Working Conditions, 187
European Free Trade
Association, 63, 64, 81
European identity, 31, 36, 57,
137, 194–200
European integration, early ideas
about, 38–41
European Investment Bank, 58,
71, 160, 185, 308
European Maritime Safety
Agency, 187
European Monetary Institute, 183
European Monetary System, 50,
57, 68–69, 248
European Monitoring Centre for
Drugs and Drug Addiction,
187

European Movement, 47–48
European Neighborhood Policy, 309
European Parliament, 5, 7, 29, 30, 136–137
  and Council of Ministers, 7, 77, 119, 121, 122
  and European Commission, 98
  and Lisbon Treaty, 85, 90, 187
  Bureau of the EP, 144
  committees, 160, 144–146
  Conference of Committee Chairs, 144
  Conference of Presidents, 144
  elections, 100, 201–205
  evolution, 59, 60, 61, 83, 138–140
  growing powers, 137–140
  how it works, 148–153
  members, 136–137, 141, 146–148
  multisite problem, 137, 142
  political groups, 205–209
  powers of the budget, 151
  powers over legislation, 148–151
  powers over other institutions, 151–153
  president, 141–144
  Secretariat, 141
  structure, 140–148
European People's Party, 141, 206, 207–208
European Police Office. *See* Europol
European Political Community, 651–52, 60, 338
European Political Cooperation, 78–79, 298
European Railway Agency, 187

European Regional Development Fund, 70–71, 169, 190, 260
European Security and Defense Identity, 302
European Security Strategy, 303–304
European single market. *See* Single European Act; Single market
European Social Fund, 58, 72, 149, 260, 265
European Stability Mechanism, 92, 253, 340
European Union
  achievements, 1, 341
  and fallout with U.S. over Iraq, 78, 86–87, 182, 221, 297, 319, 322, 333
  and United States, 7, 9–10, 84, 361–362, 365–370, 377–379
  as economic superpower, 306–307
  as international organization, 16, 25, 26, 32
  as political system, 17, 26–27
  as state, 25–26
  budget, 29, 31, 98, 103, 113, 119, 129, 137, 138, 140, 141, 182, 185, 217, 218, 230–235, 254, 338
  characteristics, 15–16
  European attitudes toward, 197–198, 202
  evolution, 19–25
  flag, 6, 31, 197–198
  significance of, 1–2
  social and economic differences, 259–260
  soft power of, 10, 296, 298, 299, 307

European Union law, 112,
    165–166
European Union of Federalists,
    20, 47
European Union, Treaty on, 5,
    57–58, 71, 77, 79–80, 178,
    195, 200, 220, 228
European United Left-Nordic
    Green Left, 206
Europeanization, 229–230
Europol, 79, 174–175, 186–187,
    227, 247
Eurosclerosis, 239
Euroskepticism, 90, 97–98, 196,
    206, 208, 249, 338–339
Eurostat, 108–109
Eurotunnel, 244
Eurozone crisis, 91, 92, 128,
    179, 183, 252–254, 279,
    272, 339–342
Exchange Rate Mechanism, 68,
    102
Eyskens, Mark, 300

Federalism, 20
    and European Union, 27–29,
        99
    compared to confederalism,
        29
    defined, 27
Finland, 42, 91, 99, 340
First and second order elections,
    202
Fiscal compact, 201
Fischler, Franz, 285–286
Fisheries Control Agency,
    282–283
Flag, European. *See* European
    Union, flag
Fontaine, Nicole, 143

Foreign policy, 70, 76–77, 84,
    298–302
    See also Common Foreign and
        Security Policy
Fouchet, Christian, 176
France
    and agricultural policy, 232,
        279, 280–281
    and euro, 252
    and European Central Bank,
        184
    and European constitution, 6,
        77, 85, 195, 200
    and European Parliament, 142
    and eurozone crisis, 91, 340
    and *franglais*, 274
    and Indochina/Suez crises, 45,
        46, 47, 62
    and Iraq war, 62, 86, 105, 319
    and NATO, 302, 304
    postwar situation, 39, 41, 43, 44
    relationship with Germany,
        39, 48, 65, 181, 274, 333
Franco, Francisco, 67
Frattini, Franco, 101
Functionalism, 20–21

Galileo, 244
Garton Ash, Timothy, 2
de Gasperi, Alcide, 40
de Gaulle, Charles, 39, 60, 138
    and British membership of
        EEC, 65, 232
    and empty chair crisis, 61, 99,
        232
General Affairs and External
    Relations Council, 179
General Agreement on Tariffs
    and Trade, 41, 60, 63, 285,
    327

Georgieva, Kristalena, 101
Germany
  and confederalism, 28, 228
  and euro, 183, 249, 252
  and eurozone crisis, 91, 254,
    339–340
  and federalism, 28, 228
  and Iraq war, 319
  and presidency of Council of
    Ministers, 128
  beer purity law, 167
  containment of, 57
  postwar situation, 2, 39–40,
    42, 44
  unification, 5, 77
Giscard d'Estaing, Valéry, 85,
  147, 176–177
Global financial crisis, 76, 78,
  82–83, 91, 252, 253, 263
Globalization Adjustment Fund,
  262
Governance, 27
Greece, 5, 21, 41, 42, 113, 181,
  226
  and eurozone crisis, 78, 91–92,
    251–253, 262, 268, 339–
    340
  accession, 5, 56–57, 65–66,
    70
  adoption of euro, 80, 249
  "Grexit," 252, 340
Green papers, 112
Greens-European Free Alliance,
  206–207
Grundtvig program, 272
GUE-NG. *See* European United
  Left-Nordic Green Left
Gulf war 1990–91, 86, 175, 297,
  298, 302, 324
Gulf War 2003. *See* Iraq war

Haas, Ernst, 23, 26, 27
Hallstein, Walter, 46, 99, 107
Havel, Václav, 329
Heath, Edward, 70
Hitler, Adolf, 39
Hix, Simon, 26
Ho Chi Minh, 46
Hoffmann, Stanley, 25, 26
Hollande, François, 91, 181, 182
Holy Roman Empire, 38
Homosexuality, 331
Hoon, Geoff, 148
Hugo, Victor, 49
Hungary, 5, 45, 47, 86, 87–88,
  181, 331
Hussein, Saddam, 84, 86, 319

Iceland, 45, 64, 71, 81, 243,
  247, 282, 309
Immigration, 79, 81, 240, 243,
  247, 270, 341
Incrementalism, 223, 228
Integrative potential, 23
Interest groups, 16, 21, 23,
  26–27, 194–195, 210–212
Intergovernmental conferences,
  71
Intergovernmentalism, 15,
  25–26, 247
International Court of Justice,
  328
International Criminal Court,
  327–328
International Monetary Fund,
  41, 254, 263, 313–314
International organizations,
  118–119
International relations theory,
  15–16, 26
International system, 362–364

Iraq, 128, 285, 328
Iraq War 2003, 62, 78, 84–87,
    105, 106, 182, 221, 297,
    299, 319–320, 323, 328, 333
Ireland, 42, 63, 68, 69, 83–84,
    90, 100, 127, 201
  accession, 56–57, 64, 65,
  economic boom and bust, 78,
    91, 252–253, 263
Italy, 40, 51, 57, 91, 253, 268,
    339

Jaeger, Marc, 165
Jeleva, Rumaina, 101
Jenkins, Roy, 107
Jobert, Michel, 176
Joint actions, 300
Joint ventures, 245
Justice and home affairs, 79, 80,
    246–248

Kaczynski, Lech, 131
Kagan, Robert, 332
Kant, Immanuel, 38, 49
Kennedy, John F., 61, 62
Kissinger, Henry, 301
Klaus, Vaclav, 90
Kohl, Helmut, 181, 182, 184,
    266
Korean War, 37, 61
Kosovo, 30, 84, 175, 300, 303,
    304, 309, 312
Kyoto protocol, 289, 327

Languages
  in European Court of Justice,
    163
  official (EU), 109, 163, 273,
    274
  training, 273–274

de Lapuerta, Rosario Silva, 183
Law. See European Union law
League of Nations, 29, 236
Lebanon, 309
Legal Service, 109, 111
Legitimacy, 225
Leonardo de Vinci program, 271
Liberal intergovernmentalism,
    25
Lifelong Learning Program, 271
Lindberg, Leon, 20–21, 26
Lipsius, Justus, 123
Lisbon Strategy, 82, 239, 241, 271
Lisbon Treaty, 6, 7, 76–77, 85,
    90–91, 104, 107, 112, 128,
    159, 197, 247, 279, 300,
    303
  and Commission, 100, 105,
    107
  and Council of the EU, 91,
    175, 177, 178, 179, 181
  and European Council,
    118–119, 124, 125, 126,
    129, 130, 301
  and European Court of Justice,
    160, 165
  and European Parliament, 91,
    121, 140, 149
Lithuania, 87–88, 113, 311
Lomé conventions, 313, 314
Luxembourg, 40–41, 128, 170
Luxembourg Compromise, 61,
    99, 121, 131

Maastricht Treaty. See European
    Union, Treaty on
MacSharry, Ray, 148
Major, John, 267
Malta, 64, 82, 87–88, 250, 260
Mancini, Federico, 166

Mansholt, Sicco, 60, 284
Marshall, George, 43
Marshall Plan, 36–37, 322
de Meana, Carlo Ripa, 148
Merger Treaty, 60, 71, 112, 120, 124, 165
Mergers and acquisitions, 242, 244–246
van Miert, Karel, 148
Merkel, Angela, 91, 128, 181, 182, 254, 311, 340
Mitrany, David, 20, 26, 27
Mitterrand, François, 79
Monnet, Jean, 48–49, 52
Monti, Mario, 91
Multilevel governance, 16, 27
Multi-speed integration, 229

Nagy, Imre, 45
Napoleon, 38
Nasser, Gamal Abdel, 46
Nationalism, 18–20, 38, 57, 130, 330, 332, 342
Neofunctionalism, 15–16, 20–21, 23–25
Netherlands, 30, 40–41, 59, 85, 86, 91, 106, 178, 181, 195, 200, 232, 300, 331, 340
New institutionalism, 26–27
New Transatlantic Agenda, 323
Nice, Treaty of, 83, 84, 130, 200
Nixon, Richard, 62, 68, 322–323
Noël, Emil, 110
Non-Attached Members (EP), 208
North American Free Trade Agreement, 17, 22, 23, 24
North Atlantic Treaty, 37

North Atlantic Treaty Organization, 37, 44, 45, 62, 67, 87, 114, 300, 301, 302, 305, 322, 323
Norway, 44–45, 65, 74–75, 77, 93
Nuclear weapons, 44, 62
Nye, Joseph, 23

Office for Harmonization in the Internal Market, 187
Ordinary legislative procedure, 133, 140, 141, 149, 150, 226, 290
Organization for Economic Cooperation and Development, 114, 263
Organization for European Economic Cooperation, 43–44, 322

Palacio, Ana, 148
Paris, Treaty of, 3, 49, 50, 71, 124, 138, 157, 160, 165, 338
Passports, European, 16, 17, 197
Patten, Chris, 324
Penn, William, 49
Petersberg tasks, 302–303
Pillars, 79, 247
Poland, 5, 87, 113, 130, 131, 144, 181, 331
Political games, 228
Political groups, 137, 143, 195, 205–209
Political parties. *See* political groups
Pompidou, Georges, 181
Poos, Jacques, 300
Portugal, 5, 21, 41, 45, 56–57, 64, 67, 69, 127, 228, 243, 288, 331

Prodi, Romano, 107, 251, 264
Progressive Alliance of Socialists
    and Democrats, 206
Public policy in the EU, 217–218
  adoption, 226
  agenda setting, 219–221
  evaluation, 227
  features of the policy process,
    227–230
  formulation, 221–225
  implementation, 226–227
  legitimation, 225–226
  policy cycle, 219–227
Putin, Vladimir, 182

Qualified majority voting, 90,
    121, 130–131

Raffarin, Jean Pierre, 148
Rahoy, Mariano, 91
Rapid Reaction Force, 303
Reagan, Ronald, 323, 329
Realism, 20–21
Recommendations and Opinions
    (EU), 112
Reding, Viviane, 148
Referendums, 30, 85, 88,
    194–195, 200–201
Regional Competitiveness and
    Employment Objective, 264
Regional integration, 19, 22, 23,
    24
Regional policy, 70, 190, 259, 262
Regulations (EU), 112
Religion in Europe, 330–331
Residence, rights of, 242
Roman Empire, 38
Romania, 103, 181, 200, 243
  Accession, 87–88

Rome, Treaties of, 46, 56,
    58–59, 60, 64, 67, 69, 70,
    138, 156, 167, 188, 240,
    247, 258, 265, 270, 278,
    282, 287, 288, 298, 306
Rousseau, Jean-Jacques, 38, 49
Rumsfeld, Donald, 86, 319
Russia, 30, 81, 87, 122, 187,
    307, 311

S & D group. *See* Progressive
    Alliance of Socialists and
    Democrats
de Saint-Simon, Comte, 38
Santer, Jacques, 107, 148
Sarkozy, Nicolas, 91, 181
Schengen Agreement, 242, 243,
    247, 272
Schmidt, Helmut, 68, 128, 176,
    181
Schröder, Gerhard, 181, 182, 303
Schuessel, Wolfgang, 105
Schulz, Martin, 141
Schuman, Robert, 48, 49, 50
Schuman Plan, 50
Security policy. *See* Common
    Foreign and Security Policy
Single European Act, 5, 56, 58,
    70–72, 77, 110, 112, 121,
    140, 149, 165
Single market, 22, 23, 51,
    57–58, 69, 70, 82, 105, 128,
    140, 149, 156, 164, 167,
    197, 229, 238–240, 241,
    266, 281, 324, 339
Skouris, Vassilios, 163
Slovakia, 82, 87–88, 250
Slovenia, 79, 82, 87–88, 113,
    160, 250, 300

Social Action Programs, 259
Social Charter, 72, 105,259, 266–267
Social policy, 72, 79, 83, 265–270
Soft power, 10, 272, 298, 299, 307
Solana, Javier, 105, 301
Solidarity Fund, 262
Sovereign debt crisis, 78, 83, 253
Sovereignty, 18, 19, 26, 67, 79, 120, 131, 158, 159, 176, 196, 227, 251
Spaak, Paul-Henri, 58
Spain, 18, 41, 42, 69, 86, 181, 200, 288, 298, 311
 and eurozone crisis, 78, 91, 252–253, 268–270, 339
 accession, 5, 56–57, 64, 67, 87
Spillover, 21, 22, 23, 230
Sputnik, 47
Stalin, Joseph, 44
State, the, 15–19
Stockholm Convention, 64
Structural funds, 72, 113, 149, 186, 234–235, 260, 263, 264, 265, 283
 See also Cohesion Fund; European Agricultural Guidance and Guarantee Fund; European Regional Development Fund; European Social Fund
Stuart, Lord McKenzie, 160
Subsidiarity, 229
Suez crisis, 37, 45, 46, 62, 63
Supranationalism, 16, 26, 29, 37, 48, 51, 98, 120, 138, 150, 156

Sustainable development, 262, 279, 290, 292
Sweden, 42, 64, 81, 82, 99, 181, 249, 300
 and euro, 80, 82, 249
 accession, 5, 81, 99
Switzerland, 30, 42, 64, 243, 247, 309, 331

Territorial Cooperation Objective, 264
Terrorist attacks of 9/11, 247, 324
Thatcher, Margaret, 234, 266, 285
Thomson Report, 70
Thorning-Schmidt, Helle, 128
Tindemans, Leo, 147, 197
Toader, Camelia, 161
de Tocqueville, Alexis, 329
Trade policy, 305–307
Transatlantic Declaration, 323
Trans-European networks, 242–244
Translation Centre, 187
Trichet, Jean-Claude, 184
Truman Doctrine, 42–43
Turkey, 42, 67, 88, 151, 273, 309–311, 331

Unemployment in the EU, 92, 69, 72, 82, 128, 220, 239, 267–268
Union of Soviet Socialist Republics, 9, 323
United Kingdom. *See* Britain
United Nations, 44, 114, 287, 326

United States
  and capital punishment, 331
  and confederalism, 30
  and European integration, 36–
    37, 43, 61, 322–326
  and EU, 7, 9–10, 36–37, 61,
    78, 318–320, 331–333
  and EU security, 44–47, 304
  and federalism, 28
  and Gay marriage, 331
  and Gulf war, 1991, 298–300
  and Iraq, 62, 78, 86, 298, 299,
    319–320, 324
  and Marshall Plan, 36–37, 43–
    44, 322
  and patriotism, 330
  and religion, 330–331
  and role of government, 331
  and trade with EU, 9–10, 325
  and US-EU free trade agenda,
    334
  differences with EU, 328–334
  disputes with EU, 326–328
  environmental policy, 289, 292
  military power, 297, 321
  nationalism in, 18
  postwar policy on Europe,
    41–47, 322
  US dollar and the euro, 285

Value-added tax, 232, 240
van Rompuy, Herman, 178
Verhofstadt, Guy, 105
Versailles, Treaty of 39
Vietnam War, 46, 62, 68, 78,
    3231, 322
Vitorino, Antonio, 148

Warsaw Pact, 45
Western European Union, 45,
    302–303
Western Union, 44
Westerwelle, Guide, 341
Westphalia, peace of, 18
White papers, 112
Winthrop, John, 329
Worker mobility
    See also Education policy;
        Social policy
World Bank, 41, 188, 313, 314
World Trade Organization, 41,
    114, 286, 307, 327
World War I, 318
World War II, 2, 3, 18, 37–38,
    39–41, 57, 280

Yaounde Conventions, 60, 78,
    313
Yugoslavia, 18, 30, 300, 339